THE BLACK FAMILY: ESSAYS AND STUDIES
SECOND EDITION

ROBERT STAPLES

UNIVERSITY OF CALIFORNIA, SAN FRANCISCO

WADSWORTH PUBLISHING COMPANY, INC., BELMONT, CALIFORNIA

Sociology Editor: Stephen D. Rutter
Production Editor: Catherine Aydelott
Designer: Nancy Benedict
Cover Photo: Paula Patterson

Printed in the United States of America
3 4 5 6 7 8 9 10—82

**Library of Congress Cataloging in
Publication Data**

Staples, Robert, comp.
  The Black family.

  Bibliography
  1. Afro-American families—Addresses,
essays, lectures. I. Title.
E185.86.S7 1978   301.41   77-21417
ISBN 0-534-00557-8

Contents

\# – CRITIQUE

Preface

There has been a significant increase in literature on Black families since 1971 when the first edition of *The Black Family* was published. Because it is a qualitatively different kind of literature, these articles reflect the new trends and concerns in the sociology of the Black family. Only three of the original articles have been retained here. Where the first edition presented articles focused on whether or not Black families constitute a form of pathology, most of the articles here are based on sound research and ideas, shunning the notion of pathology. The breadth of topics covered is the same, but these articles concentrate on the unique structure of the Black family and its evolution in meeting its own unique functional prerequisites. Problems of the Black family are put in a normative framework of Black culture and how its form is related to its own unique character and needs. I chose the articles by virtue of their quality, not the reputation of the authors. Much of the material here is original, in many cases unpublished, research by heretofore unknown but very competent authors.

In compiling this collection of articles I had the help of many friends and colleagues, whom I would like to thank here. I am grateful to Joyce Ladner, Robert Chrisman, Barbara Carter, Terry Jones, and Bill Strickland for the ideas they shared with me informally. Walter Allen, Leanor Johnson, Shirley Nuss, Marie Peters, Roger Rubin, and Patricia Bell Scott read and made comments on the original outline for the book. Robert Allen, Wendell Brooks, Beverly Edmunds, Elaine Mayberry, and Jane Usami contributed valuable technical assistance in the collection and editing of the articles.

I am most deeply indebted to Catherine Aydelott, production editor at Wadsworth, Steve Rutter, sociology editor, and particularly to his assistant, Barbara Cuttle, for their help and patience while I completed my work on the book. A special note of thanks to Bob Gormley of Duxbury Press who has inspired me to work on this anthology since 1969 and provided the resources for my efforts.

Robert Staples

Part One
The Setting

Many changes have occurred in this country since 1962, changes involving a wide array of personalities, values, and institutions, and bringing about a marked change in the functioning of society as a whole. These changes have been most dramatic within the institution of the family, where they have had a most telling effect on our personal lives. We are all, to some degree, affected by increasing sexual permissiveness, changes in sex role expectations, a declining fertility rate, altered attitudes toward child bearing and child rearing, a continuing increase in the divorce rate, and the like.

One would not expect Black families to be immune to the forces modifying our family forms; there is ample evidence that they are not. At the same time their special status as a racial minority with a singular history continues to give the Black marital and family pattern a unique character. Despite what many allege to be the positive gains of the Black liberation movements of the sixties and seventies, the problems of poverty and racial oppression continue to plague large numbers of Afro-Americans. Black Americans are still spatially segregated from the majority of the more affluent white citizenry, and certain cultural values distinguish their family life, in form and content, from the middle-class, white Anglo-Saxon model. Thus, there is still a need to look at the Black family apart from the white family.

Nevertheless, the commonality of the two may be greater than the differences. We lose nothing by admitting this. Moreover, the variations within the Black population may be greater than the differences between the two racial groups. Therefore, it becomes even more important to view the Black family from the widest possible perspective—from its peculiar history to the alternate family life styles now emerging.

The statistics on Black and white family life vividly show prolonged variations in the family life styles of the two races and lingering differences in Black and white marital and family patterns. Certain historical factors continue to affect contemporary Afro-American family patterns; these will become clear in the ensuing articles. Here, we shall summarize some of the more salient differences.

1. Increases in sexual permissiveness seem to be greater among white Americans.

2. The Black fertility rate, while still higher than that of whites, has declined faster.

3. In contrast to past years, Blacks marry later than whites, and a greater proportion remain unmarried past the age of thirty.

4. The proportion of children born out of wedlock is considerably larger for Blacks than for whites.

5. Divorce and separation rates continue higher for Afro-Americans.

6. The imbalance in the sex ratio (more men than women) grows more marked every year.

The Study of Black Families

Part One focuses on the study of Black families from several perspectives. The first selection in chapter 1 is "The Tangle of Pathology" by Daniel P. Moynihan. Although outdated and long since discredited by a number of scholars, this work is included to put in perspective most of the literature that followed its publication. Moynihan excludes middle-class Blacks from the tangle of pathology he asserts exists in Black families, yet the report was originally entitled "The Negro Family," and assumptions have been made about all Black families on the basis of his findings. Moynihan's thesis is that a weak family structure is at the root of many Black problems. In particular, he focuses on the matriarchal nature of Black families as being responsible for the "deterioration" of Black society. In most cases the articles that follow his report effectively refute his assertions.

In the article by Staples, the stages of Black family research are delineated, along with some of their characteristics and practitioners. He starts with the original studies of the Black family, which examined the relationship of the Black family to economic conditions, and goes on to describe as pathological the type of research generated by Moynihan's view of the Black family.[1] Much of the literature from 1966 to 1971 was devoted to refuting Moynihan's thesis. The following period was characterized by studies and essays outlining the strengths of Black families. Finally, certain models for studying Black family life are discussed for their strengths and weaknesses in understanding the Afro-American family.

Wade Nobles' article provides us with one of the most systematic counter-models for research on Black families. Using what Staples calls the Pan-Africanist approach, he outlines some of the deficits of past studies of Black family life. Proceeding from the premise that the Black family did not begin in America but is really a continuation of traditional African forms, he discusses the philosophical heritage that animates the family life of all groups that originated on the African continent. His contention is that 400 years in the United States may have modified but did not erase certain African values relating to the family: survival of the tribe and oneness of being.

Leanor Johnson discusses in greater detail some of the value assumptions underlying the investigation of Black family life. She points out the shortcomings of the biological model, which served to validate the supremacy of white family forms and the inferiority of Black family practices

simply because they were different. After examining the concepts of *value separation*—which denies the existence of values in social research—and *value espousal*—which advocates that the scientist explicitly state his values, she discusses the search for a distinctly Black value system to guide research on the Black family.

Historical Background

In the past decade the literature on Black families has included a new body of historical research. These historical studies served to correct many misconceptions about family life among Black slaves. As was true of other investigations of Black family life, earlier historians had constructed their view of slave family life from untested assumptions and faulty methodology. One popular theory was that slavery had destroyed the family traditions and values brought to this continent by Africans. Early historical research had found that there was no legal basis for marriage between slaves, that slave families could be and were disrupted by the sale of their members, and that the exercise of normative sex and parental roles was constrained. These early findings were based on plantation records and slaveowners' diaries. The new historical research added to these traditional sources a more extensive and reliable analysis of slave narratives and census records.

One of the groundbreakers on the subject was John Blassingame.[2] He accepted the view that slavery was, in many cases, destructive of the bondsmen's family life, but he also found that they used substantial cultural resources to maintain, in some form, many of the African family traditions brought to this country. Instead of the presumed widespread family disorganization among slaves, he discovered that the family was the one institution that met the needs of that group. Although the form of the family was modified to include a number of extended kinsmen—both real and imaginary—it was within that institution that slaves received emotional nurturance, love, and empathy, and through which children were socialized.

Whereas Blassingame corrected the myths surrounding the slave family, the exhaustive his-

[1]Daniel P. Moynihan, *The Negro Family: The Case for National Action* (Washington, D.C.: U.S. Government Printing Office, 1965).

[2]John Blassingame, *The Slave Community* (New York: Oxford University Press, 1972).

torical research of Herbert Gutman shed new light on Black family life of the immediate post-slavery years.[3] By examining census data for a number of cities between the years 1880 and 1925, he undermined the notion that slavery had created the foundation for an unstable, female-dominated Black family and for the family disorganization among Blacks in contemporary urban America. Gutman found that the simple nuclear family—two adults and their children—was the norm even in poor Black communities, and that female-headed families were hardly, if at all, more common than among comparable whites.

Eugene D. Genovese's article "The Myth of the Absent Family" is historical research that reveals a different picture of the slave family. He found that the disorganization so many historians had assumed existed among slave families was not as pervasive as the stable—though illegal—unions between male and female slaves. Moreover, these relationships were ones of affection and respect that were acknowledged by slaveowners and considered whenever a decline in fortunes caused them to sell any slaves. In general, slaves had strong feelings of affection toward their family members.

Another article in our historical section is Stanley Elkins' comparative analysis of the effect of slavery on the bondsman's family life in North and South America. According to Elkins, the principal differences between the two regions lay in the manumission process and the legal basis of marriage between slaves; that is, slaves could become free citizens more easily in South America and those who remained in bondage were permitted a legal marriage ceremony. The inviolability of the family was sanctioned in both civil law and the canons of the Catholic church. The reverse was true, he asserts, in the slave system of the United States. In reading Elkins' article you should take into account the contention of other historians that the slave code of which he speaks was not only unenforced but never promulgated in any of the South American countries. In fact, it is claimed, some of the measures encouraging marriage among slaves were designed to hold the slaves to the estates with family ties.[4]

The article by Furstenberg, Hershberg, and Modell investigates the origin of the female-headed Black family and its relation to the urban experience. Basing their analysis on samples from the decennial Federal population manuscript schedules for the period from 1850 to 1880, they look at the household structure of immigrants from Ireland and Germany and native white Americans in the city of Philadelphia. Only minor variations were found to exist among the four ethnic groups. Blacks and native whites were only slightly less likely to reside in nuclear households than were the immigrants. When property holdings were held constant, variations in family composition were negligible. It was economic status that caused most of the variations, for it led to high mortality, which in turn created problems of remarriage for Black females with children.

[3]Herbert Gutman, The Black Family in Slavery and Freedom (New York: Pantheon, 1976).

[4]Gwendolyn Midlo Hall, "The Myth of Benevolent Spanish Slave Law," Negro Digest 19 (1970): 31–38.

1

The Study of Black Families

The Tangle of Pathology

Daniel P. Moynihan

In this controversial and much-debated report on the Black family, the author claims that weaknesses in family structure account for many of the problems Afro-Americans encounter in American society. The reason for welfare dependency, out-of-wedlock children, educational failure, crime and delinquency, and so on is the unnatural dominance of women in the family structure. Without tongue in cheek the author recommends, as remedy, increased involvement of Black men in the military.

That the Negro American has survived at all is extraordinary—a lesser people might simply have died out, as indeed others have. That the Negro community has not only survived, but in this political generation has entered national affairs as a moderate, humane, and constructive national force is the highest testament to the healing powers of the democratic ideal and the creative vitality of the Negro people.

But it may not be supposed that the Negro American community has not paid a fearful price for the incredible mistreatment to which it has been subjected over the past three centuries.

In essence, the Negro community has been forced into a matriarchal structure which, because it is so out of line with the rest of the American society, seriously retards the progress of the group as a whole, and imposes a crushing burden on the Negro male and, in consequence, on a great many Negro women as well.

There is, presumably, no special reason why a society in which males are dominant in family relationships is to be preferred to a matriarchal arrangement. However, it is clearly a disadvantage for a minority group to be operating on one principle, while the great majority of the population, and the one with the most advantages to begin with, is operating on another. This is the present situation of the Negro. Ours is a society which presumes male leadership in private and public affairs. The arrangements of society facilitate such leadership and reward it. A subculture, such as that of the Negro American, in which this is not the pattern, is placed at a distinct disadvantage.

Here an earlier word of caution should be repeated. There is much evidence that a considerable number of Negro families have managed to break out of the tangle of pathology and to establish themselves as stable, effective units, living according to patterns of American society in general. E. Franklin Frazier has suggested that the middle-class Negro American family is, if anything, more patriarchal and protective of its children than the general run of such families.[1] Given equal opportunities, the children of these families will perform as well or better than their white peers. They need no help from anyone, and ask none.

While this phenomenon is not easily measured, one index is that middle-class Negroes have even fewer children than middle-class whites, indicating a desire to conserve the advances they have made and to insure that their

[1]E. Franklin Frazier, *Black Bourgeoisie* (New York, Collier Books, 1962).

Condensed from *The Negro Family: The Case for National Action,* by the Office of Policy Planning and Research, United States Department of Labor (U.S. Government Printing Office, March 1965), pp. 29–44. Tables have been deleted and footnotes renumbered.

children do as well or better. Negro women who marry early to uneducated laborers have more children than white women in the same situation; Negro women who marry at the common age for the middle class to educated men doing technical or professional work have only four-fifths as many children as their white counterparts.

It might be estimated that as much as half of the Negro community falls into the middle class. However, the remaining half is in desperate and deteriorating circumstances. Moreover, because of housing segregation it is immensely difficult for the stable half to escape from the cultural influences of the unstable one. The children of middle-class Negroes often as not must grow up in, or next to the slums, an experience almost unknown to white middle-class children. They are therefore constantly exposed to the pathology of the disturbed group and constantly in danger of being drawn into it. It is for this reason that the propositions put forth in this study may be thought of as having a more or less general application.

In a word, most Negro youth are in *danger* of being caught up in the tangle of pathology that affects their world, and probably a majority are so entrapped. Many of those who escape do so for one generation only: as things now are, their children may have to run the gauntlet all over again. That is not the least vicious aspect of the world that white America has made for the Negro.

Obviously, not every instance of social pathology afflicting the Negro community can be traced to the weakness of family structure. If, for example, organized crime in the Negro community were not largely controlled by whites, there would be more capital accumulation among Negroes, and therefore probably more Negro business enterprises. If it were not for the hostility and fear many whites exhibit towards Negroes, they in turn would be less afflicted by hostility and fear and so on. There is no one Negro community. There is no one Negro problem. There is no one solution. Nonetheless, at the center of the tangle of pathology is the weakness of the family structure. Once or twice removed, it will be found to be the principal source of most of the aberrant, inadequate, or antisocial behavior that did not establish, but now serves to perpetuate the cycle of poverty and deprivation.

It was by destroying the Negro family under slavery that white America broke the will of the Negro People. Although that will has reasserted itself in our time, it is a resurgence doomed to frustration unless the viability of the Negro family is restored.

Matriarchy

A fundamental fact of Negro American family life is the often reversed roles of husband and wife.

Robert O. Blood, Jr., and Donald M. Wolfe, in a study of Detroit families, note that "Negro husbands have unusually low power,"[2] and while this is characteristic of all low income families, the pattern pervades the Negro social structure: "the cumulative result of discrimination in jobs . . . , the segregated housing, and the poor schooling of Negro men."[3] In 44 percent of the Negro families studied, the wife was dominant, as against 20 percent of white wives. "Whereas the majority of white families are equalitarian, the largest percentage of Negro families are dominated by the wife."[4]

The matriarchal pattern of so many Negro families reinforces itself over the generations. This process begins with education. Although the gap appears to be closing at the moment, for a long while, Negro females were better educated than Negro males, and this remains true today for the Negro population as a whole.

The difference in educational attainment between nonwhite men and women in the labor force is even greater; men lag 1.1 years behind women.

The disparity in educational attainment of male and female youth age 16 to 21 who were out of school in February 1963, is striking. Among the nonwhite males, 66.3 percent were not high school graduates, compared with 55.0 percent of the females. A similar difference existed at the college level, with 4.5 percent of the males having completed 1 to 3 years of college compared with 7.3 percent of the females.

The poorer performance of the male in school exists from the very beginning, and the magnitude of the difference was documented by the 1960 Census in statistics on the number of

[2]Robert O. Blood, Jr., and Donald M. Wolfe, *Husbands and Wives: The Dynamics of Married Living* (New York, The Free Press, 1960), p. 34.
[3]*Ibid*, p. 35.
[4]*Ibid*.

children who have fallen one or more grades below the typical grade for children of the same age. The boys have more frequently fallen behind at every age level. (White boys also lag behind white girls, but at a differential of 1 to 6 percentage points.)

In 1960, 39 percent of all white persons 25 years of age and over who had completed 4 or more years of college were women. Fifty-three percent of the nonwhites who had attained this level were women.

However, the gap is closing. By October 1963, there were slightly more Negro men in college than women. Among whites there were almost twice as many men as women enrolled.

There is much evidence that Negro females are better students than their male counterparts.

Daniel Thompson of Dillard University, in a private communication on January 9, 1965, writes:

As low as is the aspirational level among lower class Negro girls, it is considerably higher than among the boys. For example, I have examined the honor rolls in Negro high schools for about 10 years. As a rule, from 75 to 90 percent of all Negro honor students are girls.

. . . .

In 1 out of 4 Negro families where the husband is present, is an earner, and some one else in the family works, the husband is not the principal earner. The comparable figure for whites is 18 percent.

More important, it is clear that Negro females have established a strong position for themselves in white collar and professional employment, precisely the areas of the economy which are growing most rapidly, and to which the highest prestige is accorded.

The President's Committee on Equal Employment Opportunity, making a preliminary report on employment in 1964 of over 16,000 companies with nearly 5 million employees, revealed this pattern with dramatic emphasis.

In this work force, Negro males outnumber Negro females by a ratio of 4 to 1. Yet Negro males represent only 1.2 percent of the males in white collar occupations, while Negro females represent 3.1 percent of the total female white collar work force. Negro males represent 1.1 percent of all male professionals, whereas Negro females represent roughly 6 percent of all female professionals. Again, in technician occupations, Negro males represent 2.1 percent of all male technicians while Negro females represent roughly 10 percent of all female technicians. It would appear therefore that there are proportionately 4 times as many Negro females in significant white collar jobs than Negro males.

Although it is evident that office and clerical jobs account for approximately 50 percent of all Negro female white collar workers, it is significant that 6 out of every 100 Negro females are in professional jobs. This is substantially similar to the rate of all females in such jobs. Approximately 7 out of every 100 Negro females are in technician jobs. This exceeds the proportion of all females in technician jobs—approximately 5 out of every 100.

Negro females in skilled jobs are almost the same as that of all females in such jobs. Nine out of every 100 Negro males are in skilled occupations while 21 out of 100 of all males are in such jobs.[5]

This pattern is to be seen in the Federal government, where special efforts have been made recently to insure equal employment opportunity for Negroes. These efforts have been notably successful in Departments such as Labor, where some 19 percent of employees are now Negro. (A not disproportionate percentage, given the composition of the work force in the areas where the main Department offices are located.) However, it may well be that these efforts have redounded mostly to the benefit of Negro women, and may even have accentuated the comparative disadvantage of Negro men. Seventy percent of the Negro employees of the Department of Labor are women, as contrasted with only 42 percent of the white employees.

Among nonprofessional Labor Department employees—where the most employment opportunities exist for all groups—Negro women outnumber Negro men 4 to 1, and average almost one grade higher in classification.

The testimony to the effects of these pat-

[5]Based on preliminary draft of a report by the President's Committee on Equal Employment Opportunity.

terns in Negro family structure is widespread, and hardly to be doubted. . . .

Duncan M. MacIntyre

The Negro illegitimacy rate always has been high—about eight times the white rate in 1940 and somewhat higher today even though the white illegitimacy rate also is climbing. The Negro statistics are symptomatic of some old socioeconomic problems, not the least of which are underemployment among Negro men and compensating higher labor force propensity among Negro women. Both operate to enlarge the mother's role, undercutting the status of the male and making many Negro families essentially matriarchal. The Negro man's uncertain employment prospects, matriarchy, and high cost of divorces combine to encourage desertion (the poor man's divorce), increase the number of couples not married, and thereby also increase the Negro illegitimacy rate. In the meantime, higher Negro birth rates are increasing the nonwhite population, while migration into cities like Detroit, New York, Philadelphia, and Washington, D.C., is making the public assistance rolls in such cities heavily, even predominantly, Negro.[6]

Robin M. Williams, Jr., in a Study of Elmira, New York

Only 57 percent of Negro adults reported themselves as married—spouse present, as compared with 78 percent of native white American gentiles, 91 percent of Italian-American, and 96 percent of Jewish informants. Of the 93 unmarried Negro youths interviewed, 22 percent did not have their mother living in the home with them, and 42 percent reported that their father was not living in their home. One-third of the youths did not know their father's present occupation, and two-thirds of a sample of 150 Negro adults did not know what the occupation of their father's father had been. Forty percent of the youths said that they had brothers and sisters living in other communities; *another 40 percent reported relatives living in their home who were not parents, siblings, or grandparents.[7]*

The Failure of Youth

Williams' account of Negro youth growing up with little knowledge of their fathers, less of their fathers' occupations, still less of family occupational traditions, is in sharp contrast to the experience of the white child. The white family, despite many variants, remains a powerful agency not only for transmitting property from one generation to the next, but also for transmitting no less valuable contracts with the world of education and work. In an earlier age, the Carpenters, Wainwrights, Weavers, Mercers, Farmers, Smiths acquired their names as well as their trades from their fathers and grandfathers. Children today still learn the patterns of work from their fathers even though they may no longer go into the same jobs.

White children without fathers at least perceive all about them the pattern of men working.

Negro children without fathers flounder—and fail.

Not always, to be sure. The Negro community produces its share, very possibly more than its share, of young people who have the something extra that carries them over the worst obstacles. But such persons are always a minority. The common run of young people in a group facing serious obstacles to success do not succeed.

A prime index of the disadvantage of Negro youth in the United States is their consistently poor performance on the mental tests that are a standard means of measuring ability and performance in the present generation.

There is absolutely no question of any genetic differential: Intelligence potential is distributed among Negro infants in the same proportion and pattern as among Icelanders or Chinese or any other group. American society, however, impairs the Negro potential. The statement of the HARYOU report that "there is no basic disagreement over the fact that central Harlem students are performing poorly in school"[8] may be taken as

[6]Duncan M. MacIntyre, *Public Assistance: Too Much or Too Little?* (New York, New York State School of Industrial Relations, Cornell University, Bulletin 53-1, December 1964), pp. 73–74.

[7]Robin M. Williams, Jr., *Strangers Next Door* (Englewood Cliffs, N.J., Prentice-Hall, Inc., 1964), p. 240.
[8]*Youth in the Ghetto* (New York: Harlem Youth Opportunities Unlimited), p. 195.

true of Negro slum children throughout the United States.

Eighth grade children in central Harlem have a median IQ of 87.7, which means that perhaps a third of the children are scoring at levels perilously near to those of retardation. IQ *declines* in the first decade of life, rising only slightly thereafter.

The effect of broken families on the performance of Negro youth has not been extensively measured, but studies that have been made show an unmistakable influence.

Martin Deutch and Bert Brown, investigating intelligence test differences between Negro and white 1st and 5th graders of different social classes, found that there is a direct relationship between social class and IQ. As the one rises so does the other: but more for whites than Negroes. This is surely a result of housing segregation, referred to earlier, which makes it difficult for middle-class Negro families to escape the slums.

The authors explain that "it is much more difficult for the Negro to attain identical middle- or upper-middle-class status with whites, and the social class gradations are less marked for Negroes because Negro life in a caste society is considerably more homogeneous than is life for the majority group."[9]

Therefore, the authors look for background variables other than social class which might explain the difference: "One of the most striking differences between the Negro and white groups is the consistently higher frequency of broken homes and resulting family disorganization in the Negro group."[10]

Further, they found that children from homes where fathers are present have significantly higher scores than children in homes without fathers.

The influence of the father's presence was then tested *within* the social classes and school grades for Negroes alone. They found that "a consistent trend within both grades at the lower SES [social class] level appears, and in no case is there a reversal of this trend: for males, females, and the combined group, the IQ's of children with

fathers in the home are always higher than those who have no father in the home."[11]

The authors say that broken homes "may also account for some of the differences between Negro and white intelligence scores."[12]

The scores of fifth graders with fathers absent were lower than the scores of first graders with fathers absent, and while the authors point out that it is cross sectional data and does not reveal the duration of the fathers' absence, "What we might be tapping is the cumulative effect of fatherless years."[13]

This difference in ability to perform has its counterpart in statistics on actual school performance. Nonwhite boys from families with both parents present are more likely to be going to school than boys with only one parent present, and enrollment rates are even lower when neither parent is present.

When the boys from broken homes are in school, they do not do as well as the boys from whole families. Grade retardation is higher when only one parent is present, and highest when neither parent is present.

The loneliness of the Negro youth in making fundamental decisions about education is shown in a 1959 study of Negro and white dropouts in Connecticut high schools.

Only 29 percent of the Negro male dropouts discussed their decision to drop out of school with their fathers, compared with 65 percent of the white males (38 percent of the Negro males were from broken homes). In fact, 26 percent of the Negro males did not discuss this major decision in their lives with anyone at all, compared with only 8 percent of white males.

A study of Negro apprenticeship by the New York State Commission Against Discrimination in 1960 concluded:

Negro youth are seldom exposed to influences which can lead to apprenticeship. Negroes are not apt to have relatives, friends, or neighbors in skilled occupations. Nor are they likely to be in secondary schools where they receive encouragement and direction from alternate role models. Within the minority community, skilled Negro "models" after whom

[9]Martin Deutch and Bert Brown, "Social Influences in Negro–White Intelligence Differences," *Social Issues,* April 1964, p. 27.

[10]*Ibid,* p. 29.

[11]*Ibid.*

[12]*Ibid,* p. 31.

[13]*Ibid.*

the Negro youth might pattern himself are rare,
while substitute sources which could provide
the direction, encouragement, resources, and
information needed to achieve skilled craft
standing are nonexistent.[14]

Delinquency and Crime

The combined impact of poverty, failure,
and isolation among Negro youth has had the
predictable outcome in a disastrous delinquency
and crime rate.

In a typical pattern of discrimination, Negro
children in all public and private orphanages are a
smaller proportion of all children than their proportion of the population although their needs are
clearly greater.

On the other hand Negroes represent a third
of all youth in training schools for juvenile delinquents.

It is probable that at present, a majority of
the crimes against the person, such as rape,
murder, and aggravated assault, are committed by
Negroes. There is, of course, no absolute evidence; inference can only be made from arrest
and prison population statistics. The data that
follow unquestionably are biased against Negroes, who are arraigned much more casually
than are whites, but it may be doubted that the
bias is great enough to affect the general proportions.

Again on the urban frontier the ratio is
worse: 3 out of every 5 arrests for these crimes
were of Negroes.

In Chicago in 1963, three-quarters of the
persons arrested for such crimes were Negro; in
Detroit, the same proportions held.

In 1960, 37 percent of all persons in Federal
and State prisons were Negro. In that year, 56
percent of the homicide and 57 percent of the
assault offenders committed to State institutions
were Negro.

The overwhelming number of offenses committed by Negroes are directed toward other
Negroes: the cost of crime to the Negro community is a combination of that to the criminal and to
the victim.

Some of the research on the effects of
broken homes on delinquent behavior recently

surveyed by Thomas F. Pettigrew in A Profile of the
Negro American is summarized below, along with
several other studies of the question.

Mary Diggs found that three-fourths—twice
the expected ratio—of Philadelphia's Negro delinquents who came before the law during 1948 did
not live with both their natural parents.[15]

In predicting juvenile crime, Eleanor and
Sheldon Glueck also found that a higher proportion of delinquent than nondelinquent boys came
from broken homes. They identified five critical
factors in the home environment that made a
difference in whether boys would become delinquents: discipline of boy by father, supervision of
boy by mother, affection of father for boy, affection
of mother for boy, and cohesiveness of family.

In 1952, when the New York City Youth
Board set out to test the validity of these five
factors as predictors of delinquency, a problem
quickly emerged. The Glueck sample consisted of
white boys of mainly Irish, Italian, Lithuanian, and
English descent. However, the Youth Board group
was 44 percent Negro and 14 percent Puerto
Rican, and the frequency of broken homes within
these groups was out of proportion to the total
number of delinquents in the population.[16]

In the majority of these cases, the father
was usually never in the home at all, absent for
the major proportion of the boy's life, or was
present only on occasion.

(The final prediction table was reduced to
three factors: supervision of boy by mother, discipline of boy by mother, and family cohesiveness
within what family, in fact, existed; it was, nonetheless, 85 percent accurate in predicting delinquents and 96 percent accurate in predicting
nondelinquents.)

Researchers who have focussed upon the
"good" boys in high delinquency neighborhoods
noted that they typically come from exceptionally
stable, intact families.[17]

[14]"Negroes in Apprenticeship, New York State," Monthly
Labor Review, September 1960, p. 955.

[15]Mary H. Diggs, "Some Problems and Needs of Negro
Children as Revealed by Comparative Delinquency and Crime
Statistics," Journal of Negro Education, 19, 1950, pp. 290–297.

[16]Maude M. Craig and Thelma J. Glick, "Ten Years
Experience with the Glueck Social Prediction Table," Journal of
Crime and Delinquency, July 1963, p. 256.

[17]F. R. Scarpitti, Ellen Murray, S. Dinitz, and W. C.
Reckless, "The 'Good' Boy in a High Delinquency Area: Four
Years Later," American Sociological Review, 25, 1960, pp. 555–
558.

Recent psychological research demonstrates the personality effects of being reared in a disorganized home without a father. One study showed that children from fatherless homes seek immediate gratification of their desires far more than children with fathers present.[18] Others revealed that children who hunger for immediate gratification are more prone to delinquency, along with other less social behavior.[19] Two psychologists, Pettigrew says, maintain that inability to delay gratification is a critical factor in immature, criminal, and neurotic behavior.[20]

Finally, Pettigrew discussed the evidence that a stable home is a crucial factor in counteracting the effects of racism upon Negro personality.

A warm, supportive home can effectively compensate for many of the restrictions the Negro child faces outside of the ghetto; consequently, the type of home life a Negro enjoys as a child may be far more crucial for governing the influence of segregation upon his personality than the form the segregation takes—legal or informal, Southern or Northern.[21]

A Yale University study of youth in the lowest socioeconomic class in New Haven in 1950 whose behavior was followed through their 18th year revealed that among the delinquents in the group, 38 percent came from broken homes, compared with 24 percent of nondelinquents.[22]

The President's Task Force on Manpower Conservation in 1963 found that of young men rejected for the draft for failure to pass the mental tests, 42 percent of those with a court record came from broken homes, compared with 30 percent of those without a court record. Half of all the nonwhite rejectees in the study with a court record came from broken homes.

An examination of the family background of 44,448 delinquency cases in Philadelphia between 1949 and 1954 documents the frequency of broken homes among delinquents. Sixty-two percent of the Negro delinquents and 36 percent of white delinquents were not living with both parents. In 1950, 33 percent of nonwhite children and 7 percent of white children in Philadelphia were living in homes without both parents. Repeaters were even more likely to be from broken homes than first offenders.[23]

The Armed Forces

The ultimate mark of inadequate preparation for life is the failure rate on the Armed Forces mental test. The Armed Forces Qualification Test is not quite a mental test, nor yet an education test. It is a test of ability to perform at an acceptable level of competence. It roughly measures ability that ought to be found in an average 7th or 8th grade student. A grown young man who cannot pass this test is in trouble.

Fifty-six percent of Negroes fail it.

This is a rate almost four times that of the whites.

The Army, Navy, Air Force, and Marines conduct by far the largest and most important education and training activities of the Federal Government, as well as provide the largest single source of employment in the nation.

Military service is disruptive in some respects. For those comparatively few who are killed or wounded in combat, or otherwise, the personal sacrifice is inestimable. But on balance service in the Armed Forces over the past quarter-century has worked greatly to the advantage of those involved. The training and experience of military duty itself is unique; the advantages that have generally followed in the form of the G.I. Bill, mortgage guarantees, Federal life insurance, Civil Service preference, veterans' hospitals, and veterans' pensions are singular, to say the least. . . .

In 1963 the Civil Rights Commission commented on the occupational aspect of military service for Negroes. "Negro enlisted men enjoy relatively better opportunities in the Armed Forces than in the civilian economy in every clerical,

[18]W. Mischel, "Father-Absence and Delay of Gratification: Cross-Cultural Comparisons," *Journal of Abnormal and Social Psychology,* 63, 1961, pp. 116–124.

[19]W. Mischel, "Preference for Delayed Reinforcement and Social Responsibility," *Journal of Social and Abnormal Psychology,* 62, 1961, pp. 1–7; "Delay of Gratification, Need for Achievement, and Acquiescence in Another Culture," *Journal of Abnormal and Social Psychology,* 62, 1961, pp. 543–552.

[20]O. H. Mowrer and A. D. Ullman, "Time as a Determinant in Integrative Learning," *Psychological Review,* 52, 1945, pp. 61–90.

[21]Thomas F. Pettigrew, *Profile of the Negro American* (New York: Van Nostrand, 1964), p. 22.

[22]Erdman Palmore, "Factors Associated with School Dropouts on Juvenile Delinquency Among Lower Class Children," *Social Security Bulletin,* October 1963, p. 6.

[23]Thomas P. Monahan, "Family Status and the Delinquent Child," *Social Forces,* March 1957, p. 254.

technical, and skilled field for which the data permit comparison."[24]

There is, however, an even more important issue involved in military service for Negroes. Service in the United States Armed Forces is the *only* experience open to the Negro American in which he is truly treated as an equal: not as a Negro equal to a white, but as one man equal to any other man in a world where the categories "Negro" and "white" do not exist. If this is a statement of the ideal rather than reality, it is an ideal that is close to realization. In food, dress, housing, pay, work—the Negro in the Armed Forces *is* equal and is treated that way.

There is another special quality about military service for Negro men: it is an utterly masculine world. Given the strains of the disorganized and matrifocal family life in which so many Negro youth come of age, the Armed Forces are a dramatic and desperately needed change: a world away from women, a world run by strong men of unquestioned authority, where discipline, if harsh, is nonetheless orderly and predictable, and where rewards, if limited, are granted on the basis of performance.

The theme of a current Army recruiting message states it as clearly as can be: "In the U.S. Army you get to know what it means to feel like a man."

At the recent Civil Rights Commission hearings in Mississippi a witness testified that his Army service was in fact "the only time I ever felt like a man."

Yet a majority of Negro youth (and probably three-quarters of Mississippi Negroes) fail the Selective Service education test and are rejected. Negro participation in the Armed Forces would be less than it is, were it not for a proportionally larger share of voluntary enlistments and reenlistments. (Thus 16.3 percent of Army sergeants are Negro.)

Alienation

The term alienation may by now have been used in too many ways to retain a clear meaning, but it will serve to sum up the equally numerous ways in which large numbers of Negro youth appear to be withdrawing from American society.

One startling way in which this occurs is that the men are just not there when the Census enumerator comes around.

[24]*Ibid,* p. 174.

According to Bureau of Census population estimates for 1963, there are only 87 nonwhite males for every 100 females in the 30-to-34-year age group. The ratio does not exceed 90 to 100 throughout the 25-to-44-year age bracket. In the urban Northeast, there are only 76 males per 100 females 20-to-24-years of age, and males as a percent of females are below 90 percent throughout all ages after 14.

There are not really fewer men than women in the 20-to-40 age bracket. What obviously is involved is an error in counting: the surveyors simply do not find the Negro man. Donald J. Bogue and his associates, who have studied the Federal count of the Negro man, place the error as high as 19.8 percent at age 28; a typical error of around 15 percent is estimated from age 19 through 43.[25] Preliminary research in the Bureau of the Census on the 1960 enumeration has resulted in similar conclusions, although not necessarily the same estimates of the extent of the error. The Negro male *can* be found at age 17 and 18. On the basis of birth records and mortality records, the conclusion must be that he is there at age 19 as well.

When the enumerators do find him, his answers to the standard questions asked in the monthly unemployment survey often result in counting him as "not in the labor force." In other words, Negro male unemployment may in truth be somewhat greater than reported.

The labor force participation rates of nonwhite men have been falling since the beginning of the century and for the past decade have been lower than the rates for white men. In 1964, the participation rates were 78.0 percent for white men and 75.8 percent for nonwhite men. Almost one percentage point of this difference was due to a higher proportion of nonwhite men unable to work because of long-term physical or mental illness; it seems reasonable to assume that the rest of the difference is due to discouragement about finding a job.

If nonwhite male labor force participation rates were as high as the white rates, there would have been 140,000 more nonwhite males in the labor force in 1964. If we further assume that the 140,000 would have been unemployed, the unem-

[25]Donald J. Bogue, Bhaskar D. Misra, and D. P. Dandekar, "A New Estimate of the Negro Population and Negro Vital Rates in the United States, 1930–1960," *Demography,* Vol. 1, No. 1, 1964, p. 350.

ployment rate for nonwhite men would have been 11.5 percent instead of the recorded rate of 9 percent, and the ratio between the nonwhite rate and the white rate would have jumped from 2:1 to 2.4:1.

Understated or not, the official unemployment rates for Negroes are almost unbelievable.

The unemployment statistics for Negro teenagers—29 percent in January 1964—reflect lack of training and opportunity in the greatest measure, but it may not be doubted that they also reflect a certain failure of nerve.

"Are you looking for a job?" Secretary of Labor Wirtz asked a young man on a Harlem street corner. "Why?" was the reply.

Richard A. Cloward and Robert Ontell have commented on this withdrawal in a discussion of the Mobilization for Youth project on the lower East Side of New York.

What contemporary slum and minority youth probably lack that similar children in earlier periods possessed is not motivation but some minimal sense of competence.

We are plagued in work with these youth, by what appears to be a low tolerance for frustration. They are not able to absorb setbacks. Minor irritants and rebuffs are magnified out of all proportion to reality. Perhaps they react as they do because they are not equal to the world that confronts them, and they know it. And it is the knowing that is devastating. Had the occupational structure remained intact, or had the education provided to them kept pace with occupational changes, the situation would be a different one. But it is not, and that is what we and they have to contend with.[26]

Narcotic addiction is a characteristic form of withdrawal. In 1963, Negroes made up 54 percent of the addict population of the United States. Although the Federal Bureau of Narcotics reports a decline in the Negro proportion of new addicts, HARYOU reports the addiction rate in central Harlem rose from 22.1 per 10,000 in 1955 to 40.4 in 1961.[27]

There is a larger fact about the alienation of Negro youth than the tangle of pathology described by these statistics. It is a fact particularly difficult to grasp by white persons who have in recent years shown increasing awareness of Negro problems.

The present generation of Negro youth growing up in the urban ghettos has probably less personal contact with the white world than any generation in the history of the Negro American.[28]

Until World War II it could be said that in general the Negro and white worlds lived, if not together, at least side by side. Certainly they did, and do, in the South.

Since World War II, however, the two worlds have drawn physically apart. The symbol of this development was the construction in the 1940's and 1950's of the vast white middle- and lower-middle class suburbs around all of the Nation's cities. Increasingly, the inner cities have been left to Negroes—who now share almost no community life with whites.

In turn, because of this new housing pattern—most of which has been financially assisted by the Federal government—it is probable that the American school system has become *more,* rather than less segregated in the past two decades.

School integration has not occurred in the South, where a decade after *Brown* v. *Board of Education* only 1 Negro in 9 is attending school with white children.

And in the North, despite strenuous official efforts, neighborhoods and therefore schools are becoming more and more of one class and one color.

In New York City, in the school year 1957–58 there were 64 schools that were 90 percent or more Negro or Puerto Rican. Six years later there were 134 such schools.

Along with the diminution of white middle-class contacts for a large percentage of Negroes, observers report that the Negro churches have all but lost contact with men in the Northern cities as well. This may be a normal condition of urban life, but it is probably a changed condition for the Negro American and cannot be a socially desirable development.

[26]Richard A. Cloward and Robert Ontell, "Our Illusions about Training," *American Child,* January 1965, p. 7.
[27]*Youth in the Ghetto, op cit.,* p. 144.

[28]Nathan Glazer and Daniel Patrick Moynihan, *Beyond the Melting Pot* (Cambridge, Mass.: M.I.T. Press, 1965).

The only religious movement that appears to have enlisted a considerable number of lower-class Negro males in Northern cities of late is that of the Black Muslims: a movement based on total rejection of white society, even though it emulates white mores.

In a word: the tangle of pathology is tightening.

The Black Family Revisited

Robert Staples

The author presents a historical review of Black family research and discusses four evolved stages of research: poverty-acculturation, the pathologists, the reactive period, and Black nationalist family studies. He explains the historical conditions surrounding the popularity of these stages. Three conceptual models for studying Black families are examined: Pan Africanism, historical materialism, and domestic colonialism.

For seventy years the Black family has been the subject of scientific investigation. This study has had a variety of purposes, methodologies and conclusions. Concomitant with these have been the prevailing state of race relations and the circumstances of the Black population. This observation is congruent with Mannheim's thesis (1936) that ideas are a function of environment, that the nature of a society influences the kind of knowledge that the individual is exposed to contingent on his location in a certain milieu within the social structure.

This obviously raises the question of what type of Black family really exists in the United States. Probably there is no monolithic Black family grouping that we can use as a model, since there are numerous differences in family organization and functioning within the Black community. These variations exist by class, religious and regional lines, and so on. However, there are similar conditions which all Black families encounter; adaptations to these circumstances will produce similarities in their family life styles.

Another problem is that the study of Afro-American families has always used the white, middle-class family as a referent. Black families will always be perceived negatively with this yardstick, because the white, middle-class family is only an analytical construct, an ideal type which does not fit the majority of white families in this country. Moreover, even in white circles the ideal family form has come under attack for contributing to the suppression of women, producing neurotic and battered children and inhibiting individual sexual expression (Gordon 1972).

In this paper we review the past stages of Black family research and the social conditions at the time. Then, we propose some alternative conceptual models for studying Black families and discuss the strengths and weaknesses of each approach. Finally, we examine some of the future trends of Black family life as they relate to traditional patterns, along with the social forces influencing changes in the organization and functioning of Black families.

Stages of Black Family Research

Poverty-Acculturation

The original studies of Black family life by DuBois (1909) and Frazier (1932, 1939) focused on the economic conditions of the Black population which allegedly brought about their family "disorganization." It is important to note that these studies were undertaken at a time when urbanization was having its most devastating effect on the Black community. DuBois, in particular, wrote his classic "The Negro American Family" at a time when the massive Black migration

Condensed and revised from *Journal of Social and Behavioral Sciences* 20 (Spring 1974): 65–78. © 1974 by the Association of Social and Behavioral Scientists. Reprinted by permission.

from an agrarian setting to the city was taking place. Hence, it is not surprising that he found much higher rates of illegitimacy and female-headed households than in the previous century, when free Black families lived in the rural South. He was not studying a stable group of Blacks but one that was being uprooted from its folk culture and forced to the cities, where it was becoming part of the landless, urban proletariat.

But much of their family organization was a continuation of African values relating to family life. Because DuBois, Frazier and others believed that the solution to Black poverty was the integration of Blacks in the white world, they placed their emphasis on Black family norms coming into conformity with white, middle-class family behavior. At the same time they gave recognition to the African past, although in different ways, and noted the variety of Black family types that existed. Moreover, they believed that the disorganization of Black families was a result of slavery, racism and poverty. Family disorganization was not cited as a major cause of Black poverty and oppression by Black scholars during that period (Bracey et al. 1971).

The Pathologists

The pathologists' approach is primarily identified with Daniel Moynihan's (1965) report on the Negro family, which contained the thesis that at the heart of the deterioration of the Black community are weaknesses in the Black family. While using many of the same indices of family disorganization as the poverty-acculturation approach, it is differentiated by at least three other factors: (1) it occurred in a different era and had significant import for the formulation of public policy, (2) most of the scholars using this model were white and (3) in effect, it placed the blame for Black oppression on the Black family and, specifically, on Black women.

Moynihan and his followers (Aldous 1969, Bernard 1966, Rainwater 1970) initiated the study of Black families as a pathological form of social organization at precisely the time when Blacks were beginning to indict institutional racism as the cause of their oppression. The Civil Rights Movement was moving into a militant phase when the government-subsidized Moynihan study made public the assertion that it was weaknesses in the

Black family, for example, illegitimacy, female-headed households, and welfare dependency, that were responsible for poverty, educational failures and lack of employment in the Black population. His efforts put Blacks on the defensive and diverted their energy into responding to his charges (Rainwater and Yancey 1967).

In the mid-sixties the Moynihan thesis was taken up by a number of white behavioral scientists who found it easy to get funds to study Black family dysfunctions. During this period one found the strange situation of the majority of white family research being based on middle-class, white families and almost all of the studies of Black families dealing with the lower 25 percent of the Black class strata.

The Reactive Period

Behavioral scientists during the reactive period (roughly 1966 to 1971) included Blacks and whites. Basically this group argued that Black families were much like white families except for their impoverished status and history of slavery. Although there were exceptions, most agreed that permissive sex, out-of-wedlock children and female-headed households were undesirable and that improved economic conditions would diminish their prevalence among Black families. In some cases they denied any significant distinction between Black and white families. If one considered social class differences, Black families were much the same as white families (Rodman 1963). Even upper-lower-class Black families were found to have the same value system as white families (Liebow 1966, Willie 1970).

While research and theory during this period portrayed the Black family as victim rather than criminal, it still gave no positive value to the unique traits of Black family structure. For the most part it apologized for the political–economic system that had imposed these "undesirable" family characteristics on Afro-Americans. It was rare for any members of this group to call into question the value of the dominant groups' form of family organization. To have done so would have been to undermine the dominance of the Anglo-Saxon values that had prevailed from the first white settlement on these shores (Davidson 1969). However, as the white youth of America began to reject traditional family life styles, the emerging forms of marriage and the family approximated those of Black families. Hence, what had been negatively labeled when associated with Blacks had to be validated when it became part of the white cultural system.

What was known as the notorious matriarchy among Blacks is now regarded as women's liberation in the white community. The common-law marriages (or shacking up) that existed among Blacks has been redefined and re-evaluated as heterosexual cohabitation for whites. In the past, Black involvement in premarital sex was seen as immoral and licentious. Today, it is interpreted as part of the sexual freedom movement and has become an annual two and one half billion dollar industry for whites. All of these changes may be perceived as part of a domestic colonialism that denies legitimacy to the colonized's value system unless or until it becomes a part of the dominant group's culture.

Black Nationalist Family Studies

Black nationalist family research not only considered Black families non-pathological but began to delineate their strengths as well. The first significant work was that of Andrew Billingsley (1968), in the era of Black power movements. Billingsley's work was a combination of the reactive and nationalist orientations. He challenged the Moynihan report for its depiction of the Black family as pathological but continued to accept many normative values of middle-class, white family life. He was, however, one of the first scholars to perceive the Black family as viable and to indict the political and economic system for its oppression of Black families. His initial study was elaborated on and extended by other Black scholars.

In the post-Billingsley period, the most significant works on Black families were produced by young Black scholars. A large number of articles and books were devoted to the strengths of Black women (Cade 1970, Ladner 1971, Reid 1972, Staples 1973). In general these studies focused on the severe conditions that Black women encountered and their courage and strength in overcoming those obstacles. Another landmark study was by Robert Hill (1972), who was the first Black scholar to systematically define and examine the

strengths of the Black family. Furthermore, he used quantitative data to support his propositions about the positive values in Afro-American family life.

Studies of Afro-American families have generally considered them as a deviant American family type. Although recent works have attempted to refute many of the negative stereotypes in the research literature, few have set forth counter-models that describe the nature and function of Black families historically, or that provide us with new insights into the Afro-American family as an autonomous social system.

Conceptual Models for Studying Black Family Life

We are concerned here with conceptual models that can be used to understand the structure and dynamics of Black family life—not systematic theories of Black family life but concepts that alert the sociologist to what is important when studying Black family relationships (Zetterberg 1965). Thus, we are interested in using historical materialism not as a holistic theoretical framework but rather to help us determine the effect of economic forces in shaping a groups' family pattern. The three conceptual models to be considered are *Pan Africanism, historical materialism* and *domestic colonialism.*

Pan Africanism

Pan Africanism has become the dominant conceptual model among Black scholars studying the Black family. While the Pan-Africanist perspective is more commonly associated with a political program, it also has value as a conceptual model. The Pan-African philosophy holds that people of African descent have a common culture as well as a common history of racist oppression that has culminated in a shared destiny. In relation to the Black family, people of African descent are perceived as part of the diaspora wherever they are found and in whatever form.

This conceptual model allows us to study the Afro-American family as representing a continuity of African family patterns. The focus is on comparative study of Black families in the United States, the West Indies and Africa. Instead of measuring and evaluating Afro-American families according to white, middle-class family norms, the task is to find the similarities and contrasts with African family patterns throughout the world.

Cultural variations can be determined by studying the different forms of family behavior found among peoples of African descent. This means not only the variations within Africa (for example, matrilineal and patrilineal systems), but also the different types of African family forms in other parts of the world. For instance, in the United States one might compare Muslim with Christian families, lower-class with middle-class families, rural with urban families.

The Pan-African approach liberates the study of Afro-American families from the domination of white referents in the study of Black life. A comparison of Blacks and whites in America is useful for illustrating the effects of racial oppression, but if a meaningful analysis of Black cultural forms is what we want, the focus must be on those cultural traditions that are maintained in institutions such as the family (Ladner 1971, Nobles 1972).

Whereas the Pan-Africanist perspective is valuable for understanding the family traditions that remained intact or were modified in the diaspora, the political and economic forces that the Afro-American family encountered that influenced its character need to be understood. Pan-Africanism as a conceptual model has concentrated more on cultural forms than on the effect of a society's political economy. Moreover, historical and anthropological methodologies have to be refined and strengthened so that contemporary Afro-American families can be understood in light of historical and cross-cultural facts.

Historical Materialism

This concept, attributed primarily to the socialist theoretician Karl Marx (1936), views the family institution as a product of economic forces. According to Marx, the functions of the family are determined by class relationships. In capitalist societies women and children are mere appendages of machines, to be used as a reserve labor supply in cases of economic expansion. He believed that the capitalist economic order made family life almost impossible for the working class since women were forced to work, and their employment ipso facto destroys the family. Engels,

his collaborator, asserted (1950) that the working man was dependent on the family and that this resulted in a continual succession of family troubles: domestic quarrels, neglect of domestic duties, an increase in juvenile delinquency and child mortality, and the like.

Historical materialism's emphasis on political and economic influences on family life has considerable significance for understanding variations among Black families of the diaspora. There are indications, for instance, that the matricentric family is partially related to wage-labor systems that require the mobility of the male labor force, which produces an imbalance in the sex ratio (Staples 1972a). In North America the political system may have produced the same results (Jackson 1971, Staples 1973).

This model also has import for understanding the nature of family conflict, the suppression of women, and other forces that act on the family. A good combination of Pan-Africanist and historical materialist elements would be a syncretic model that shows how economic forces act on family relations, counteracted by cultural adaptations to each event. Moreover, we might analyze families of the diaspora by economic epoch and study the modification of family forms in response to those vagaries. However, economics is not the only cause of the historical movement and transformation of Black families. Other elements of a given society also influence the quality of a group's family life. Economic factors do not sufficiently distinguish the Black family from poor white families. Another pre-eminent force in American life is white racism.

Domestic Colonialism

Domestic colonialism contains some of the essential elements of historical materialism but focuses on the use of racism for political and economic exploitation. A colonial system typically places racial groups into superordinate and subordinate categories, with the racially subordinate group being denied equal participation in society and the dominant group accorded special privileges at their expense (Blauner 1972). Central to the understanding of Afro-American family life are the concepts of "racial privilege" and "cultural domination."

As Blauner (1972) has noted, domestic colonialism is distinguished from capitalism by its use of culture as an instrument of domination. In the case of Afro-American families, the Anglo-Saxon family pattern was imposed on them while attempts were made to destroy the African family system. A good example is the vitiation of the parent's rights in their children under the system of slavery. The husband's domestic rights in his wife were also eliminated, being abrogated to the slavemaster. The continuation of white cultural domination is seen in the negative labeling of Black families who do not conform to Anglo-Saxon family norms. Furthermore, the conditions necessary for approximating the middle-class family model are denied many Black Americans, since the economic needs of the ruling class take precedence over Black family needs.

The domestic colonialism model may explain other aspects of Black family behavior in addition to the motivation behind the pathological approach to studying Afro-American family patterns. We might better understand Black family violence, the middle-class Black family's contradictions and how the strengths of Black families have been defined by white racism. This approach, however, needs to be developed theoretically, lest it be applied mechanically to the American experience, specifically Afro-American family life.

A further limitation of this model is its emphasis on the negative and oppressive aspects of Afro-American life. It needs to be combined with the Pan-Africanist perspective in order to understand the continuity of cultural strands as well as the imposition of Anglo-Saxon cultural forms which threaten to destroy the African cultural heritage. . . .

Summary

In this paper we have tried to put the study of Black families into its proper historical and theoretical perspective. This can only be seen as a small, initial effort in the development of a Black Nationalist family study. While our critics will condemn us for imposing ideology on a discipline bounded by the concept of a value-free science, it is at least an honest effort to confront those who have prostituted science in the service of an oppressive, white-dominated system. The question of what is truth can be left to those who can afford the luxury of a search for abstractions in this time of compelling social unrest and who have no interest that takes ascendency over this elusive quest.

The control of Black family studies is now in the hands of those whose destiny is affected by the nature of what we choose to investigate and the problems that seek resolution. If the Marxist dictum that the knowledge of a society reflects the needs of its ruling class is true, we must stand fast to his other maxim: some men seek to understand society, our task is to change it.

References

Aldous, Joan
1969 "Wives' Employment Status and Lower Class Men as Husband-Fathers: Support for the Moynihan Thesis." *Journal of Marriage and the Family* 31 (August): 469–476.

Bernard, Jessie
1966 *Marriage and Family Among Negroes.* Englewood Cliffs, New Jersey: Prentice-Hall.

Billingsley, Andrew
1968 *Black Families in White America.* Englewood Cliffs, New Jersey: Prentice-Hall.

Blauner, Robert
1972 *Racial Oppression in America.* New York: Harper & Row.

Bracey, John, et al.
1971 *The Black Sociologists: The First Half Century.* Belmont, Calif.: Wadsworth.

Cade, Toni
1970 *The Black Woman: An Anthology.* New York: Signet Books.

Davidson, Douglas
1969 "Black Culture and Liberal Sociology." *Berkeley Journal of Sociology* 15:164–183.

DuBois, W. E. B.
1909 *The Negro American Family.* Atlanta: Atlanta University Press.

Engels, Frederick
1950 *Conditions of the Working Class in England.* London: Oxford University Press.

Farley, Reynolds
1970 *Growth of the Black Population.* Chicago: Markham.

Frazier, E. Franklin
1932 *The Negro Family in Chicago.* Chicago: University of Chicago Press.
1939 *The Negro Family in the United States.* Chicago: University of Chicago Press.

Gordon, Michael
1972 *The Nuclear Family in Crisis.* New York: Harper & Row.

Heer, David
1966 "Negro–White Marriage in the United States." *Journal of Marriage and the Family* 28 (August):262–273.

Hill, Robert
1972 *The Strengths of Black Families.* New York: Emerson-Hall.

Jackson, Jacquelyne
1971 "But Where Are the Men?" *The Black Scholar* 2 (December):30–41.

King, Mae
1973 "The Politics of Sexual Stereotypes." *The Black Scholar* 4 (March–April):12–23.

Ladner, Joyce
1971 *Tomorrow's Tomorrow: The Black Woman.* New York: Doubleday.

Liebow, Eliott
1966 *Tally's Corner.* Boston: Little, Brown.

Mannheim, Karl
1936 *Ideology and Utopia.* New York: Harcourt, Brace and World.

Marx, Karl
1936 *Capital.* New York: Modern Library.

Moynihan, Daniel P.
1965 *The Negro Family: The Case for National Action.* Washington, D.C.: U.S. Government Printing Office.

Nobles, Wade
1972 "African Root and American Fruit: The Black Family." Paper originally presented at a conference on the Black Family, Laguna Beach, California.

Rainwater, Lee
1970 *Behind Ghetto Walls: Black Families in a Federal Slum.* Chicago: Aldine.

Rainwater, Lee, and Yancey, William
1967 *The Moynihan Report and the Politics of Controversy.* Cambridge: M.I.T. Press.

Reid, Inez
1972 *Together Black Women.* New York: Emerson-Hall.

Rodman, Hyman
1963 "The Lower Class Value Stretch." *Social Forces* 42 (December):205–215.

Staples, Robert
1972a "The Matricentric Family: A Cross-Cultural Examination." *Journal of Marriage and the Family* 34 (February):156–165.
1972b "The Sexuality of Black Women." *Sexual Behavior* 2 (June):4–15.
1973 *The Black Woman in America.* Chicago: Nelson-Hall.

Willie, Charles V.
1970 *The Family Life of Black People.* Columbus, Ohio: Charles E. Merrill Books.

Zelnik, Melvin, and Kantner, John
1972 "Sexuality, Contraception and Pregnancy among Young Unwed Families in the United States." Paper prepared for the Commission on Population Growth and the American Future (May).

Zetterberg, Hans
1965 *Theory and Verification in Sociology.* New York: Bedminister Press.

Africanity:
Its Role in Black Families

Wade Nobles

The author offers the notion that the Black family should be defined in relation to its African ancestry. He shows a parallel between African tribalism and the Black family unit, in terms of an intrinsic ability to extend kinship to non-relative members, a sense of oneness in the purpose of survival, and a flexibility of family roles.

For close to seventy-five years, the black family has been the subject of scientific investigations; and for close to seventy-five years, social scientists have offered "evidence," "information," and "analyses" concerning the so-called problems inherent in black family systems. As early as 1909, DuBois and later Frazier (1932, 1939) focused on the economic conditions of the black family which they related to the *problems* of "family disorganization." More recently investigators have claimed that the root cause of the deterioration of the black community was not to be found in its political and economic subjugation by a hostile wider (white) society, but rather the cause of the conditions of black communities is found in the nature of black families (cf: Moynihan, 1965).

Historically, the black family has generally been studied as a pathological form of social organization and the so-called *problems* (e.g., illegitimacy, female-headed households, welfare dependency, etc.) reportedly characteristic of black families were viewed or interpreted as being responsible for poverty, educational failures, unemployment, and crime in black neighborhoods.

Though some researchers have argued that the cause of the observable differences between white and black families is the fact of previous historical servitude and current economic impoverishment, the major trend of building upon the problem-oriented analysis of black families which assumes that they are no more than "sick" white families (cf: Scanzoni, 1971; Liebow, 1966;

Willie, 1970) continues to characterize the literature.

Professor Cedric X (Clark) has argued for an epistemological differentiation between the *study of black people* and *black studies* (cf: Clark, 1972). He notes in this regard that the *study of black people* takes as its interpretative framework the nature of non-black people while *black studies* should take as its interpretative framework the nature of black people. Consequently, the overweighted emphasis on the study of *negativity* in black family research is especially interesting in light of Professor X's recognition that all knowledge is rooted in social relations, particularly as these are determined by racial classifications and the Mannheim (1936) thesis that the nature of a society influences the kind of knowledge its people are exposed to. In further recognition of the social relativity of knowledge or information concerning the black family, Dr. Staples (1971) argues that the imposition of ethnocentric (white) values on the analyses of black family life precludes the application of much if not most of the previous and current research and theory concerning the black family. Several black scholars (Billingsley, 1966; Ladner, 1971; Staples, 1973; Hill, 1972; Nobles, 1974) have in fact suggested that the major problems in the studies of black families may not be problems intrinsic to the family itself but rather *problems* in or with the assumptions implicit in the theoretical analysis of the black family.

In recognizing, therefore, this methodological and theoretical "problem," one can also recognize the distortion given to family welfare, and/or education systems where the major portion of professional training activity and program development has used as its source of knowledge the understanding of the black family from white analytical frameworks. Naturally, these customary

From *The Black Scholar* 9 (June 1974):10–17. © 1974 by the Black World Foundation. Reprinted by permission.

analytical frameworks offer a *distorted perspective* to the total reality and complexion of the black family system. In reviewing the seventy-five years of research conducted on black families (i.e., the study of black families a la Cedric X), it becomes evident that the information collected by most researchers of black family life reflects more of the researchers' *mis*perceptions of black social reality and less representative exemplification of black family life. This fact alone stands in stark relief as the most notable critique of research on the black family.

Of equal importance in black family research is the fact that seldom has any investigator until very recently (cf. Shimkin, 1974) taken seriously the realization that the American black family, its definition, character, form and function did not begin with the American experience of slavery and that as a system it has an historical continuation extending back in history to traditional Africa and its culture. Furthermore, the black family, we contend, can only be understood or is best understood as a unit or system deriving its primary characteristics, form and definition from its African nature. Consequently, and in accordance with Professor X's caution, analysis of it must take as its interpretative framework the nature of black (African) families.

It is, therefore, suggested that what determines the special form black families take and the unique relational patterns expressed by black families is primarily the sense of *Africanity* or being in tune with or responsive to an African worldview or sense of the universe. It is important to note here that in speaking of a sense of "Africanity" in black families one does not require the presupposition of a singular, monolithic, homogeneous black family type. There is diversity in black families. However, within the diversity one is able to discern a comprehensive cultural unity which has historically characterized black families. It is this commonality which is referred to as the sense of "Africanity," and it is this sense of Africanity in black families which has served as the hidden force in our struggle. However, before offering evidence for this latter point, a brief description of the analytical framework for understanding African-based black family systems should be made.

For purposes of analytical clarity, family systems should be distinguished according to their own intrinsic definitions and natures. Accordingly, one should conceptually discuss the analytical framework of a family system primarily from the indices of its own intrinsic definition. Given, therefore, that the nature of a family system is culturally bound to its ethnic definition, the analytical framework for understanding the family system should be consistent with the intrinsic ethnic nature and definition of the family. Even though the black family unit is, as Dr. Billingsley (1966) has pointed out, only one element embedded in a network of mutually interdependent relationships with the black community and wider white society, it cannot be totally and only understood or interpreted from non-black (white-oriented) analytical frameworks. Black family systems can be thought of as African in nature and American in nurture (cf. Nobles, 1974). For this reason it is necessary that the analytical framework reflect the African-based reality.

Essentially, our argument suggests or presupposes that the African cultural heritage or philosophical worldview was *not* severed by the "horrors of the middle passage" nor the cruelty of the West Indian seasoning camps and New World plantation life. It is rather suggested that the continuance of the traditional African worldview has and still does define the basic structures and functions of black family units.

The African Philosophical Heritage

Traditional African social reality was, in fact, defined by a particular philosophical orientation generally described as "the understanding, attitude of mind, logic and perception behind the manner in which African peoples think, act or speak in different situations of life" (cf. Mbiti, 1970). As suggested elsewhere (Nobles, 1972), this philosophical definition implies an *ethos* or common guiding principle which permeated the life spaces of African peoples. It was further suggested that the African ethos or guiding principle could be perceived as defining or determining two operational orders: (1) *the survival of the tribe,* and (2) *the Oneness of Being*. Couple these guiding principles with the several African philosophical, cosmological, and behavioral principles (i.e., unity, cooperative effort, mutual responsibility, reconciliation, etc.) and one is able to understand or put in perspective most, if not all, aspects of traditional and contemporary African social reality.

Both the ethos and philosophical behavioral principles were primarily reflected in and reinforced by a deep sense of family or kinship (Osei, 1970) and the philosophical orientation, as reflected by the family, defined, regulated and controlled all the relations in traditional communities (cf: Mbiti, 1970). Consequently, the family was probably one of the strongest cohesive devices in traditional African life.

The traditional family system structurally stretched *horizontally* in every direction as well as *vertically* in both directions taking into account every member of the community. A person was related to the tribal ancestors as well as to those persons yet-to-be-born (vertical relations) and to every living person in the tribe (horizontal relations). The knowledge of one's tribal or family genealogy not only reflected and showed the importance of the *interconnectedness* of all elements of the family (tribe), it also was thought to impart the sense of sacred obligation to extend and continue one's genealogical line (see Mbiti, 1970). Individual persons recognized that their very existence depended not only on those who conceived and personally nourished them but every member of the tribe—living and dead. The structural definition of the family is best reflected in a belief the Ashanti share with all Akan peoples and which is typically held by Africans in general. This is the belief that "the dead, the living and those still-to-be-born of the tribe are all members of *one* family." The traditional family is thus defined as constituting the several "households" which make up a particular community (cf: Osei, 1970). Accordingly, the black African family has been defined as simply a group of persons related by marriage and/or ancestry (cf: Nobles, 1974).

Functionally, the purpose of the traditional family unit was to fulfill certain tasks, responsibilities, and/or basic needs of its members. For analytical purposes, one can divide the functional character of the family unit or system into two areas: the *pragmatic* functions and the *psychological* functions. Pragmatically, the family insures the provision of food, shelter, clothing and protection. Psychologically, the family unit offers a sense of belonging. It is via the psychological functions of the family system that its members

become conscious of their own being, purpose, and responsibilities toward oneself and other people.

In addition to recognizing that the family unit has the capacity to sustain its members economically (pragmatic function) and enhance the emotional inter- and intra-relationships (psychological function), we can further note that the structure of traditional African families was based on the *union* of elements. That is, the important feature in the structure was the way in which the elements (people, functions, rules, etc.) *united* together to make the whole. Each family function in a way "flowed" rhythmically into each other function.

Conceptually speaking, therefore, African-based family systems can be thought of as a *"Continual Flexibility in Circularity."*[1] By this we mean the nature of the system is *appositional*. It is based on the "continuity" and "union" of people, functions, roles, relationships and processes. Each element in African-based families is not distinct or separate from other elements. In a sense the "elemental" structure of African families is continuous or spiralling. Family elements spiral or flow into each other. The functions of the family are likewise "fluid" with all relationships and subsequent roles having the quality of being "flexible" and "interchangeable." Therefore, the intrinsic nature of black (African-based) families is its *sense of* Africanity or what we've operationally called the *"Continual Flexibility in Circularity."*

Africanity in Black Families

Even though some scholars would argue that mutual aid is prerequisite to survival for minority status groups in a hostile environment and

---

[1]In conceptual contrast, we can see that the European-based family system can be thought of as a *"Limited Flexibility in Laterality."* By this, it is meant that the typical family here is *oppositional* in nature. European-based families are based on the "contrarity" and "polarity" of elements (people, functions, roles, etc.) with rectilinear structures having each element stand in sharp contrast or opposition to each other element. The functions of the family system are "concrete," "exact," or "distinct." The "concreteness" of the European-based family is most typically illustrated in its expressions of intra-familial relationships wherein one finds fixed and generally restrictive familial roles and relationships. Though one could carry the implications implicit in the comparison of African-based and European-based family system to varied and multiple interpretations of differences in black and white families, that is not the intention of this essay.

the fact of hostility alone strengthens the ties of kinship, Matthews (1972) and Nobles (1973) argue that the strong kinship bonds found in black extended families (cf. Shimkin, 1974) are positive functional reflections of the sense of Africanity in black communities. Prof. Matthews for instance notes that the individual person in the black community is always relating to the remainder of the total black community and that "Black Togetherness" is at the heart of black social organizations. In socializing its members to "see no *real*" or important distinction between the personal self and other members of the family, I have discussed the importance of kinship in terms of its psychological ability to enhance the emotional relationships of the family. In noting the particular practice in black family systems of referring to and seriously regarding non-blood relatives as kinsmen, Prof. Staples (1974) has pointed out a well-known (at least in black communities) yet unique feature of black kinship networks. Staples notes that these "para-kinship" ties (or what anthropologists in studying traditional African societies call "kin-like" relations) where males and females who are "unrelated" to one another "go for" or have "play" brothers and sisters who have the same loyalties and responsibilities as "blood" relations, seem to serve as a validating and facilitating agent for black life in the United States.

What seems most clear is that the actuality of black kinship bonds and the sense of extended family are exemplifications of the sense of Africanity in black families. Earlier, we noted for instance that the African ethos (survival of the tribe and Oneness of Being) and various philosophical and/or behavioral principles (unity, mutual responsibility) were primarily reflected in and reinforced by the sense of family or kinship. Is not the practice of "ain't none of my children no better than the others" an expression of the "oneness of being," and is not the practice of informal adoption, (i.e., "one more child ain't gonna make no difference") a behavioral and attitudinal expression of survival of the tribe and collective responsibility? The ability to expand and accept other "non-related" members is itself possible because of the continued expression in black families of the "Continual Flexibility in Circularity."[2]

The findings of Stone and Schlamp (1966) that it was not at all uncommon to find black men engaging in "expressive" or domestic and/or emotional functions generally assigned to women in this society and for black women to be engaged in "instrumental" or economic and/or support functions generally assigned to men in this society are of particular interest when they are interpreted in the analytical framework reflecting a family structure wherein family roles are *interchangeable* and *flexible* and the overall structure is spiralling in that each element flows into and is not distinct from other elements. Hill (1972) further establishes this flexibility of roles and tasks in black families by noting that even children participate fully and integrally in family affairs.

The myth of the black matriarch has been challenged too often to even require mentioning. However, for the purposes of perspective, we note that the critical issue is not the household *makeup* but the household *process*. Recent research (Hyman and Reed, 1969; Mack, 1971; Middleton and Putney, 1960) shows that the process in most black families is typified by an *egalitarian pattern* of relations. Staples (1974) notes that the myth of the black matriarch has been reinforced by the failure of scholars and researchers to distinguish between the terms "dominant" and "strong." He contends, along with Prof. Ladner (1971), that while the black woman has needed to be "strong" in order for the family to survive, she has not necessarily been "domineering." What is important to understand, in this society particularly, is that what has been critical in black families is not whether it's female-headed or male-headed, but whether the *survival of the tribe* (family) was maintained.

The inability to appropriately reflect the actuality of black family systems is probably always linked to the scholar's failure to respect the sense of Africanity in black people and families. A good example of this is found in Frazier's (1962) classic study of the black middle class. In terms of consumptive patterns, Frazier described the lack of regard for the Protestant Ethic (which emphasizes the accumulation of capital wealth) as an index of the Black Bourgeoisie's, failure to internalize "genuine" middle-class values. He concluded this in terms of black consumptive activities. What he failed to understand was that black consumptive activity was not an indicator of black families failing to be like white families but rather the possible expression of a trait that is related to the African heritage and philosophical orientation of black families. African peoples traditionally are not a money-oriented people (in the sense of hoarding money for the sake of having money). Money itself is not most important. The value of money is in its provision of goods and services. Money, therefore, is not generally saved for saving's sake. *It is consumed.* Similarly, Matthews (1972) and Murray (1970) have noted that for black people the critical standard for evaluating other people is not their wealth but their feelings toward other people. That is, the evaluation standard is *affective* rather that *economic.*

In reconsidering the conceptual and theoretical bases of studies on black families, Turner (1972) noted that the intricate meaning and emotional dynamics of black relationships—particularly sexual relations—are seldom captured in most black family studies. In terms of family intrarelationships, the importance of the childhood experiences and unique child-rearing practices are also areas of questionable and special consideration. It appears for instance that the special bond between the black mother and her child or children is not, as previously thought, the consequence of slavery *legally* defining the family as a mother and her child. Rather, or more correctly, this special bond is deeply rooted in our African heritage and philosophical orientation which as Brown and Forde (1967) note, places a special value on children because they represent the continuity of life. Motherhood itself has historically been an important role (some suggest even more important than the role of wife) for black women (cf: Bell, 1971).

Though the unique child-rearing practices or techniques found in black families are fundamental reflections of the sense of Africanity, they are also in part determined by the keen sociopolitical observations and interpretations by black parents about the state of contemporary reality (i.e., white racism and economic oppression). As such, these child-rearing practices are in part geared to prepare black children for a particular kind of existence in a hostile environment. They are not distortions of white child-rearing techniques. Black children are prepared to take on the appropriate sex and age roles (which by historical and philosophical definition are flexible, interchangeable and fluid) as well as the racial roles (which by social and political definition are ones of resistance, suspicion and caution).

The African philosophical notion of the *interdependence of universal elements* is best seen in the black family in terms of the aged. The black elderly (unlike the white elderly who are institutionally cared for) have traditionally been an integral part of the total family structure. Staples (1974) notes that even though most aged black parents live separately from their children (in terms of households) they remain in close contact with them. It is in fact the case that most aged blacks have a significant amount of interaction with their children; and where no *blood* children are present or near, the black elderly interact with neighbors or "para-kinsmen."

In reflecting on the notion of interdependence, the structure of the family in black communities plays an important part in buttressing the psychological isolation, economic oppression and social loneliness found in various strata within family systems—particularly the elderly. The black family system itself teaches (socializes) its members to deal with the daily realities of white racism (cf: Staples, 1974). This fact coupled with the sense of Africanity as reflected by various contemporary expressions of *survival of the tribe* and *the oneness of being* is the real hidden force or strength in the black struggle.

We contend that the black African definition of the family, prior to the intrusion of the European presence on the continent, included every member of the tribe. Many scholars (Frazier, 1939, 1940; Johnson, 1941; and Davis and Dollard, 1942) have suggested that upon being transplanted in the Western world, the evil and inhumanity of Western—particularly American—slavery destroyed the sense of family, amongst the new-world slaves. In noting, as do other commentators on the black family, that the practice of separating people belonging to the same tribe was designed purposely to break down the collective reinforcement of a common definition, we still contend that the experiences of new-world slavery did not significantly disrupt the traditional philosophical orientation wherein kinship or the family system bound the life and existence of each individual. Consequently, by philosophical definition, for the African, the "I" was really a "We." That is, for traditional Africans, it was the community or the family which defined the individual. Consequently, group identity was the most important identity and it was reinforced by the African ethos which operationally related to the *survival of the tribe.*

Several sources suggest that slavery in the United States slowly came to define itself in terms of black people; and we note that, as the system moved closer and closer to its final definition of slave meaning Africans or black people in bondage, the "slaves" themselves were moving closer to African or black as the definition of tribe or family. The principle underlying the family system (i.e., the traditional ethos of "survival of the tribe") was not altered by the forced separation. Whether "Ibo" or "Fulani" or "Igbera," as tribesmen were regrouped, each came to the new group with the same underlying "hidden strength" or guiding principle. Consequently, the Euro-American forced separation of tribal members was nothing more than a re-organization (retribalization) of tribal affiliation.

Even though all families have undergone severe challenges to their integrities as a consequence of the introduction of technological society, the black family has been additionally burdened with the effects of Euro-American racism. Technological society[3] primarily introduced or heightened the idea of a *money economy* and the perspective that *time* can be defined as a "commodity" which in turn can be bought and sold.

It has been the incorporation of the notions of "money economy" and "time as a commodity" which have offered the greatest challenge to black families. The philosophy of "individualism" found in modern technological societies demands its own code of ethics. In traditional life, for instance, the individual was defined by the family. However, as a result of technological society and its intrinsic conception of "time" as a commodity and "money" as an economy, *individualism* (with its "do your own thing" principle) allowed and determined that one's identity would be a personal creation. Consequently, these twin "evils" of

modern technology have heightened for black families the importance of the "individual" and subsequently lowered the collective resistance to racism and oppression. Clearly the sense of individualism has been detrimental to the black family and destructive to the buffer it provides against a hostile and racist society. The ill effects this will have on black people, in general, are only now being uncovered.

Hidden Strength in Black Families

The sense of "Africanity," we contend, is nevertheless the hidden strength in black families and has served as the underlying force in the "struggle." It is, however, only when the interpretative framework for one's analysis is based on the nature of black people as suggested by Professor X, that the varied expressions of that hidden strength are revealed. For instance, overarching the notion of family is the concept of kinship which as a system was based on the philosophical principle of the "Oneness of Being" or *one with nature.* Behaviorally and structurally this principle translated into the idea of interdependence. That is, all elements are interdependent and interconnected. Structurally, the individual is embedded in a web of "interdependent" relations with all the other elements of the family. The idea of family or kinship consequently assigned to each individual their position in the system of descent and marriage, while at the same time it defined attitudes, functions and behaviors. Psychologically, the individual existed insofar as he belonged to a family line and was *situated* in interdependent relations to others within the family or kinship line. The family is, therefore, experienced not only on a quasi-biological level by all its members, but it is also experienced as a veritable institution of *social solidarity* and *psychological security.* The subsequent social relations and organizations which are influenced by the family not only reflect this sense of security and solidarity, but they, in many ways, are the consequences of them.

Clearly, the sense of social solidarity and psychological security can be seen now as part of the underlying force or strength in the black (African) struggle for liberation and human dignity. Equally clear should be the relationship of the sense of Africanity to the hidden strength in

---

[3]Modern technology and development have been accompanied by new societal and institutional models, new types of behavior, new values and new ideas. It is recognized that technological developments and the combined thrust of racism and oppression have severely challenged the African-based black family and like the plethora of new behaviors, values and ideas, a new analysis is necessary to accommodate the historical fact that African-based families have been oppressed by European-based social conceptions of reality. Naturally, the effect of this change, if allowed to go unchecked, will not only result in a retribalization of black families but a detribalization as well.

black families. Without this hidden force, no movement would have emerged and no struggle would have materialized.

References

Bell, Robert, "The Relative Importance of Mother and Wife Roles Among Negro Lower Class Women," in Robert Staples' *The Black Family, Essays and Studies,* Belmont, Calif.: Wadsworth, 1971, pp. 248–256.

Billingsley, Andrew, *Black Families in White America,* Englewood-Cliffs, New Jersey: Prentice-Hall, 1966.

Brown, Radcliffe R., and Forde, D., *African Systems of Kinship and Marriage,* New York: Oxford University Press, 1967.

Clark, Cedric C., "Black Studies or the Study of Black People," in Reginald Jones (ed.) *Black Psychology,* New York: Harper & Row, 1972.

Davis, A., and Dollard, J., *Children of Bondage,* Washington, D.C.: American Council on Education, 1942.

DuBois, W.E.B., *The Negro American Family,* Atlanta: Atlanta University Press, 1909.

Frazier, E. Franklin, *Black Bourgeoisie,* New York: Collier Books, 1962.

Frazier, E. Franklin, *The Negro Family in Chicago,* Chicago: University of Chicago Press, 1932.

Frazier, E. Franklin, *The Negro Family in the United States,* Chicago: University of Chicago Press, 1939.

Frazier, E. Franklin, *Negro Youth at the Crossways: The Personality Development in the Middle States* (prepared for the American Youth Commission, American Council on Education), New York: Schocken Books, 1940.

Hill, Robert, *The Strengths of Black Families,* New York: Emerson Hall, 1972.

Hyman, Herbert, and Reed, John S., "Black Matriarch Reconsidered: Evidence for Secondary Analysis of Sample Surveys," *Public Opinion Quarterly,* 33 (Fall, 1969), pp. 354–364.

Johnson, C.S., *Growing Up in the Black Belt,* Washington, D.C.: American Council on Education, 1941.

Ladner, Joyce, *Tomorrow's Tomorrow: The Black Woman,* Garden City, New York: Doubleday, 1971.

Liebow, Elliot, *Tally's Corner,* Boston: Little, Brown and Co., 1966.

Mack, Deloris, "Where the Black Matriarchy Theorists Went Wrong," *Psychology Today,* 4 (January, 1971), p. 24.

Mannheim, Karl, *Ideology and Utopia,* New York: Harcourt, Brace and World, 1936.

Matthews, Basil, "Black Perspectives, Black Family and Black Community," a paper presented to the Annual Philosophy Conference, Baltimore, April, 1972.

Mbiti, John S., *African Religions and Philosophies,* New York: Anchor, 1970.

Middleton, Russell, and Putney, Snell, "Dominance in Decisions in the Family: Race and Class Difference," *American Journal of Sociology,* 29, (May, 1960), pp. 605–609.

Moynihan, Daniel P., "Employment, Income and the Ordeal of the Negro Family," *Daedulus,* 94 (Fall, 1965), pp. 745–770.

Murray, Albert, *The Omni-Americans,* New York: Outerbridge and Dienstfrey, 1970.

Nobles, Wade W., "African Philosophy: Foundations for Black Psychology," in Reginald Jones (ed.), *Black Psychology,* New York: Harper & Row, 1972.

Nobles, Wade W., "African Root and American Fruit: The Black Family," *The Journal of Social and Behavioral Sciences,* 20 (June, 1974), pp. 66–77.

Nobles, Wade W., "Psychological Research and the Black Self-Concept: A Critical Review," *Journal of Social Issues* 29 (1), 1973.

Osei, G.K., *The African Philosophy of Life,* London: The African Publican Society, 1970.

Scanzoni, John, *The Black Family in Modern Society,* Boston: Allyn & Bacon, 1971.

Shimkin, D.B., Louie, G.L., and Frute, D.H., "The Black Extended Family: A Basic Rural Institution and a Mechanism of Urban Adaptation," reprinted in *Ebony,* March, 1974.

Staples, Robert, *The Black Family, Essays and Studies,* Belmont, Calif.: Wadsworth, 1971.

Staples, Robert, *The Black Woman in America,* Chicago: Nelson-Hall, 1973.

Staples, Robert, "Strength and Inspiration: Black Families in the United States," in Robert Habenstein and Charles Mindel (eds.), *American Minority Lifestyles,* New York: Elsevier, 1976.

Stone, Robert, and Schlamp, F.T., *Family Lifestyles Below the Poverty Line,* a Report to the State Social Welfare Board from the Institute for Social Science Research, 1966.

Turner, C.R., "Some Theoretical and Conceptual Considerations for Black Family Studies," *Black Lines,* 2 (Winter, 1972), pp. 13–28.

Willie, Charles, *The Family Life of Black People,* Columbus, Ohio: Charles E. Merrill Books, 1970.

The Search for Values in Black Family Research

Leanor B. Johnson

This article discusses three models for examining the Black family—value rejection, value espousal and value separation—and shows their inapplicability in Black family research. The alternative approach of symbolic interaction is suggested for more reliable study of the Black family.

It is necessary for us to develop a new frame of reference which transcends the limits of white concepts . . . we must abandon the partial frame of reference of our oppressors and create new concepts which will release our reality, which is also the reality of the overwhelming majority of men and women on this globe. We must say to the white world that there are things in the world that are not dreamt of in your history and your sociology and your philosophy. (Lerone Bennett, The Challenge of Blackness)

The role of the social scientist and the relationship between the researcher's own values and the data under his investigation has been a sporadic yet unabated controversy since Lundberg (1939) and MacIver (1942). Christensen (1964, 973–974) categorized the debate into three camps: *Value Rejection, Value Espousal,* and *Value Separation.* Those adhering to a *Value Rejection* stance search for facts with the expectation that these facts will lead to a rational ordering of social life. Using the natural sciences as their model, they believe that a lack of concern for both moral problems and the end results of their research is essential to objectivity. A number of early American sociologists promoted this position. A later version of this stance, *Abstract Empiricism* (Mills, 1959), attempts to verify theoretical propositions by a canonization and controlling of facts through statistical manipulation. A positive relationship is presumed to exist between statistical control of facts and objectivity. This method has resulted in partial investigation (without much hope of unification), a historical analysis, and a lack of critical thought concerning the relationship between the biography of men and the social structure. Supporters of *Value Separation* acknowledge values as legitimate data, but believe that the scientist should compartmentalize his citizen-self from his scientist-self, thus avoiding a scientist-activist role. Adherents of the *Value Espousal* position argue that values are an intricate part of the scientist, thus, cannot be compartmentalized. The scientist must state his value position in order

Paper presented to the Annual Meeting of the National Council on Family Relations, October 24, 1974, St. Louis, Missouri.

to aid his audience in interpreting his research. Verstehen/empathy is considered a virtue or asset in the understanding of the meaning of the situation to the subjects under investigation. Involvement with issues and problems in the community is considered necessary for germane and objective research.

Nowhere in the academic community have these value positions been so intertwined with the survival and well being of a people than in Black family research and theory. The claims made by researchers of the Black family are often put into practice, at times inadvertently, by policy makers and social service agencies. If these claims stem from fallacious assumptions, unvalidated generalizations, and biased values, the present and future functionality of Black families is negatively affected. From the inception of sociology as a field of scientific investigation, efforts were made to study the Black family from an objective perspective. Each of the aforementioned camps has had its stab at an objective interpretation of Black family life, but only the last position, *Value Espousal,* seems to hold any hope for a sociology that will promote the well being of Black families as well as lead to incisive theoretical propositions and accurate conceptualizations.

This paper will briefly trace the struggle by researchers to rid the Black family field of values and models which block the development of systematic sociology of the Black family and which present superficial and inaccurate analyses, as well as to present an approach which will help illuminate rather than obscure the true nature of Black family life in its sundry forms.

The greatest threat to the well being and survival of Black family life has been various derivations of the *Value Rejection* position,[1] with its notion of objectivity. This position was taken by the early "biological determinates" and is locked into the acculturation model employed by Frazier and his disciples.

At the turn of the century the first model of the Black family emerged through a seemingly sincere scientific spirit to search for the facts "without prejudice" (Odum, 1910:20) and "to know more of the Negro from impartial sources . . ." (Odum, 1910:21). Scholars of the best universities were determined to take the

Negro question out of the heated arena of politics, society, and popular religious discussion and put it into science (Odum, 1910). Thus, it was hoped that an emphasis on objectivity, keeping to the facts, and value rejection would lead to a moral solution to the so-called "Negro problem."

The result of this scientific stance was "biological determinism" or what Frazier referred to as "Blood will tell" theory. Biological determinism held that Blacks' immorality was not only a function of the conditions of slavery, but was a genetic adaptation of Black people to the hot climate of Africa. This climate was conducive to the preservation of those with hotter sexual passions and richer fertility (Dow, 1922). A representative scholar of this period states:

Soberly speaking, negro nature is so craven and sensuous in every fibre of its being that negro manhood with decent respect for chaste womanhood does not exist. . . . Women unresistingly betray their wifely honor to satisfy a bestial instinct. . . . So deeply rooted in immorality are our negro people that they turn in aversion from any sexual relation which does not invite sensuous embraces (Thomas, 1910:187).

This same scholar warns that neither a social class theory nor any theory based on external societal conditions as the causal factor in Negro deprivation and immorality will lead to a greater understanding of the "negro."

Marital . . . immoralities, however, are not confined to the poor, the ignorant, and the degraded among the freed people, but are equally common among those who presume to be educated and refined. . . . The truth is that negroes have not yet realized that their inefficiency is due to fundamental and inherent conditions (Thomas, 1910:187).

Thus, he strongly proposes the framework and basic assumption which should guide any critical analysis of the "negro" people:

Negro social conditions will, however, be but dimly understood, even in their more conspicuous phases, unless we are prepared to realize at every step in our investigation that physical excitation is the chief and foremost

---

[1]Since the end result of both value rejection and value separation is much the same, only the most extreme of these two positions is discussed—*Value rejection.*

craving of the freedman's nature (Thomas, 1910:189).

The American Journal of Sociology published a plethora of statistical data on illegitimacy, hyper-sexuality, and other so-called pathologies which support this framework. So alarming were the facts that several scholars warned of a degeneration of the "negro" people that would in the near future, if the rate continued, lead to an extermination of the Black race.

It becomes lucid in the concluding chapters of many of these scholars' works that their supreme commitment was not to science and objectivity, but to the values sustaining the American system. For example, Thomas (1901) writes:

We conclude a discussion in which we have sought to solve complex problems—not in the depth of racial bigotry, but elevated by fraternal patriotism, by observing that our indigenous toilers, the brawny Blacks, have both place and duty in America's development (pp. 430–431).

The logical solution based on "biological determinism" was miscegenation, but this was rejected on the instinctual repulsion assumed to be shared by both Blacks and Whites. Thus, the more racist scholars concluded that assimilation was an impossibility and racial segregation and political disenfranchisement were necessities; while others diverted from the theory to suggest that:

The future American negro will part, undoubtedly, with many of his racial characteristics as he approximates in color and conduct the White race. . . . In a word, a radical regeneration, not in color, but in conduct, is the absolute need of our freedmen. . . . The redemption of the negro is . . . possible and assured through assimilation of the thought and ideals of American civilization. (Thomas, 1901:401, 431).

Despite their avowedly objective stance, this and other early racial inferiority theories are based on blatant subjective notions and loyalty to what was considered the supreme end of the Darwinian evolutionary process—the White family. Although Jensen (1969) and Shockley (1972a)

have recently reclaimed this genetic model and have attracted a number of disciples, such theories are often dismissed by many of us with a chuckle and a sigh of relief that social scientists have come of age through the burial of such value-laden theories. However, "racial-biological determinism" has been replaced by a more subtle perspective, "social determinism" and the consequences are much the same. This is not to imply that no significant progress has been made towards understanding the nature of the Black family. Despite the fact that phenomenologists have warned of the reality that is ignored when one accepts "social determinism," much of social science, especially the studies on Black family by Frazier and others who use an "acculturation model," implicitly employ this perspective.

The first definitive challenge to the "racial-biological determinism" theory came from E. Franklin Frazier (1932). His works emerged during the 1930's when Black Americans for the first time were experiencing the cruel effects of the combination of urbanization, poverty, and discrimination. The basic assumption/values shared by White social scientists prevented any scholarly support necessary to alleviate the Black man's burden. Frazier recognized that to establish a sociology of the Black family within the general framework of a theory of race relations, he must first dismiss the "racial-biological determinism" model. This was done through presenting available census data to support the concept of "social disorganization." Viewing the city of Chicago as concentric zones, Frazier, in the spirit of scientific detachment, demonstrated that a movement from the poverty-stricken central city where the new immigrants settled, to the periphery where the more acculturated Blacks moved, decreased the rate of familial and social disorganization (e.g., female-headed households and illegitimacy, delinquency, and crime associated with this family form). Thus, E. W. Burgess states that Frazier "shows quite conclusively that certain behavior popularly attributed to the Negro varies almost, if not quite, as widely within the Negro group as within the White group" (Frazier, 1932:xi).

If Frazier had here ceased his search for a new perspective and in the tradition of DuBois urged specific recommendations for social change, the reexamination of his work in the last few years may not have been so harsh. However, he attached the "acculturation" model to his analysis and allowed the inherent assumption of White supremacy to creep in to destroy the opportunity of viewing Black families in their own right. Acculturation referred to the adoption of the values and norms of the dominant White culture. This adoption was deemed necessary in order to divorce Blacks from their primitive folk culture and to place them in harmony with the modern urban and industrial society. Although Frazier indicated that the writings of Thomas (1901), Odum (1910) and others were "merely rationalizations of the existing racial situation" (1947:268), he accepted their conclusions concerning the pathological characteristics of the Black family and suggested the same solution—acculturation. He differed from these scholars in his identification of the causal factor creating the pathology, thus he exchanged "biological determinism" for "social determinism." Contributing to his arrival at the acculturation solution was Frazier's commitment to objectivity and the "natural history" framework developed by his mentor, Park. This framework emphasized the historical context (e.g., slavery, emancipation, migration, and urbanization) in which Black families evolved and claimed that this history shaped their primitive and pathological form. Both Moynihan (1965) and Rainwater (1970) employed this historical sequence, focused on the same so-called "pathologies" of illegitimacy, matrifocality, male marginality, sex-role confusion, and delinquency. Rainwater indicted the socio-economic structure, Moynihan the Black family, and both researchers found Black salvation in acculturation.

The accuracy of this historical description of the influence of slavery and emancipation on the Black family formation has recently been questioned by Turner (1972), who states that "certainly these accepted theories of the effects of historical occurrences on the family structure of Black Americans warrant close examination in light of the most recent research and findings of several historians and sociologists" (p. 15), such as Gutman (1973), Abzug (1971), and Anderson (1971) which reveal little evidence of a matriarchal family structure during and immediately following slavery.

Since most studies of the post-Frazier era have followed Frazier's orientation, it is important to point out the shortcomings. Not only is White moral supremacy maintained, but greater insight into the nature of Black family life is hindered by 1)

a general acceptance of the family as passive, reactive, and dependent; 2) a focus on the family as an institution rather than on the search for internal dynamics (e.g., norms/values) which may be a causal nexus of observed psychological and social behavior and family structure; and 3) a focus on one-system analysis which yields mere description and prevents the development of testable explanatory propositions (see Christensen, 1969).

The *Value Rejection* stance has taken the posture of "do what I say" (e.g., thou shall not make any value judgments), "but not as I do" (e.g., promoting the values of vested interest groups). It has failed as an adequate tool for analyzing the nature of Black family life because it has placed unlimited faith in the ability of facts to order truth and has ignored the influence of environment on the structure of ideas. Myrdal (1944) argues that "blases in social science cannot be erased simply by 'keeping to the facts,' and by refined methods of statistical treatment of the data. Facts, and the handling of data, sometimes show themselves even more pervious to tendencies towards bias than does 'pure thought' " (p. 1041). I believe that all scientific and nonscientific investigations are based on an explicit conception of reality—a philosophy or ideology. Science itself is a value judgment and, more often than not, varies with economic, social, and political climate. Whether he is aware of it or not, or desires it or not, the scientific investigator carries with him a conception of man which reflects not only the investigator's inner spirit, but his place in history and the social structure, and the prevailing ideology of his time (Thomas, 1971; Mills, 1959; Sorokin, 1957; Mannheim, 1936). This is especially evident when race is a factor. Thomas (1971) argues that race determines race-specific communication patterns which in turn create different realities or distinct groups. Thus, to speak of an absolute objectivity is absurd. At every step of the research process (e.g., in the selection of a problem, the framing of hypotheses, in choosing a theoretical orientation, and in interpretations), values are shaping conclusions. Thus, the question is whose values will be chosen (cf. Almeida, 1974).

Motivated by the adverse implications Moynihan's (1965) "Tangle of Pathology" thesis had on government policies for Black Americans, a large segment of the Black leadership community began a critical analysis of the values underlying traditional theoretical orientations to the study of Black family life. A strong Black response was made possible by a growing number of Black scholars and was influenced by the advent of the Black nationalistic ideology.

The first comprehensive critique came from Billingsley, a Black social scientist. Unlike Scanzoni (1972), Moynihan (1965), and Liebow (1967), Billingsley does not deny the existence of a partially autonomous Black subculture, but suggests that our society consists of interdependent institutions of which the Black family is one. He is then able to argue that the behavior and structure of Black families is partially influenced by the racist economic exploitative dominant White culture. Much of what is considered pathological behavior is explained by Billingsley as positive functions needed for the survival of the Black family and the Black community. Thus, husbands and wives interchanging expressive and instrumental roles is not a sign of sex-role confusion, but is a positive adaptive function to counteract the economic system that requires both parents and sometimes the entire family to work in order to remain above the poverty line. Billingsley's (1968) thesis was a much needed change in perspective, but it never elaborated upon the Black family's effect on the greater society and more seriously did not fully challenge the basic values of White supremacy. Billingsley accepts White middle-class values as the aspirations of Black families and devotes a section of his book to describing the opportunity screens that have made it possible for Blacks to leave the lower-class family form.

The Billingsley study generated several studies by Black social scientists which capitalized on the notion of "strengths." Hill (1972) identifies five strengths: adaptation of family roles, strong kinship bonds, strong achievement orientation, strong work orientation, and strong religious orientation. Ladner (1971) suggests that if Blacks were only viewed within the context of their history of racial oppression that Black children would perhaps be seen not as having incomplete personality formation, but as possessing a more integrated personality and emotional stability than White children. Staples (1972) claims that the lack of a double sexual standard among Blacks is indicative of meaningful and guiltless sex relationships. Johnson (1974) contends that illegitimacy is not a sign of generational acceptance of pathological behavior, but reflects a

respect for life at its conception. No doubt there is a need to refute myths and redefine faulty concepts, but there is a need to move beyond polemical issues. "Our polemics," Turner (1972) warns, "have often bound us more closely to the parochial views of some colleagues than I think we realize, insuring that our response would be opposite although equal to theirs in content and generalities" (p. 22). We need to move towards developing theoretical frameworks that will provide a systematic examination of the Black family. The *"notion of 'strength' is a value judgment that gives no frame of reference for understanding the Black family"* (Garnes, 1969:2). Garnes and others are realizing that as long as scholars embrace concepts that are solely based on reaction to White racism and oppression they will never completely break the chains which bind Black family research to anachronistic theories and faulty and imprecise methodological procedures, and which restrain researchers from fully seeking out the nature of Black families relative to values within the Blacks' own subculture.

Value Espousal

The search is now on for values that will undergird the frame of reference used to guide research on the Black family. With the onset of Black Nationalism a growing number of scholars are choosing Black Cultural Nationalism (BCN) as their point of departure from the White middle-class ethnocentrism expressed by those adhering to the *Value Rejection* stance. There are three prerequisites for adopting this framework: 1) recognition of a distinct Black subculture 2) adherence to the *Value Espousal* position and 3) a commitment to searching out the values shaping the Black ethnic subculture.

Scholars accepting BCN have rejected Moynihan and Glazer's (1963) conclusion that Blacks are Americans and nothing else and have taken Billingsley and Turner's position. Billingsley states (1968): "Even when the income levels are similar for the White and the Negro samples, the two groups are not comparable. . . . For the Negro group must reflect its experience with the caste barrier as well as its distinctive history, both of which set the conditions for growing up black in white America" (1968:201). These two unique conditions provide a sense of "peoplehood," "a special sense of both ancestral and future-oriented identification with the group" (Gordon, 1964). The assumptions of BCN are delineated by Garnes (1969) and Turner (1972):

Nationalism is a belief that Black people in this country make up a cultural Nation. The cultural nation is a people with a common past, a common present and, hopefully, a common future. Our society may be American, but our values must be Afro-American. Black values can only come through a Black culture.

. . . we stress culture because it gives identity, purpose and direction. It tells you who you are, what you must do, and how you can do it.

Without a culture Black people are only a set of reactions to White people (Garnes, 1969:5).

Black cultural Nationalism is an expression of the desire of Afro-Americans to decide their own destiny through control of their own political organizations and the formation and preservation of their cultural economic and social institutions (Turner, 1973:252).

Thus, social scientists become instruments in assisting Blacks in achieving self-defined goals. Social scientists who accept this framework have then adopted the *Value Espousal* position, for their values are explicitly stated in a political ideology of survival and culture and they advocate decisive involvement. In the past few years they have organized symposia, conferences, and workshops with the purpose of clarifying the role of the social scientist in the Black liberation struggle. They deem it necessary to be activists as well as researchers and despise the concept of "detached scientist." They claim that to be Black is *not* sufficient, but to be Black and involved is necessary. They are realizing as DuBois did that the conservative tools of social science cannot grasp all of reality. There is a crucial point where the ethical and moral implications of the researcher's work must be acted out. They are convinced that the field of the social sciences "must redeem itself from the fact that it rose 'to its present prosperity and eminence on the blood and bones of the poor and oppressed, it owes its prestige in this society to its putative ability to give information and advice to the ruling class of the society about ways and means to keep people down.'" (Forsythe, 1973:221). Consequently, they are developing new concepts/frameworks based on Black history, are seeking to take leadership in interpreting Black reality to the masses, and are providing any knowledge necessary to obtain self-defined goals.

The BCN framework is without doubt an ethnocentric orientation. Thus, it may be viewed as a reversal in discrimination. Not so! It merely means that if the social scientist desires to report on the behavior of a culture other than his own, then he must not use his own cultural framework and definitions to explain that behavior (Wheeler, 1973). In other words, Black Cultural Nationalism cannot be used to explain White social patterns, only Black. It does not deny the necessity of other approaches but deems them insufficient. Thus, the problem or issue becomes *not one of objectivity,* but the search for *value-laden concepts and models* which will promote the well being and viability of a pluralistic society and a search for values which have and are presently shaping the Black ethnic subculture.

In seeking an approach that would accelerate the search for the true nature of Black families, it is clear that merely substituting qualitative for quantitative data will not suffice to differentiate between faulty and correct conclusions. Hill (1972) demonstrated family strengths and Moynihan (1965) family weaknesses, yet both utilized the same U.S. census data. Similarly, Rainwater's use of participatory observation yields much the same erroneous conclusions as Moynihan. Hill differed from the other two researchers in recognizing that the Black rather than the White cultural value system must be the foundation for interpretations of Black family life. Thus, it is necessary to turn to a cultural framework. Those using the Black cultural perspective would profit by taking advantage of existing, established, and viable conceptual frameworks. For example, Hill's (1949) use of the symbolic interaction framework in the study of conditions and consequences of Family crises provides Black family researchers with an approach for seeking out values/norms which aid in determining the family's internal dynamics and its interaction with other units in its environment. Using his approach on Black family research would require an acceptance of the family as both reactor and actor and requires that Black family researchers seek out three definitions of the family situation: "the ob-

jective definition of the family situation formulated
by an impartial observer (I would add statistical
trends), the cultural definition formulated by the
community, and the subjective definition formulated by the family'' (150–151). In considering the
later definition which Hill considers most important, the researcher should focus on the individual, dyadic, and family level. Further development of the framework of ethnomethodology
should aid in defining the subjective. The symbolic interaction should be coupled with an analysis of the major historical phases through which
the family has passed as well as a comparative
examination of other family systems. An historical
analysis should not be confined to the industrialization and urbanization processes which have
influenced the Black family. Turner asserts that
"no scientific study of human social behavior can
be called adequate unless it deals with the religious and philosophical foundations of the institutional and cultural pattern in a society''
(1972:25). Legend, folklore, and mythology
handed down through oral tradition have given
definition to Black family forms (Turner, 1972). In
this regard, rich resources are available from
qualitative data drawn from printed matter—letters, diaries, and manuscripts (Lipset, 1958), as
well as from the aged Black who has been neglected as both source and subject of sociological research.

In short, the search for values and the
internal dynamics of the Black family promises to
be complex and difficult, requiring precise methodological procedures, time, and money. But, if
there is no struggle, there is no progress (Frederick Douglas). Searches which produce fruitful
returns are never easy.

References

Abzug, Robert H.
1971 "The Black Family During Reconstruction." In Nathan I. Huggens, Martin Kelson
and Daniel M. Fox (eds), *Key Issues in the
Afro-American Experience*. New York: Harcourt Brace Jovanovich, pp. 26–39.

Almeida, Eleanor E.
1974 "Whose Values?: Racial Chauvinism in Research on Black Families." Paper presented to the 1974 Annual Meeting of the
American Sociological Association, Caucus of Black Sociologists (August 27),
Montreal, Quebec, Canada.

Anderson, C. H.
1971 "Black Americans." In *Towards a New Sociology: A Critical View*. Homewood, Illinois: The Dorsey Press.

Billingsley, Andrew
1968 *Black Families in White America*. New
Jersey: Prentice-Hall.

Christensen, Harold T., (ed).
1964 *Handbook of Marriage and the Family*. Chicago: Rand McNally.
1969 "Normative Theory Derived from Cross-
Cultural Family Research," *Journal of Marriage and the Family* 31 (May): 209–222.

Davidson, Douglas
1969 "Black Culture and Liberal Sociology,"
Berkeley Journal of Sociology 14: 165–
175.

Dow, Grove S.
1922 *Society and Its Problems*. New York:
Crowell.

Drake, St. Clair (audiotape)
1971 "The Role of the Black Scholar in the
Struggle of the Black Community." Atlanta: Institute of the Black World.

DuBois, W. E. B.
1899 *The Philadelphia Negro: A Social Study*.
Philadelphia: University of Pennsylvania
Press.
1940 *Dusk of Dawn*. New York: Harcourt, Brace
and World.

Fontaine, William
1940 "An Interpretation of Contemporary Negro
Thought from the Standpoint of the Sociology of Knowledge," *Journal of Negro History* 2 (January): 6–13.

Forsythe, Dennis
1973 "Radical Sociology and Blacks." In Joyce
A. Ladner (ed.), *The Death of White Sociology*. New York: Vintage Books, pp. 213–
233.

Frazier, E. F.
1932 *The Negro Family in Chicago*. Chicago:
University of Chicago Press.
1947 "Sociological Theory and Race Rela-

tions," *American Sociological Review* 12 (June): 265–271.
1949 "Race Contacts and the Social Structure," *American Sociological Review* 14 (February): 1–11.

Garnes, James M.
1969 "The Strength of Black Family." Paper presented to the National Conference of Black Social Workers, Philadelphia (February).

Gordon, Milton M.
1964 *Assimilation in American Life.* New York: Oxford University Press.

Gutman, Herbert
1973 *The Negro Family.* New York: Pantheon Books.

Hill, Mazell
1957 "Research on the Negro Family," *Marriage and Family* (February): 25–31.

Hill, Robert
1972 *The Strengths of Black Families.* New York: Emerson-Hall.

Hill, Rueben
1949 *Families Under Stress.* New York: Harper & Row.

James, C. L. R. (audiotape)
1971 "The Role of the Black Scholar in the Struggles of the Black Community." Atlanta: Institute of the Black World.

Jensen, Arthur
1969 "How Much Can We Boost I.Q. and Scholastic Achievement?" *Harvard Educational Review* 39 (Winter): 1–123.

Johnson, Leanor B.
1974 "Afro-American Premarital Sex Attitudes and Behavior: A Comparison with Midwestern and Scandinavian Whites." Unpublished Ph.D. dissertation, Purdue University.

Ladner, Joyce A.
1971 *Tomorrow's Tomorrow: The Black Woman.* New York: Doubleday.

Lieberman, Leonard
1973 "The Emerging Model of the Black Family," *International Journal of Sociology of the Family* 3 (March): 10–22.

Liebow, Elliot
1967 *Tally's Corner.* Boston: Little, Brown.

Lipset, C. Martin
1958 "A Sociologist Looks at History," *Pacific Sociological Review* 1 (Spring): 13–17.

Lundberg, G. A.
1939 *Foundations of Sociology.* New York: Macmillan.

MacIver, Robert M.
1942 *Social Causation.* Boston: Ginn and Co.

Mannheim, Karl
1936 *Ideology and Utopia.* London: Routledge and Kegan Paul.

Mills, C. W.
1959 *The Sociological Imagination.* New York: Grove Press.

Moynihan, Daniel
1965 *The Negro Family: The Case for National Action.* Office of Policy Planning and Research, United States Department of Labor.

Moynihan, Daniel, and Nathan Glazer
1963 *Beyond the Melting Pot.* Cambridge, Mass.: M.I.T. Press.

Odum, Howard
1910 *Social and Mental Traits of the Negro: Research into the Conditions of the Negro Race in Southern Towns.* New York: A.M.S. Press.

Rainwater, Lee
1970 *Behind Ghetto Walls.* Chicago: Aldine.

Scanzoni, John H.
1971 *The Black Family in Modern Society.* Boston: Allyn & Bacon.

Shockley, William
1972a "I.Q. and Race," *The Humanist* 32 (January–February).
1972b "A Debate Challenge," *Phi Delta Kappan* 53 (March): 415–420.

Sorokin, Pitirim
1957 *Social and Cultural Dynamics.* New York: American Books.

Staples, Robert
1972 "The Sexuality of Black Women," *Sexual Behavior* (June): 4, 6, 8–11, 14–15.
1973 "Towards a Sociology of the Black Family: A Theoretical and Methodological Assess-

ment," *A Decade of Family Research and Action*. Minneapolis: National Council on Family Relations, pp. 141–160.

Stocking, George
1966   "Franz Boas and Culture Concept in Historical Perspective," *American Anthropology* 68 (August): 867–882.

Thomas, Charles W.
1971   *Boys No More*. Encino, California: Glencoe Press.

Thomas, William H.
1910   *The American Negro: What He Was, What He Is, and What He May Become*. New York: Macmillan.

Turner, C. R.
1972   "Some Theoretical and Conceptual Considerations for Black Family Studies," *Black Lines* (Winter): 13–26.

Turner, James
1972   "The Sociology of Black Nationalism." In Joyce Ladner (ed.), *The Death of White Sociology*. New York: Vintage Books, pp. 234–252.

Waller, W., and R. Hill
1938   *The Family: A Dynamic Interpretation*. New York: Dryden.

Wheeler, William H.
1973   "The Black Family in Perspective." Unpublished Ph.D. dissertation, Arizona State University.

2

Historical Background

The Myth of the Absent Family

Eugene D. Genovese

This article examines some common myths about the Black family during the period of slavery. Genovese finds that despite considerable constraints on their ability to carry out normative family roles and functions, the bondsmen created impressive norms of family life and entered the post-emancipation era with a strong respect for the family and a comparatively stable family base.

The recent controversy over the ill-fated Moynihan Report has brought the question of the black family in general and the slave family in particular into full review. Largely following the pioneering work of E. Franklin Frazier, the report summarized the conventional wisdom according to which slavery had emasculated black men, created a matriarchy, and prevented the emergence of a strong sense of family.[1] Historians and sociologists, black and white, have been led astray in two ways. First, they have read the story of the twentieth-century black ghettos backward in time and have assumed a historical continuity with slavery days. Second, they have looked too closely at slave law and at the externals of family life and not closely enough at the actual temper of the quarters. During the twentieth century blacks went north in great waves and faced enormous hardship. The women often could find work as domestics; the men found themselves shut out of employment not so much by their lack of skills as by fierce racial discrimination. Some disorientation of the black family apparently followed; evaluation of its extent and social content must be left to others who can get beyond simple statistical reports to an examination of the quality of life.[2] But those inclined to read the presumed present record back into the past have always had a special problem, for by any standard of judgment the southern rural black family, which remained closer to the antebellum experience, always appeared to be much stronger than the northern urban family.[3]

The evidence from the war years and Reconstruction, now emerging in more systematic studies than were previously available, long ago should have given us pause.[4] Every student of the Union occupation and early Reconstruction has known of the rush of the freedmen to legalize their marriages; of the widespread desertion of the plantations by whole families; of the demands by men and women for a division of labor that would

[1] Lee Rainwater and William L. Yancey, *The Moynihan Report and the Politics of Controversy* (Cambridge, Mass., 1967), which includes the text of the report; Frazier, *Negro in the United States* and *Negro Family*; Elkins, *Slavery*.

[2] For a brief general critique of prevailing notions of family disorganization see Charles V. Willie, "The Black Family in America," *Dissent*, Feb., 1971, pp. 80–83. The specialized literature is growing rapidly. For one of the most careful and responsible of the older studies see Drake and Cayton, *Black Metropolis*, II, 582–583.

[3] See, e.g., Myrdal, *American Dilemma*, p. 935; Jessie Bernard, *Marriage and Family Among Negroes* (Englewood Cliffs, N.J., 1966), p. 21; Powdermaker, *After Freedom*, p. 143.

[4] See esp. Peter Kolchin, *First Freedom: The Responses of Alabama's Blacks to Emancipation and Reconstruction* (Westport, Conn., 1972), Ch. 3.; Herbert G. Gutman, "Le Phénomène invisible: La Composition de la famille et du foyer noirs après la Guerre de Sécession," *Annales: Economies, Sociétés, Civilisations*, XXVII (July–Oct., 1972), 1197–1218. Of special interest in these studies are the data from marriage certificates in the Union archives, which show an impressive number of cases in which slaves had lived together for ten years and longer, sometimes much longer.

send the women out of the fields and into the homes; of the militancy of parents seeking to keep their children from apprenticeship to whites even when it would have been to their economic advantage; and especially of the heart-rending effort of thousands of freedmen to find long-lost loved ones all over the South. These events were prefigured in antebellum times. Almost every study of runaway slaves uncovers the importance of the family motive: thousands of slaves ran away to find children, parents, wives, or husbands from whom they had been separated by sale. Next to resentment over punishment, the attempt to find relatives was the most prevalent cause of flight.[5]

These data demand a reassessment of slave family life as having had much greater power than generally believed. But a word of warning: the pressures on the family, as E. Franklin Frazier, W. E. B. DuBois, Kenneth M. Stampp, Stanley M. Elkins, and other scholars have pointed out, were extraordinary and took a terrible toll. My claims must be read within limits—as a record of the countervailing forces even within the slavocracy but especially within the slave community. I suggest only that the slaves created impressive norms of family life, including as much of a nuclear family norm as conditions permitted, and that they entered the postwar social system with a remarkably stable base. Many families became indifferent or demoralized, but those with a strong desire for family stability were able to set norms for life in freedom that could serve their own interests and function reasonably well within the wider social system of white-dominated America.

The masters understood the strength of the marital and family ties among their slaves well enough to see in them a powerful means of social control. As a Dutch slaveholder wrote from Louisiana in the 1750s: "It is necessary that the Negroes have wives, and you ought to know that nothing attaches them so much to a plantation as children."[6] No threat carried such force as a threat to sell the children, except the threat to separate husband and wife. The consequences for the children loomed large in the actions of their parents. When—to take an extreme example—a group

of slaves planned a mass suicide, concern for their children provided the ground for sober second thoughts.[7]

Evidence of the slaveholders' awareness of the importance of family to the slaves may be found in almost any well-kept set of plantation records. Masters and overseers normally listed their slaves by households and shaped disciplinary procedures to take full account of family relationships. The sale of a recalcitrant slave might be delayed or avoided because it would cause resentment among his family of normally good workers. Conversely, a slave might be sold as the only way to break his influence over valuable relatives.[8] Could whites possibly have missed the content of their slaves' marital relationships when faced with such incidents as the one reported by James W. Melvin, an overseer, to his employer, Audley Clark Britton?

[*Old Bill*] breathed his last on Saturday the 31st, Jan. about 8–½ o'clock in the morning. He appeared prepared for Death and said he was going to heaven and wanted his wife to meet him there. When he took sick he told all it would be his last sickness—I was very sorry to lose him.[9]

The pretensions of racist propagandists that slaves did not value the marriage relation fell apart in the courts, which in a variety of ways wrestled with the problems caused by the lack of legal sanction for slave marriages. However much they insisted on treating the slaves' marriages as mere concubinage, they rarely if ever denied the moral content of the relationship or the common devotion of the parties to each other. Thus, Georgia and Texas illogically and humanely would not permit slave wives to testify against their husbands while continuing to insist that their relationship had no standing at law. The high courts of South Carolina and other states took a more consistent stand on the question of testimony but repeatedly acknowledged the painful problems caused by the lack of legal sanction for relation-

---

[5]Mullin, *Flight and Rebellion*, p. 109; Sydnor, *Slavery in Mississippi*, p. 103; Bancroft, *Slave Trading*, p. 206.

[6]Quoted in M. Le Page Du Pratz, *History of Louisiana or of the Western Parts of Virginia and Carolina* (London, 1924), p. 365.

[7]WPA, *Negro in Virginia*, p. 74; Fisk University, *Unwritten History of Slavery*, p. 136.

[8]See, e.g., Agnew Diary, Aug. 19, 1862 (II, 124a–124b); Sitterson, *Sugar Country*, pp. 103–104; the correspondence of Charles C. Jones, Jr., and C. C. Jones, Oct., 1856, in Myers, ed., *Children of Pride*.

[9]James W. Melvin to A. C. Britton, Feb. 11, 1863, in the Britton Papers.

ships everyone knew to be meaningful and worthy of respect.[10]

Many slaveholders went to impressive lengths to keep families together even at the price of considerable pecuniary loss, although, as Kenneth Stampp forcefully insists, the great majority of slaveholders chose business over sentiment and broke up families when under financial pressure. But the choice did not rest easy on their conscience. The kernel of truth in the notion that the slaveholders felt guilty about owning human beings resides largely in this issue. They did feel guilty about their inability to live up to their own paternalistic justification for slavery in the face of market pressure.[11]

The more paternalistic masters betrayed evidence of considerable emotional strain. In 1858, William Massie of Virginia, forced to decrease his debts, chose to sell a beloved and newly improved homestead rather than his slaves. "To know," he explained, "that my little family, white and *black,* [is] to be fixed permanently together would be as near that thing happiness as I ever expect to get. . . . Elizabeth has raised and taught most of them, and having no children, like every other woman under like circumstances, has tender feelings toward them."[12] An impressive number of slaveholders took losses they could ill afford in an effort to keep families together.[13] For the great families, from colonial times to the fall of the regime, the maintenance of family units was a matter of honor.[14] Foreign travelers not easily taken in by appearances testified to the lengths to which slaveholders went at auctions to compel the callous among them to keep family units together.[15] Finally, many ex-slaves testified about masters who steadfastly refused to separate families; who, if they could not avoid separations, sold the children within visiting distance of their parents; and who took losses to buy wives or husbands in order to prevent permanent separations.[16] Stampp's insistence that such evidence revealed the exception rather than the rule is probably true, although I think that exceptions occurred more frequently than he seems to allow for. But it does demonstrate how well the whites understood the strength of the slaves' family ties and the devastating consequences of their own brutal disregard of the sensibilities of those they were selling.

Masters could not afford to be wholly indifferent to slave sensibilities. "Who buys me must buy my son too," a slave defiantly shouted from an auction block. Better to buy in Virginia than Louisiana, wrote J. W. Metcalfe to St. John R. Liddell, for we stand a better chance of buying whole families, whose attachments will make them better and less troublesome workers. Enough slaves risked severe punishment in demanding that their families be kept intact to make masters thoughtful of their own self-interest.[17] So far as circumstances permitted, the slaves tried to stay close to brothers and sisters, aunts and uncles.[18] A woman with a husband who struck her too freely might turn to her brother for protection. A widowed or abandoned aunt could expect to live in a cabin

[10]Catterall, ed., *Judicial Cases,* I, passim; III, 89–90, 160; V, 182; also C. P. Patterson, *Negro in Tennessee,* pp. 57, 154.

[11]Kenneth Stampp, having studied the wills of a large number of slaveholders, concludes that the financial return to the heirs constitutes the overriding consideration; see *Peculiar Institution,* p. 204. But see also J. B. Sellers, *Slavery in Alabama,* p. 168, for a somewhat different reading.

[12]Quoted in Phillips, *Life and Labor,* p. 243.

[13]For some evidence of masters who went to great lengths to keep the families of even recalcitrant slaves together, or who took financial losses to avoid separations, see the Witherspoon-McDowall Correspondence for 1852; Richard Whitaker to A. H. Boykin, Nov. 17, 1843, in the Boykin Papers; J. B. Hawkins to Charles Alston, Nov. 28, 1847, in the Alston Papers; William Otey to Octavia A. Otey, Nov. 20, 1855, in the Wyche-Otey Papers; Ernest Haywood Correspondence, 1856–1857; Lewis Stirling to his son, Jan. 10, 1843; Henry A. Tayloe to B. O. Tayloe, Jan. 5, 1835; Correspondence of Joseph Bryan of Savannah, Ga., a slave trader, in the Slave Papers, Library of Congress; Gavin Diary, July 2, 1857; George W. Clement to Capt. John P. Wright, Oct. 28, 1849, in the Pocket Plantation Record. For evidence and analyses in secondary works see esp. R. H. Taylor, *Slaveholding in North Carolina,* p. 85; Phillips, *Life and Labor,* pp. 274–275; McColley, *Slavery and Jeffersonian Virginia,* pp. 66–68.

[14]See, e.g., Morton, *Robert Carter of Nomini Hall,* p. 111; Joseph Clay to Edward Telfair, Dec. 6, 1785, in the Telfair Papers; Heyward, *Seed from Madagascar,* p. 88; W. T. Jordan, *Hugh Davis, passim;* Myers, ed., *Children of Pride, passim;* John Lynch to Ralph Smith, Oct. 13, 1826, in Pocket Plantation Record; J. B. Grimball Diary, June 20, 1835, Jan. 11, 1860, July 17, 1863; C. C. Mercer to John and William Mercer, July 28, 1860; wills dated Dec. 12, 1849, July 9, 1857, Feb. 2, 1862, in the Lawton Papers; A.G.G. to Thomas W. Harriss, Oct. 28, 1848, in the Harriss Papers; Gavin Diary, Sept. 9, 1856; William McKean to James Dunlop, April 4, 1812, in the McKean Letterbook; Eaton, *Henry Clay,* pp. 120–121; John Kirkland to his son, Sept. 15, 1858, in the Wyche-Otey Papers.

[15]See, e.g., Lyell, *Second Visit,* I, 209–210; Stirling, *Letters from the Slave States,* p. 260.

[16]Fisk University, *Unwritten History of Slavery,* pp. 1, 33: Rawick, ed., *S.C. Narr.,* II (1), 206; III (3), 2; *Texas Narr.,* IV (2), 110; *Indiana Narr.,* VI (2), 10; George Teamoh Journal, Pts. 1–2, p. 31, in the Woodson Papers.

[17]Schoepf, *Travels in the Confederation,* II, 148; Metcalfe to Liddell, June 24, 1848, in the Liddell Papers. Also Charles M. Manigault to Louis Manigault, Jan. 8, 1857; John W. Pittman invoice and note, in the Slave Papers, Library of Congress.

[18]In general see Rawick, *Sundown to Sunup,* p. 90.

with an affectionate niece and her husband. An old slave without spouse or children could expect attention and comfort from nieces, nephews, and cousins when facing illness and death.[19] Brothers looked after their sisters or at least tried to. An overseer killed a slave girl in Kentucky and paid with his own life at the hands of her brother, who then made a successful escape. In Virginia terrible whippings could not prevent a young man from sneaking off to visit a cherished sister on another plantation.[20]

The more humane masters took full account of their slaves' affection for and sense of responsibility toward relatives. Charles West wrote to the Reverend John Jones of Georgia to ask if a certain Clarissa was alive and about, for her sister, Hannah, in Alabama wanted to visit her during the summer. Dr. Bradford, a slaveholder in Florida, hired out three sisters at a lower price than he could have gotten because he would not separate them even for a year.[21] Few slaveholders took such pains to respect the strong ties of brothers and sisters, but fewer still could claim as excuse that they did not have evidence of the slaves' feelings. Three-quarters of a century after slavery, Anne Harris of Virginia, at age ninety-two, told her interviewer that no white person had ever set foot in her house.

Don't 'low it. Dey sole my sister Kate. I saw it wid dese here eyes. Sole her in 1860, and I ain't seed nor heard of her since. Folks say white folks is all right dese days. Maybe dey is, maybe dey isn't. But I can't stand to see 'em. Not on my place.[22]

In the late antebellum period several states moved to forbid the sale of children away from their mother, but only Louisiana's law appears to have been effective. At that, Governor Hammond of South Carolina had the audacity to argue that the slaveholders deserved credit for efforts to hold slave families together and that the slaves themselves cared little.[23]

Masters not only saw the bonds between husbands and wives, parents and children, they saw the bonds between nieces and nephews and aunts and uncles and especially between brothers and sisters. Nowhere did the slaveholders' willful blindness, not to say hypocrisy, concerning the strength of their slaves' family ties appear so baldly as in their reaction to separations attendant upon sales. They told themselves and anyone who would listen that husbands and wives, despite momentary distress, did not mind separations and would quickly adjust to new mates. Not content with this fabrication, some slaveholders went so far as to assert that separation of mothers from children caused only minimal hardship. Most slaveholders knew this claim to be nonsense, but they nevertheless argued that the separation of fathers from their children was of little consequence.

From time to time a slave did prefer to stay with a good master or mistress rather than follow a spouse who was being sold away. In these cases and in many others in which slaves displayed indifference, the marriage had probably already been weakened, and sale provided the most convenient and painless form of divorce. Such incidents reveal nothing about the depth of grief aroused by the sale of cherished wives and husbands. The slaveholders knew that many slave marriages rested on solid foundations of affection. Slaves on all except the most entrenched and stable plantations lived in constant fear of such separations and steeled themselves against them. When the blow came, the slaves often took it with outward calm. A discernible decline in a master's fortune or growing trouble with the overseer or master might have given warning of what was coming. If the slaves suffered quietly and cried alone, their masters had an excuse to declare them indifferent.

No such excuses, frail as they were, could explain the slaveholders' frequent assertions that mothers and children adjusted easily to separa-

---

[19]For illustrations of each of these cases see Fisk University, *Unwritten History of Slavery*, pp. 140, 143; Phillips, *Life and Labor*, p. 270; Henry [the Driver] to William S. Pettigrew, July 1, 1857, in the Pettigrew Papers; Eliza G. Roberts to Mrs. C. C. Jones, May 20, 1861, and Mary Jones to Mary S. Mallard, Nov. 7, 1865, in Myers, ed., *Children of Pride*.

[20]Rawick, ed., *Kansas Narr.*, XVI, 71; *Ohio Narr.*, XVI, 12.

[21]Charles West to John Jones, July 23, 1855, in the John Jones Papers; Chatham, "Plantation Slavery in Middle Florida," unpubl. M.A. thesis, University of North Carolina, 1938, p. 80. See also *Father Henson's Story of His Own Life*, pp. 147–148, 157; Fisk University, *Unwritten History of Slavery*, p. 78.

[22]WPA, *Negro in Virginia*, p. 34.

[23]*DBR*, VIII (Feb., 1850), 122. For a discussion of the state laws designed to protect families from separation see Bancroft, *Slave Trading*, pp. 197–199.

tions. The slaveholders saw the depth of the anguish constantly, and only the most crass tried to deny it. John A. Quitman said that he had witnessed the separation of a family only once. It was enough: "I never saw such profound grief as the poor creatures manifested." Mary Boykin Chesnut remarked to a visiting Englishwoman as they passed a slave auction, "If you can stand that, no other Southern thing need choke you."[24]

John S. Wise's testimony may stand for many others. An apologist who put the best face he could on the old regime, he described an auction in which a crippled man of limited use was in danger of being separated from his wife and children. Israel, the man, spoke up in his own behalf:

"Yes, sir, I kin do as much ez ennybody; and marsters, ef you'll only buy me and de chillum with Martha Ann, Gord knows I'll wuk myself to deth for you." The poor little darkeys, Cephas and Melinda, sat there frightened and silent, their white eyes dancing like monkey-eyes, and gleaming in the shadows. As her husband's voice broke on her ear, Martha Ann, who had been looking sadly out of the window in a pose of quiet dignity, turned her face with an expression of exquisite love and gratitude towards Israel. She gazed for a moment at her husband and at her children, and then looked away once more, her eyes brimming with tears.[25]

Wise's story—of course—ended happily when a slaveholder accepted a loss he could not easily afford in order to buy the family as a unit. But Wise, a man of the world, had to know, as Brecht later reminded us, "In real life, the ending is not so fine/Victoria's Messenger does not come riding often."

John Randolph of Roanoke, a slaveholder himself, who had known Patrick Henry, Henry Clay, and all the great political orators of the day and who himself ranked at the top, was asked whom he thought to have pride of place. "The greatest orator I ever heard," he replied, "was a

woman. She was a slave and a mother and her rostrum was an auction block."[26]

All except the most dehumanized slaveholders knew of the attachments that the slaves had to their more extended families, to their friends, and to most of those who made up their little communities and called each other "brother" and "sister." Kate Stone wrote in 1862, "Separating the old family Negroes who have lived and worked together for so many years is a great grief to them and a distress to us."[27] Those who pretended that the separations came easy never explained why so many ruses had to be used to keep men and women occupied while one or another of their children was being whisked off. Robert Applegarth, an Englishman, described a common scene in which slaves suffered threats and punishments at auctions in response to their wailing and pleading to be kept together.[28] So well did the slaveholders understand the strength of these family ties that the more humane among them found it useful to argue against separations on the grounds of economic expediency by pointing out that the slaves worked much better when kept together.[29]

The extent of separation of wives from husbands and children from parents will probably remain in dispute. The impressive econometric work by Robert Fogel and Stanley Engerman suggests that separations occurred less frequently than has generally been believed, but the data do not permit precise measurement.[30] The nostalgic son of an antebellum planter did not fear contradiction when he recalled long after emancipation: "Were families separated by sale, etc.? Yes, quite often."[31] The potential for forced sepa-

[24]Quitman as quoted in Bancroft, *Slave Trading*, p. 308; Chesnut, *Diary from Dixie*, p. 18.

[25]Wise, *End of an Era*, p. 84; also pp. 85–86.

[26]As quoted by R. E. Park in his introduction to Doyle, *Etiquette of Race Relations*, p. xxvii.

[27]Kate Stone, *Brokenburn*, p. 84. Or see the remarks of the court in *Nowell* v. *O'Hara* (S.C.), 1833, in Catterall, ed., *Judicial Cases*, II, 352.

[28]See Applegarth's statement in the Slave Papers, Library of Congress.

[29]See, e.g., Judge DeSaussure of South Carolina in *Gayle* v. *Cunningham*, 1846, in Catterall, ed., *Judicial Cases*, II, 314; or Judge Slidell of Louisiana in *Bertrand* v. *Arcueil, Ibid.*, III, 599–600.

[30]Fogel and Engerman, *Time on the Cross*, pp. 126–144. See also the suggestive article by William Calderhead, "How Extensive Was the Border State Slave Trade: A New Look," *CWH*, XVIII (March, 1972), 42–55.

[31]J. A. McKinstry to H. C. Nixon, Feb. 11, 1913, in Correspondence: Slavery, Tennessee State Library and Archives. In general see Bancroft, *Slave Trading*, esp. Chs. 2 and 10.

ration—whatever the ultimate measure of its realization—struck fear into the quarters, especially in
the slave-exporting states of the Upper South. If
the rich and powerful Pierce Butler of the Sea
Islands had to sell hundreds of slaves to cover
debts in the 1850s, was anyone safe? Even planters willing to take financial losses to keep families
intact could not always control events. Once
slaves passed out of the hands of their old masters, their fate depended upon the willingness of
professional traders to honor commitments to
keep families together or upon the attitude of new
masters. And many masters did not respect their
slaves' family feelings and did not hesitate to sell
them as individuals.

Frederick Douglass referred to "that painful
uncertainty which in one form or another was ever
obtruding itself in the pathway of the slave."[32]
Perhaps no single hardship or danger, not even
the ever-present whip, struck such terror into the
slaves and accounted for so much of that "fatal-
ism" often attributed to them. If the spirit of many
did crack and if many did become numb, nothing
weighs so heavily among the reasons as the
constant fear of losing loved ones. In the weakest
slaves it instilled reckless irresponsibility and a

fear of risking attachments—of feeling anything—
and in the strongest, a heroic stoicism in the face
of unbearable pain. A majority of the slaves probably suffered from some effects of these fears, but
their vibrant love of life and of each other checked
the slide into despair.

But the pain remained, and the slaveholders
knew as much. Is it possible that no slaveholder
noticed the grief of the woman who told Fredrika
Bremer that she had had six children, three of
whom had died and three of whom had been sold:
"When they took from me the last little girl, oh, I
believed I never should have got over it! It almost
broke my heart!"[33] Could any white southerner
pretend not to know from direct observation the
meaning of Sojourner Truth's statement: "I have
borne thirteen chillun and seen 'em mos' all sold
off into slavery, and when I cried out with a
mother's grief, none but Jesus heard. . . ."[34]
Whatever the whites admitted to others or even
themselves, they knew what they wrought. And
the slaves knew that they knew. A black woman,
speaking to Lucy Chase, recalled her first husband's being sold away from her: "White folks got
a heap to answer for the way they've done to
colored folks! So much they won't never pray it
away!"[35]

[32]*Life and Times of Frederick Douglass*, p. 96.
[33]Bremer, *Homes of the New World*, II, 93.

[34]Quoted in Du Bois, *Gift of Black Folk*, p. 143.
[35]Swint, ed., *Dear Ones at Home*, p. 124.

Slavery in Capitalist and Noncapitalist Cultures

Stanley M. Elkins

*In this article, Elkins shows that the position of the
slave in this society was precarious at best. The
position of the slave family in the U.S., according
to Elkins, was based on the market economy of
slavery, in contrast to other societies, notably
Brazil.*

The four major legal categories which defined the
status of the American slave may be roughly

classified as "term of servitude," "marriage and
the family," "police and disciplinary powers over
the slave" and "property and other civil rights."
The first of these, from which somehow all the
others flowed, had in effect been established
during the latter half of the seventeenth century; a
slave was a slave for the duration of his life, and
slavery was a status which he transmitted by
inheritance to his children and his children's children.

From *Slavery: A Problem in American Institutional and Intellectual Life* (Chicago: University of Chicago Press, 1968), pp. 52–55

and 72–74. Copyright © 1968, The University of Chicago. Reprinted by permission. Footnotes have been renumbered.

It would be fairest, for several reasons, to view the remaining three categories in terms of the jurisprudence of the nineteenth century. By that time the most savage aspects of slavery from the standpoint of Southern practice (and thus, to a certain extent, of law) had become greatly softened. We may accordingly see it in its most humane light and at the same time note the clarity with which its basic outlines remained fixed and embodied in law, much as they had been laid down before the middle of the eighteenth century.

That most ancient and intimate of institutional arrangements, marriage and the family, had long since been destroyed by the law, and the law never showed any inclination to rehabilitate it. Here was the area in which considerations of humanity might be expected most widely to prevail, and, indeed, there is every reason to suppose that on an informal daily basis they did: the contempt in which respectable society held the slave trader, who separated mother from child and husband from wife, is proverbial in Southern lore. On the face of things, it ought to have been simple enough to translate this strong social sentiment into the appropriate legal enactments, which might systematically have guaranteed the inviolability of the family and the sanctity of the marriage bond, such as governed Christian polity everywhere. Yet the very nature of the plantation economy and the way in which the basic arrangements of Southern life radiated from it made it inconceivable that the law should tolerate any ambiguity, should the painful clash between humanity and property interest ever occur. Any restrictions on the separate sale of slaves would have been reflected immediately in the market; their price would have dropped considerably. Thus the law could permit no aspect of the slave's conjugal state to have an independent legal existence outside the power of the man who owned him: "The relation of master and slave is wholly incompatible with even the qualified relation of husband and wife, as it is supposed to exist among slaves."[1] Marriage, for them, was denied any standing in law. Accordingly, as T. R. R. Cobb of Georgia admitted, "The contract of marriage not being recognized among slaves, none of its

consequences follow."[2] "The relation between slaves," wrote a North Carolina judge in 1858, "is essentially different from that of man and wife joined in lawful wedlock . . . [for] with slaves it may be dissolved at the pleasure of either party, or by the sale of one or both, depending on the caprice or necessity of the owners."[3]

It would thus go without saying that the offspring of such "contubernial relationships," as they were called, had next to no guarantees against indiscriminate separation from their parents.[4] Of additional interest is the fact that children derived their condition from that of their mother. This was not unique to American slavery, but it should be noted that especially in a system conceived and evolved exclusively on grounds of property there could be little doubt about how such a question would be resolved. Had status been defined according to the father's condition—as was briefly the case in seventeenth-century Maryland, following the ancient common law—there would instantly have arisen the irksome question of what to do with the numerous mulatto children born every year of white planter-fathers and slave mothers. It would have meant the creation of a free mulatto class, automatically relieving the master of so many slaves on the one hand, while burdening him on the other with that many colored children whom he could not own. Such equivocal relationships were never permitted to vex the law. That "the father of a slave is unknown to our law" was the universal understanding of Southern Jurists.[5] It was thus that a father, among slaves, was legally "unknown," a husband without

[1]*Howard* v. *Howard*, 6 Jones N.C. 235 (December, 1858), quoted in Helen T. Catterall, *Judicial Cases concerning American Slavery and the Negro* (Washington: Carnegie Institution, 1926 ff.), II, 221.

[2]Thomas R. R. Cobb, *An Inquiry into the Law of Slavery in the United States of America* (Philadelphia: T. & J. W. Johnson, 1858), p. 246.

[3]Quoted in Catterall, *Judicial Cases*, II, 221.

[4]The few exceptions—none of which meant very much in practice, except perhaps the law of Louisiana—are discussed in Bancroft, *Slave-trading*, pp. 197–221. "Louisiana, least American of the southern States," writes Mr. Bancroft, "was least inhuman. In becoming Americanized it lost many a liberal feature of the old French *code noir*, but it forbade sale of mothers from their children less than ten years of age (and *vice versa*) and bringing into the State any slave child under ten years of age without its mother, if living. The penalty for violating either prohibition was from $1,000 to $2,000 and the forfeiture of the slave. That would have meant much if it had been strictly enforced" (p. 197). Louisiana's Spanish and French background, plus the fact that in both the legal and social senses slavery in Latin America generally was very different from slavery in North America, may furnish significant clues to some of the idiosyncrasies in the Louisiana code. See below.

[5]*Frazier* v. *Spear*, 2 Bibb (Ken.), 385 (Fall, 1811), quoted in Catterall, *Judicial Cases*, I, 287.

the rights of his bed,[6] the state of marriage defined as "only that concubinage . . . with which alone, perhaps, their condition is compatible,"[7] and motherhood clothed in the scant dignity of the breeding function. . . .[8]

Neither in Brazil nor in Spanish America did slavery carry with it such precise and irrevocable categories of perpetual servitude, "durante vita" and "for all generations," as in the United States. The presumption in these countries, should the status of a colored person be in doubt, was that he was free rather than a slave.[9] There were in fact innumerable ways whereby a slave's servitude could be brought to an end. The chief of these was the very considerable fact that he might buy his own freedom. The Negro in Cuba or Mexico had the right to have his price declared and could, if he wished, purchase himself in installments. Slaves escaping to Cuba to embrace Catholicism were protected by a special royal order of 1733 which was twice reissued. A slave unduly punished might be set at liberty by the magistrate. In Brazil the slave who was the parent of ten children might legally demand his or her freedom.[10] The medieval Spanish code had made a slave's service terminable under any number of contingencies—if he denounced cases of treason, murder, counterfeiting, or the rape of a virgin, or if he performed various other kinds of meritorious acts. Though all such practices did not find their way into the seventeenth- and eighteenth-century legal arrangements of Latin America, much of their spirit was perpetuated in the values, customs, and social expectations of that later period. It is important to appreciate the high social approval connected with the freeing of slaves. A great variety of happy family events—the birth of a son, the marriage of a daughter, anniversaries, national holidays—provided the occasion, and their ceremonial was frequently marked by the manumission of one or more virtuous servitors. It was considered a pious act to accept the responsibility of becoming godfather to a slave child, implying the moral obligation to arrange eventually for its freedom. Indeed, in Cuba and Brazil such freedom might be purchased for a nominal sum at the baptismal font.[11] All such manumissions had the strong approval of both church and state and were registered gratis by the government.[12]

In extending its moral authority over men of every condition, the church naturally insisted on bringing slave unions under the holy sacraments. Slaves were married in church and the banns published; marriage was a sacred rite and its sanctity protected in law. In the otherwise circumspect United States, the only category which the law could apply to conjugal relations between slaves—or to unions between master and slave—was concubinage. But concubinage, in Latin America, was condemned as licentious, adulterous, and immoral; safeguards against promiscuity were provided in the law,[13] and in Brazil the Jesuits labored mightily to regularize the libertinage of the master class by the sacrament of Christian marriage.[14] Moreover, slaves owned by different masters were not to be hindered from marrying, nor could they be kept separate after marriage. If the estates were distant, the wife was to go with her husband, and a fair price was to be fixed by

[6]"A slave has never maintained an action against the violator of his bed. A slave is not admonished for incontinence, or punished for fornication or adultery; never prosecuted for bigamy, or petty treason for killing a husband being a slave, any more than admitted to an appeal for murder." Opinion of Daniel Dulany, Esq., Attorney-General of Maryland, quoted in William Goodell, *The American Slave Code in Theory and Practice* (New York: American and Foreign Anti-Slavery Society, 1853), pp. 106–107.

[7]*State* v. *Samuel (a slave)*, 2 Dev. and Bat. (N.C.), 177 (December, 1836), quoted in Catterall, *Judicial Cases*, II, 77.

[8]The picturesque charge that planters deliberately "bred" their slave women has never been substantiated, and Avery Craven's point that white women bred about as young and as often as their black sisters is a sensible one. But with no law to prevent the separation of parents and children, and with the value of a slave being much in excess of what it cost to rear him, the temptation to think and talk about a prolific Negro woman as a "rattlin' good breeder" was very strong.

[9]"In the Cuban market freedom was the only commodity which could be bought untaxed; every negro against whom no one had proved a claim of servitude was deemed free." William Law Mathieson, *British Slavery and Its Abolition* (London: Longmans, Green, 1926), pp. 37–38.

[10]Johnston, *Negro in the New World*, p. 89.

[11]What I have said in this paragraph is virtually a paraphrase of the information which Mr. Tannenbaum has collected and so skillfully summarized on pp. 50, 53–54, 57–58 of *Slave and Citizen.*

[12]Johnston, *Negro in the New World*, p. 42.

[13]"The master of slaves must not allow the unlawful intercourse of the two sexes, but must encourage matrimony." Spanish slave code of 1789, quoted in *ibid.*, p. 44. Although slaves were allowed "to divert themselves innocently" on holy days, the males were to be kept apart from the females. *Ibid.*, p. 44.

[14]Freyre, *The Masters and the Slaves*, p. 85.

impartial persons for her sale to the husband's master.[15] A slave might, without legal interference, marry a free person. The children of such a

[15]Johnston, *Negro in the New World,* pp. 44–45. A diocesan synod of 1680 in Cuba issued weighty regulations on this subject which were supposed to supplement and have equal force with civil law. "Constitution 5 established that 'marriage should be free' and ordered that 'no master prohibit his slaves from marriage, nor impede those who cohabit therein, because we have found that many masters with little fear of God and in grave danger of their consciences, proscribe their slaves from marrying or impede their cohabitation with their married part-

marriage, if the mother were free, were themselves free, inasmuch as children followed the condition of their mother.[16]

ners, with feigned pretexts'; and also prohibited 'that they go away to sell them outside the city, without that they take together husband and wife.' " Ortiz, *Los Negros Esclavos,* p. 349. The church even made some concessions here to African tribal marriage arrangements, to the extent that a slave with multiple wives might—if the first-married wife's identity could not be ascertained—pick out the one he preferred and have his marriage with her solemnized under the sacraments. *Ibid.,* p. 349.

[16]Tannenbaum, *Slave and Citizen,* p. 56.

The Origins of the Female-Headed Black Family: The Impact of the Urban Experience

Frank F. Furstenberg, Jr., Theodore Hershberg, and John Modell

Examining census data of Philadelphia from 1850–1880 the authors uncovered some interesting facts concerning Black family structure as compared to that of other ethnic groups. Results showed that most households across all ethnic groups, Blacks included, were couple-headed. The large number of Black female-headed households were a consequence of the higher mortality rate among Black males.

The link between family structure and social mobility has been a topic of considerable sociological speculation. For some years now, there has been a running controversy among scholars working in the area of the family as to whether certain kinship arrangements are especially conducive to success in an industrial society. Specifically, a general proposition was set forth, principally by Parsons that the most prevalent family form in this society—the nuclear household—emerged at about the time of industrialization in response to demands of the economy for a highly flexible, mobile, emotionally bonded, small kin unit. Parsons contends that extended family forms restrict social mobility by subordinating immediate economic motives to longer range familial interests. Strong commitment to kin, according to this line of reasoning, detracts from unqualified commitment to economic achievement, for it fosters a sense of collectivity rather than individualism, an emphasis on personal qualities rather than on general performance.[1]

Although the functional explanation for the family in contemporary Western society has a plausible ring, empirical support has been conspicuously absent. Indeed, many of the studies on the relationship of the economy, family forms, and social mobility have failed to confirm even basic assumptions underlying the evolution of the contemporary Western family: (1) several historical

[1]Talcott Parsons, "Age and Sex in the Structure of the United States," *American Sociological Review,* VII (1942), 604–616; Parsons and Robert F. Bales, *Family, Socialization and the Interaction Process* (New York, 1965), ch. 1.

From *The Journal of Interdisciplinary History* 6 (1975), 211–233. Reprinted by permission of *The Journal of Interdisciplinary History* and The M.I.T. Press, Cambridge, Massachusetts.

The authors wish to express their appreciation to the Center for the Study of Metropolitan Problems, National Institute of Mental Health, the financial support of which (MH16621) has made this research possible. An earlier version of this paper was presented at the 1973 annual meeting of the American Sociological Association.

The data presented here were collected by the Philadelphia Social History Project, directed by Theodore Hershberg. They are part of a larger study of the impact of urbanization,

industrialization, and immigration on social and family structure, the formation and transformation of neighborhoods, the organization of and journey to work, the development of an intra-urban transportation network, and patterns of migration and social mobility. To study these topics, a massive machine-readable data base has been created describing individual persons, families, businesses, manufacturing firms, and transportation facilities. See Theodore Hershberg, "The Philadelphia Social History Project: A Methodological History," unpub. Ph.D. diss. (Stanford, 1973). The authors are indebted to the critical readings of Etienne van de Walle and John Durand.

studies have cast doubt on the proposition that the traditional family in Western society was extended and non-nuclear in form in preindustrial society; (2) cross-cultural comparisons suggest that although the form of the family is changing in many societies in response to economic conditions, various family forms can co-exist with industrialized economies; (3) relations with extended kin abound in contemporary society, indicating that the family is not so nuclear or isolated as was supposed in the classic formulation; (4) extensive kinship relations may promote social mobility by providing economic resources and social support not available in a small family unit.²

The evidence which runs counter to the classic formulation of the functional relationship between industrialization and social mobility is still inconclusive; nevertheless, it suggests that it is a sociological problem that bears further consideration. Until further historical data are assembled, there is little basis to select among the conflicting interpretations or to develop a more integrative theory.

In recent years, however, another even more compelling reason for gathering further information on this problem has arisen. As attention shifted in the 1960s from an undifferentiated examination of the experience of the "American family" to a more detailed inspection of the subcultural variations in family form, a bitter debate erupted on one aspect of the broad question of the articulation of economy, family, and social mobility. At the locus of this disagreement was the question of whether "structural defects" in the black family accounted for the economically disadvantaged position of blacks in American society. Even before and especially since the earlier writings of Frazier, the sociological writings on the black family were heavily laced with references to the destructive legacy of slavery, the missing male, and the matrifocal character of black family

life.³ However, Frazier's observations were amplified and extended in the early 1960s in Nathan Glazer and Daniel P. Moynihan's widely acclaimed book, *Beyond the Melting Pot* (Cambridge, Mass., 1964). While acknowledging the impact of prejudice and economic discrimination, Glazer and Moynihan, following Frazier, traced the current position of blacks in America back to slavery. They contended that the black family, weakened by slavery, could not withstand the pressures of urban life.

In reviewing the Glazer/Moynihan section on the condition of the black family in the nineteenth century, it is impossible not to be impressed by the absence of supporting data. Both the propositions that slavery resulted in a permanent deterioration of the black family structure and that family structure accounts for economic disadvantage are accepted uncritically. Several years later, the Glazer/Moynihan thesis was restated in the report on the black family that Moynihan prepared for the Johnson administration. In this later document, the argument is further amplified and family structure is accorded even greater importance in accounting for the current fate of black Americans:

> *Obviously, not every instance of social pathology afflicting the Negro community can be traced to the weakness of family structure. . . . Nonetheless, at the center of the tangle of pathology is the weakness of the family structure. . . . It was by destroying the Negro family under slavery that white Americans broke the will of the Negro people. Although that will has reasserted itself in our time, it is a resurgence doomed to frustration unless the viability of the Negro family is restored.*[4]

Needless to say, the Moynihan report has engendered a heated discussion of a number of crucial issues: What was the impact of slavery on the family structure of Afro-Americans? How does family structure shape prospects of economic success in American society? How do the answers to these questions contribute to our understanding of the potential effect of various strategies for

---

[2] Ethel Shanas and Gordon F. Streib (eds.), *Social Structure and the Family: Generational Relations* (Englewood Cliffs, N.J., 1965); Marvin B. Sussman, "The Isolated Nuclear Family: Fact or Fiction?" *Social Problems,* VI (1959), 333–340; Sussman and Lee Burchinal, "Kin Family Network: Unheralded Structure in Current Conceptualizations of Family Functioning," *Marriage and Family Living,* XXIV (1962), 221–240; Eugene Litwack, "Occupational Mobility and Extended Family Cohesion," *American Sociological Review,* XXV (1960), 9–21; Elizabeth Bott, *Family and Social Network* (London, 1957); William J. Goode, *World Revolution and Family Patterns* (New York, 1963). See also Michael Gordon and Tamara K. Hareven (eds.), "New Social History of the Family," special issue of *Journal of Marriage and the Family,* XXXV (1973).

[3] E. Franklin Frazier, *The Negro Family in the United States* (Chicago, 1939).

[4] Lee Rainwater and William Yancey (eds.), *The Moynihan Report and the Politics of Controversy* (Cambridge, Mass., 1967), 76.

ameliorating economic disadvantage? In a very real sense, these questions raised by the Moynihan thesis are specifications of the general problem of how family structure is linked to economic success in American society. Are certain forms of the family more or less conducive to social mobility in an industrialized economy? Specifically, is there reason to believe that the couple-headed nuclear family is better equipped to utilize economic resources and confer special advantages on their offspring than a non-couple-headed or non-nuclear family structure?

A few contemporary studies have explored the link between family structure and social mobility with largely inconclusive results.[5] The most penetrating historical studies have so far concentrated on questioning the link between slavery and black family structure.[6] As yet, little historical information has been brought to bear on the status of the black family relative to other ethnic groups and the economic consequences of family structure for people of different ethnic backgrounds. Thus, it is not even known whether sizable variations existed in the structure of families among various ethnic groups prior to this century, much less whether such variations influenced the mobility patterns of these different populations.

This paper examines how family structure and family composition varied by ethnic group in the second half of the nineteenth century in Philadelphia, the nation's second largest city. Our analysis is based on samples drawn from the decennial Federal population manuscript schedules for 1850 through 1880. The black sample consists of all black households; the white ethnic samples are drawn systematically from the whole number of households headed by immigrants from Ireland and Germany, and by native white Americans. None includes fewer than 2,000 households for each census year.[7]

The Structure of the Household

Although our information does not reach back into the early nineteenth century, it does lend further support to the position that complex households were less common than simple nuclear structures, at least in one major urban area.[8] When we examined the 1880 data from Philadelphia, several interesting observations came to light. First, considering only those families in which a child was present, more than three-fourths of the households in Philadelphia consisted of nuclear families, that is families comprised of parents and children with no other relatives present in the home. Of greatest significance is our finding that only minor variations exist among the four ethnic groups (Table 1). Blacks and native whites were slightly less likely to reside in nuclear households than the Irish and German, probably in large measure because the latter groups—more recent immigrants to Philadelphia—had less time for extended kin to develop in this country.

Extended families were the second most common household arrangement. Approximately 14 percent of the sample resided in three-generation families, a figure somewhat greater than the proportion in the current census of Philadelphia. Again we find little variation among the different ethnic groups in the proportion of extended households. Blacks had the highest proportion (17.3 percent); the lowest were German immigrants, of whom 10.2 percent were residing in three-generation families. Expanded families made up only 7 percent of the households. Again, no conspicuous differences appear among ethnic groups. In particular, blacks were about as likely as other ethnic groups to be organized in complex households, and the patterns between the blacks and native white Americans are almost identical. Thus, whatever the benefits or liabilities of the nuclear family in promoting economic mobility, the household structure cannot explain the differential patterns of social mobility which emerge in the latter part of the nineteenth century.

[5]O. D. Duncan and Beverly Duncan, "Family Stability and Occupational Success," *Social Problems*, XVI (1969), 273–285.

[6]Herbert Gutman, "Persistent Myths about the Afro-American Family," above, 181–210. See also Theodore Hershberg, "Free Blacks in Antebellum Philadelphia: A Study of Ex-slaves, Freeborn and Socioeconomic Decline," *Journal of Social History,* V (1971), 183–209; Elizabeth Pleck, "The Two-Parent Household: Black Family Structure in Late Nineteenth-Century Boston," *Ibid.* VI (1972), 3–31.

[7]About 4 percent of the city's population were neither black, Irish, German, nor native white. For a detailed description of how the samples were drawn, see Hershberg, "Philadelphia Social History Project," ch. 2.

[8]For purposes of this analysis, a detailed code of family forms was developed. Families are classified into nuclear, extended (households of three or more generations), and expanded (households with additional relatives but which do not extend generationally). These family types are further subdivided into couple-headed, male-headed, and female-headed. This distinction allows us to look at the family composition within the three different structural forms. For each of these nine types, a further breakdown is made between those families with and without children.

Table 1 Household Structure by Ethnicity, 1880[1]

	Black	Irish	German	NWA
Nuclear	75.2%	82.2%	84.5%	73.1%
Extended	17.3	10.6	10.2	17.0
Expanded ·	7.5	7.3	5.3	9.9
	N = 2,949	N = 1,637	N = 1,766	N = 1,730

[1]. The figures in this and the following tables refer only to households with children. Here and throughout tables, decimals in total percentage are due to rounding.

Changes in Household Structure Over Time

Of course, it is possible that, by 1880, many changes had already taken place in the structure of the family, that our snapshot was taken after the action occurred. In particular, one might speculate that it was too late to detect the damage done to the black family by slavery. Even if this were the case, it would represent a finding of great worth, suggesting that the presumed effects of slavery were quickly erased and that the structure of the contemporary black family could hardly be traced in an unbroken line back to slavery. Our evidence, however, casts doubt even on this hypothesis. When the household composition of the black family in 1880 is compared with the structure of the black household in the antebellum period in 1850, we discover a remarkable degree of continuity. Virtually the same proportion of blacks were living in nuclear households in 1850 as in 1880. Indeed, if anything, there had been a slight decrease in nuclear households.

Other ethnic groups revealed a slight trend toward nuclearity; however, the increase in each case was only a few percentage points (Table 2). Apart from the information that these figures provide about the black family, the comparisons of household structure over time are significant in another respect. They offer little support for the proposition that household structure was changing, at least within the urban areas, as a result of increasing industrialization. This finding, again, seems to run counter to the widely held view that

Table 2. Household Structure by Ethnicity, 1850 and 1880

Inferred Relationships, 1850[1]	Black	Irish	German	NWA
Nuclear	60.6%	60.6%	61.4%	45.6%
Extended	6.6	4.4	3.5	4.7
Expanded	32.8	35.0	35.0	49.7
	N = 1,739	N = 1,844	N = 1,564	N = 1,648
Inferred Relationships, 1880	Black	Irish	German	NWA
Nuclear	57.6%	67.1%	65.5%	52.4%
Extended	4.9	5.6	4.3	5.3
Expanded	37.6	27.2	30.2	42.3
	N = 3,206	N = 1,637	N = 1,726	N = 1,680

[1]. The Federal population manuscript schedules of the United States Census became for the first time in 1850 an enumeration of every inhabitant of the nation, and recorded important information describing each individual within each household unit; but it was not until 1880 that the relationship of each member of the household to the household head was recorded. Researchers using the schedules for 1850, 1860, and 1870, therefore, must *infer* these relationships from the information which was included, such as surname, age, sex, position of listing in the household, etc. The PSHP has developed a computer program to make these inferences; see Theodore Hershberg, "A Method for the Computerized Study of Family and Household Structure Using the Manuscript Schedules of the U.S. Census of Population, 1850–1880," *The Family in Historical Perspective, An International Newsletter,* I (1973), 6–20; Buffington Clay Miller, "A Computerized Method of Determining Family Structure from Mid-Nineteenth Century Census Data," unpub. M.S. diss. (Moore School of Electrical Engineering, University of Pennsylvania, 1972). For the analysis of the 1880 data presented in this paper, however, we have used the given relationships, as recorded in the 1880 manuscript census. In the 1850 and 1880 "inferred" tables, individual relationships which cannot be determined by the computer program (such as "Servant," "Brother-in-Law") are categorized as "Others." The computer program assigns households with "Others" to the expanded category (households with relatives), thus considering all "Others" as relatives. The expanded category, therefore, is inflated by the number of households with only non-relative "Others" (boarders and servants). This can be seen by comparing Table 2 for 1880 based on "inferred" relationships with Table 1 based on "given" relationships.

the American family evolved from an extended family to a nuclear family in response to changing industrial conditions. Of course, the findings here are limited, not only in time, but, more significantly, to an urban population. Quite possibly the impact of industrialization on family structure was accomplished by migration from rural America to the rapidly growing cities.

Our data do not permit a direct test of the effects of industrialization on the family. In subsequent analyses, however, we shall be able to examine the link between the occupational and family structure within the city of Philadelphia during the middle and latter part of the nineteenth century. Although not definitive, this forthcoming analysis should provide some clue to the effect of industrialization on the American family in urban areas of the country.

Ethnicity and Family Composition

Earlier we drew a distinction between household structure and family composition (referring to the membership of the family unit). Most contemporary research on the black family has been concerned, not with the issue of household structure, but with that of family membership. In particular, researchers have been preoccupied with the question of who heads the family unit. As we noted earlier, there is reason to wonder whether this question deserves the prominence that it has received. Reserving our judgment on this issue, we shall in this section examine whether the family composition of blacks differs significantly from other ethnic groups before the turn of the century.

Households were divided into three categories: couple-headed households in which a male was head and in which his wife was listed as present in the home; male-headed households in which the wife was not listed as present in the home; female-headed households. This basic division does not take into account whether the households were nuclear or some complex unit. Furthermore, we again considered only those households in which children were present.[9]

Using this simple classification scheme, there is a noticeable relationship between family composition and ethnicity in the 1850 and 1880 census data (Table 3). German Americans are most likely to be living in couple-headed house-

Table 3. Family Composition by Ethnicity, 1850 and 1880

Inferred Headship, 1850[1]	Black	Irish	German	NWA
Female head	22.5%	13.4%	3.3%	13.3%
Male head	6.0	7.2	3.2	4.0
Couple head	71.5	79.4	93.5	82.6
	$N = 1,739$	$N = 1,844$	$N = 1,564$	$N = 1,648$
Given Headship, 1880	Black	Irish	German	NWA
Female head	25.3%	12.7%	8.3%	13.6%
Male head	5.9	7.5	5.3	6.2
Couple head	68.8	79.8	86.5	80.2
	$N = 2,949$	$N = 1,637$	$N = 1,766$	$N = 1,730$

[1]. Although inferring household *structure* by computer is difficult, inferring household *headship* is simple and certain. Results derived by such an inference are almost exactly those found from "given" relationships. Were we to use "inferred" figures for headship in 1880, the percentage of female heads would be 24.5, 12.6, 8.5, and 11.5 for the blacks, Irish, Germans, and native whites, respectively.

[9] In two recent studies on black family structure (Gutman, "Persistent Myths"; Pleck, "Two-Parent Household"), the proportion of female-headed households is misrepresented because the calculations include couple-headed households *without* children. We disagree with this procedure for three reasons. First, to include childless couples but not households with a single member biases the proportion of female heads substantially downward. Second, the assumption that underlies the association of the female-headed household with a set of negative social consequences is that the absence of a father adversely affects the socialization of the young. To include childless families, therefore, introduces an irrelevant compo-nent. Third, this irrelevant component has a downward bias because childless families tend to be younger and less likely to have experienced family dissolution. A further refinement might have been to remove from consideration those families where the youngest child in the household was presumably beyond the age of childhood socialization. Among the 1880 blacks, applying age 20 as the cutoff point would have removed almost 15 percent of the families from consideration. Such a procedure, however, would have affected almost exclusively the oldest categories of families, and would leave untouched the distinctions and trends treated in this paper.

holds, followed by native whites, closely in 1880 but less so in 1850. Irish households were somewhat less likely to be couple-headed and blacks had the lowest proportion of families in which both parents were present. Thus, the contemporary pattern of a high prevalence of matrifocal households among blacks is visible before the turn of the century and before the arrival in the city of numbers of freedmen.

It is one thing to demonstrate the existence of this pattern and quite another to interpret its significance. In the first place, the magnitude of the difference can be seen in two quite separate lights. We could say that blacks are more than twice as likely as foreign and native-born white Americans to live in households headed by a female. Such a statement emphasizes the differential. Alternatively, we could point out that the great majority of all ethnic groups live in couple-headed households. Even among blacks, only one-fourth of the households were headed by a female. Moreover, among the various ethnic groups there is a difference of only 17 percentage points between the group with the lowest proportion of female-headed households—the German Americans—and that with the highest, black Americans. Obviously, this characterization tends to minimize the differences by underscoring the similarities. The only reasonable way of resolving this issue of interpretation is to delve further into the source of these differences. To us, their significance is to be found more in how they came about than in their magnitude.

Contemporary research on female-headed families has demonstrated the existence of a strong link between economic status and family composition. Male absence is far more prevalent in the lower class than in the middle class. Accordingly, differences in female-headedness between blacks and whites diminish sharply under conditions of economic parity. This finding has caused many to question the position that variations in family composition can be traced to divergent subcultural standards. In many respects the argument that the roots of the black matrifocal family are to be found in slavery represents an extension of the subcultural argument, and the same criticisms that pertain to the subcultural explanation can be applied historically.

New historical studies provide compelling reason to question the destructive impact which slavery allegedly had on the black family. One of the major conclusions reached by econometric historians Fogel and Engerman is that the slave family was considerably stronger than has been believed. Further evidence which challenges the standing interpretation comes from research conducted by Gutman whose data are consistent with conclusions reached by Fogel and Engerman. In groundbreaking essays, Gutman examined "the family patterns of those Negroes closest in time to actual chattel slavery," and did not find "instability," "chaos," or "disorder." Instead, in fourteen varied Southern cities and counties between 1865 and 1880, Gutman found viable two-parent households ranging from 70 to 90 percent. The empirical picture presented here is staggering. Gutman's data make clear that the vast majority of black families were headed by both parents, and they convincingly contradict the view that slavery "destroyed" the black family.[10]

The data for Philadelphia, moreover, are consistent with the findings of Gutman, and Fogel and Engerman. We know from unique information on status-at-birth reported in a Quaker census of Philadelphia blacks in 1847 that only 10 percent of all of the city blacks had been born slaves. More importantly, however, these ex-slaves were *more* likely than the freeborn to have two-parent households. However unrepresentative of all slaves the ex-slaves in Philadelphia's population may have been, direct contact with slavery cannot explain the degree of matrifocality which existed at mid-century.[11] In 1880, one out of every two Philadelphia blacks had been born in the South. Although it is impossible to know with absolute certainty who among these immigrants had been freeborn or slaveborn, place of birth constitutes a plausible proxy for ex-slave status, especially when considered in conjunction with illiteracy.[12] Therefore, if the slavery argument is valid, this

[10]Robert William Fogel and Stanley L. Engerman, *Time on the Cross: The Economics of American Negro Slavery* (Boston, 1974), I, 5, 126–144; Gutman, "Persistent Myths."

[11]Hershberg, "Free Blacks," 192–204.

[12]See Pleck, "Two-Parent Household," 18–19; note 3, above. Although there are problems in this approach, combining the variables of place of birth and illiteracy brings us closer to identifying accurately those blacks most likely to have been slave-born. There were slightly more female illiterates among both northern-born and southern-born black Philadelphians, but this difference was not at all of a magnitude to suggest that the relationships shown in Table 4 are spurious.

Table 4. Black Family Composition by Literacy and Place of Birth, 1880[1]

	Literate			Illiterate		
		Other			Other	
	Pa.	North	South	Pa.	North	South
Female head	25.8%	23.4%	18.3%	46.9%	47.9%	31.9%
Male head	6.6	4.4	5.3	3.5	4.2	6.6
Couple head	67.5	72.2	76.4	49.7	47.9	61.5
	N = 798	N = 158	N = 1,103	N = 143	N = 48	N = 636

[1] Literacy and place of birth refer to the household head.

segment of the population should account for a disproportionate share of the female-headed households. Yet this, in fact, was *not* the case: southern-born illiterate blacks were *less* likely than their northern-born counterparts to have female-headed families (Table 4).

Family Composition and Economic Condition

In place of the subcultural "legacy of slavery" explanation for disorganization in the black family, we wish to argue for the primacy of urban economic and demographic factors. The vast majority of Philadelphia's blacks faced a life of abject poverty. Job discrimination was ubiquitous in the economy. Of every ten black males in the labor force, eight worked at unskilled jobs; the comparable figure for the Irish was five, and for the Germans and native whites fewer than two (see Table 5). When converted to wages and yearly income, these figures bear stark testimony to the difficulty black men faced in attempting to raise and provide for their families. Although there is some disagreement over the amount of a subsistence income for families in 1880, it is quite clear that unskilled laborers were faced with a serious shortfall.[13] In such grim economic circumstances, the conditions for the maintenance of stable family life were at best precarious.

These economic circumstances bear a di-

Table 5. Occupational Structure by Ethnicity, 1880 (for Males 18 Years and Older)

	Black	Irish	German	NWA
Professional high white collar	1.1%	1.6%	1.6%	5.1%
Proprietary[1] low white collar	4.4	13.4	17.5	27.8
Skilled	13.7	31.5	59.7	45.3
Unskilled	79.2	50.1	15.3	17.2
	N = 8,700	N = 36,333	N = 25,172	N = 90,756

[1] Percentages do not add up to 100; the missing percentages—1.6, 3.5, 5.9, and 4.6—for the four groups, respectively, represent a category of ambiguous occupational designation such as "liquor store." Based on other characteristics of this category, we suspect that such individuals were in fact proprietors and should be added to the "proprietary" category.

[13]Eudice Glassberg calculates the subsistence income for a family of five in "Philadelphia's Poverty Line, 1860 and 1880: A Comparison of Earnings and Minimum Standard of Living," unpub. paper, PSHP (Oct. 1973). Unskilled workers rarely made as much as $400 a year. Using Glassberg's figures, the shortfall is about 40 percent. Most families were able to compensate in a variety of ways, which included working wives and children, the pooling of income in expanded and extended families, the taking in of boarders, etc.

rect and powerful relationship to the incidence of female-headed families. This can be seen in Table 6A, which relates wealth (real and personal property holdings) to family composition. Wealth data are not reported in the manuscript schedules for 1880, but they are for 1870. In that year, as in 1880, a greater percentage of black families with children were headed by females (27.1) than for the Irish (16.9), Germans (5.9), and native whites (14.3). Female-headedness varies inversely with wealth. They were found far less often among families with property valued at more than $500 than among propertyless families: half as often for the blacks and Irish; two-thirds as often for the native whites; and one-third as often for the Germans. Table 6B focuses on a special group of household heads, those 30–39 years of age. By examining this group, we eliminate variations which arise from different age structures among the four ethnic groups—an important control because age structure is strongly related both to mortality and to the acquisition of wealth. The same inverse relationship between female-headedness and wealth is found in the 30–39 age group, but the strength of the relationship is far more pronounced.

Table 7 presents these same data in a different form, as the percent differences in female-headedness between blacks and each of the three white groups. Using different wealth categories Table 7B shows that the original variation observed between all black and Irish families with children—9.3 percent—is reduced: to 4.5 percent among holders of "any wealth" and yet further to 4.0 percent among holders of "wealth greater than $1,000." The same is true for the variation observed between blacks and Germans: the 18 percent separating them is reduced to 7.0 among holders of "any" wealth and 2.8 percent among holders of "wealth greater than $1,000." Most striking, however, is the reduction of the variation between blacks and native whites. The observed variation for all families is reduced to 1.2 percent among holders of "any" wealth, and for those owning more than $1,000 the relationship is reversed: native whites in this category were more likely than blacks to have female-headed families. Among the propertied across the entire ethnic spectrum, then, most of the variation in female-headedness is eliminated.

Although the economic data presented in Tables 6 and 7 describe the dramatic reduction of

Table 6.   Proportion of Household Heads Female, by Ethnicity and Wealth, 1870[1]

A. All households with children

$ Wealth	Black		Irish		German		NWA	
0	31.2	(1,414)	21.3	(889)	9.6	(616)	18.8	(674)
100–199	20.2	(129)	15.9	(113)	8.3	(96)	16.7	(96)
200–299	18.7	(91)	12.9	(101)	4.5	(132)	8.3	(157)
300–499	14.6	(48)	10.7	(75)	3.2	(156)	10.6	(179)
500–999	8.3	(72)	9.3	(75)	3.7	(189)	10.5	(143)
1,000 +	17.0	(206)	10.6	(378)	3.5	(633)	12.8	(695)
All	27.1	(1,962)	16.9	(1,636)	5.9	(1,825)	14.3	(1,946)

B. Households with children headed by 30–39 year olds

	Black		Irish		German		NWA	
0	25.8	(395)	18.1	(282)	6.1	(212)	14.2	(211)
100–199	11.1	(36)	5.7	(35)	5.4	(37)	9.1	(33)
200–299	8.0	(25)	7.9	(38)	0	(54)	6.9	(58)
300–499	7.1	(14)	4.8	(21)	0	(43)	3.4	(58)
500–999	15.0	(20)	0	(22)	1.5	(65)	8.1	(62)
1,000 +	6.3	(32)	2.3	(86)	3.5	(172)	10.1	(178)
All	21.8	(522)	12.5	(488)	3.8	(583)	10.3	(600)

[1] Wealth consists of all real and personal property holding reported in the census manuscripts. Figures shown are percentages of all households in a particular ethnic wealth category headed by women; the figures in parentheses are the Ns for these classes.

Table 7.   Percentage Difference in Female-Headedness by Property Holdings between Blacks and the White Ethnic Groups, 1870

	All Households	Without Any Wealth	With Any Wealth	With Wealth Greater Than $1,000
A. All households with children				
Black-Irish	10.2	9.9	4.8	6.4
Black-German	21.2	21.6	12.5	13.5
Black-Native white	12.8	12.4	4.7	4.2
B. Households with children headed by 30–39 year olds				
Black-Irish	9.3	7.7	4.5	4.0
Black-German	18.0	19.7	7.0	2.8
Black-Native white	11.5	11.6	1.2	-3.8

observed variation in female-headedness among holders of property, among the propertyless little or none of the variation is eliminated. There remains, in other words, a variation of 11.5 percent between blacks and native whites, and 9.3 and 18.0 percent respectively, between blacks and the Irish and Germans. There are two reasons for this residual variation. The substantial portion is accounted for by differential mortality which we discuss in detail below. The remainder is at least in part an artifact of the way property holding was reported in the Federal population manuscript schedules. Census marshals were instructed not to record property holding in amounts less than $100. When we observe the category "without property," we are in fact looking at *two* groups:

those with some property worth less than $100 and those without any property at all. This distinction is an important one to bear in mind. Table 8 displays data describing all black families with children in Philadelphia, collected in 1838 by the Pennsylvania Abolition Society and in 1847 by the Society of Friends.[14] Unlike the Federal population manuscript schedules, these forms report property holding down to amounts of $5, and permit the study of variation in female-headedness along a rank order of wealth which includes 95 percent of all black families.

As with the 1870 Federal census, female-headedness and property holding are negatively related (see Table 8). Significantly, this negative relationship is visible for sums of less than $100,

Table 8.   Proportion of Black Household Heads Female by Wealth, 1838 and 1847

	Families with		
	1838	1847	
Wealth	All Children	Children 0–4	Children 5–14
$0–50	31.4 (570)	27.8 (298)	37.9 (610)
50–99	24.2 (241)	12.0 (150)	22.3 (350)
100–499	13.3 (420)	6.1 (181)	17.3 (567)
500 . . .	8.5 (216)	16.3 (49)	10.6 (254)

Sources: 1838: Manuscript Census, Pennsylvania Abolition Society.
1847: Manuscript Census, Society of Friends.

[14]See Hershberg, "Free Blacks," 184–185; *idem*, "Free-Born and Slave-Born Blacks in Antebellum Philadelphia," in Eugene D. Genovese and Stanley L. Engerman (eds). *Race and* *Slavery in the Western Hemisphere: Quantitative Studies* (Princeton, 1975), 395–426.

so that in 1838, for example, black families with $50–$99 of property were only about three-fourths as likely to be female-headed as families with less than $50. If, as we have good reason to suppose in light of the occupational distributions of the several groups, whites in the 1870 "less than $100" category clustered at its higher reaches, while blacks were far more prevalent at the bottom, then an unknown but sizable proportion of the black–white variation among the 1870 "propertyless" can be understood.

Family Composition and Mortality

Differential wealth thus accounts for the observed disparity between Philadelphia's blacks and whites in family composition. Contemporary studies of family life among the poor tend to stress illegitimacy, desertion, and divorce in understanding female headship, but in the nineteenth century a different consideration was the major link between female headship and the poverty cycle: mortality. Today, family instability can be traced to the limited economic prospects that the poor recognize for themselves; in the last century sickness and death played the more important part.[16] Those most ravaged were the urban poor blacks, irregularly employed, segregated, and neglected in matters of public health.

Table 9 seeks to elucidate the contribution of widowhood to female-headedness among black families in Philadelphia in 1880 by examining the reported marital status of each female-headed household (for families with children). Though, as we have seen, females constituted a larger minority of all household heads among blacks than in other ethnic groups, Table 9 shows that for blacks as for the others, widowhood overwhelmingly predominates among female household heads. In each ethnic group, most of the remaining female heads are married women whose spouses are absent—presumably deserted in some cases, with husbands temporarily away at work in others. When we combine the separated, divorced, and single mothers, they constitute only one-fourth of all female heads. It is to widowhood, therefore, that we must attribute the excess of female-headedness among black families with children. This stands in stark contrast with today, when among blacks widowhood is overshadowed by separation and single parenthood as a source of family breakup.

Mortality, of course, increases sharply with age. Had the black population been notably older than other groups, their age distribution might account for the prevalence of widowhood. But this is not the case. Table 10 presents the composition of families by age, measuring age according to the female's age when she is present, and accord-

Table 9.   Reported Marital Status of Female Household Heads, Households with Children, by Ethnicity, 1880

	Black	Irish	German	NWA
Widowed	74.3%	79.5%	77.8%	75.0%
Single	5.0	1.4	3.3	2.5
Divorced	1.1	0.9	0.7	1.0
Married	19.7	18.3	18.3	21.5
	$N = 747$	$N = 219$	$N = 153$	$N = 200$

[15] For evidence of the extraordinary mortality differentials by race (esp. in infant mortality), see the 1879 life tables for Baltimore and Washington (which had more blacks than Philadelphia, but similar mortality experiences) in U.S. Census Office, *Census of 1880,* XII: *Mortality and Vital Statistics* (Washington, 1883), pt. 2, 773–777. See also W. E. B. DuBois' excellent discussion of health and mortality differentials in Philadelphia, in which he lays the blame immediately on the ignorance of

hygiene among the victims and on the uneven distribution of public-health effort (*The Philadelphia Negro: A Social Study* [New York, 1967], ch. 10).

[16] See Frank F. Furstenberg, "Work Experience and Family Life," in James O'Toole (ed.), *Work and the Quality of Life* (Cambridge, Mass., 1974), 341–360; Reynolds Farley, *Growth of the Black Population* (Chicago, 1973).

ing to the male's age when she is not.[17] At every age, the composition of black families is different, with an increasing excess of widows. So fierce was the mortality among Philadelphia's blacks that at least a quarter of the married Negro women in families with children were widowed by their 40s.[18]

Table 10, however, goes beyond the obvious and the awful. We note, for instance, that despite the extraordinarily high incidence of widowhood among blacks, *widowerhood* is rarer among them than in the other groups. This requires explana-

tion. The figures presented are on reported marital status at a given moment in time. Thus, the number of widows counted would (under ideal census conditions) be equal to the number of persons ever widowed, less the number who had remarried; likewise for widowers. Sex differentials in black mortality cannot account for so large a difference. One implication of these statistics is that black men could remarry with relative ease, but black women could not. Another is that a larger proportion of black men than black women who were left with children by the deaths of their

Table 10.   Sex and Marital Status of Heads of Households (with Children) by Age of Head and Ethnicity, 1880[1]

Headed by	Age of Head				
	Less Than 30	30–39	40–49	50–59	60 +
Couples					
Black	84.5	77.2	62.0	44.8	31.0
Irish	90.7	93.5	83.5	75.5	39.5
German	93.4	90.4	82.9	71.2	45.0
NWA	93.8	92.5	84.3	73.5	44.2
Widows					
Black	4.2	11.4	20.8	29.1	35.5
Irish	1.1	3.2	8.6	10.3	16.8
German	2.0	5.4	9.9	11.4	19.3
NWA	0.6	4.4	8.8	10.7	25.1
Other females					
Black	6.7	5.3	6.1	5.7	4.7
Irish	2.3	1.0	1.4	1.8	0.8
German	1.6	1.2	2.7	3.2	4.2
NWA	0.9	1.4	1.8	2.7	2.5
Widowers					
Black	0.1	0.8	2.7	4.6	12.5
Irish	0.4	1.3	3.0	7.3	26.6
German	0.4	1.3	1.3	7.1	15.8
NWA	0	1.4	2.8	5.3	15.0
Other males					
Black	3.9	3.6	4.2	5.0	6.0
Irish	5.2	1.7	1.9	5.0	4.8
German	2.7	1.9	2.1	3.2	5.0
NWA	4.8	1.2	1.3	5.3	6.7
Ns					
Black	899	887	526	281	168
Irish	265	418	369	220	124
German	256	470	374	253	120
NWA	336	517	394	226	120

1. Female's age for couples, widows, and other female heads; male's age for widowers and other male heads. Figures shown are percentages.

[17]The same finding appears when, to avoid the clumsiness of measuring "age" of the family sometimes by the woman, sometimes by the man, we measure it by the age of the oldest child, as a proxy of how long the marriage has been established.

[18]When all households, and not just those with children, are examined, quite the same white/black pattern of differences obtains.

spouses found it impossible or inadvisable to raise the children while unmarried, and left them with relatives or others.

Data on marital status by age strongly bear this out, and point as well to a sex ratio considerably favoring the marriage and remarriage chances of males. These imbalances can be seen in Table 11. Taking all blacks in Philadelphia as our base, and not just those living in families with children (for the former constitute the marriage pool), we find that by ages 35–39, more than one-fifth of all black women were living as widows. Overall in this age group, four in ten black women were, for one reason or another, not currently married; this is so for only a quarter of the men.[19] Black women generally married men older than themselves by an average of about three years; therefore, we should treat the next older age category as the most likely remarriage pool for widowed black women. By this reasoning, 35–39 year-old widows looked to remarry 40–44 year-old men. This group, however, was smaller to begin with because of differential inmigration by sex. Because they were older, because males generally suffer higher mortality, and because of the physically taxing nature of "nigger work," the pool experienced still further attrition. Very nearly half of Philadelphia's large number of widows,

then, can be "explained" by their inability to find suitably aged mates.

Aggravating the situation even more is the fact that black males may have had more reason to leave the city than females when their spouses died, or to have placed their children with friends or relatives, rather than raise them alone on a scant and uncertain income. Women more easily than men could find jobs and at the same time support their children. (It is also possible that Philadelphia attracted an immigration of widowed women. A detailed analysis of the widowed black population of Philadelphia, however, indicates that unlike native whites, black immigrants who were widowed were, if anything, *less* likely at given ages than those born in Pennsylvania to be household heads, and among those who were household heads, less likely to have children.) Many of the female heads of families were employed as seamstresses and domestics, or were able to take in boarders, thus making it possible for them not to remarry. Unless female kin were available to serve as parent surrogates, men undoubtedly found it more difficult to remain unmarried, especially with young children. Finally, men had a further advantage in the remarriage market because they could more actively initiate a marriage contract. Women without means com-

Table 11.   Marital Status by Age and Sex, Blacks, 1880

	Married		All Unmarried		Widowed Only	
	Males	Females	Males	Females	Males	Females
15–19	13	143	925	1,434	1	9
20–24	426	986	1,147	1,574	8	79
25–29	929	1,206	806	947	44	158
30–34	939	937	464	577	41	207
35–39	970	839	333	549	52	288
40–44	641	513	211	486	62	293
45–49	425	325	124	397	47	285
50–54	376	257	114	453	48	338
55–59	196	144	78	251	45	207
60–64	184	74	70	275	43	229
65–69	101	45	36	174	27	147
70 +	114	43	91	397	70	340
TOTAL	5,314	5,512	4,399	7,514	488	2,580

[19]This argument rests on the fact that the effective marriage pool for blacks was other blacks. See Theodore Hershberg, "Mulattoes and Blacks: Intra-Group Color Differences and Social Stratification in Nineteenth-Century Philadelphia," *Journal of American History* (forthcoming).

manded little bargaining power and therefore were in an especially weak position to attract a mate.

We have chosen to accept as *prima facie* evidence the marital status recorded by census marshals a hundred years ago. We have not done so naively. We recognize the likelihood that at least some black female respondents may have told the census marshals what they thought they wanted to hear, explaining by "widowhood" the absence of a male household head, whatever the real reason.[20] But we can validate the plausibility of the claims of widowhood by reference to death statistics contained in other documents and to known patterns of mortality by age. Our procedure has been to construct estimates of joint survival probabilities for a hypothetical population

of black couples, which will allow us to suggest, at appropriate levels of mortality, the likely, or "expected" proportion of widows among the once-married female population, assuming for the moment that remarriage is negligible.[21] Table 12 compares the "expected" proportions of widows at this level of mortality with that measured for the whole black female population of Philadelphia in 1880; we have also prepared a slightly more severe mortality schedule displayed in the same Table.

The findings are unequivocal. By far the greatest part of reported "widowhood" can readily be explained by the level of mortality among black Philadelphians. To be sure, there was some remarriage of widows, which would suggest a somewhat greater discrepancy between stated "widows" and the proportion expected by mor-

Table 12. "Expected" Proportion of Widows among Ever-Married Black Women, 1887, at Two Levels of Mortality, Compared with Proportion Recorded in the 1880 Census, by Age[1]

Age	"Expected" at South Level 3 Mortality	"Expected" at South Level 2 Mortality	"Measured," 1880 Census
25–29	7.2	14.8	11.5
30–34	14.1	21.6	18.1
35–39	21.3	28.7	25.4
40–44	29.1	36.5	36.1
45–49	37.5	45.6	46.6
50–54	47.0	53.4	56.5
55–59	57.8	63.5	59.0
60–64	69.9	74.6	75.3
65–69	81.8	84.3	76.2

1. Figures shown are percentages.

[20]We would expect that among female heads with children, the proportion of widows would increase with the age of the youngest child of the female head, since (assuming no illegitimacy) the younger the child, the fewer the elapsed years since the female head's husband surely was alive. Trends along these lines are present but quite weak and irregular; they are, however, virtually identical for each of the four ethnic groups. If we have not in this fashion gained greater confidence in the literal meaning of census "widowhood," we have discovered that its meaning seems to have been similar across ethnic lines.

[21]Mortality for "colored" persons (including negligible numbers of Chinese, Japanese, and Indians) for Philadelphia in 1890 and for the six years preceding 1890 are derived from registration materials tabulated in U.S. Census Office, *Eleventh Census, 1890* (Washington, 1895), IV: *Mortality*, 662, 1046–1047. John S. Billings, who supervised the 1890 vital statistics volumes, noted that, as in the other 27 cities to which he devoted a volume, registration of deaths was "based upon certificates of deaths by physicians, [collected] under a compulsory registration law." The crude colored death rate in Philadelphia, 30.1, can be compared with the rate there for whites, 23.0, and with colored death rates of 32.9 in Baltimore, 34.0 in Washington,

34.6 in New York, and 30.9 for all 28 cities studied (U.S. Census Office, *Report on Vital and Social Statistics of the United States at the Eleventh Census: 1890, Part II—Vital Statistics. Cities of 100,000 Population and Upward* [Washington, 1892], 1–5). The age-specific figures, distributing the unknown ages, and taking the average one-year level from the figures for the six-year period, were then compared with linearly interpolated estimates for 1887 of the Philadelphia black population by age and sex, based on PSHP grid-square tallies for 1880 and U.S. Census Office, *Population, 1890*, II, 127. The age-specific mortality rates were matched with model life tables in Ansley J. Coale and Paul Demeny, *Regional Model Life Tables and Stable Populations* (Princeton, 1966), and a good match was found on ages 20–50 at South Level 3, a severe mortality regime where the high rate of infant and child mortality proved closer to the observed Philadelphia black mortality than did the West series tables, more often applied to American populations. Good matches were also found between South Level 3 and the black life tables centering on 1879 for Baltimore and Washington, cited above, note 15. South Level 3 implies an expectation of life at birth of 25 years; Level 2 implies 22.5 years.

tality alone. Table 12 shows a close fit at all ages between expected and observed widowhood, suggesting that a fraction of declared widows were not so, but rather were unmarried or deserted women hiding their actual condition from the census taker.

Variant Patterns in Family Composition

In bringing out the excess of widowed female heads among blacks, the data presented in Table 10 also reveal a persistent difference in headship by "other females," most of whom are married without spouse (Table 9). The proportion of "other female" headship for blacks is about 5 or 6 percent, unvarying with age. We have here what might be considered a variant pattern.

In our attempt to probe the source of this variant pattern, we examined marital status by age of non-widowed female heads. Divorcées at every age represent an insignificant proportion of this group. Unmarried mothers, although constituting almost a quarter of all female heads less than 30, virtually disappear at older ages. Separated women are at every age the largest proportion of non-widowed female heads, but their numbers, too, decline with age. This decline cannot be explained by mortality alone. These patterns are identical across ethnic groups.

Had there been cultural support within the black community for female-headed families (whatever the reason), we should have found a growing number of families of this type with advancing age. Instead, they decline, doing so in the face of a remarriage market that offered them extremely limited prospects. In summary, the data provide no evidence for believing that Philadelphia's blacks valued anything distinct from what poverty and death often denied them: to raise their children in stable and continuous families.

Much of the speculation about the origins of the matrilocal black family has been uninformed by systematic historical data. In recent years, historians have begun to correct this situation. It is becoming increasingly clear with each new study that misconceptions about the past have resulted in certain erroneous interpretations of the present. The PSHP data indicate that the household

Philadelphia Social History Project (PSHP)

structure in 1850, 1870, and 1880 was highly similar among each of the ethnic groups. Black families were just as likely to be organized in nuclear households, and, hence, were not more or less able to adapt to conditions created by industrialization than other ethnic groups. A somewhat higher proportion of black families were headed by a female than was true for other ethnic groups. However, we argue that a cultural explanation cannot account for this disparity.

In the first place, the great majority of black families were couple-headed. Second, ex-slaves were more likely to reside in couple-headed households. Third, when property holding among the different ethnic groupings was held constant, variations in family composition largely disappeared. Finally, we were able to show that economic status had a powerful effect on the structure of the black family because blacks suffered extremely high mortality and females with children faced difficulties in remarrying. To the extent that the female-headed family appeared during this period, it emerged, not as a legacy of slavery, but as a result of the destructive conditions of northern urban life.[22]

With a few important exceptions, students of black history have not adequately appreciated the impact of the urban experience. In part, this is because the institution of slavery has so dominated the history of Afro-Americans. Ever since the 1920s when justification for the low status of black Americans shifted from a genetic to an environmental interpretation, scholars have for the most part accepted without question the slavery hypothesis. After all, it followed logically that any institution as morally reprehensible as slavery also had to be destructive.

We do not wish to imply that the institution of slavery was *not* brutalizing and dehumanizing. Yet, one must not convert a sense of moral outrage into a monolithic interpretation of the black

[22] This interpretation finds support in the statistics offered by Gutman, "Persistent Myths," above. Of all of the urban and rural communities that he studied, those with the highest percentages of female-headed households were cities: Natchez (30%), Beaufort (30%), Richmond (27%), and Mobile (26%), although the percentages for rural areas were all below 19%. These percentages, moreover, if re-calculated after childless households are removed (see note 9 above), may increase as much as 8 percentage points. The cities varied widely in their size, type of economy, and rate of growth, to be sure; nonetheless, some differential process must have been operating to generate these statistics.

experience. Once we recognize that the matrifocal black family is a product of economic discrimination, poverty, and disease we cease to blame the distant past for problems which have their origins in more recent times. It was, and still is, much easier to lament the sins of one's forefathers than to confront the injustices of more contemporary socioeconomic systems.

Part Two
The Dyad

Premarital Dating Patterns

Each family unit begins as a dyad, usually two members of the opposite sex who occupy a range of roles based on the stage of their relationship. The first stage in the formation of a family has traditionally been that of dating and courtship. Recent changes in attitudes toward the family, however, have altered dating and courtship practices—the participants are different, the purpose is different, the form is different. For instance, dating now involves not only the very young. More and more people remain unmarried longer, and a dating partner could as easily be 38 as 18. The rising divorce rate and the low remarriage rate add further to the pool of dating partners.

Dating now often exists only for the moment, for sexual or recreational purposes and is no longer an automatic prelude to courtship or marriage. Men and women now often get together without having made prior arrangements for an evening out. Much of this description is true for the white middle class, with its new ideology about dating. When we discuss Black dating, however, lack of information limits the generalizations we can make.

Black dating practices vary by region, epoch, and social class. In the past, when Blacks formed a small, cohesive community in the rural or urban South, dating centered around the neighborhood, church, or school. It was a casual process whereby men and women met, formed emotional attachments, and later married. Most participants came from larger social units whose members or reputations were known to the community. As Blacks moved into urban areas outside of the South, the anonymity of the setting modified dating patterns. The school and the house party became centers for socializing, particularly in the lower class. In the middle class, dating took on the characteristics of the mainstream culture—movies, dances, bowling, and the like.

Among our selections on dating, the work by Staples explains some of the dynamics of what he calls *the dating game*. From his perspective, because of the differential socialization of men and women in our society, dating is often laden with conflict. Once dating ceased to be a means to marriage, it became more exploitative; men were oriented toward sexual dalliance and women sought commitment. The greater power accorded men in our society, along with the greater number of women, has created a dating game in which individuals attempt to maximize their gains while minimizing their efforts.

Dickinson's article reports the findings of one of the few empirical studies comparing Black and white dating practices. His thesis is that desegregation of public schools and other public facilities has made Black dating patterns more like those of the majority culture. His findings, based on a sample of Texas high school students, indicate that with increased income and freer access to public facilities, Black dating behavior has become more like that of whites, although the reverse is not true. His conclusion is that with increased interaction between the two racial groups, Blacks now use whites as their reference group.

In the article by Schulz we see the variety of behaviors exhibited by men who play the "boyfriend" role. This behavior ranges from attempting to exploit women for financial gain to forming liaisons with single mothers for their economic maintenance. This wide variation in the boyfriend role illustrates the problem Black men have in reconciling an exploitative ethic with the impulse to love and take care of a woman. It also demonstrates how informal arrangements take care of the problems faced by women who ostensibly raise children alone.

Sexual Behavior

Black sexuality is another neglected area in the study of Black family life. This is particularly difficult to understand in light of the cultural myth that the Black is a peculiarly desirable or different sexual object. Yet, while we have witnessed a full-blown sexual revolution, at least in the media, there is no reliable study of Black sexuality. Blacks are rarely included in the many studies on white sexual attitudes and behavior. There has been so little research on Black sexuality that it is difficult to assess what, if any, changes have occurred as a result of the widespread transformation of sexual attitudes and practices.

We do know that, in the past, Black sexuality differed from its white counterpart in a number of ways, beginning with the African versus European conception of human sexuality. While Europeans have viewed sex as inherently sinful, the African view was that sex was a natural function and should be enjoyed as such—a case of permissiveness versus puritanism. Within Africa, however, a wide range of sexual codes and practices coexisted.

Slavery exercised another influence on Afro-American sexuality. Women in bondage had no way to protect their sexual purity, a fact that led many to assume that Black women did not value their sexual integrity. This assumption ignores the existence of a moral code related to sex in the Black community, which, though different from mainstream norms, does regulate the sexual activity of both men and women.

The three articles in this section give us some insight into the nature of Black sexuality. The address by Bell gives the results of previously unreported data on Black sexual experiences collected by the Institute for Sex Research headed by the late Alfred Kinsey. Even though the information is dated (having been collected between 1942 and 1949), it provides us with knowledge unavailable anywhere else. After describing racial differences in sexuality, Bell concludes that the stereotype of Black hypersexuality is largely a myth, that the two racial groups may differ in their form of sexual expression but not in their morals or desires.

A more recent study of Black sexual patterns was conducted by Leanor B. Johnson. Comparing the premarital attitudes and behavior of Afro-Americans with those of white Americans and Scandinavians, she found that culture and gender often influenced sexual attitudes and behavior more than race. Some significant racial differences are found and explained by the peculiar function of sexual performance for Black males and the imbalanced sex ratio that is unique to the Black community.

In the final paper of this section, Staples assesses the impact of the so-called sexual revolution on Blacks. He finds Blacks under-represented and under-involved. Blacks relate to the full realm of sexual experiences, but their participation in some of the alternate sexual life styles is less frequent and of a different form from that of their white counterparts. Certain elements in Black culture responsible for the lack of participation in the sexual revolution are delineated and the variety of sexual types are described.

Male Sex Roles

In recent years, sex roles and their definition have received a lot of attention. While the discussion has centered on the issue of female subordination and male dominance and privilege, Blacks have considerably different problems of sex role identity. First, they have to overcome certain disabilities based on racial membership, not gender affiliation. However, that does not mean that sex role identities within the Black community do not carry with them advantages and disadvantages. But equality with Black males would still leave Black women in a low status. Black men, for example, must contend with the plaguing problems of an unemployment rate as high as 25 percent. Related to high unemployment are other problems: declining life expectancy of Black men, rising drug abuse, suicide, crime, and widespread educational failure. This situation does not support a movement to equalize the condition of men and women in the Black community.

Along with the economic conditions that

impinge on their role performance, Black men are saddled with a number of stereotypes that label them as irresponsible, criminalistic, hypersexual, or lacking in masculinity. Some of these stereotypes are self-fulfilling, for the dominant society is structured so as to prevent many Black men from achieving the goals of manhood. At the same time, the notion of the castrated Black male is largely a myth. Even though mainstream culture has deprived many Black men of the economic wherewithal for normal masculine functioning, most of them still gain the respect of their mates, children, and community.

The article by Staples examines some of the myths related to the alleged impotency of the Black male, beginning with slavery. Staples demonstrates that despite systematic efforts to undermine the Black male's role in the family and slave community, the male slave found ways to assert his will and gain the respect of his family. The article goes on to show that in spite of the barriers to manhood placed in his way, the Black male has not become the emasculated creature depicted in the social science literature. Stereotypes of Black males as effeminate, irresponsible, and unexposed to adequate role models are exploded, and alternative norms and role functions in the Black community are described.

The selection by Sizemore further refutes the notion of a castrated Black male. She raises the issue of Black male chauvinism and contends that male superiority is an institutional value into which Black men are socialized. While Black men are denied many of the ordinary perquisites of manhood, they are still elevated above the status of Black women on the basis of gender affiliation alone. Using the statements of certain Black male leaders, she advances the argument that Black women must not allow Black men to define the role of women as subordinate and unequal. She suggests that Black women hold their men accountable for their actions and demand parity in decision making and leadership organizations.

A major reason for whatever power Black men have is the imbalanced sex ratio, which has put Black women in the position of competing for the limited pool of Black males eligible as lovers and mates. Jacquelyne Jackson examines this shortage of Black males and its implications for the Black family, including the time span in which it has existed, the sex ratio in various age ranges,

and its variation by geographical location. She suggests that Black women consider moving to areas where the men are, or developing alternative familial forms.

Female Sex Roles

Along with all the changes in American society, there are slow but perceptible alterations in the role of the Black woman. The implications of these changes are profound, especially when we consider how central the woman is in the family life of Black people. Traditionally, the Black woman has been a source of strength for the Black community. From the time of slavery onward, she has resisted the destructive forces of American society. During the period of slavery she fought and survived the attacks on her dignity, and she relinquished the passive role ascribed to her gender so as to ensure the survival of her people. Also, she tolerated the culturally induced irresponsibility of her man in recognition of this country's relentless attempts to castrate him.

Too often the only result of her sacrifices and suffering has been an invidious and inaccurate labeling of her as a matriarch, a figure deserving of respect but not love. In reality, the Black woman in America occupies the lowest rung of the socioeconomic ladder and has the least prestige. The double burden of gender and race has put her in the category of super-oppressed. Considering the disrespect to which she is subjected, one would expect her to be well represented in the women's liberation movement. Yet, that movement remains primarily white and middle class. This is due in part to a difference of objective—white feminists relate to psychological and cultural factors such as language and sexist behavior and Black women are concerned with economics.

There is common ground on issues like equal pay for equal work, child care facilities, and female parity in the work force. Instead of joining the predominantly white, middle-class women's movement, many Black women have formed their own organizations, such as the Welfare Rights Organization, Black Women Organized for Action, and the Black Feminist Alliance. There is little question that there is a heightened awareness among Black women of the problems they face based on sex role alone. Whether the struggle of

Black women for equal rights will come into conflict with the movement for Black liberation remains to be seen. It is fairly clear that Black women have to be freed from the disabilities of both race and sex.

The articles in this section deal with several aspects of the Black female experience: In the first selection, Frances Beale discusses how Black women suffer double victimization by virtue of being both Black and female. In addition to economic exploitation, they are subjected to psychological manipulation and the abuse of their bodies through unnecessary sterilization. The paper by Carol Stack shows how Black women form an extensive network of friends and kinfolk to overcome some of the problems of poverty and of rearing children alone. Through this network, poor women are able to draw on a number of economic and psychological resources and collectively adapt to their situation. The study by Slaby and Sealy indicates that Black female college students used to be generally more concerned with Blackness than with women's liberation. The trend now is toward increasing Black female involvement in women's issues.

Husbands and Wives

We are all aware that marriages are fragile these days. Fewer people are marrying and divorce is at an all-time high. It is estimated that the majority of marriages will not last a lifetime. There are many forces responsible for this changing pattern, including changing attitudes and new laws on divorce, changing and conflicting definitions of sex roles and their functions in the family, economic problems, and personality conflicts. Although divorce and its increase cut across race and class lines, it is still more prevalent among Blacks. Only one of every three Black couples will remain married longer than ten years.

It is not easy to pinpoint causes of marital dissolution unique to Blacks. In some cases it is the severity of the problems they face. Financial problems are a major factor in marital conflict and there are three times as many Blacks as whites with incomes below the poverty level. The tensions of coping with pervasive racism often have ramifications in the marital arena. A special problem Blacks face is the imbalanced sex ratio, which

places many women in competition for the available males. Too often the males they compete for are already married, and this places serious pressure on those marriages.

Still, most adult Blacks are married and have positive and loving relationships with their spouses. There is practically no research on marital adjustment and satisfaction among Blacks, but what there is indicates that Black wives are generally less satisfied than white wives with marriage. Their dissatisfaction often stems from poverty and racism.

The articles included in this section present the normative aspects of Black marriages. In an article entitled, appropriately, "Ordinary Black Husbands: The Truly Hidden Men," Jacquelyne Jackson attempts to correct the imbalance of research on Black families. Through her study of 170 married Black males, she gives us a good picture of how Black husbands function in the family. Their activities range from shopping for groceries to making joint decisions with their wives on important matters. The study by Delores Mack on the power relationship in Black and white families found that working-class husbands are significantly more powerful than middle-class husbands and that class differences far outweigh racial differences.

Black and White: Sex and Marriage

The last decade has witnessed a significant increase in interracial dating and marriage, no doubt an effect of the desegregation of the public school system, the work force, and other social settings. In these integrated settings Blacks and whites have met as equals, thus facilitating homogeneous matings. The liberation of many white youths from parental control and racist values has also affected Black/white dating patterns.

Not only has the incidence of interracial relations increased, but their character has changed as well. Ten years ago the typical interracial pair was a Black male and a white female, with the male partner generally of higher status. This pattern was so common that social theorists even developed a theory of racial hypergamy. In essence, they assumed that the high-status Black male was exchanging this status for the privilege of marrying a woman of a superior racial group.

Contemporary interrace relations are much more likely to involve people of similar educational background and occupational status.

Although no research has yielded any data on the subject, there appears to be a decline in Black male/white female couples and an increase in Black female/white male pairings since 1970. Several factors account for this modification of the typical pattern. Many Black women are gravitating toward white men because Black males are in short supply or because they are disenchanted with those they have access to. In a similar vein some white men are dissatisfied with white females and their increasing and vociferous demands for sex role parity. At the same time there is a slight but noticeable decrease in Black male/white female unions. Possibly it is no longer so fashionable. Also, much of the mutual attraction of the partners was based on customary inaccessibility plus the stereotype of Black men as superstuds and white women as forbidden fruit. With more extensive interaction the myths were exploded and the attraction consequently diminished.

Although there may be relatively normal reasons for interracial attractions and matings, it would be naive not to assume that special factors are involved in our racially stratified society. Given the persistence of racism, many interracial marriages still face difficulties. In addition to the normal problems of a marital relationship, interracial couples still have to cope with ostracism and isolation. Recently there has been an increase in hostility toward such unions by the Black community, forcing some interracial couples into a marginal existence. It is such pressures that cause the interracial marriage rate to remain low. Less than five percent of marriages involving a Black person are interracial.

The article by Staples summarizes many of the factors and problems associated with interracial dating. Because of the unique and historical relationship between the races, interracial dating practices often differ in motivation and character from those involving members of the same race. Heer's article analyzes census data to interpret the changes in interracial marriages in the period from 1960 to 1970. He finds a shift of such marriages from the South to the North, an increase in Black male/white female unions, and a fairly high rate of dissolution of such marriages.

3
Premarital Dating Patterns

The Black Dating Game
Robert Staples

The author stresses the importance of "the game" for many Blacks engaged in dating. This is a problem for society as a whole, but an even greater problem for many Blacks. The article focuses on the negative effects of gaming, and the author is pessimistic about the future.

Even the most casual observer has probably noted the growing polarization of Black men and women. There are a broad set of forces responsible for this schism between the sexes, forces which are not unique to Black people. In fact, the Black man–woman conflict is not as severe as in the white community. Compared to whites, Black men and women are moving closer together, not further apart. But the sad truth is that they are not as close as they were in the past—and sexual conflict plays an important part in the separation process.

American society creates the basis of this hostility between the sexes by the different values it places on sex for men and women. Even in our era of sexual liberation, young Black girls are socialized to believe that sexual activity is related to love or marriage. The realities of the dating game force them to accept sex either as a value in itself or for other things—companionship, affection, money, or just a "good time." The contradiction between what they have been reared to believe and what they are ultimately forced to accept places many Black women in the painful dilemma of having sex without emotional fulfillment, physical pleasure, or marriage.

Meanwhile, Black boys learn early that sex contains a great deal of private pleasure for them.

They also learn that sex is a way to win a reputation with fellow males. In "bullshit" sessions, reputations are won or lost on the number of girls allegedly "ripped off." Much of this sexual activity is mythical, leading to the oft-repeated charge of "lying on the dick." Still, "ripping off" women becomes a central concern of the Black male as his self-image and group-image come to depend on the number of his sexual conquests. He also comes to learn that his sexual prowess can be translated into psychological control over a woman.

Hence, Blacks enter the dating game with these presocialized values and attitudes. Many Black females lose their virginity not as a result of falling in love or getting married, but as a consequence of male pressure to "give it up." This initial loss of virtue can be time consuming and can involve a lot of negotiation. After the first initiation comes the game playing. She becomes more sophisticated in what sex is all about and he starts to develop his skills in order to successfully "rip off" as many women as physically possible.

Making a date and going out on one can be fright inducing for both men and women. In a large city, people often find it difficult to meet members of the opposite sex. It is somewhat easier for Black people, since they do not view each other as complete strangers because of the commonality of their blackness. Yet, securing that first date can be an ordeal—especially for the Black male. While many Black men have a bravado that makes approaching a woman for a date easy, shy Black males find the process painful.

Society decrees that the male must be the aggressor and pursue the woman, while she must

Adapted from *Essence* (October 1973): 92–96. © 1973 by Robert Staples.

remain a passive object, accepting or rejecting his invitation. There are many men who do not know how or when to request a date. Moreover, those who do know find it a problem because of the rules of the dating game. For example, out of the total number of women a man meets daily, which one will be willing to go out with him? Usually she gives cues about her readiness, commonly friendliness. Most males take a woman's willingness to engage in a lengthy conversation as a sign of her receptivity for further social interaction. Since not all such friendly females are available for his company, he runs the risk of having his invitation rejected.

While being turned down for a date need not signify a rejection of him personally, many men take it that way. It is an ego-deflating process which affects different men to varying degrees. Some retreat into a shell and wait for women who make unmistakable cues of their availability for a date. Some drop out of the heterosexual dating game because they find it too oppressive. Some find other mechanisms to shield the hurt. Getting sympathy from other men is one way; adopting a cynical and exploitative attitude toward all women is another.

The manner in which some Black women reject requests for dates tends to arouse male hostility. Many women are not content to simply refuse an invitation but feel compelled to humiliate the man in the process. Some even give false cues of friendliness to lure males into their waiting trap. Women are often known to brag about the number of men who have tried to date them. One male reaction is to proposition women indiscriminately, to give the impression that they don't care whether an individual woman accepts or not.

Although their passive role in the dating game protects women, it also restricts their freedom of choice. In theory they must wait to be asked by a man whom they find desirable. Sometimes the invitation never comes. Most women manage to get around the restrictions placed on them. Older Black women are likely to make the first move. Their role as receptor, however, places many in the position of having to deal with undesirable types who may proposition them in a most offensive manner. It also leaves many a woman at home alone or tolerating a man she would never have selected if given a free choice.

A common complaint of Black dating partners is that dates fail to appear. This practice is epidemic on the college campus and tends to increase when people make multiple dates for the same evening to ensure their entertainment for the night. The reason for not keeping a date may be legitimate but in most cases it is simply irresponsible behavior. A woman who has accepted a date because she could not refuse may use her absence to signal her real feelings. A man may not show because he has gotten involved with another woman, who is "better" than his date. Sometimes a man is having too much fun with the brothers, drinking or playing cards, to put in an appearance.

Once individuals do get into a steady dating relationship, they start to bargain for their individual needs and goals. Under normal circumstances, with the right man, her long-term goal is marriage. His short-term purpose is to "get over," that is, have sex. These different goals may be compatible, but rarely are in the beginning of the dating game. Regardless of her feelings or desires about sex, she knows that men rarely consider marrying a woman who is an easy conquest— despite their persistent demands for immediate sexual gratification. At the same time, she cannot absolutely rule out sex before marriage if she wants to maintain his interest. Assuming they have some interest in each other, she tries to extract some kind of commitment from him while he attempts to whittle away her resistance to sexual relations.

In this bargaining process one person usually has the balance of power. The contemporary Black dating game gives most of this power to the Black male. A central reality of most Black women in the dating game is a serious shortage of eligible Black men. In some areas—and for certain age groups—one finds a ratio as low as five Black women to every Black male. Unfortunately, the ratio of Black men to Black women will be even more imbalanced in the future. For unknown reasons, the majority of Black births are female. Added to this are the high death rate of young Black males, the number of men in prison and the military, increasing Black male homosexuality, decreasing life expectancy of Black males, and a rising number of interracial marriages.

To bargain effectively the Black woman must use the enticement of sex—if the man waits long enough. Given the abundance of women around, he does not have to wait too long, and her alternatives are limited because of the shortage of men.

After losing a couple of men who could not wait, many Black women cut short the waiting time. Also, Black women often want the security of a steady dating partner, because playing the field can be a terrifying ordeal—never knowing what kind of man they will wind up with next. Hence, it is wiser at times to deal with a known though undesirable male than to chance an unknown.

There are two major complaints Black men and women have about one another. Her primary grievance is about his desire to practice polygamy while restricting her to monogamy. Male infidelity often means boredom with the same sexual partner. The Black male is surrounded by alluring women who seem more attractive—or different—than his own. And the shortage of men has made Black women very competitive for the available men.

Attempting to restrict his main woman to himself alone is hardly defensible. In most cases it is a power play. If the woman wants to keep his affection, he expects her to be faithful to him—or at least discreet. Sometimes the penalty for female "tipping-out" is violent retaliation, the fear of which keeps some women in line. The Black male's justification for his behavior is that he will lose face if his main woman is known to be dating other men. Yet, some Black men are known to be possessive of a woman they just met, or a woman who is number fifty on their list of "squeezes." This attitude of "woman as property" represents male chauvinism at its worst.

Probably the most common complaint of Black men about Black women is the "gold digger" tendency. Black women are charged with looking for men with money and then helping them spend all of it as soon as possible. Certain cities, such as New York and Chicago, are rumored to have large numbers of such Black women. The "gold digger" demands money or material goods after she has given her body. Such practices, it should be noted, are most prevalent among the Black bourgeoisie.

It is clear that some Black women use sex for economic gain. Most of them find very early that it is a commodity for which men will pay. Some use it because it is their only weapon over men. Others, because they find the sexual relationship unfulfilling and think they ought to get *something* out of it since love, fidelity, or marriage cannot be expected. Sex for such purposes, however, leads Black men to view women as enemies and allows them to justify their own exploitative behavior.

A recent phenomenon is the growth of the pimp among Black men—using Black women for material gain. This pimp complex has become so popular that even Black professional men who do not need the money have become fascinated with its results. The shortage of Black males has given them this opportunity to use Black women. Even on some college campuses Black women hustle for a Black man to buy his dope or fine clothes.

There are other sources of Black male-female discontent. For example, instead of withholding sex from the male, many Black women enjoy it and are quite willing to indulge. Some are often left sexually frustrated because drugs have depressed the sexual desire of many Black men. Even the marijuana smoker is occasionally more preoccupied with his "high" than with sex. A recent complaint of Black women is the increasing number of sexually impotent Black men. Moreover, when found in this embarrassing situation the man blames the woman for "turning him off." Some even physically attack their partner. Even without the drug problem, many Black women report that their sexual relations are unsatisfying. Premature ejaculation is frequently mentioned; so is inconsiderate behavior. The men complain that if Black women were more supportive of them, they might be more considerate.

Another problem stemming from these sexual demands by Black women is the increasing number of Black male homosexuals. (There is no corresponding increase in the number of Black lesbians.) Many Black male homosexuals are involved with white partners. Among Black homosexuals there is a fairly high suicide rate: Herbert Hendin found about half the Black male suicides in New York were homosexuals.

A pervasive complaint of Black women is that Black men have deserted them en masse for white women, a topic that deserves more attention than I can give it here. Its importance is illustrated by the reports—still unconfirmed—that some Black women have spent their entire undergraduate college careers without one date with a Black male. The latest United States census reported that the number of interracial marriages of Black men doubled in the past decade, while those of Black women declined. Moreover, the majority of these Black men were in high educational and income brackets.

That all is not well with Black men and women is not a figment of my imagination. Statistics show the following:

1. The highest increase in the suicide rate in the last decade occurred among Black women.

2. At least two out of three Black women under thirty who marry will divorce.

3. Less than 75 percent of Black college-educated women will marry by the age of thirty.

4. Of all sex-race groups, Black males are most likely to reach the age of thirty without marrying.

5. There has been a serious increase of Black women suffering from depression and other nervous disorders.

6. The interracial marriage rate of Black men has doubled in the last decade.

These statistics translate into large numbers of lonely Black women who cannot find eligible men and into an increase in Black male homosexuality. Another statistic which tragically reflects the Black male–female tension is that homicide is the second leading cause of death among Black males age 15 to 30, and the majority of these homicides involve Black women as the defendant.

Black people cannot afford such internal tensions. We have to accept responsibility for eliminating the sources of these male–female conflicts, and, the best place to begin is at home.

Dating Behavior of Black and White Adolescents Before and After Desegregation

George E. Dickinson

Black and white adolescent dating behavior before and after desegregation in a Northeast Texas community is analyzed in this selection. Evidence was found to support the hypothesis that Blacks' dating behavior has changed in the direction of whites, while whites' has changed only slightly over time. It is suggested that reference group theory helps to explain this change.

Adolescence in American society has always been a time of breaking away from or joining with established modes of living. . . .

The winds of change are blowing particularly hard in the South, shaking the roots of old mores and laws almost out of their soil, leaving them exposed and tender. Southern adolescents . . . are perhaps the most vulnerable to these changes. (Powell, 1973: 46–47)

Some evidence in the literature suggests a change in behavior of blacks in the direction of the numerically dominant group. For example, Frumkin (1954) found that a change in black family organization is taking place in the direction of "white norms and ideals." Frumkin's conclusion is substantiated in a more recent study by King, Abernathy, and Chapman (1974). The importance of both the family and peer group in the development of values of the adolescent has been pointed out, but most investigations have concentrated upon the influence of the family (Wilson, 1959). However, a growing body of research points to the conclusion that peers in some areas are at least as effective if not more potent than parents in their capacity to influence the behavior of the child (Bronfenbrenner, 1970:232).

"Now there is evidence that modern youth have organized themselves into an adolescent society, which has its own status rewards, its own power structure, and its own norms" (Ramsey,

Condensed from *The Journal of Marriage and the Family* 37 (August 1975): 602–608. Copyright © 1975 by National Council on Family Relations. Reprinted by Permission. Tables have been deleted and some footnotes renumbered.

1969:28). The present study seeks to determine if this "adolescent society" exists between racial groups soon after desegregation by ascertaining if the peer influences regarding dating behavior are interracial. The 1964 study by the author revealed significant differences in black and white dating behavior in a racially segregated community.[1]

With black and white adolescents being placed in the same social milieu of the desegregated school and thus being in situations like sitting in the same classroom, having lockers next to each other, eating in the same cafeteria, playing on the same athletic teams, participating in the same musical groups, and being members of the same voluntary organizations, it is assumed that interaction between racial groups will have increased over previous levels when the schools were segregated. With increased social intercourse the two racial groups will have the opportunity to observe the behavior of each other. Through such observations over time, the norms of one group could be internalized by the other.

Despite the continuance of interracial dating after desegregation, it is hypothesized that since the white group is dominant, dating behavior of blacks will have changed more over time than whites and the direction of change will be toward whites' behavior.[2]

The dependent variables are age at first date, frequency of dating, activity on dates, parking on dates, requirement to be home at a certain time, specific time required to return home, and going steady; independent variables are race (white and black) and time (1964 and 1974).

Methodology

.   .   .   .

Source of Data

The population from which data were obtained for this investigation was composed of the sophomore, junior, and senior classes of the two high schools in 1964 and the desegregated high

school in 1974 in a northeast Texas community (population in 1970 was 5007). The school system was desegregated in 1970. The number of respondents in 1964 was 367 (260 whites and 107 blacks) with a total of 432 adolescents (289 whites and 143 blacks) responding in 1974. The respondents both in 1964 and 1974 constituted 87 per cent of the student enrollment. Less than one per cent of the students present on the days the questionnaires were administered refused to complete the questionnaires. The other students were absent on the days of administration. No attempt was made to follow up the absentees.

Research Instrument

The research instrument was a questionnaire administered during the school day by the author in all English classes of the tenth, eleventh, and twelfth grades in both the 1964 and 1974 studies. The 18 multiple-choice questions in the 1974 survey were taken from the 1964 questionnaire which contained a total of 56 questions.

Findings

Age at First Date

. . . The mean age of first date for blacks changed from 14.91 years in 1964 to 13.93 in 1974. This difference was significantly different. . . . While age for first date lowered for blacks over the decade, whites changed less with the age actually increasing slightly—from 13.59 in 1964 to 13.88 in 1974. This difference was not statistically different. A statistical difference between whites and blacks was found for 1964, . . . while no statistical difference was found for 1974 suggesting that the gap between the races for the age at first date has narrowed considerably over time. While blacks are beginning to date a year earlier than in 1964, whites are actually dating slightly later than in 1964. These data give support to the hypothesis that black dating behavior has changed more over time than for whites with the direction of change being toward white behavior.

Frequency of Dating

. . . [T]he difference in frequency of dating for blacks and whites over time is slight and does

---

[1]See Dickinson (1971) for details of these differences.

[2]Two-thirds of the high school population is white. It should also be noted that the school system is dominated by whites with an all-white school board, a white superintendent, and a white high school principal. Thus, with decision-makers of the school system being white, political dominance by whites is suggested.

not show an interaction of time and race. . . . Thus, these data do not support the hypothesis that black dating behavior has changed more over time than white behavior.

Activity on Dates

Most frequent type of activity on dates for blacks and for whites revealed a statistically significant change in distribution over time. . . . Whites changed slightly from 13 per cent attending parties and dances in 1964 to 17 per cent in 1974 while the most frequent activity of blacks changed from 75 per cent going to parties and dances in 1964 to only 38 per cent in 1974. Blacks in 1974 tend to participate more in activities which require money like movies and driving around. These data suggest that dating activities of blacks and whites are becoming more similar with blacks changing more than whites with the direction of change being toward white behavior. Thus, support is found for the stated hypothesis.

Each respondent was asked if he/she "parked" on dates. Since the two-way analysis of variance of parking on dates revealed a significant interaction . . . between race and time, . . . the simple effects were analyzed by means of one-way analyses of variance. A statistical difference . . . for blacks over time was found while no statistical difference for whites over time was shown.

. . . [We find] further evidence of these differences with the response of white adolescents remaining basically unchanged over the decade (81 per cent "parked" in 1964 and 78 per cent in 1974) while blacks went from only 44 per cent "parking" in 1964 to the majority (76 per cent) "parking" in 1974. In looking at racial differences within specific years a statistical difference . . . was noted for 1964 but not for 1974, again suggesting that the gap between the two racial groups is narrowing. Thus, "parking" in both racial groups is found to be to nearly the same degree today. This supports the hypothesis that black dating behavior is changing more than whites and the direction of change is in the direction of white behavior.

Required to be Home at Certain Time from a Date

The majority of whites responded in the affirmative regarding the requirement to be home at a certain time from a date both in 1964 (72 per cent) and in 1974 (70 per cent) as did the blacks in 1964 (89 per cent) and in 1974 (53 per cent). . . . The . . . analysis of blacks' requirement to be home at a certain time showed a significant difference over time, . . . while no statistical difference was found for whites over time. A statistical difference . . . was found between blacks and whites for the year 1964, but no statistical difference was found between blacks and whites for the year 1974. Thus, analysis of the data pertaining to the requirement to be home from a date at a certain time supports the hypothesis that blacks' dating behavior is changing more than whites' and in the direction of whites.

When asked about a specific time to return home from a date, . . . whites in both surveys had fewer than eight per cent who were required to be in prior to ten o'clock. For blacks in the 1964 survey 40 per cent had to be in prior to ten o'clock, but in 1974 only seven per cent had to be in prior to ten o'clock. . . . A significant difference was found for blacks over time . . . regarding specific time to be in from a date and for whites . . . over time. Thus, both blacks and whites reveal significant differences over time regarding specific time to be in from a date. . . . [O]ver time both blacks and whites changed regarding specific time to be home from a date, but the difference between the races is less today than in 1964. This lends further support to the stated hypothesis. . . . Blacks actually show more independence than whites in 1974 regarding the requirement to be home at a certain time from a date and the specific time.

Going Steady

Both whites and blacks are "going steady" more today than they were a decade ago. The percentage of white students going steady has increased from 61 to 80 and for black students from 54 to 68 over the decade. . . . [An] analysis . . . did not indicate an interaction between race and time; however, a significant main effect was revealed for both variables, . . . suggesting that both groups are changing over time but in the same direction. Support for the hypothesis that black dating behavior is changing more than whites' with the direction being toward whites' is not supported by "going steady" behavior.

Conclusions

Some of the dating behavior variables cited in the present study give support for the hypothesis that dating behavior of blacks today is more like that of whites prior to desegregation while white behavior regarding dating patterns has changed less in a decade. Variables supporting the hypothesis are age at first date, parking on dates, requirement to return home from a date at a certain time, and specific time required to return home from a date (using analyses of variance). Activity on dates showed a statistically significant difference . . . for both blacks and whites over time indicating change for both races over time. The frequency of dates showed no statistically significant difference over time for whites or blacks while the going steady behavior data revealed changes for blacks and whites in the same direction. These changes in blacks could lead one to believe that the behavior is due in part to desegregation. Since dating in this school is intraracial, this suggests that blacks *may* be using the dominant group as their reference group.[3]

In suggesting that black dating behavior in this desegregated school system may be a function of dominant group norms, Merton and Rossi (1966) lend some support when they state that an individual may adopt the values of a group to which he aspires but does not belong. Further, Shibutani (1955) suggests that in some transactions one may assume the perspective attributed to a social category such as a social class or ethnic group rather than his membership group. All forms of social mobility may be regarded essentially as displacements of reference groups since they involve a loss of responsiveness to the demands of one social world and the adoption of the perspective of another. Through social participation the perspectives shared in a group are internalized.

More recently Levin and Leong (1973:294) gave support to Shibutani's assertion when they found in a study of minority members (Chinese-American high school and college students) that reference group behavior tended to increase as minority group members became assimilated into American society. Further, their study showed that

minority group members were more likely to select the dominant group for comparison purposes as comparison processes became heightened by means of assimilating either in terms of the internalization of dominant values or, more so, the establishment of interaction patterns with members of the dominant group. The findings of the current study suggest that through interaction with members of the dominant group in the sociocultural milieu of the school, the perspectives of whites *may* be internalized by the blacks and that blacks are "selecting" the dominant group for comparison purposes regarding dating behavior.

In further trying to explain the changes—in some cases extreme—of black dating behavior over time, the changing economic situation gives support to the preceding argument. Blacks are making more money now with the median gross family income going from less than $2000 to over $5000 in a decade while white median gross family income went from over $4000 to nearly $7000 according to the 1960 and 1970 census for the county in which this high school is located. According to Floyd and South (1972:628–629):

If it is true that children from all social class levels are taught to "need" the same things from the system, and if some classes are better equipped to actually provide these needs than are others then the better providers should be more highly esteemed and thus the greater source of orientation.

Thus, blacks *may* be orienting their dating behavior toward that of the "better equipped" whites. The increase in income for blacks gives some explanation for a shift in more expensive dating activities for blacks and for a much higher number of blacks "parking" on dates since an automobile is required for this behavior.

The independence extended to black adolescents in 1974 that was not present in 1964 is revealed in the questions regarding whether or not one has a time to be in from a date, the specific time required to be in from a date, and the much earlier dating patterns of blacks today. This independence might be partially explained by a more just treatment extended to blacks in the country in general, thus perhaps giving them a greater sense of security than was found in the early 1960's.

---

[3]Shibutani (1962:132) defines a reference group as "any audience consisting of real or imaginary personification, to whom certain values are imputed. It is an audience before whom a person tries to maintain or enhance his standings."

In summary, changes for blacks in dating behavior over time are evident with some support being found for the hypothesis that the direction of change is toward whites' behavior. These data indicate changes in black dating behavior in a decade—changes which reveal more homogeneous patterns for blacks and whites. The data suggest a need for further study in this area to determine if, in fact, reference group theory explains as much of this change as is suggested here. Powell's assertion is warranted, at least in this study: the winds of change in the South *are* blowing particularly hard—especially for the black adolescent.

References

Bronfenbrenner, Urie
1970   "The psychological costs of quality and equality in education." In N. S. Smelser and W. T. Smelser (eds.), *Personality and Social Structures.* New York: Wiley, pp. 223–235.

Dickinson, George E.
1971   "Dating patterns of black and white adolescents in a southern community." *Adolescence 6* (Fall): 285–298.

Dunlap, William P.
1974   "*F* and *Chi*-square as approximate tests with binomial data." Paper delivered at the Annual Meeting of the Eastern Psychological Association. Philadelphia, Pennsylvania.

Floyd, H. Hugh, and Donald R. South
1972   "Dilemma of youth: the choice of parents or peers as a frame of reference for behavior." *Journal of Marriage and the Family* 34 (November): 627–634.

Frumkin, Robert M.
1954   "Attitudes of Negro college students toward intrafamily leadership and control." *Journal of Marriage and the Family* 16 (August): 252–253.

Hsu, Tse-Chi, and Leonard S. Feldt
1969   "The effects of limitations on the number of criterion score values on the significance level of the *F*-test." *American Educational Research Journal 6* (November): 515–527.

King, Karl, Tom Abernathy, and Ann Chapman
1974   "Adolescent perception of power structure in the black family: a replication 1963 and 1973." Paper delivered at the Annual Meeting of the Midwestern Sociological Society, April 3–6. Omaha, Nebraska.

Levin, Jack, and William J. Leong
1973   "Comparative reference group behavior and assimilation." *Phylon* 34 (September): 289–294.

Merton, Robert K., and Alice R. Rossi
1966   "Reference group theory and social mobility." Pp. 510–515 in Reinhard Bendix and Seymour Lipset (eds.), *Class, Status and Power.* 2nd Ed. New York: The Free Press.

Powell, Gloria J.
1973   *Black Monday's Children.* New York: Appleton-Century-Crofts.

Ramsey, Charles
1969   *Problems of Youth.* Belmont, Calif.: Dickenson.

Shibutani, Tamotsu
1955   "Reference groups as perspectives." *American Journal of Sociology* 60 (May): 562–569.

1962   "Reference groups and social control." Pp. 128–147 in Arnold Rose (ed.), *Human Behavior and Social Processes.* Boston: Houghton Mifflin.

Wilson, Alan B.
1959   "Residential segregation of social classes and aspirations of high school boys." *American Sociological Review* 24 (December): 836–845.

The Role of the Boyfriend in
Lower-Class Negro Life

David A. Schulz

The author develops a typology of boyfriends based on the longevity of their liaisons and the extent of their economic support of the female partner. He shows that in these relationships the male is either contributing to the economic maintenance of the female partner, or he is attempting to exploit her for economic gain.

The importance of the boyfriend's role becomes apparent when one realizes that four of the five women in this group who are now heading households receive support from boyfriends. The amount of support and the type of relationship that exists vary considerably and suggest a typology consisting of four different roles which a boyfriend may play and for which there is some support from segments of this population. These types are: the quasi-father, the supportive biological father, the supportive companion, and the pimp. The image of the pimp has dominated the literature thus far. In this relationship the male is largely exploitive.

However, there is also in the literature some evidence that these nonmarital liaisons between men and women of the Negro lower class are more stable than is commonly acknowledged. In *Blackways of Kent,* Lewis mentions in passing that "gifts and some degree of support from the male are taken for granted and freely discussed. There is some informal ranking of men on a basis of the regularity and amount of gifts or support."[1] In this section fuller documentation of this support in nonmarital liaisons will be presented. In so doing,

we hope to make it apparent that the lower-class Negro man contributes to the welfare of his woman more than is commonly acknowledged, and plays an important role of surrogate father to her children.

The Quasi-Father

The distinguishing marks of the quasi-father are that (1) he supports the family regularly over long periods of time (eleven years is the longest known, though this was interrupted by a short marriage; five years is the longest consecutive time known at present). Often he will go with his woman to the store and buy her week's food. (2) His concern extends directly to her children as well. He will give them allowances or spending money, attempt more or less successfully to discipline them, and will take them out to the park, to the movies, or to other places for entertainment. (3) He frequently visits the family during the week, and may or may not reside with them in the project--usually not. The relationship is not ordinarily conducted clandestinely, but in full knowledge of kin on both sides—particularly the parents, if they reside in the same city with the couple. In return for this he receives (1) his meals (some or all if residing with the family); (2) washing and ironing; (3) sexual satisfaction; and (4) *familial companionship.* In short, he seems to be bargaining for more than just a woman in seeking intimacy in the context of a family. To illustrate let us take the example of Jay and Ethyl.

Ethyl Perry (thirty-three) went with Jay (twenty-four) for over five years. During that time he took her out, bought her the majority of her furniture, and supplied her with fifteen to twenty dollars per week, usually by means of buying her week's food. In addition his family contributed several pieces of furniture and invited Ethyl over

---

[1]Hylan Lewis, *Blackways of Kent* (Chapel Hill: University of North Carolina Press, 1961), p. 84. See also E. Franklin Frazier, *The Negro Family in the United States* (Chicago, University of Chicago Press, 1939), and St. Clair Drake and Horace Cayton, *Black Metropolis* (New York: Harcourt, Brace and Company, 1945).

From David A. Schulz, *Coming Up Black: Patterns of Ghetto Socialization,* pp. 136–144. © 1969. Reprinted by permission of   Prentice-Hall, Inc., Englewood Cliffs, New Jersey.

for meals on occasion. None of her six children is his. Ethyl describes Jay as a "nice person . . . kind-hearted" and by this she means that ". . . he believes in survival for me and my family, me and my kids. He don't mind sharing with my youngsters. If I ask him for a helping hand, he don't seem to mind that. The only part of it is that I dislike his drinking." It's not the drinking as such that Ethyl dislikes, but the man Jay becomes when he drinks. He becomes angry and quick tempered, but has yet to beat Ethyl when in such a state.

Jay's concern for Ethyl's children is expressed in various ways. As Dovie, Ethyl's fifteen-year-old daughter, sees Jay, he tends to be bossy. "He be all right sometimes but he drinks and that's the reason I don't like him. . . . He tries to boss people. Like if my boyfriends come over here he be saying I can't have no company." But Mary, her eighteen-year-old daughter, revealed that Jay gave her a small washing machine for her baby's diapers. She said, "My mother's *boyfriend* bought it. . . . It was about three days after my baby was born."

Jay's concern is expressed in other ways as well. He took the children to the movies, to the park, gave them a small allowance as spending money each week when he bought the groceries, and once, when Ethyl was sick, he took care of the youngest two for nearly a month while she was in the hospital. During the years that they were going together Jay visited the family several times a week, most frequently spending the weekend with them. He continually asked Ethyl to marry him, though Ethyl felt he was only half serious. Jay was asked why he bothered to take care of Ethyl and he replied, "That's a personal question. . . . Well, first of all I help her because I love her and we're going to get married sometime, but not just now because we can't afford it."

A second example is that of Tilly (thirty-three) and Sam (thirty-four—looks twenty-five). Tilly has been going with Sam for over eleven years—even while married to her second husband, whom she finally left for Sam. He helps the budget regularly out of his pay as a dock worker in a river barge yard. Tilly says, "Sam gives me thirty dollars a week." He has also bought several small pieces of furniture and takes her out almost every weekend. He lives just around the corner with his cousin, visits the family almost every night, and sometimes spends the night, though he usually sleeps with his cousin.

Tilly feels that Sam "treats her kids better than their daddy do. He buys them certain things [such as] clothes. He spanks them. . . . He takes them different places." She further feels that it is very important that a man treat her kids right. "If they don't care for the kids or anything then that's a bad man. . . . First he's got to love your kids before he loves you."

Her sons Richard (ten) and William (seventeen) confirm the fact that Sam is concerned about the children. Richard says, "He takes up for us when we get a whipping. . . . He tells her not to whip us this time." When asked, "Does he have pretty good control over the kids?" William replied, "They do what he say most of the time. Irvin [eighteen] don't, but the rest of them will."

They are still going together and Sam proposes marriage with some regularity, but Tilly shies away. "I think I'm better off just not having a husband. . . . I wouldn't definitely say I would get a good one. I might get a bad one. I don't want to take a chance." Even though she has known Sam since childhood, she is not certain about him. He drinks a lot but is not to her knowledge the violent type—at least he is not as a single man. Her fear is that when he "has papers on her" he might change. Her experience with her second husband taught her how quickly a man could change on her.

And so Ethyl broke up with Jay, never having seriously considered marriage while going with him, and Tilly says that *maybe* in three or four years she will be ready for marriage to Sam. Marriage has not yet resulted because in both instances the family is doing better under the combined resources of welfare and the boyfriend's assistance than they could do under his wages alone, and in both instances the woman is afraid of the man's drinking behavior. In both instances the boyfriends are well known by the women's families and visit frequently with them.

Since breaking with Jay, Ethyl has been living with a new boyfriend, Raymond (twenty-nine), and says that she is seriously considering marriage to him—at least to the extent that she has decided to get a divorce. Thus, marriage may or may not be a result of a quasi-father relationship, but it does provide the context in which a woman with children is likely to make up her mind one way or another about a man. It is interesting to remember here that three of the five women [in the study] still living with their husbands began their relationship "common law." Only one of the quasi-fathers at present lives with his woman.

The Supportive Biological Father

A second type of boyfriend is the supportive biological father. Here the concern of the man— and largely that of the woman also—is to support the children that they have brought into the world without seriously considering marriage to one another. In some instances the man or woman may well be married to someone else. The man's support may be voluntary, as in the case of Edward Patterson, or it may be as the result of a voluntarily signed acknowledgment that the children are his.

In the case of Leona Wards (fifty) and Larry (forty-nine), Leona was married once and had four children by her first husband. His "cutting out" and drinking led to a separation and Leona took up with Larry, who gave her three children, in ages now from eighteen to thirteen, before he married another woman a couple of years ago. He played the role of supportive biological father before he married. They had been going together for nearly *sixteen* years, though only Leona was true to the relationship. She has never remarried and claims that even now she has no boyfriend because they are too much trouble at her age, although she admits that she would enjoy a companion in her declining years.

Larry has taken the children on long trips, such as the one to Arizona in 1963, he has bought them clothes, especially at Christmas time, and has paid regularly the amount of fifteen to twenty dollars a week for their support since 1954. At that time he acknowledged that the children are his and the court fixed the amount for their support.

Leona's being true to Larry is a part of her rearing as she sees it. Her mother died in 1927 and "daddy went haywire," so she went to live with her maternal aunt and her husband, Uncle Paul— "gentle Paul"—who was a Baptist minister. Her aunt was a very strict woman and quite respectable.

Leona's marriage lasted fourteen years, and at the end she left her husband because he was undependable in his support of her and the children. While separated she met Larry, her boyfriend:

At the time I met Larry, my first husband and I wasn't together. I met Larry through the [same] church. He asked me [to marry] and I told him not until my husband's children got off my hands and out of the way. I never wanted a stepfather over my children . . . it was something that Lewis and I have always said.

Her main departure from her rearing was having children out of wedlock, and while she loves the children, she regrets the departure:

That's the only thing in life I didn't want— to have children without being married. I just wasn't reared like that. But they are all by one man. They're not by this, that one, nor the other one. They're all by one man.

Leona is proud to be able to say, "I have been by Larry as if he and I were married." But he was not true to her. She broke off their relationship by cutting him with a knife.

While it is true that Larry is legally obligated to care for his children, it is noteworthy that he claimed them as his in the first place and that he supports them in gifts over and above his legal obligations. His inability to believe that Leona was true to him, plus her reluctance to have a stepfather over her husband's children, at least one of whom has not yet left home, contributed to the factors other than economic that mitigated against their marriage—but did not prevent them from courting for sixteen years.

Most of the care that fathers give to their outside children seems to be much less regular than Larry's, but is, nevertheless, largely voluntary. Edward Patterson, for example, has three by two different women. His outside children live with their mothers, and when he gets tired of his wife he moves out and lives with Leddie B., by whom he has had two children. His legitimate children complain that when he goes to visit one of the outsiders, he gives her and her siblings more money for spending than he gives his legitimate children. His wife protests that he stole their TV set and gave it to the mother of one of these children, and his son claims that when he returned to his home in the country recently, he bought several dresses for his outside child living there. Mr. Patterson will not speak of these outsiders and keeps his money matters to himself. His wife has opened letters from the mothers of these children requesting regular support, but does not know if he is giving only to them. She believes that he spends most of the $406 a month take-home pay he earns from his job on these women and their children.

The Supportive Companion

A less durable relationship exists in the case of the "supportive companion" who "keeps a woman." Here the concern of the male is mainly to have a good time with a clean woman. The concern of the woman is for support and companionship. Such a relationship is not to be confused with prostitution, for it is not a mere matter of a business transaction but a search for intimacy on both parts, a search conducted in the context of severe economic and emotional handicaps. In this community such a relationship is likely to occur between an older man (late twenties, early thirties) and a younger woman (early twenties, teens) who has had children outside of wedlock.

In such a relationship, the man rarely keeps the woman in her own apartment, as would be the case in more solvent circumstances, where the woman is usually single and without children. Rather, he provides a regular "weekend away" at his apartment or other suitable place where they can be together away from the children. He takes her out, provides her with spending money and a good time. Should she conceive a child, he is least likely of all types to want to assume support of the child. Responsibility is what he is trying to avoid.

The example of Madeline (sixteen) and Jerry (twenty-three) is a case in point. They knew each other about a year during 1959–1960. Madeline had already had two children by two other men. Jerry came by for dinner occasionally, but usually he made the weekend scene at a motel apartment he rented for the occasion. When Friday came round, he would give Madeline money which she often turned into dresses or other items to enhance her appearance. Madeline says, "Jerry's not like a lot of men that you find. A lot of men, if they do something for you they feel they own you." Jerry gave her "fifteen or twenty dollars, sometimes more" each week and had keys to a two-room kitchenette for the weekend. Madeline says "We were always together [on the weekend]. Where I went he usually went, where he went I went. We'd go to the apartment and everything. But lots of times we would go and just watch TV or

sit and talk or have a drink or something. Then we would go—especially in the summertime—we'd go there because they had air conditioning."

The Pimp

. . . The pimp is characteristic of the young man of the street who lives off the labors of prostitutes or off women who are able to earn their own way through wages or welfare. He is kept by his woman and dresses like a dandy. None of the women living in broken homes has had a pimp, but Andrew Buchanan claims he was one as a youth. The pimp relationship may be, for the man at least, quite often a *premarital* experience. . . .

Speculation on Extensiveness and Relationship in Time

While there is no accurate measure of the prevalence of these four types of boyfriends, the data are suggestive. The pimp is the most talked about male-female nonmarital relationship in the literature. These data, however, suggest that it is not as prevalent in the project as is commonly assumed. It is possible that pimping may be more or less restricted to the younger men and may phase out into less exploitive relationships with females as the men grow older. Therefore, the frequency of the pimping relationship may well be exaggerated, since the younger men tend to be more vocal about their exploits, and the older men who now view such activity with a certain resentment may bewail the fact that "things used to be much better."

A man may play one or more boyfriend roles in his life. We can thus see these types as phases in a developmental sequence. The pimp is an early role of the young man of the street who would rather "live sweet" than work, or who has found that his value on the love market is greater than it is on the labor market. The data suggest that such a relationship is quite likely to terminate when the man reaches his mid-thirties. He may then decide to marry the woman he has pimped off because by then he has had one or more children by her, or because he is, after having sown his wild oats, seeking now a more intimate and lasting relationship. If he does marry her, then he comes under the norm that it is "unfair" to pimp off a woman you are married to.

No one, however, has gone from a pimping relationship directly to marriage with the same woman. In the case of Edward Patterson, who pimped off several women for several years before marriage, a quasi-father relationship was entered into with another woman for four or five years before he married her as the result of an unwanted pregnancy. This marriage has lasted nineteen years.

The quasi-fathers are in their late twenties or early thirties, and in one of the three instances, marriage is actively sought by the woman. In the other two the males are still being tested. This opportunity to get to know a man under near familial situations is a boon to these women, who have been disappointed in marriage one or more times. He can prove that he is a good provider and a gentle, "good" man. Not all quasi-father relationships terminate in marriage.

The supportive companion is, if the data from these inferences are correct, more likely to be the relationship that exists between an older man (late twenties or early thirties) and a younger woman (late teens, early twenties). It may be an alternative for a rejected quasi-father, who sought but could not obtain marriage, and whose income is stable enough to permit such indulgence. Finally, most men can play, if they so desire, the role of supportive biological father throughout most of their lives, since almost every male has had at least one child outside of wedlock. For some who never marry, this may be the extent to which their craving for familial companionship is expressed—the occasional gift to an illegitimate child.

4

Sexual Behavior

Black Sexuality: Fact and Fancy

Alan P. Bell

This article explores the myths of Black sexuality in comparison to white sexuality. Some facts and figures that give rise to the myths about Black sexuality are put into proper perspective. The author places emphasis on individual differences in sexual experience of Blacks and whites alike.

. . . [M]uch of what can be said about the white's stereotypes of the black is related directly to a physical and/or sexual imagery. The black, according to Jerome Davis, is seen as "a sexual superman, the uninhibited expressionist." Thomas Jefferson wrote of Negroes being "more ardent after their female." Draw up a list of the stereotypes, and you will be impressed by their explicitly sexual imagery: 1) the first and foremost preoccupation of black males is to have sex relations with white women; 2) the reproductive instinct of the black male is colossal; 3) black males have sex organs which dwarf those of white men; 4) this makes [their] potency or virility greater; 5) the black man is more animalistic in bed than the white man. Black women are not viewed dissimilarly: 1) all black women want to sleep with anyone who comes along; 2) black women respond instantly and enthusiastically to all sexual advances. . . .

. . . What are the facts? What do we know about black sexual attitudes and behaviors versus those of whites? Before I begin reeling off my impressions of the facts, allow me to quote the late Alfred Kinsey: "It is impossible to generalize concerning the behavior of a whole race." Statistically significant differences between groups of

people tend to blur the extent to which large numbers in both groups feel and act similarly. In a very real sense one can say that there is no such thing as black or white sexuality. There is only individual sexuality whose motivations and conflicts and values and attitudes and behaviors—at least in a way they hang together—are, like the palm of the hand, entirely idiosyncratic. This must be understood at the start. If one explores oneself or another deeply enough, one will become increasingly aware of the extent to which we are a secret to each other. We may say the same things, wear the same clothes or even the same skin, knock on the door of the same whorehouse, but our experience of the moments which we think we share is utterly different. Sex, like chow mein, means different things to the homosexual than it does to the heterosexual, to the adult than it does to the adolescent, to the black than it does to the white, to the male than it does to the female. But if the truth were known, even these customary dichotomies must be abandoned if the mystery of each of us is even to be imagined. But we rebel at this kind of request for further inquiry. We want labels that fit. But there are none, nothing under the sun which can justify a single stereotype of the white or of the black.

. . . [W]ith this introduction let [us] look at differences between blacks and whites in terms of their sexual experience which, in the telling of it, will probably render us blind to their similarity and certainly to the complexity of meaning associated with the events which will be reviewed. . . .

There are . . . some data that I would share with you tonight, data that has not been reported

Abridged from an address originally presented at the "Focus: Black America" Series at Indiana University, Fall 1968. The author presented it orally, which accounts for the informal language. Reprinted by permission.

or published by the Institute for Sex Research. The data were gathered from approximately 6,000 white males (about 80% of whom had attended college), 6,000 white females (about 75% of whom had attended college), 496 black males (about 45% of whom had attended college), and 498 black females (about 50% of whom had attended college). Subjects ranged in age from approximately 13 to 65 with the majority between the ages of 15 and 30. They were interviewed chiefly between the years 1942 and 1949. While a larger percentage of the blacks than the whites was rural, better than three fourths of both groups were urban. The data in their present form allow us to distinguish the college from the non-college-educated whites, but this is not possible when it comes to the blacks. Finally, a handful of what I designate as the black group was Oriental, a fact which may diminish or enhance the differences between the two groups. . . .

Since the prominent impression of blacks is that of their sexual precocity, of an early physical maturity with an excessive biologically grounded libidinal urge, it is interesting to note from the data the tendency for non-white males to reach puberty at later ages than their white counterparts. This tendency, which is probably a function of poorer nutrition, is reflected again in the tendency for non-white males to experience their first ejaculation from any source at later ages than the white male. It seems that the non-white's sexual career in terms of certain biological requirements is not launched at an earlier age than the white's! There is no evidence of an animal-like and rapid physical maturity on the part of blacks which many whites suppose is the case. And this lack of precocity goes beyond the physical consequences of second-class citizenship. For example, white males and females tend to learn about menstruation at slightly earlier ages than non-whites; white males and females also tend to learn about fertilization, pregnancy, and abortion at slightly earlier ages than non-white males and females. At least on this level, when it comes to sexual sophistication in childhood and adolescence, it can surely be said that non-whites do not lead the whites. We find white males learning about condoms at earlier ages than non-white males. We find white non-college females much more likely to have learned about penis erection by observing this phenomenon than non-white

females who were more likely to have learned about this through discussions with their female peers. Despite the imagery which is recalled by ape-man films and despite white notions of the pre-fig-leaf eras of man which supposedly persist in Africa and the vestiges of which they think are surely to be found in Afro-American homes, we find non-white females reporting *less* nudity in their childhood homes than white females. We find non-white males and females much less likely to sleep in the nude than their white counterparts. Apparently, if the non-white possesses a raw sexuality which the white does not, it is at least not expressed in the raw!

In fact, let us take a look at the evidence with regard to the matter of the non-white's raw sexuality, at the white man's image of the black man or woman who is "turned on" sexually by most erotic stimuli. Larger percentages of white males and females reported ever being sexually aroused by being bitten during sexual activity. Larger percentages of white males and females than black males and females reported that they were much aroused sexually by seeing a member of the opposite sex in a social situation. Larger percentages of white males than black males reported being much aroused from seeing themselves nude in the mirror or from seeing another male's erect penis. White males appeared to experience more sexual arousal from hearing risqué stories than their black counterparts. Larger percentages of white males and females reported sexual arousal from sadomasochistic literature or pictures than non-white males and females. And what I think is of particular interest is the fact that, despite the many areas in which white males and females exceeded the non-whites in their sexual arousal by various stimuli, larger percentages of whites also reported that they were offended and disgusted by the various stimuli in question. Which leads me to what I believe is one of the most important differences between the two groups.

As I think of white versus black sexuality, I am really impressed by the extent to which white preoccupations have made us whites a race of fetishists who recoil from explicit and frank sexual experience, and who manage to find only partial satisfaction, a juvenile titillation, in a host of substitutes: in our guarded conversations, in our dirty stories, in verbal and artistic imagery which are pale imitations of direct experience, and, yes, in all that we imagine about the black which threatens the bejesus out of us. The stereotypes themselves are, I think, evidence of the white fetishism to which I would draw your attention. As James Weldon Johnson—a black man—put it, "An examination of the vast number of salacious white periodicals published in the United States would incline one to think that sex has gone to the white man's head. . . . When sex goes to the head, it loses its lusty, wholesome quality and begins to fester, to become maggoty. Sex with us is, in large measure, still in the lusty, wholesome state. Let's keep it there as long as we possibly can." The white—ground under by his so-called civilized attitudes—resorts to fantasies of unbelievable proportions in which his sexual energies erupt in masturbatory activities or wet dreams beneath the sheets. White heterosexual encounter prior to marriage becomes a fetishistic enterprise in which the finger substitutes for the penis and in which petting has been developed to such an art that each female orifice is penetrated by inadequate substitutes for fear of a lost virginity.

The evidence indicates that we would do well to refrain from thinking of the moral versus the immoral when it comes to white versus black sexual behavior. There are differences born of custom, differences which are a function of different rewards and punishments, differences which make the way we manage our sexuality a little easier for us to survive as whites among whites or blacks among blacks.

The black male tends to learn about coitus at an earlier age than the white male. Coitus is much more likely to be the source of the male's first ejaculation for the non-white than for the white for whom masturbation serves as such a source. For example, coitus was the source of the first ejaculation for less than 1% of white college males, for 4% of the white non-college males, but for 33% of the non-white males. A much larger percentage of non-white females report being aroused in heterosexual contact by the age of 14 than white females. A greater proportion of premarital coital acts result in orgasm for the non-white females and a larger percentage of white females reported that they had not reached orgasm at all prior to marriage. There is little doubt but that non-whites tend to reach full genital engagement at earlier ages, to participate in premarital coitus more frequently, and to reach

orgasm more frequently in premarital coitus than their white counterparts. Holman and Schaffner report in the *American Journal of Sociology* a virginity rate of less than 1% for black males versus 21% for white males by age 21. The Institute for Sex Research reports that by age 20, among college-educated females, 25% of the whites versus 50% of the blacks had had sexual intercourse.

The point that I would like to make, however, is that since blacks have not taken over the white substitutes of masturbation and fellatio in their sexual repertoires their illegitimate birth rates are consequently higher than those of the whites. I suppose this is one of the reasons for the persistence of myths regarding black sexuality. White fetishism gives birth to fewer babies than black genitality. And speaking of genitals, the *majority* of both white and non-white penises in our sample measured less than or equal to four and a half inches in their flaccid state and less than or equal to seven inches in their erect state. However, three times the percentage of non-whites (versus whites) had penises which measured more than seven inches in their erect state. The Masters and Johnson report, however, indicates that penises are much like intelligence quotients: any increment beyond a certain point has no noticeable effect on performance. Also, if you are inclined to look at the matter even further, it would appear that whites report longer continuous erections in sociosexual activities than non-whites who, again, may be more direct and to the point in their sexual expressions.

What, then, can be said by way of summary? Is the sexual experience of whites and blacks different from each other? Yes. Is it a difference which supports the usual stereotype which the white man has of black sexuality? No.

If I were to summarize what I have been saying, it would be simply this. White virginity or asexuality is a myth—uncovered long ago by Kinsey and his associates—just as the black's overabundance of sexuality is a myth. Although their sexuality tends to take different forms, neither involves any more self-control or moral heroism than the other. There is little evidence, in other words, which supports the notion of delayed gratification on the part of middle-class whites versus the black man's quest for immediate gratification. The means by which sexual gratification is accomplished are simply different. For example, although we have not compared the frequencies of orgasm in black and white adolescents and young adults, we at the Institute suspect that there are no significant differences between the two groups.

Finally, I suppose that I am more impressed by our ignorance of the matters which have been discussed than by the capsule of knowledge which we possess. For example, what changes in black sexuality have taken place since the fifties? What differences exist between the sexual perspectives of the black radical and the black middle-class conservative and what effects do these have upon their social encounters? To what ex-tent have the white's stereotypes of the black changed, and what is the relationship between those stereotypes and "white" views about integration and black civil rights? How much investment does the black himself have in the sexual legends which whites have of him? To what extent do they reflect or reinforce black-white alienation? What does the future hold for us? A greater repressiveness for blacks or less repressiveness on the part of whites? The answers which are found to these questions and to many others may have profound consequences for the nation, indeed, for the world.

Sexual Behavior of Southern Blacks

Leanor B. Johnson

The author in this study compares attitudes towards premarital sex and premarital sex behavior among Scandinavian, southern Black, and midwestern white students. The findings point up a number of unexpected variables that affect the students' premarital sexual behavior.

The present study is an attempt to retest and extend a normative theory of premarital sexual behavior developed by Harold T. Christensen (1969) approximately eighteen years ago. His studies were based upon three 1958 samples of American and Danish University students, replicated in 1968 at these same universities plus several others (e.g., the Swedish University and Black Southern College utilized in the present study). Generally Christensen found that sexual permissiveness of respondents varied with the assumed overall sexual norms of their respective societies. Some specific results from his general findings are as follows: the more liberal the culture, the higher the incidence of premarital coitus, the greater the male–female congruence with regard to sexual behavior, the greater the amount of permissiveness with commitment, and the lower the negative effects following first premarital coital experience.

In order to extend this analysis to Afro-Americans, the present writer in 1973 read-ministered essential portions of the questionnaire to student samples at the same Midwestern University and at one of the two Black colleges that Christensen surveyed in 1968. Christensen's 1968 Swedish data were used for cross-cultural comparisons, and his 1968 Southern Black and White Midwestern samples were used for both cross-cultural and across-time analyses. This paper is limited to the 1968 data alone. Our primary focus is upon variations of Afro-Americans' premarital behavior as compared to two White samples— Midwestern United States and Scandinavia. Christensen's generalizations, cited above, are employed as working hypotheses, with the exception that conservative Midwesterners are expected to be more committed in premarital coitus than the more liberal Afro-American males. These samples enable us to look at the Afro-American subculture in relationship to the dominant and more conservative norms of the White American as well as the more permissive norms of the Scandinavian society. Because the latter society

Revised and reprinted by permission. This research constituted the writer's 1974 doctoral dissertation, completed at Purdue University with Harold T. Christensen serving as major professor.

Eugene G. Sherman, Jr., gave valuable assistance by administering the questionnaire at the Black college. Footnotes have been renumbered.

is removed from the historical-cultural and geographical experience of both American groups, it is expected that comparisons with it should highlight near universals in premarital sexual patterns.

Before proceeding with our analysis a brief and selective overview of each of the socio-cultural milieus is warranted.

Afro-Americans: Socio-Cultural Context

There is a small body of research evidence, as well as a large collection of non-scientific literature, which shows that Afro-Americans of the lower-class attach limited value to sexual abstinence prior to marriage. Gebhard (1958) calls attention to the fact that the Black middle class have just recently experienced vertical social mobility and thus retain vestiges of the sexual patterns of the lower class. Also, de facto residential segregation has operated to create sexual attitudes among Black Americans which cut across socio-economic lines. Thus, the children of middle-class Blacks are exposed to the more permissive sexual patterns of their lower-class neighborhood playmates (Moynihan, 1965; Staples, 1966). Elsewhere, social class along with religiosity is perceived to be a powerful determinant of the level of sexual permissiveness (Dollard, 1937; Kardiner and Ovesey, 1951; Kinsey, 1953; Frazier, 1957; Bell, 1966; and Poussaint, 1971). Frazier (1961), for example, observed that although the middle class reject the permissive sex life of Black "folks," it is only the religious middle class who maintain sexual conduct consistent with conservative, middle-class White America. Reiss' study (1967), the most extensive published empirical evidence available on Afro-Americans, does not fully support Frazier, Kinsey, or the others. His data led him to conclude that in contrast to the White society, strong ecclesiastical authority over sex is generally lacking in the Black community. Traditionally, Black churches have served as a source of tension reduction rather than as enforcers of a puritanical code of sexual ethics. The churches which strive to reduce sexual permissiveness are blocked by the strong and long tradition of liberal Afro-American sexual patterns. Controlling for Afro-American religiosity, Reiss (1971) found that little difference in the degree of acceptance of premarital coitus occurred between low and high church attenders.

Reiss' data also revealed that lower-class Blacks possessed more liberal attitudes towards premarital sex than their White counterpart. A historical reason is often given for such a finding. To illustrate, Staples (1971a) contends that

The flagrant violation of the Black woman's body during the slavery era served to devalue the worth of virginity to her. What good was it to value something one was not allowed to have? As a consequence the deeply rooted feelings of guilt about sex never became entrenched in the psyche of Black women as they did in her White counterpart (p. 120).

Much the same can be said of the Afro-American male. The Black male's family commitment was limited under slavery. His rewards were primarily based on his studability and labor output to the master. This pattern is believed to have been maintained through economic deprivation, the social caste system and the myths surrounding his sexuality.[1]

Only a few scientific studies focus on commitment in premarital coitus.[2] As early as 1944 Myrdal (1944) noted that "fly-by-nite," "fast women," and cohabitation with more than one person at a given time was against the mores of rural Southern Blacks. The later studies by Reiss (1967), Zelnik and Kantner (1972), and Ladner (1971) support Myrdal's observation. This discriminate permissiveness standard no doubt applies to females more than males (Liebow, 1966; Bell, 1970). Reports which show a higher degree of indiscriminate permissiveness among Blacks than among Whites may partly be explained in terms of the shortage of males in the Black population (Cox, 1940; Jackson, 1972). Since 1940 this ratio has become worse. The competition for male mates is intensified by the unwillingness of some men to marry at all (Broderick, 1965) and the increase of Black male-White female marriages (Heer, 1966). Although the total number of intermarriages are small, they tend to occur in those classes (college levels) in which the number of potential husbands is the smallest. If a Black female does not give in to demands for sexual gratification by a Black male, it seems there are

[1]Black males are assumed to be "super-studs": oversexed, with large phalluses.
[2]Most non-scientific accounts describe Afro-Americans as being highly noncommitted in both premarital and marital relationships.

plenty of other women who will. In short, Staples (1971) and others conclude that Black women are left with less bargaining power in the competitive husband and male companion market.

White: Socio-Cultural Context

The Judeo-Christian tradition has played an important role in tempering the sexual patterns of Whites. Although Jesus did not make any anti-feminist statements nor explicitly condemn pre-marital sex, the Apostle Paul developed a per-spective on sexuality and marriage which set the stage for many White churches today. Paul pro-claimed, "To the unmarried and widows I say that it is well for them to remain single as I do. But if they cannot exercise self-control, they should marry. For it is better to marry than to be aflame with passion" (1 Corinthians 7:8–9 RSV). Thus, it is argued that Paul implicitly states that premarital sex is a sin. Later the Stoic Musonius and the Catholic Church declared premarital coitus to be a manifestation of spiritual weakness and estab-lished sex as sacred only when it functioned for procreation within the doors of marriage. Fornica-tion outside marriage was placed in the same category as bloodshed and apostasy. This atti-tude is also strong in the churches of Sweden. In 1965 they reaffirmed their 1951 authoritarian position which declared all premarital sex against the will of God. In view of the pluralistic, demo-cratic, and experimental life style of the Swedes, this anachronistic stance has appealed only to a small number (Ferm, 1971). Recently, social and technological developments have functioned to further weaken this concept of sex, but the legacy of the Judeo-Christian sexual code still influences many of those high on religiosity.

There is ample support for the presumption that premarital coitus has been the rule rather than the exception for the majority of Scandina-vians (Croog, 1952). This sexual liberalism is said to be the result of both the lack of control religion has over Scandinavian lives and the deeply in-grained peasant rural tradition of "free sex" which the middle class and urban milieu has been un-able to alter. It is believed that the increasing use of contraceptives by the upper class and the predominant social democratic political parties have aided in propagating this liberal stance (Sim-enson and Geis, 1956).

In line with the English code laws, the early American colonial period was characterized by the double sexual standard which dictated chas-tity for women and allowed or encouraged males to "sow their wild oats." History testifies to the fact that most males who remain single up to age 21 are acceptably not virgins at the moment of matrimony. On the other hand, females who were not virgins or, worse yet, who had a premarital pregnancy, damage their chances of obtaining a husband. Thus, females more than males have traditionally been inculcated with the idea that positive identity, self-respect, and respect from others are dependent upon decorum in sexual matters. Recent research shows that the Amer-ican female's identity is heavily dependent upon her ability to get married and to perform her "natural career" of satisfying a husband and rearing children (Bardwick, 1971). Reiss (1971) contends that as long as females are oriented to marriage and the family as a career (as is the case for women in present-day United States) it is doubtful whether sex can be viewed by her as merely a source of pleasure.[3]

Gagnon and Simon (1970) claim that during 1964–1970 (the period in which our present sam-ples were drawn) there were enormous changes in the representation and definition of sex in the cultural life of Americans. Luckey and Nass (1969), Davis (1969), and Christensen and Gregg (1970a) present empirical evidence which indi-cates that this revolution has been rampant in the 1960s and has drawn its primary vanguard from college students, especially coeds. These studies suggest that behavior is now catching up with attitude, show that there is a reduction in guilt feelings following premarital coitus and that a mass retreat from premarital chastity may be oc-curring. Reiss, however, asserts that the sexual revolution of the 1960s is a myth.[4] What he per-ceives is an evolution in sexual standards result-ing from youth assuming more responsibility for their own standards.

The degree of differential gender role ex-pectation is not as pervasive in the sexual realm of

[3]Noted is the fact that Scandinavians have also had traditional sex role socialization, but it has been mitigated by their governments' strong efforts toward sexual equality.

[4]Recently, Reiss (1972) has conceded that a change in sexual behavior may have taken place during the last few years.

Scandinavian lives as is the case in the United States. For example, unlike couples in the U.S., Scandinavian couples share any expenses incurred from courting or dating. Rarely does the male pay all the expenses. While the sexual interaction of American couples is characterized by extensive kissing in the initial stages of courtship and at later stages heavy petting (thus, technically preserving the female's virginity), Scandinavians reserve kissing for later stages, but socially endorse full sexual relations during the typically long engagement period.[5] Given that the majority of Scandinavian marriages are entered into after the female becomes pregnant (usually five months later), little shame is felt by either gender as a result of this event (Croog, 1952; Svalastoga, 1954; Anderson and Anderson, 1960; Christensen, 1960).

As with the case of the Afro-Americans, Scandinavians have also had a history of sex ratio imbalance. The 1866–1913 high emigration of Scandinavian males to the United States left a surplus of females in the urban areas and a deficit in the rural communities. Recent demographic data *(U.N. Demographic Yearbook, 1972)* show a leveling of this imbalance only in the cities. This situation may present problems for each gender. However, it is important not to equate the consequences of Scandinavian regional sex ratios with the results of the Afro-American gender imbalance, for the total number of males of marriageable age in each of the Scandinavian countries exceeds their female counterparts.

In sum, all three cultures have been touched by the Judeo-Christian experience. However, traditionally it appears that Midwestern White Americans' sexual life is most influenced by religion and Scandinavians' least. Afro-Americans and Scandinavians have a liberal tradition of sexual patterns. The Afro-American pattern is believed to be rooted in slavery and the Scandinavians' in their peasant rural background. The Scandinavian culture has been characterized by high permissiveness *with* commitment and Afro-Americans' high permissiveness *without* commitment (more so in the non-scientific literature than in the scientific). Unique to the Afro-American experi-

ence, and assumed to be influencing their sexual patterns, is the surplus of marriageable-age females and the mystique surrounding the males' sexuality. Given these general characteristics it is expected that Afro-American sexual patterns will tend to resemble those of Scandinavians more than those of their American counterpart. We will now turn our attention to the findings.

Samples

Harold Christensen, with the assistance of an American and a Swedish professor, drew a non-random sample from the population of social science students in three universities—a predominantly Black Southern college, a predominantly White Midwestern university, and a university located in Sweden. The questionnaire employed was the one developed in 1958 by Christensen and Carpenter. (For a brief discussion of the construction and testing of this instrument see their 1962 article). The sample (total $N = 1113$) included 51 male and 123 female Afro-Americans, 245 male and 238 female Midwestern White Americans, and 206 male and 250 female Scandinavians.

Background

Frequent dating is a common experience for all three groups. Expectedly, fewer males than females are in a commitment relationship—the difference between the genders is least in the Scandinavian culture and greatest in the Afro-American subculture. The socio-economic data clearly indicate a basic difference in the sociocultural context within which heterosexual relationships are structured. When asked for their subjective social class rankings the majority of Afro-Americans reported lower- or working-class membership, while the majority of the other two groups reported middle- or upper-class. Afro-American and Midwestern males are approximately equal in age (21 or older: Blacks, 54.9 percent; Whites, 51.8 percent), Afro-American females tend to be older (21 or older: 47.9 percent) than their American female counterpart (21 or older: Blacks, 47.9 percent; Whites, 24.9 percent), and Scandinavians are considerably older

---

[5]In that rings are exchanged, engagements are more formal in Scandinavia than in the United States. The majority of engagements last one or more years with four or more years not too uncommon.

(21 or older: males, 84.5 percent; females, 65.2 percent) than the Americans. Scandinavians are also far less likely to be high on church attendance, while Black and White American males are virtually identical on low church attendance (percentages, respectively: 41.2 and 42.4), and Black females are the highest of all gender-culture groups. Males attend church less often than females; however, there is no meaningful difference in the low church attendance of males and females in Scandinavia (percentages, respectively: 91.7 and 90.8).

Measurement

A percentage difference (dyx) is used as a measure of association in the majority of the contingency tables. Behavior was measured by actual reported behavior. In general, those respondents stating experience in premarital coitus are considered permissive; while those engaging in necking or petting only are considered conservative. Other behavioral measures include response to questions concerning number and identity of coital partner, positive or negative con-

sequences following first coital experience, and frequency of church attendance.

Analyses

Table 1 presents premarital coital experience by culture. Culture makes its greatest impact on behavior when Afro-Americans are compared with Midwesterners. The most striking observation is the great deal of premarital experience Afro-American males have had relative to all other cultural-gender groups. While Afro-American females are noticeably more permissive than White Americans of both genders, they are less permissive than Scandinavian females.

Male–Female Congruence

Male–female congruence as related to premarital behavior is presented in Table 2. Although Scandinavians, as expected, show the greatest male–female congruence, not expected is the lowest degree of male–female congruence occurring among Afro-Americans.

Table 1.   Premarital Coital Experience as Related to Culture, by Sex, 1968

	Afro-American	Midwestern	Scandinavian
	a	b	c
Males			
Premarital coital experience	96.1%	50.2%	87.0%
No premarital coital experience	3.9	49.8	13.0
	100.0	100.0	100.0
N	(51)	(241)	(200)
		a, b: dyx = −45.9	
		a, c: dyx = −9.1	
Females			
Premarital coital experience	67.2%	34.3%	80.7%
No premarital coital experience	32.8	65.7	19.3
	100.0	100.0	100.0
N	(122)	(236)	(249)
		a, b: dyx = −32.9	
		a, b: dyx = 13.5	

Table 2.   Male–Female Congruence in Premarital Coital Experience as Related to Culture, 1968

	Afro-American		Midwestern		Scandinavian	
	%	N	%	N	%	N
Premarital coital experience						
Males	96.1	(51)	50.2	(245)	87.0	(206)
Females	67.2	(123)	34.3	(238)	80.7	(250)
dyx	28.9		15.9		6.3	

Commitment

The relationship between culture and commitment, as measured by two items, is presented in Table 3. The Afro-American male definitely shows a trend which is distinctly different from Midwestern and Scandinavian males. For example, a shift from one or two partners to six or more *increases* the number of Afro-American males 88.4 percent, *decreases* the number of Midwestern males 29.7 percent, and creates no meaningful change for Scandinavians. Black males are exceedingly more likely than any gender-culture group to have six or more partners and to have their first coital experience with a partner to whom they were not committed. By both measures, the most committed among the males are the Midwesterners. Although Afro-American females tend to have more partners than their White female American counterpart, they are virtually identical to them in confining their first premarital coital experience to a steady or fiance. Since Black females are not only older in age, but begin their sexual activities earlier than White females, they have had a greater length of time to accumulate more partners than their White female counterparts. Scandinavian females tend to have more partners and to more frequently have their first experience in a non-committed relationship than the American female subjects.

The high number of partners which Black males claim is partly due to their beginning sexual activities at an earlier age than any of the other groups. The overwhelming majority (71.4 percent) of Black males have had premarital coitus by age 15, while the majority of White males (Midwestern-

Table 3.   Commitment in Premarital Coital Experience as Related to Culture, by Sex, 1968

	Males			Females		
	Afro-American	Midwestern	Scandinavian	Afro-American	Midwestern	Scandinavian
	a	b	c	a	b	c
Number of partners						
1–2	2.3%	50.0%	34.8%	75.0%	83.8%	54.2%
3–5	7.0	29.7	31.7	13.9	11.3	27.9
6 or more	90.7	20.3	33.5	11.1	5.0	17.9
	100.0	100.0	100.0	100.0	100.1	100.0
N	(43)	(118)	(161)	(72)	(80)	(190)
First premarital coital experience confined to steady or fiance(e)						
Yes	17.0%	54.3%	46.5%	90.0%	89.6%	77.0%
No	83.0	45.7	53.5	10.0	10.4	23.0
	100.0	100.0	100.0	100.0	100.0	100.0
N	(47)	(116)	(170)	(80)	(77)	(200)
		a, b: dyx = 37.3			a, b: dyx = .4	
		a, c: dyx = 29.5			a, c: dyx = 13.0	

ers, 56.4 percent; Scandinavians, 51.3 percent), Scandinavian females (51.3 percent), and Black females (63.0 percent) begin between 16 and 18, and White American females (50.6 percent) at age 19 or older. In all cultures most non-virgins had premarital coitus by age 22.

Negative Feelings

It was expected that the more liberal the culture the less the negative effect following first premarital experience. Table 4 shows that just the opposite is true among the males. However, the differences between the Afro-American males and the other male groups are not great. Within the female samples Scandinavians are, as expected,

the lowest in negative feelings and Afro-Americans are surprisingly high in negative feelings. It is important to note that the Afro-American group has the greatest degree of male-female discrepancy in negative feelings.

Religiosity

Our earlier discussion of religiosity leads us to hypothesize that religiosity influences Scandinavians least, Midwesterners most and Afro-Americans moderately or intermediate to these two cultures. However, this did not consistently hold. The sexual behavior of Afro-Americans is not influenced more than that of Scandinavians by religiosity. In fact, the permissive behavior of the

Table 4.   Feelings Accompanying First Premarital Coitus as Related to Culture, by Sex, 1968

	Afro-American a	Midwestern b	Scandinavian c
Males			
First experience followed by tenseness, remorse, guilt, disgust, fear of others knowing, of pregnancy, or of religious punishment[1]	21.3%	18.5%	23.5%
No negative feelings, or a mixture of positive and negative feelings followed first experience[2]	78.7	81.5	76.5
	100.0	100.0	100.0
N	(47)	(119)	(170)
		a, b: dyx = −2.8	
		a, c: dyx = 2.2	
Females			
First experience followed by tenseness, remorse, guilt, disgust, fear of others knowing, of pregnancy, or of religious punishment[1]	53.2%	39.0%	25.0%
No negative feelings or a mixture of positive and negative feelings followed first experience[2]	46.8	61.0	75.0
	100.0	100.0	100.0
N	(79)	(77)	(200)
		a, b: dyx = −14.2	
		a, c: dyx = −28.2	

[1]. Represents all those who experience *only* negative feelings.

[2]. Regardless of culture, males had more positive feelings than mixed feelings, while among the females, Scandinavians were the only culture that had more positive feelings than mixed feelings. Moving from column a to column c, the percentages of positive feelings were 51.1, 52.1, and 58.8 for males and 19.0, 24.7, and 53.5 for females.

Table 5.   Premarital Coital Experience as Related to Culture, by Church Attendance and Sex, 1968

	Afro-American Church Attendance		Midwestern Church Attendance		Scandinavian Church Attendance	
	Less Than Once a Month	Once a Month or More	Less Than Once a Month	Once a Month or More	Less Than Once a Month	Once a Month or More
Males Premarital coital experience	95.2%	96.7%	63.1%	40.6%	90.8%	43.8%
No premarital coital experience	4.8	3.3	36.9	59.4	9.2	56.2
	100.0	100.0	100.0	100.0	100.0	100.0
N	(21)	(30)	(103)	(138)	(184)	(16)
	dyx = 1.5		dyx = −22.5		dyx = −47.0	
Females Premarital coital experience	64.7%	67.6%	46.1%	28.8%	82.7%	59.1%
No premarital coital experience	35.3	32.4	53.9	71.2	17.3	40.9
	100.0	100.0	100.0	100.0	100.0	100.0
N	(17)	(105)	(76)	(160)	(226)	(22)
	dyx = 2.9		dyx = −17.3		dyx = −23.6	

few Scandinavians that are high on religiosity is considerably lower than those who are low—this is especially true among Scandinavian males. Males, an exception being the Afro-American, tend to be more influenced by religiosity than are females.[6] Black females tend to be highly resistant to the influence of religiosity.

Summary and Discussion

The expectations from Christensen's findings were not consistently supported. In a few cases gender rather than culture served as the discriminating variable. Using church attendance as a control on sexual behavior, the data generally showed religiosity to influence the sexual permissiveness of males more than females. There are at least two studies, Gregg (1971) and Robinson et al. (1972), which are consistent with this finding. However, the bulk of empirical research demonstrates that not only are females more

[6]A check on the influence of religiosity on sexual attitude showed Black males to be considerably more influenced by religiosity than Black females.

influenced by religiosity, but they are more likely to attend church than males. Perhaps the pattern which is present here can be explained through cognitive balance theory (Aronson and Mills, 1959; Sampson, 1963). This theory suggests that individuals establish relationships between themselves and others that could be characterized as balanced. Thus, there is a tendency for individuals to reduce dissonance when it occurs. For example, Aronson and Mills (1959) found that there is a more positive attraction by members of an organization which rendered severe initiation rituals than organizations that are less severe. They interpreted their findings to mean that it would be dissonant to maintain the belief that one endure such a severe initiation for so unimportant a group. Therefore, those members receiving severe initiation act and talk as if their organization is highly meaningful and important. Perhaps, in the present study, church is like the organization and when a male attends he is going against the expectation of his male subculture. It would be dissonant not to adhere to religious codes after going against the expectation of the male peer group. Thus, it may be that the males who are high on religiosity have given a greater degree of thought to church attendance and tend to attach greater meaning and importance to religious values than do females. This same theory can also explain the profound impact of religion on the sexual lives of church-going Scandinavians. After all, it is in Scandinavia that the overwhelming percentage of the population believes that church attendance is neither a status symbol nor a majority folkway (Locke and Karlsson, 1952).[7]

Regardless of culture, females were more committed in first premarital coitus than males. This finding brings to mind Kinsey's statement on promiscuity:

Among all peoples, everywhere in the world, it is understood that the male is more likely than the female to desire sexual relations with a variety of partners (1953:682).

Kinsey suggested that psychologic conditioning is the primary source of the male's erotic response to a variety of partners. The implication is that this conditioning is the same regardless of culture. Although the data in Table 3 give support to Kinsey's statement, they also suggest that psychologic conditioning does not necessarily create any meaningful difference between males and females of different cultures. For example, on the first measure of commitment (see Table 3) there is a marked similarity between Midwestern males and Scandinavian females.

As an explanation for Black males' high degree of noncommitment relative to the other groups, the "super-stud-compensation" theory has been a popular one in the Black–White literature. For example, Frazier (1961) asserts that the Black male frequently uses sex to manifest his masculinity and to overcome his inferior status in the family as well as in the White world (also see Liebow, 1966). A derivation of this same stream of thought is given by Hare and Hare (1970). They contend that 200 years of brainwashing in the myth of Black male sexuality has forced the Black male to prove his "super-stud" ability. Thus, the Black male is a puppet in a self-fulfilling prophecy. Bell (1968) asserts that the Black female has no

part in the myth—because relative to the Black male and the sex symbol White female she comes across as sexless.

Frazier's thesis is weakened somewhat by the fact that the Black male does not hold the lowest rung of the socio-economic ladder—the Black female does (U.S. Census, 1972). One might then interpret Frazier to mean that the Black male's position relative to the White male forces him to compensate for a sense of inferiority. But even this interpretation is weakened by the growing evidence that the Black male does not perceive the White society as his reference group nor, when compared with Whites and the Black female, does he show lower self-esteem (Billingsley, 1968; Friedman, 1969; Rich, 1973). In addition, at least one study (Rich, 1973) gives evidence which weakens the theory of an "overly masculine" self-image of the Black male as compared to the White male. As a final note, there is some evidence which shows that the Black male's sexual behavior may be affected by the White female who may have been seen as a "forbidden fruit" that is now accessible (Sebald, 1971). Staples (1972c) states that some Black males date only White females because: (1) they are more sexually accessible, (b) they are less likely to use commitment as a condition for sex relations, and (c) the probability of demands for marriage are low.

It is understandable that in the Scandinavian culture where the super-stud myth is relatively absent, where basically all women have been eligible sexual partners, and where premarital coitus is expected within a steady or engaged relationship, there are just as many Scandinavian males with six or more partners as those with one or two partners.

Gender rather than culture was most important in differentiating negative and positive feelings following first premarital coitus. Within each culture males had fewer negative feelings than did females. The differences were considerable in the American groups, especially among the Afro-Americans, and minimal among the Scandinavians. Apparently, the double standard has allowed a broader range of socially acceptable premarital sexual behavior for males. Thus, when a male violates his own sexual code it is probably not as liberal as society's code for him, and he then has greater justification for his actions. This

---

[7]Although 90.0 percent of this present sample of Scandinavians are affiliated with the State Church, few (8.3 percent, males; 9.02 percent, females) attend. These percentages reflect the general pattern in Scandinavia.

double standard, more pervasive in America than in Scandinavia, is reflected in the greater male-female incongruence in the former country. The greater adverse consequences among Afro-American females may be associated with the imbalance in the sex ratio which forces them to go against their own sexual code in lieu of losing their partner to other more permissive females.

Based on Christensen's (1969) proposition 3, it was assumed that greater permissiveness in sexual norms would converge behavior as between males and females. Thus, we should have expected Blacks to have greater male–female congruence than White Americans, and Scandinavians more than Americans. Although Scandinavians were highest on male–female congruence, the Midwestern culture as compared to Afro-Americans' had greater male–female congruence.

In reevaluating Tables 2 through 4, it is evident that Afro-Americans show the greatest male–female incongruence. This incongruence reaches its peak in their commitment relationships. On both measures there is a 73 percent difference between the genders and this difference is far greater than that which occurs among the other two cultures. It has been noted in several recent Black popular publications that a major grievance the Black female has against the Black male is his insistence that she be faithful to him while he "raps" with many women. It may be the commitment phenomenon which is the major difficulty between the genders. The question is then, will controlling for various measures of commitment level bring Afro-American males and females together with regard to attitude and behavior? This check is now in process. The preliminary results of such a check on related 1972 samples show that courtship stage was the only one of three variables which brought Afro-Americans together with regard to both attitude and behavior.

Since commitment was the variable which resulted in the greatest differentiation between Black males and females, it may be that Christensen's proposition 3 should be revised to state that greater permissiveness in norms converge male and females with regard to attitude and behavior if the norms include adherence to a standard of commitment which applies to both genders.

References

Alvarez, R.
1971   Cited in J. Lever and P. Schwartz, "Sex Sacred? Or Just a Good Way to Get Acquainted?" *New Woman* (August): 108.

Anderson, R., and F. Anderson
1960   "Sexual Behavior and Urbanization in a Danish Village." *Southwestern Journal of Anthropology* 16 (Spring): 93–109.

Aronson, E., and J. Mills
1959   "The Effect of Severity of Initiation on Liking of a Group." *Journal of Abnormal Social Psychology* 59 (September): 177–181.

Bardwick, J.
1971   *Psychology of Women.* New York: Harper & Row.

Bell, A.
1968   "Black Sexuality: Fact and Fancy." Paper presented to "Focus: Black America" Series, Indiana University, Bloomington, Indiana.

Bell, R.
1966   *Premarital Sex in a Changing Society.* Englewood Cliffs, New Jersey: Prentice-Hall.

Bell, R., and J. Chaskes
1970   "Premarital Sexual Experience Among Coeds." *Journal of Marriage and the Family* (February): 81–84.

Billingsley, A.
1968   *Black Families in White America.* Englewood Cliffs, New Jersey: Prentice-Hall.

Breed, W.
1956   "Sex, Class & Socialization in Dating." *Marriage and Family Living* 18 (May): 137–144.

Broderick, C.
1965   "Social Heterosexual Development among Urban Negroes and Whites." *Journal of Marriage and the Family* 27 (May): 200–203.

Burgess, E., and P. Wallin
1953   *Engagement and Marriage.* Philadelphia: Lippincott.

Christensen, H.
1960   "Cultural Relativism and Premarital Sex

Norms.'' *American Sociological Review* 25 (February): 31–39.

Christensen, H. (ed.)
1964   *Handbook of Marriage and the Family.* Chicago: Rand McNally.
1969   ''Normative Theory Derived from Cross Cultural Family Research.'' *Journal of Marriage and the Family* 31 (May): 209–222.

Christensen, H., and G. Carpenter
1962   ''Value-Behavior Discrepancies Regarding Premarital Coitus in Three Western Cultures.'' *American Sociological Review* 27 (February): 66–74.

Christensen, H., and C. Gregg
1970a ''Changing Sex Norms in America and Scandinavia.'' *Journal of Marriage and the Family* 32 (November): 616–627.
1970b ''Changing Sex Norms in America and Scandinavia.'' Mimeographed paper. Lafayette, Ind.: Purdue University, Institute for the Study of Social Change.

Clark, K.
1965   *Dark Ghetto.* New York: Harper & Row.

Clemensen, C.
1956   ''State of Legal Abortion in Denmark.'' *American Journal of Psychiatry* 112 (March): 662–663.

Cox, Oliver
1940   ''Sex Ratio and Marital Status Among Negroes.'' *American Sociological Review* 5:937–947.

Croog, S. H.
1952   ''Premarital Pregnancies in Scandinavia and Finland.'' *American Journal of Sociology* 57 (January): 358–365.

Davis, K. B.
1929   *Factors in the Sex Life of Twenty-Two Hundred Women.* New York: Harper & Row.

Davis, K. E.
1969   ''Sex on Campus: Is there a Revolution?'' *Medical Aspects of Human Sexuality* 3 (Winter): 55–60.

Debman, J.
1959   ''The Relationship between Religious Attitude and Attitude Towards Premarital Sex Relations.'' *Marriage and Family Living* 21 (May): 171–176.

De Rachewitz, B.
1964   *Black Eros.* New York: Lyle Stuart.

Dollard, J.
1937   *Caste and Class in a Southern Town.* New York: Doubleday.

Drake, St. C., and H. Cayton
1945   *Black Metropolis.* Chicago: University of Chicago Press.

Ehrmann, W.
1959   *Premarital Dating Behavior.* New York: Holt, Rinehart and Winston.
1964   ''Marital and Nonmarital Sexual Behavior.'' Pp. 585–622 in H. Christensen (ed.), *Handbook of Marriage and the Family.* Chicago: Rand McNally.

Ferm, W.
1971   *Responsible Sexuality—NOW.* New York: Seabury.

Festinger, L.
1957   *A Theory of Cognitive Dissonance.* New York: Harper & Row.

Frazier, E.
1948   *The Black Family in the United States.* Chicago: University of Chicago Press.
1957   *The Black Bourgeoisie.* New York: Collier Books.
1961   *The Negro Church in the United States.* Liverpool: Liverpool University Press.

Freedman, M.
1965   ''The Sexual Behavior of American College Women. An Empirical Study and an Historical Survey.'' *Merrill-Palmer Quarterly of Behavior and Development* 11 (January): 33–48.

Friedman, N.
1969   ''Africa and the Afro-American: The Changing Negro Identity.'' *Psychiatry* 32: 127–136.

Gagnon, J., and W. Simon
1970   *The Sexual Scene.* Chicago: Aldine.

Gebhard, P., W. Pomeroy, C. Martin, and C. Christenson
1958   *Pregnancy, Birth, and Abortion.* New York: Harper & Row.

Glasser, B., and A. Strauss
1967   *The Discovery of Grounded Theory.* Chicago: Aldine.

Gregg, C.
1971   "Premarital Sexual Attitudes and Behavior in Transition: 1958 and 1968." Ph.D. dissertation, Purdue University.

Hamilton, G.
1929   *A Research in Marriage.* New York: Albert and Charles Boni.

Hammond, B., and J. Ladner
1969   "Socialization into Sexual Behavior in a Negro Slum Ghetto." Pp. 46–52 in J. Bernard and C. Broderick (eds.), *The Individual, Sex, and Society.* Baltimore: Johns Hopkins University Press.

Hare, N., and J. Hare
1970   "Black Women." *Transaction* (November): 66–70.

Heer, D.
1966   "The Prevalence of Black–White Marriage in the United States, 1960 and 1970." *Journal of Marriage and the Family* 36 (May): 246–259.

Heltsley, M., and C. Broderick
1969   "Religiosity and Premarital Sexual Permissiveness: A Re-Examination of Reiss' Traditionalism Proposition." *Journal of Marriage and the Family* 31 (August): 441–443.

Himes, J.
1964   "Some Reactions to a Hypothetical Premarital Pregnancy by 100 Negro College Women." *Journal of Marriage and the Family* 26 (August): 344–346.

Inghe, J., and A. Joachin
1971   Cited in Birgitta Linner. *Society and Sex in Sweden.* Stockholm: Swedish Institute for Cultural Relations. P. 19.

Jackson, J.
1972   "Where Are the Black Men?" *Ebony* (March): 99–106.

Johnson, C.
1934   *Shadow of the Plantation.* Chicago: University of Chicago Press.

1941   *Growing Up in the Black Belt.* Washington, D.C.: American Council on Education.

Kardiner, A., and L. Ovesey
1951   *The Mark of Oppression.* New York: Norton.

Kinsey, A., W. Pomeroy, C. Martin, and P. Gebhard
1948   *Sexual Behavior in the Human Male.* Philadelphia: Saunders.

1953   *Sexual Behavior in the Human Female.* Philadelphia: Saunders.

Ladner, J.
1971   *Tomorrow's Tomorrow: The Black Woman.* Garden City, New York: Doubleday.

Landis, J., and M. Landis
1958   Building a Successful Marriage. Englewood Cliffs, New Jersey: Prentice-Hall.

Lever, J., and P. Schwartz
1971   "Sex Sacred? Or Just a Good Way to Get Acquainted?" *New Woman* (August): 38–43, 108–109.

Lewis, H.
1960   "The Changing Negro Family." Vol. 1. In Eli Ginzberg (ed.), *The Nation's Children.* New York: Columbia University Press.

Liebow, E.
1966   *Tally's Corner.* Boston: Little, Brown.

Linderfield, F.
1960   "A Note on Social Mobility, Religiosity, and Students' Attitude toward Premarital Sexual Relations." *American Sociological Review* 25 (February): 81–84.

Linner, B.
1971   *Sex and Society in Sweden.* Stockholm: Swedish Institute for Cultural Relations.

Locke, H. J., and G. Karlsson
1952   "Marital Adjustment and Prediction in Sweden and the United States." *American Sociological Review* 17 (February): 10–17.

Lower, G.
1973   *Feelings of Regret Involved in Premarital Intercourse.* New York: Poet's Press.

Luckey, E., and G. Nass
1969   "A Comparison of Sexual Attitudes and Behavior in an International Sample." *Journal of Marriage and the Family* 31 (May): 364–379.

Middendorp, C., W. Brinkman, and W. Koomen
1970   "Determinants of Premarital Sexual Permissiveness: A Secondary Analysis." *Journal of Marriage and the Family* 32 (August): 369–379.

Moskin, R.
1971 "Sweden: The Contraceptive Society." Pp. 187–193, in A. Skolnick and J. Skolnick (eds.), *Family in Transition*. Boston: Little, Brown.

Moynihan, Daniel
1965 *The Negro Family: The Case for National Action*. Washington, D.C.: Office of Policy Planning and Research, United States Department of Labor.

Myrdal, G.
1944 *An American Dilemma*. New York: Harper & Row.

Pope, H.
1967 "Unwed Mothers and Their Sex Partners." *Journal of Marriage and the Family* 29 (August): 555–567.

Pope, H., and D. Knudsen
1965 "Premarital Sexual Norms, the Family, and Social Change." *Journal of Marriage and the Family* 27 (August): 314–323.

Poussaint, A.
1971 "Blacks and the Sexual Revolution." *Ebony* (October): 112–120.

Rainwater, L.
1960 *Premarital Sexual Standards in America*. New York: Free Press.
1968 "Crucible of Identity: The Negro Lower-Class Family." Pp. 102–127 in Robert Winch and Louis Goodman (eds.), *Selected Studies in Marriage and the Family*. New York: Holt, Rinehart and Winston.

Reiss, I.
1964 "Premarital Sexual Permissiveness among Negroes and Whites." *American Sociological Review* 29 (October): 688–698.
1967 *The Social Context of Premarital Sexual Permissiveness*. New York: Holt, Rinehart and Winston.
1968 "How and Why America's Sex Standards Are Changing." *Transaction* (March): 26–32.
1971 "Premarital Sex Codes: The Old and the New." In D. Grummon and A. Barclay (eds.), *Sexuality: A Search for Perspective*. New York: Reinhold.
1972 *Readings on the Family System*. New York: Holt, Rinehart and Winston.

Rich, P.
1973 "Self-Structure and Social Structure: A Study of Self-Identification and Self-Evaluation among Black and White College Students." Ph.D. dissertation, Purdue University.

Robinson, I., K. King, C. Dudley, and F. Clune
1972 "The Premarital Sexual Revolution among College Females." *The Family Coordinator* 21 (April): 189–194.

Rockwood, L., and M. Ford
1945 *Youth, Marriage, and Parenthood: The Attitudes of 364 University Juniors and Seniors toward Courtship, Marriage and Parenthood*. New York: Wiley.

Rubin, I.
1965 "Transition in Sex Values—Implications for the Education of Adolescents." *Journal of Marriage and the Family* 27 (May): 185–189.

Sampson, E.
1963 "Status Congruence and Cognitive Consistency." *Sociometry* 26 (June): 146–162.

Schulz, D.
1969 *Coming Up Black*. Englewood Cliffs, New Jersey: Prentice-Hall.

Sebald, H.
1971 "Patterns of Interracial Dating and Sexual Liaison of White and Black College Men." Unpublished manuscript. Tempe, Ariz.: Arizona State University.

Simenson, W., and G. Geis
1956 "Courtship Patterns of Norwegian and American University Students." *Marriage and Family Living* 18 (November): 334–338.

Skolnick, A., and J. Skolnick
1971 *Family in Transition*. Boston: Little, Brown.

Staples, R.
1966 "Sex Life of Middle-Class Negroes." *Sexology* 33 (September): 86–89.
1970 "A Study of the Influence of Liberal-Conservative Attitudes on the Premarital Sexual Standards of Different Racial, Sex-Role, and Social Class Groupings." Ph.D. dissertation, University of Minnesota.
1971a "Towards a Sociology of the Black Family: A Theoretical and Methodological Assessment." Pp. 144–160 in Carlfred B.

Brockerick (ed.), *A Decade of Family Research and Action.* Minneapolis: National Council on Family Relations.

1971b *The Black Family: Essays and Studies.* Belmont, California: Wadsworth.

1972a "Do Blacks Have More Fun: Sex and Race in America." Unpublished manuscript. University of California, San Francisco.

1972b "Research on Black Sexuality: Its Implication for Family Life, Sex Education, and Public Policy." *The Family Coordinator* 21 (April): 183–187.

1972c "The Sexuality of Black Women." *Sexual Behavior* (June): 4, 6, 8–11, 14–15.

1973 "The Black Dating Game." *Essence* (October): 40.

1974 "Has the Sexual Revolution Bypassed Blacks?" *Ebony* (April): 111–114.

Sutker, P., and R. Gilliard
1970 "Personal Sexual Attitudes and Behavior in Blacks and Whites." *Psychological Reports* 27 (February): 753–754.

Sutker, P., L. Sutker, and D. Kilpatrick
1970 "Religious Preference, Practice and Personal Sexual Attitudes and Behavior." *Psychological Reports* 26 (October): 835–841.

Svalastoga, K.
1954 "The Family in Scandinavia." *Marriage and Family Living* 16 (November): 374–380.

Terman, L.
1938 *Psychological Factors in Marital Happiness.* New York: McGraw-Hill.

United States Bureau of the Census
1972 *The Social and Economic Status of the Black Population in the United States.* Series P-23, No. 38. Washington, D.C.: U.S. Government Printing Office.

Weinstein, N.
1971 "Psychology Constructs the Female, or the Fantasy Life of the Male Psychologist." Pp. 271–286 in E. Showalter (ed.), *Women's Liberation and Literature.* New York: Harcourt Brace Jovanovich.

Whyte, W.
1949 "A Slum Sex Code." *American Journal of Sociology* 49 (July): 24–31.

Zelnick, M., and J. Kantner
1972 "Sexuality, Contraception and Pregnancy among Young Unwed Females in the United States." Washington, D.C.: Commission on Population Growth and the American Future (May).

Has the Sexual Revolution Bypassed Blacks?

Robert Staples

A sexual revolution, according to the author, is questionable in terms of its effect on the Black community. The discussion centers around the trappings of the sexual revolution that have found popularity among whites: singles bars, swingers, gay life style, and so on. The sexual and moral codes of Blacks are different. Blacks give more emphasis to long-term, stable relationships than to one-night stands. The author suggests that perhaps the two groups differ in their cultural attitudes toward sex. Blacks who are interested in interracial relationships are more inclined to sexual expression like that of white society.

Only a hermit would be unaware of the changes occurring in American sexual attitudes and behavior. This sexual revolution, as it is generally called, is visible everywhere in the form of erotic movies, books on sex, sex-oriented magazines, and scanty female clothing. A whole three-and-one-half-billion-dollar industry has developed

Adapted from an article originally published in *Ebony* (April) 1974): 111–114. © 1974 by Johnson Publishing Company, Inc.

Reprinted by permission.

from this trend and this figure does not include sex-related industries such as advertising, motels, and singles bars. Since Blacks have long been identified in the public mind with sexual permissiveness and potency, one would expect them to have a significant participation in this revolution. Yet, they are conspicuously underrepresented or absent in most of the sex industry. Has the sexual revolution passed Blacks by? Was Wilt Chamberlain correct when he accused Black women of having sexual hangups? To answer these questions we need to understand what the sexual revolution is all about.

Authorities in the field of sexology are not in agreement that there has been a sexual revolution. Some contend that sexual behavior has not changed, but that now it is more open. Most of the changes relate to lifting the restrictions on female premarital sexual behavior. No longer is she expected to be a virgin at marriage, with the male getting his premarital sexual experiences from prostitutes or "loose" women.

Sex plays a very important role in the movie industry. Most of the major money-making pictures include some nudity, profane language, or sexual involvement. Moreover, almost all Blaxploitation films have heavy doses of sexual action. This has led to criticism in some quarters of the Black community of the heavy emphasis on interracial sex and the portrayal of the Black woman as sex object rather than as meaningful personality in the Black male's life.

Some of this criticism is justified, because white women have alternative roles in films as wives and mothers to counteract their sexual image. But Black women appear to be portrayed exclusively as sex objects in the Blaxploitation films, and this reinforces the image of them as morally loose. The strong emphasis on interracial sexual encounters only encourages the false notion that white women make better sexual partners for Black males. It is worth noting that most of these films are produced and controlled by whites—they may be projecting their sexual fantasies into these films.

When it comes to the sex book and magazine industry, Blacks are simply not involved at all. Despite the thousands of books written on white sexuality, many of them bestsellers, there is not yet one book on Black sexual patterns. Several books have been written on interracial sexual

activity by white authors. Calvin Hernton, the one Black author who has dealt with Black sexuality, has done so in a sensational way, using personal experiences and friends as his source. Few white authors or social scientists have the intimate understanding of Black culture and values to write such a book. And Black authors avoid this explosive issue because there is little Black agreement about how it should be handled and because some fear how it will be interpreted.

There is probably more Black involvement in pornography. Quite a few recent porno films have featured Black male actors, most of them in interracial sexual action. The same is true of pornographic books, obviously aimed at the white reader. The Presidential Commission on Obscenity and Pornography reported that the typical patron of porno films and books was a white, middle-aged, middle-class married male. While there is nothing particularly wrong or harmful in viewing sexually arousing films, the regular white patron is often sexually frustrated or bored. Hence, the low number of Black patrons could indicate a more gratifying sex life.

One area of the sexual revolution is practically unheard of among Blacks: group sex. There is no research concerning the role of Blacks in group sex. One occasionally hears rumors about some middle-class Black couples that have exchanged spouses. If these couples exist, they are quite secretive about their group sex activities. In my own extensive research on Black sexuality, I have been unable to find one Black couple to interview about this type of behavior. It is estimated that over eight million white couples have participated in wife swapping; apparently Blacks are rare among such swingers. In his book *Group Sex*,[1] Bartell reported that some interracial couples were involved in swinging and noted that there was "hearsay evidence" that middle-class Blacks participated on a Blacks-only basis.

Several factors account for the non-involvement of Blacks in swinging. Bartell found that most of the white swingers were racists. It should be noted that swingers are not free of sexual hangups. The man in particular is often quite anxiety-ridden about whether the man with whom he has exchanged places will be a better sexual partner and steal his wife's affections. One way to

[1]Gilbert D. Bartell, *Group Sex*, New York: Wyden, 1971.

avoid this possibility is to engage in "open swinging," whereby all sexual activity takes place in one room. Considering the Black male's image as superstud, the ordinary white male assumes that he will lose in any sexual competition with a Black man.

Economics must also be a factor behind the low number of Blacks involved in swinging. Swinging often requires a large outlay of cash. One has to pay to advertise for couples in swinging magazines. If there are children involved, the couple must pay for a third place to swing in privacy. This can mean a lot of money for meals, travel, and so on. As with porno films and books, some people turn to swinging as a substitute for a sexually unfulfilling marriage. Since the available research indicates Blacks receive more sexual satisfaction in marriage, they are not as likely to need this type of outlet.

People who are lonely and sexually frustrated have another alternative of the sexual revolution—the singles bars. Here again, we find almost no Black patronage, except for Blacks interested in interracial sexual action. Why? First, Blacks are not likely to be as lonely as whites, even in the largest cities. There is a sense of community among Blacks that makes it easier to meet other Blacks. Just being Black gives one an entry to many Black social circles.

Even lonely Blacks forsake singles bars. They are more likely to turn to cabarets and social clubs. Many Black women in particular refuse to go to singles bars because they dislike going unescorted and putting themselves on display like merchandise. Some object because they regard it as unladylike, while others do not trust people unless they meet them through somebody they know and trust. Being picked up by a stranger is more dangerous for Black women because of the large criminal element in some Black communities.

One outcome of the sexual revolution is an increase in visible homosexuality. This is probably the one part of the changing sexual values that has significant Black participation. Now, Black men are assuming the gay life style. It is not known how many exclusive homosexuals exist in the United States. Estimates range from 5% to 20% of the total population. There is reason to believe that there is a lower proportion of Black male homosexuals than white. It is difficult to speculate

on what the figure is. We also can assume that the proportion of bisexual Black males is higher than that of whites.

Despite a shortage of Black males, very few Black women have joined the lesbian community. In fact, the ratio of Black male homosexuals to Black female homosexuals could be as high as 50 to 1. These Black lesbians often use Black superstuds or pimps as their role models. Because they are not as visible as many Black male homosexuals, their number is hard to determine. As with Black male homosexuals, many Black lesbians are deeply involved in the white homosexual community and, hence, are not as observable as other Blacks.

The Black man who is homosexual is usually different from the average Black male. Prison is one of the greatest sources of homosexuality. Some Black men who have adopted homosexuality in prison continue after their release. Their motive for assuming a homosexual life style may be to escape responsibilities to family and society and to get money through acquiring a rich patron or through prostitution. Black male homosexuals are more likely to be involved in interracial associations, sexual or otherwise. Their primary identity is often with the gay community, not the Black community.

What about actual changes in sexual attitudes and behavior among Blacks compared with whites? A recent *Playboy* survey[2] found that over 70% of white American women had engaged in premarital sex. My own research shows Blacks are more likely to have engaged in premarital sex than whites. This does not mean they are more permissive, since these statistics reveal nothing about the frequency of premarital sex or the number of sexual partners.

Looking further at these statistics we find that the sexual revolution has not affected all whites equally. Among certain segments of the white population there still exists a conservative moral code, particularly in the South and Midwest and among Mormons and Catholics. In fact, my own study of Black and white college students found the largest differences in premarital sexual behavior were not between Blacks and whites but between white women in the South and those in

[2]Morton Hunt, *Sexual Behavior in the 1970's*, Chicago: Playboy Press, 1974.

California.[3] Only 12% of white Southern females had premarital sexual experiences compared to 75% of the white California females. The regional differences for Blacks were slight.

If one considers other aspects of premarital sexual behavior, it appears that Black women are falling behind in the sexual revolution. Several studies reveal that white females are becoming more sexualized, participating more often in premarital sex with a larger number of partners, and practicing a variety of sexual techniques. An often-used rationale for Black males dating white females is that they "get over" quicker sexually. At least one study has documented that the majority of Black males dating interracially had participated in one-night flings.[4]

This type of situation makes it difficult for the Black woman to compete for the Black man's attention. Most Black women are still committed to getting married and they think a brief sexual involvement will jeopardize their chances. Unlike white women, they do not have the alternative of turning to white men after the sexual fling is over. The conflict between Black male sexual demands and Black female resistance has led to the deteriorating relationships between the sexes. One prominent Black leader told me that Black men and white women are now the most sexually compatible duo. This statement does not address the question of whether a relationship can be based solely on sex.

This situation, however, highlights what many of us have known all along. Despite the public stereotype of Black women as morally loose, they impose considerable restraint on their sexual activity. Most Black mothers raise their daughters to use caution and discretion in their relations with men. One finds a high degree of sexual modesty among Black women. Reginald Hayes of *Jet* magazine recalls the difficulty they once had there in getting Black women to pose in bikinis. A Black *Playboy*-type magazine would have been impossible ten years ago. Such modesty may have originated in the South, where it

was considered unladylike to indulge in such behavior.

One finds a variety of sexual types among Black females. Some of them are:

The *conservative* woman adamantly refuses to consider sex until after marriage. Rare in the Black community, she is likely to be a Seventh-Day Adventist, a Jehovah's Witness, a Catholic or a Muslim. Or she may have a neurotic fear of sex, instilled by a traumatic experience in childhood or by stern warnings from parents.

The *moderate* woman's ideal is sex after marriage but she is willing to compromise after the man has made a serious commitment (for example, going steady or engagement). She believes that true love must be present before sex can take place. In some cases she has no real convictions about love and sex but uses them as a deliberate strategy to entice the male into marriage. With a serious shortage of Black males, this type is rapidly disappearing.

The *liberal* woman, given the existence of affection and desire, is willing to participate in premarital sex after a certain length of time, generally more than one night but less than three months. This woman recognizes her sexual needs and refuses to repress them just for a chance at marriage, which may not be the best thing for her. Probably the majority of Black females are beginning to fall into this category.

The *radical* famale: if desire exists, she is ready. She has discovered the beauty of sex and does not want to be inhibited by any male double standard. She willingly accepts an invitation to stay at a male's residence, with the clear implication that sex will take place. She will go on a trip with a man and stay in the same room with him. Often she lives with a man without marriage. This behavior is radical because of the lack of game playing. The male does not have to seduce her by deceit or the pretense of love. Older Black women, some of whom have been married before, are more likely to be in this category.

In sum, the sexual revolution for whites is here; Blacks had theirs centuries ago. Much of the new sexual freedom is a striving for sexual thrills after centuries of sexual repression. Because Blacks came from a continent where sex was

[3]Robert Staples, "A Study of the Influence of Liberal-Conservative Attitudes on the Premarital Sexual Standards of Different Racial, Sex-Role, and Social Class Groupings," Ph.D. dissertation, University of Minnesota, 1970.

[4]Hans Sebald, "Patterns of Interracial Dating and Sexual Liaison of White and Black College Men." Unpublished manuscript, Arizona State University, 1971.

always considered a natural act, they do not have the same impulse to uncover all the mysteries of sex through porno movies and books, group sex, or other acts of sexual curiosity. To the extent that Blacks want to integrate into white society, they may become involved in these new forms of sexual expression. But, if the sexual revolution consists only of an endless quest for new but meaningless sexual thrills, perhaps Blacks had better wait for the next train.

5

Male Sex Roles

The Myth of
The Impotent Black Male

Robert Staples

The author examines stereotypes of the Black male. He begins with myths about the Black male slave as docile personality, and goes on to critique assumptions that Black men are effeminate, irresponsible, and oversexed. He concludes with an analysis of the social forces responsible for the unique expressions of Black manhood.

In white America there is a cultural belief that the black community is dominated by its female members, its men having been emasculated by the historical vicissitudes of slavery and contemporary economic forces. This cultural belief contains a duality of meaning: that black men have been deprived of their masculinity and that black women participated in the emasculinization process. The myth of the black matriarchy has been exploded elsewhere.[1] Black female dominance is a cultural illusion that disguises the triple oppression of black women in this society. They are discriminated against on the basis of their sex role affiliation, their race and their location in the working-class strata of this upper-class–dominated country.

The assumption that black men have been socially castrated has yet to be challenged. Before examining the fallacies of black male castration, it is important to understand the function of these cultural images of black men and women for maintaining the status quo of black deprivation and white privilege. Most of these theories of black life come from the field of social science, a

discipline ostensibly dedicated to the pursuit of truth. It would be more realistic to view social science research as a form of ideology, a propaganda apparatus which serves to justify racist institutions and practices. Social science as ideology is a means of social control exercised by white America to retain its privileges in a society partially sustained by this ideology. As one observer noted:

Social scientists and journalists in America generally operate under an ideology-laden code of professional conduct that requires objectivity. . . . But this objectivity is in effect a commitment to the ruling class.[2]

Stereotypes of the black male as psychologically impotent and castrated have been perpetuated not only by social scientists but by the mass media, and they have been accepted by both blacks and whites alike. This assault on black masculinity is made *precisely because black males are men,* not because they are impotent; that is an important distinction to make. As one sociologist candidly admits, "Negro men have been more feared, sexually and occupationally, than Negro women."[3] She further admits that the Negro man had to be destroyed as a man to "protect" the white world.[4] It should be added that the attempt to destroy him failed but the myth of

[1]Robert Staples, "The Myth of the Black Matriarchy," *The Black Scholar,* February, 1970, pp. 9–16.

[2]William Ellis, *White Ethics and Black Power,* Chicago: Aldine Publishing Company, 1969, p. xiii.

[3]Jessie Bernard, *Marriage and Family Among Negroes,* Englewood Cliffs, New Jersey: Prentice-Hall, Inc., 1966, p. 69.

[4]*Ibid,* p. 73.

Adapted from *The Black Scholar* 10 (June 1971): 2–9. © 1971 by the Black World Foundation. Reprinted by permission.

his demasculinization lingers on. One can see in this myth an unmitigated fear of black male power, an unrelenting determination on the part of white America to create in fiction what it has been unable to accomplish in the empirical world.

From a historical perspective, the black male's role has changed as he has moved from the African continent to the shores of North America. This span of time has introduced the forces of slavery, racism and wage exploitation in the determination of his masculine expressions. In Africa, he resided in a male-dominated society. Although women had an important place in African society, most important decisions were made by male members of the community.[5]

Forcibly uprooted from his native Africa, the black man experienced radical changes in status. In the beginning of the period of slavery, black men greatly outnumbered black women. (It was not until 1840 that there was an equal sex ratio among blacks.[6]) As a result of this low sex ratio, there were numerous cases of sex relations between black slaves and indentured white women. The intermarriage rate between black men and white women increased to the extent that interracial marriages were prohibited. Previously, black men were encouraged to marry white women in order to augment the human capital of the slave-owning class.[7]

After black women were brought to the New World, they served as breeders of children, were treated as property, and as the gratifiers of the carnal desires of white plantation owners. More importantly, they became the central figures in black family life. The black man's only crucial function within the family was to sire children. The mother's role was far more important than the father's. She cleaned the house, prepared the food, made clothes and raised the children. The husband was at most his wife's assistant, her companion and her sex partner. He was often thought of as her possession, as was the cabin in which they lived. It was common for a mother and her children to be considered a family without reference to the father.[8]

Under slavery the role of father was, in essence, institutionally obliterated. Not only was the slave father deprived of his sociological and economic functions in the family but the very etiquette of plantation life eliminated even the honorific attributes of fatherhood from the black male, who was addressed as boy—until, when the vigorous years of his prime were past, he was permitted to assume the title of uncle. If he lived with a woman, "married," he was known as her husband (e.g., Sally's John), again denying him a position as head of the household.[9]

That black men were reduced to a subordinate status in the family is quite true. That they abdicated their responsibility to their families probably highlights the unusual—not the prosaic behavior of black men. Although somewhat unusual, for example, was the case of a black slave who, when his wife complained of the beating she had taken from the overseer, took her to a cave away from harm. He fixed it up for her to live in, he brought her food, he protected her. Three children were born in the cave and only with emancipation did the family come out to rejoin him.[10]

There are those who say that slavery prevented black men from coming to emotional maturity, that they were childlike, docile creatures who were viewed not as objects of fear or hatred but as a source of amusement.[11] In conflict with this view is the observation that:

In spite of all attempts to crush it, the slave had a will of his own, which was actively, as well as passively, opposed to the master's. And it is this stubborn and rebellious will— tragic, heroic, defeated or triumphant—that, more than all else . . . haunted the master, frustrating his designs by a ceaseless though perhaps invisible countermining. . . . The slave expresses his hatred of enslavement and his contempt for his enslaver in less subtle and more open ways, such as taking what belonged to him, escaping or assisting others to escape, secretly learning or teaching others to read and write, secret meetings, suicide, infanticide, homicide, and the like.[12]

[5]John Hope Franklin, *From Slavery to Freedom,* New York: Random House, 1947.

[6]*Ibid.*

[7]E. Franklin Frazier, *The Negro Family in the United States,* Chicago: University of Chicago Press, 1939.

[8]Maurice Davie, *Negroes in American Society,* New York: McGraw-Hill, 1949, p. 207.

[9]Stanley M. Elkins, *Slavery: A Problem in American Institutional and Intellectual Life,* New York: Grosset and Dunlap, Inc., 1963, p. 130.

[10]B. A. Botkin, *Lay My Burden Down,* Chicago: University of Chicago Press, 1945, pp. 179–80.

[11]Elkins, *op. cit.,* p. 128.

[12]Botkin, *op. cit.,* pp. 137–38.

In addition to this covert resistance the so-called "docile" slave put together a number of elaborate conspiracies and insurrections. According to Aptheker, over 250 slave revolts were planned.[13] After slavery, however, the black male continued to encounter assaults on his manhood. In every aspect of his life, white America has tried to subjugate him. The historical literature, for instance, suggests that Jim Crow was directed more at the black male than the black female.[14] Black women, in a very limited way, were allowed more freedom, suffered less discrimination and were provided more opportunities than black men.

The structural barriers to black manhood were great. In a capitalistic society, being able to provide basic life satisfactions is inextricably interwoven with manhood. It is the opportunity to provide for his family, both individually and collectively, which has been denied the black man. After emancipation, the economic role of the black woman was strengthened as blacks left the rural areas and migrated to the cities, where it was difficult for black men to obtain employment. Although they had previously held jobs as skilled craftsmen, carpenters, etc., they were forced out of these occupations by a coalition of white workers and capitalists. In some instances they found employment only as strike-breakers.[15]

Through systematically denying black men an opportunity to work, white America has thrust the black woman into the role of family provider. This pattern of female-headed families has been reinforced by the marginal economic position of the black male. The jobs available to him lack the security and income necessary to maintain a household and in some cases are simply not available. Additionally, certain jobs performed by black men (e.g., waiter, cook, dishwasher, teacher, or social worker) often carry a connotation in American society as being woman's work.[16]

Economically destitute black families may be forced into a welfare system where it makes "sense" in terms of daily economic security for black men to leave their families. An example is this black woman who refused to permit her husband back into the family after he got a job. She said:

Not me! With him away I've got security. I know when my welfare check is coming and I know I can take him to court if he doesn't pay me child support. But as soon as he comes back in, then I don't know if he's going to keep his job; or if he's going to start acting up and staying out drinking and spending his pay away from home. This way I might be poor, but at least I know how much I got.[17]

White society has placed the black man in a tenuous position where manhood has been difficult to achieve. Black men have been lynched and brutalized in their attempts to retain their manhood. They have suffered from the cruelest assault on mankind that the world has ever known. For black men in this society it is not so much a matter of acquiring manhood as a struggle to feel it their own. As a pair of black psychiatrists comment:

Whereas the white man regards his manhood as an ordained right, the Black man is engaged in a never-ending battle for its possession. For the Black man, attaining any portion of manhood is an active process. He must penetrate barriers and overcome opposition in order to assume a masculine posture. For the inner psychological obstacles to manhood are never so formidable as the impediments woven into American society.[18]

After placing these obstacles to manhood in the black man's way, white America then has its ideology bearers, the social scientists, who falsely indict him for his lack of manhood. There are various sociological and psychological studies which purport to show how black males are demasculinized, in fact may be latent homosexuals. The reason they cite is that black males reared in female-centered households are more likely to acquire feminine characteristics because there is no consistent adult male model or image to shape

[13]Herbert Aptheker, *American Negro Slave Revolts,* New York: International Publishers, 1963.

[14]C. Vann Woodward, *The Strange Career of Jim Crow,* New York: Oxford University Press, 1966.

[15]C. F. Pierre Van Der Berghe, *Race and Racism,* New York: John Wiley, 1967.

[16]Harold Proshansky and Peggy Newton, "The Nature and Meaning of Negro Self-Identity," in *Social Class, Race, and Psychological Development,* Martin Deutsch et al., eds., New York: Holt, Rinehart and Winston, 1968.

[17]William Yancey, Vanderbilt University, personal communication, 1971.

[18]William H. Grier and Price M. Cobbs, *Black Rage,* New York: Basic Books, 1968, p. 49.

their personalities.[19] One sociologist stated that since black males are unable to enact the masculine role, they tend to cultivate their personalities. In this respect they resemble women who use their personalities to compensate for their inferior status in relation to men.[20]

If the above reasoning seems weak and unsubstantiated, other studies of black emasculation are equally feeble. Much of this supposition of the effeminate character of black men is based on their scores on the Minnesota Multiphasic Inventory Test (MMPI), a psychological instrument that asks the subject the applicability to himself of over five hundred simple statements. Black males score higher than white males on a measure of femininity. As an indicator of their femininity, the researchers cite the fact that black men more often agree with such feminine choices as "I would like to be a singer" and "I think I feel more intensely than most people do."[21]

This is the kind of evidence that white society has marshalled to prove the feminization of the black male. The only thing this demonstrates is that white standards cannot always be used in evaluating black behavior. Black people live in another environment, with different ways of thinking, acting and believing than the white, middle-class world. Singers such as James Brown represent successful role models in the black community. Black male youth aspire to be singers because this appears to be a means to success in this country—not because they are more feminine than white males. Additionally, music is an integral part of black culture.

One can easily challenge the theory that black males cannot learn the masculine role in father-absent homes. Black people are aware—if whites are not—that in female-headed households in the black community, there is seldom one where adult males are totally absent. A man of some kind is usually around. He may be a boyfriend, an uncle or just the neighborhood bookie. Even if these men do not assume a central family role, the black child may use them as a model for masculine behavior.[22]

Furthermore, men are not the only ones who teach boys about masculinity. Sex roles can also be learned by internalizing the culturally determined expectations of these roles. Consequently, black mothers can spell out the role requirements for their fatherless sons. They can symbolically communicate to him the way that men act. He will be shown the way men cross their legs, how they carry their books, the way they walk, etc. Through the culture's highly developed system of rewards for typical male behavior and punishment for signs of femininity, the black male child learns to identify with the culturally defined, stereotyped role of male.[23]

Black males are put in the psychological trick-bag of being "damned if they do, damned if they don't." If they acted effeminate they would be considered effeminate. Because they act like real men, they are charged with an exaggeration of normal masculine behavior to compensate for, or disguise, their femininity. The psychologists ignore one of their own tenets in this case: if men define situations as real, then they are real in their consequences.[24] If men define their behavior as masculine, for all practical purposes it becomes masculine to them. For black men, masculinity is the way they act. White America's definition of masculinity is of little importance to them.

The myth of the black matriarchy is accompanied by the falsehood that the modal black father has abdicated his paternal responsibilities. That this is untrue is confirmed in a study by Schulz which found that most black men assume a very responsible quasi-father role for their women and her children. Black men, however, have to spend a large part of their lives bargaining for a familial relationship, the major impediment being a limited income that cannot equal the combined resources of their present job plus their woman's welfare check. These men, who are not officially father or husband, play a more supportive role than is generally acknowledged.[25]

While some black men relinquish their paternal role functions, most black men perform ably in that role, considering the circumstances

[19]Thomas Pettigrew, *A Profile of the Negro American,* Princeton, New Jersey: D. Van Nostrand Company, 1964, pp. 17–22.

[20]E. Franklin Frazier, *Black Bourgeoisie,* New York: Crowell-Collier Publishing Co., 1962, p. 182.

[21]J. E. Hollanson and G. Calder, "Negro-White Differences on the MMPI," *Journal of Clinical Psychology,* 1960, pp. 32–33.

[22]Ulf Hannerz, "The Roots of Black Manhood," *Transaction,* October, 1969, p. 16.

[23]David Lynn, "The Process of Learning Parental and Sex Role Identification," *Marriage and Family Living,* 28, November, 1966, pp. 466–570.

[24]C. F. W. I. Thomas and Florence Znaniecki, *The Polish Peasant in Europe and America,* New York: Alfred A. Knopf, 1927.

[25]David Schulz, "The Role of the Boyfriend in Lower Class Negro Life," in *The Family Life of Black People.* Charles \ Willie, ed., Columbus, Ohio: Charles E. Merrill, 1970, pp. 231–46.

under which black families must live. Typical of the black father's concern for his children is this man's statement:

My youngest boy is seven. All my kids are in school. I try to instill in their minds that the only sound way to succeed is by laying a good foundation of learning and then to get actual experience. I hope to be able to see them all through college. I own property where I live and have a few dollars in the bank. I own a car, too. My greatest ambition is to see my children come along and keep this cleaning and pressing business of mine going, or else get into something they like better.[26]

That many black fathers never realize their aspirations for their children can be attributed to America's racist social structure. Instead, black women are charged with complicity with white men to subordinate the black male to his lowly position. Contrary to this assumption, one finds that when the Afro-American male was subjected to such oppression, the black woman was left without protection and was used—and is still being used—as a scapegoat for all the oppression that the system of white racism has perpetrated on black men. The system found it functional to enslave and exploit them and did so without the consent, tacit or otherwise, of black women. Moreover, while black men may be subjected to all sorts of dehumanizing practices, they still have others below them—black women.[27]

Nevertheless, black women have had a variety of responses to the plight of black men. Some black women accepted the prevailing image of manhood and womanhood that depicted black men as shiftless and lazy if they did not secure employment and support their families as they ought to. There are reported instances of the black male ceasing to provide any economic support for the family and having his wife withdraw her commitment from him and from the marriage.[28] Other black women have ambivalent

feelings about black men and remember painful experiences with them. They believe that black men do not fully appreciate the role of black women in the survival of the black race. Some even internalize white society's low regard for black men but are bothered by their appraisals.[29]

These attitudes on the part of black women are understandable. There are many conflicts between black men and women which are a result of their oppressed condition. Under a system of domestic colonialism, the oppressed peoples turn their frustrations, their wrath, toward each other rather than their oppressor.[30] Being constantly confronted with problems of survival, blacks become more psychologically abusive toward their spouses than they would under other circumstances.

On the other hand some black women are very supportive of their men. As Hare notes, black women realize that they must encourage the black man and lay as much groundwork for black liberation as he will let her lay. She realizes that it is necessary to be patient with black men whenever they engage in symbolic assertions of manliness. Her role is to assist strongly but not dominate.[31] Black women, however, may not realize the contradiction between their desire for a comfortable standard of living and wanting the black man to exercise his masculinity. The expression of black masculinity can frequently be met with the harshest punishment white society can muster. Physical punishment, and economic deprivation, are frequently the white response to expressions of black manliness.

Whatever the role of the black woman, she realizes that the mythical castrated black male can rarely be dominated. In the dating situation, he has the upper hand because of the shortage of black men in the society. The black woman, if she wants a black man, frequently has to accept the relationship on male terms. If she does not give in to his demands, there are always other women who will. The henpecked black husband is usually a mythical figure. That black wives carry a slightly

[26]St. Clair Drake and Horace Cayton, *Black Metropolis,* Chicago: University of Chicago Press, 1945, p. 665.

[27]Frances Beal, "Double Jeopardy: To Be Black and Female," *New Generation,* 51, Fall 1969, pp. 23–28.

[28]Lee Rainwater, "Crucible of Identity: The Negro Lower Class Negro Life," in *The Family Life of Black People,* Charles V.

[29]Nathan and Julia Hare, "Black Women 1970," *Transaction,* 8, November, 1970, pp. 66–67.

[30]C. F. Frantz Fanon, *The Wretched of the Earth,* New York: Grove Press, 1966.

[31]Hare, *Loc. cit.*

larger share of the housework than white wives,[32] while not a particularly desirable situation, effectively dispels any notion of the black husband as domestic servant.

It was mentioned earlier that the attempt to emasculate the black male was motivated by the fear of his sexual power. As Bernard has stated, "the white world's insistence on keeping Negro men walled up in the 'concentration camp' was motivated in large part by its fear of their sexuality."[33] One needs a deep understanding of the importance of sex in the United States in order to see the interrelationship of sex and racism in American society. In a society where white sexuality has been repressed, the imagined sexual power of the black male poses a serious threat. According to Hernton:

There is in the psyche of the racist an inordinate disposition for sexual atrocity. He sees in the Negro the essence of his own sexuality, that is, those qualities that he wishes for but fears he does not possess. Symbolically, the Negro at once affirms and negates the white man's sense of sexual security. . . . Contrary to what is claimed, it is not the white woman who is dear to the racist. It is not even the black woman toward whom his real sexual rage is directed. It is the black man who is sacred to the racist. And this is why he must castrate him.[34]

Whether the white woman is dear to the racist is debatable. It certainly appears that he is concerned about preserving the purity of white womanhood. Since 1698 social censure and severe penalties were reserved for the association of black men and white women.[35] The evidence for these suppositions is voluminous, and includes the accusations by lynch mobs that the black man raped or threatened to rape the white woman, the white South's obsession with the purity of white womanhood, the literal castration of black men for centuries, and the death of Emmet Till, who was killed for looking at a white woman. As Fanon comments, the white man fears that the black man will "introduce his daughter into a sexual universe for which the father does not have the key, the weapons, or the attributes."[36]

The question might be posed: what is the empirical basis of black male sexual superiority? Contrary to prevailing folklore, it is not the size of his genitalia. According to the Kinsey Institute, the majority of both white and black penises measured in their sample were less than or equal to four and a half inches in the flaccid state and less than or equal to seven inches in the erect state.[37] However, three times as many black males had penises larger than seven inches in length. The Masters and Johnson Report indicates no particular relationship between penis size and sexual satisfaction except that induced by the psychological state of the female.[38]

What, then, can be said about the sexual abilities of white men and black men? First, it must be acknowledged that sexual attitudes and behavior are culturally determined, not inherent traits of a particular group. But—sex relations have a different nature and meaning to black people. Their sexual expression derives from the emphasis in the black culture on feeling, of releasing the natural functions of the body without artificiality or mechanical movements. In some circles this is called "soul" and may be found among peoples of African descent throughout the world.

This means that black men do not moderate their enthusiasm for sex relations as white men do. They do not have a history of suppressing the sexual expression of the majority of their women while singling out a segment of the female population for premarital and extramarital adventures. This lack of a double standard of sexual conduct has also unleashed the sexual expression of black women. Those black women who have sexual hangups acquired them through acculturation of the puritanical values of white society.

The difference between black men and white men in sexual responses may be under-

[32]Robert O. Blood, Jr. and Donald M. Wofe, "Negro-White Difference in Blue Collar Marriages in a Northern Metropolis," Social Forces, 48, September, 1969, pp. 59–63.

[33]Bernard, op. cit., p. 75.

[34]Calvin Hernton, Sex and Racism in America, Garden City, New York: Doubleday, 1965, pp. 111–12.

[35]Frazier, The Negro Family in the United States, op. cit., pp. 50–51.

[36]Frantz Fanon, Black Skin, White Masks, New York: Grove Press, 1967, p. 163.

[37]Allan Bell, Black Sexuality: Fact and Fancy, a paper, Black America Series, Indiana University, Bloomington, Indiana, 1968.

[38]William Masters and Virginia Johnson, Human Sexual Response, Boston: Little, Brown and Co., 1966.

stood by realizing that for white men sex has to be fitted into time that is not devoted to building the technological society, whereas for black men it is a natural function, a way of life. The white man, when confronted with his woman's state of sexual readiness, may say business first, pleasure later. The black man when shown the black woman's state of sexual excitation manages to take care of both the business and the pleasure. If one is left unfinished, it is unlikely that the black woman is left wanting.

It is this trait of the black male that white society would prefer to label sexual immorality. The historical evidence reveals, however, that the white man's moral code has seldom been consistent with his actual behavior. The real issue here is one of power. In a society where women are regarded as a kind of sexual property, the white male tries to ensure that he will not have to compete with black men on an equal basis for any woman. Not only may the white male experience guilt over his possession of black womanhood but he fears that as the black man attains bedroom equality he will gain political and economic equality as well.

Sexual fears, however, do not totally explain the attempted castration of black men. White society realizes quite well that it is the men of an oppressed group that form the vanguard, the bulwark, of any liberation struggle. By perpetrating the myth of the impotent black male on the consciousness of black and white people, they are engaging in wishful thinking. It is patently clear that men such as Nat Turner, Denmark Vesey, Frederick Douglass and Malcolm X were not impotent eunuchs. The task of black liberation has been carried out by black men from time immemorial. While black women have been magnificently supportive, it is black men who have joined the battle.

Sexism and the Black Male

Barbara Sizemore

The charge of sexism is heard as frequently as the charge of racism. Many Blacks think that sexism concerns only whites. This article, however, focuses on sexism among Black males. The author is critical of many Black nationalist leaders in their treatment of women within their movements. She further provides a list of goals for Black women within the Black Struggle.

Sexism is the belief that one sex is superior to another. In our society the value of male superiority is held. Women are considered inferiors, and are relegated to the lowest rungs on economic and social ladders. Last to be hired, first fired, they are discriminated against in pay, hiring and by laws.

Male superiority is an institutional value, and Wheelis suggests a conceptualization which offers the opportunity to examine alternate sets of values at the same time. He explains that there are institutional values and instrumental values. Institutional values are generally regarded as more important than instrumental values but he says that "any value which organizes, directs and integrates other values, in respect to those other values, is higher."[1]

Wheelis points out that institutional values derive from the activities associated with myth, mores and status. The choice involved purports to be final. Such values do not refer to, but transcend, the evidence at hand. "They claim absolute status and immunity to change, but are, in fact, relative to the culture that supports them: Christian sacraments are without validity in India,

[1]Allen Wheelis, *The Quest for Identity*, N.Y.: Norton, 1958, p. 182.

Abridged from *The Black Scholar* 4 (March–April 1973): 2–11. © 1973 by the Black World Foundation. Reprinted by permission.

Footnotes have been renumbered.

and suttee has achieved no validity in the western world. The final authority of such values is force."[2] Instrumental values are derived from tool-using, observation and experimentation. They are temporal, matter-of-fact and secular. According to this definition, equality, liberty, fraternity and justice would be instrumental values. Instrumental values do not transcend the evidence at hand, but derive from progressively refined attention to such evidence. They possess transcultural validity.

They are, however, relative to the state of empirical knowledge at any given time, and change as that knowledge is enlarged. The final authority of such values is reason.[3]

The institutional values of the American society are: male superiority, white European superiority and the superiority of people with money. These values are derived from myths, mores and status and transcend the evidence at hand. Their final authority is force. From these values an ascribed status can be assigned to each individual. Arranged on a continuum, the highest order human being would be the white man of European descent with money. The lowest order human being in the male universe is the black man with no money. The highest order human being in the female universe is the white woman with money, and the lowest order human being in the social order is the black woman with no money. . . .

Some black spokesmen show little awareness of the plight of black women in America. Those which have adopted capitalist models have relegated women to the loser group. Capitalism is based on a contriently interdependent competitive model wherein when A wins B loses. A represents the groups with power and B stands for those with no power. Inherent in the model are always losers. If men are A and women are B, when men win women lose. Such a model has been embraced by the Nation of Islam. In his *Message to the Blackman in America* Elijah Muhammad[4] openly states that women are property. He says "The woman is man's field to produce his nation." He speaks of women as things,

comparable to crops and children with great needs for protection and control. He says:

Is not your woman more valuable than the crop of corn, that crop of cotton, that crop of cabbage, potatoes, beans, tomatoes? How much more valuable is your woman than these crops, that you should keep the enemies from destroying the crops. Yet you are not careful about your women.

Further along he argues that the first step is the control and protection of women in order to return to the land with a thorough knowledge of "our own" selves. He says:

Our women are allowed to walk or ride the streets all night long, with any strange men they desire. They are allowed to frequent any tavern or dance hall they like, wherever they like. They are allowed to fill our homes with children other than our own. Children that are often fathered by the very devil himself.

He orders the men of the Nation to put the women under guard, to keep them imprisoned in order to protect and control them. Inherent in the *Message* is the warning that women are evil and given to sin while men are noble and given to righteousness.

The story of the beginning in *Message* differs little from that of Christianity as far as women are concerned. Mr. Muhammad sees women as the weaker part of man. He perpetrates the untruth that black women make higher salaries than black men and he denigrates the black woman by seeing her as immoral and ignorant.

In the section on "Program and Position," Mr. Muhammad says that the Muslims want freedom, full and complete; justice under the law applied equally to all regardless of creed, class or color and equality of opportunity. None of these are applied to women. Over and over in *Message* women are mentioned only in terms of protection. It is easier to protect women if they are not free. Kept at home in semi-purdah, men do not need to confront the dangerous white man over her safety. To become good Muslims, black women must

[2]*Ibid.*, p. 179.
[3]*Ibid.*
[4]Elijah Muhammad, *Message to the Black Man in America,* Chicago: Muhammad Mosque of Islam #2, 1965, p. 58.

become chattel once again, with good and loving masters, to be sure, but chattel nevertheless.

Imamu Baraka states seven values: Umoja, Kujichagulia, Ujima, Ujamaa, Nia, Kuumba and Imani.[5] However, he fails to address himself to the issue of black female humanity. The small pamphlet, *Mwanamke Mwananchi,* outlines the Baraka program for the nationalist woman. While it says that the nationalist roles for men and women does not mean that one is superior or inferior to the other but complementary to the whole, the program specifies submissiveness as a fundamental and natural female trait. It says:

Nature has made women submissive—she must submit to man's creation in order for it to exist.[6]

The nationalist woman cannot create or initiate. Her main life's goal is to inspire and encourage man and his children.

Sisters in this movement must beg for permission to speak and function as servants to men, their masters and leaders, as teachers and nurses. Their position is similar to that of the sisters in the Nation of Islam. When Baraka is the guiding spirit of national conferences only widows and wives of black martyrs such as Malcolm X and Martin Luther King, Jr., and Queen Mother Moore can participate. Other women are excluded. In the recent National Black Political Convention, black women politicians were often ignored and Shirley Chisholm failed to get the support of the convention even though some blacks were backing her.

Other black men generally make superhuman demands of black women, even those who reject Sapphire. George Jackson in *Soledad Brother* wrote the following to Angela Davis:

The blacks of slave society, U.S.A., have always been a matriarchal subsociety. The implication is clear, black mama is going to have to put a sword in that brother's hand and stop that "Be a good boy" shit. Channel his spirit instead of break it, or help to break it, I should say. . . . All of the sisters I've ever known personally and through other brothers'

accounts begged and bullied us to look for jobs instead of being satisfied with the candy-stick take. The strongest impetus a man will ever have, in an individual sense, will come from a woman he admires.[7]

The question to be answered is, "What does the father do?" In most societies there are rituals or *rites de passage* which define manhood. Certain tasks must be performed in order to enter the ranks of warriors. These are designed by men based on their cultural values. What is the responsibility of black men toward the construction of these rituals? What is their responsibility in the training? Can women confer manhood?

Later, however, in another letter, George Jackson said that he fully understood that the role of the black woman should be the very same as the man's. He said that there was very little difference between man and woman intellectually and that the differences we see in bourgeois society are all conditioned and artificial. He acknowledged the fact that black women had to assume the responsibility of socialization through default and insisted on socializing black men to be warriors.

There is very little in the literature to describe these rites and rituals. The generally accepted argument is that the socialization of the child is the female responsibility. Men want none of it. Yet, world wide, the values of a society emanate from male expression and aggression. Sékou Touré defines culture as the creative action springing from a universal imperative and culture, which in its reflection subject and effect, both constitute universal realities. As the expression of the relationship between man and society, between man, society and nature, culture poses in the most pressing terms the problem of the dialectic of the general and the particular. Culture is an expression in particular, specific forms, of a general problem—that of the relationships linking man to his environment.[8]

If black boys are to be socialized as warriors, black men must enter into the dialogue which will define the relationships linking black men to their environment and their land.

Recently, the argument in the black commu-

[5]Imamu Ameer Baraka, "A Black Value System," *The Black Scholar,* November, 1969, pp. 54–60.

[6]*Mwanamke Mwananchi* (The Nationalist Woman) by Numininas of Committee for Unified New Ark, Newark, N.J.: 1971, p. 7.

[7]George Jackson, *Soledad Brother,* N.Y.: A Bantam Book, 1970, p. 217.

[8]Sékou Touré,"A Dialectical Approach to Culture," *The Black Scholar,* November, 1969, p. 13.

nity over "Sweetback" reflected the posture of many black men vis-a-vis black womanhood. Some black men felt that the picture denigrated black women, depicting them as whorish, licentious, immoral and evil. Others felt that the picture was real and reflected the way it "tis" in the black community. The picture was real to the extent that black women are held to be the lowest order human beings in the universe, that women in general are held to be sinful and immoral, that women are seen as things to be used by men. This is a true reflection of the American social order's ascription for women. The picture was unreal to the extent that it reflected the black prostitute as stupid and unintelligent. The black prostitute, as most black men know, is one of the most clever and resourceful individuals in the black community often outwitting her pimp, which feat takes some doing. The black prostitute seldom gives away anything much less her main commodity. The first time Sweetback climbed onto the first black prostitute he lost his freedom to a $300 reward from the local white police.

"Sweetback" also brought into clearer focus the relationship between black men and white women which both Eldridge Cleaver and Frantz Fanon discussed. Many black leaders are married to white women. What does it mean when a black man spurns his own women for outsiders? How can a black man lead black women to a black nation with white women as queens? What does this say to black women?

Frantz Fanon, who himself was married to a white woman, observed that the black man wants to be like the white man. There is only one destiny, and it is white. Having admitted the unarguable superiority of the white man, all his efforts are aimed at achieving his existence.[9]

Fortunately, Fanon's position changed when he joined the FLN of Algeria. Other Africans who searched for their manhood in the white womb are Leopold Senghor, Eduardo Mondlane and Amilcar Cabral. Americans married to whites are: James Farmer, Edward Brooke, Harry Belafonte, John A. Williams, Nathan Wright, James Forman, Julius Lester, Sam Greenlee.

Everyday Black brothers blame women for their problems many times because they see themselves as helpless to improve the situation.

One brother who had deserted his six-month pregnant wife and twenty-two month old son told the white marriage counselor, assigned to him by the divorce court, that his problem was his mother-in-law who found out about his extra-marital relationships and told his wife. He argued that everything would have been all right if his wife had remained ignorant. This brother could not deal with the real fact that he had married the sister so she would finance his last year at college and now that he was graduated he didn't need her any longer. He couldn't deal with the responsibilities, obligations and burdens that the black family imposed upon his individual narcissistic desires and aspirations.

Another brother in prison at Jackson, Michigan wrote the following in a letter:

The black woman sees the black man dependent upon the white male—the white male is the ruler, he is independent and it is he who controls education in America. The educational institutions in America teaches thoughts coming from the mind of the white male, the conquerors and our former slavemasters. The docile black male slave after being taught in these schools which was designed to push white rule has an effeminate effect on the black male. The conqueror has it so that more black women are trained in his school than black males—it is our woman or the woman of any nation that give the children their first teaching—actually the women spend the most time with the youth.[10]

This brother in prison writes that the black woman has the ideas of the white male conquerors in her mind so that the black man doesn't have his own ideas in his own black woman's mind. When the black woman teaches her son, she teaches him ideas taught her by the white male further making a sissy out of him, making him look up to the white male thinker.

This prisoner is brainwashed with the white man's myths about black women and though unable to see the fallacy in his thinking he writes later:

To destroy the oneness between the black man and the black woman by splitting their

[9]Frantz Fanon, *Black Skin, White Masks*, N.Y.: Grove Press, Inc., 1967, pp. 9–14.

[10]Letter written to Barbara A. Sizemore from Lee X Smith, April, 1972.

family life and their man and woman relationship is like the Europeans fission method of dividing the proton from the electron in the atom. The black man and the black woman need an ideology that will unite them together as concrete as a brick wall and create a beautiful energetic community without loose moral corruption and social pollution—together with a stronger family is the key.

What the brother in prison failed to see was the necessity for respect and parity between man and woman for such a unity.

Essie Branch caused controversy in the black community when she wrote about a black family in *My Name is Arnold.* Mrs. Branch listened to conversations of black eight-year-olds about their families in a Chicago housing project. Her book is a composite of many childrens' conversations for the construction of one black family. She depicts a black daddy, Willie D., in the following description given by an eight-year-old:

I have a daddy named Willie D. Porter. He live on the west side. Somedays he comes by to see us and always cusses and make Mama cry. I sure don't love him. Willie D. is a motherfucker. [11]

Ironically, some of the black men who felt that "Sweetback" was a piece of the real black community didn't feel the same about Willie D. Many black men empathize with the pimp, the stud and the deserter. This empathy impedes the implementation of UMOJA.

Black men who are labeled intellectuals often defend the position because they too may have deserted a family and left a black sister to socialize sons alone. More study needs to be carried on in this area to reconcile the differing concepts of masculinity and Umoja.

Black women cannot allow men to dominate completely the definitions of black womanhood, UMOJA and UJAMAA. Politicizing of women is necessary for thinking about their problems and resolutions. This paper has discussed sexism and the black male but black females have seldom been aggressive in demanding their rights and, as

Shirley Chisholm stated in *Unbought and Unbossed,* have cooperated in their own enslavement. She says:

They submitted to oppression, and even condoned it. But women are becoming aware, as blacks did, that they can have equal treatment if they will fight for it, and they are starting to organize. To do it, they have to dare the sanctions that society imposes on anyone who breaks with its traditions. This is hard, and especially hard for women, who are taught not to rebel from infancy, from the time they are first wrapped in pink blankets, the color of their caste. Another disability is that women have been programmed to be dependent on men. They seldom have economic freedom enough to let them be free in more significant ways, at least until they become widows and most of their lives are behind them. [12]

In view of the facts presented in this analysis and the myths perpetrated by the white European man with money, the following recommendations are offered for the survival and liberation of black people in America.

There are more black women than men in the society. Research should be conducted to find out where the men are. There has been research to indicate that the black men are committing suicide, [13] that 30 percent of the prison population is black, [14] that more black men are killed in Vietnam than their percentage of the soldier population warrants, and that more black men are killed by police than white men.

Secondly, since black women outnumber black men and are 2.2 years older on the average, an increase in illegitimacy as defined by the larger culture and in the number of female-headed households should be anticipated. Additionally, as the ratio of white men to white women declines, more white women from this surplus population will become available for black men. Blacks should drive for increased opportunities for women, equal salaries for female occupations, equal pension rights and laws for women and an

[11]Essie Branch, *My Name is Arnold,* Chicago: DuSable Museum of Negro History, 1971, p. 17.

[12]Shirley Chisholm, *Unbought and Unbossed,* Boston: Houghton Mifflin Co., 1970, p. 164.

[13]Herbert Hendin, *Black Suicide,* N.Y.: Harper Colophon Books, 1969.

[14]Angela Y. Davis, *If They Come in the Morning,* N.Y.: Third Press, 1971.

increase in the number of women in higher educational institutions and the higher professions. Females should be encouraged to go into dentistry, medicine and law. More black men should be prepared in these professions also. The number of blacks in colleges is declining. As Jacquelyne Jackson has recommended this trend needs to be studied. Increased educational opportunities must be created by the black community to assure higher education to blacks, both male and female. Alternative institutions for education must be created and implemented as a guarantee.

The declining sex ratio and the increase in mixed marriages especially between black men and white women should force many women into untenable positions unless abortion is given as a right. No woman should be forced into 21 years of child care alone as long as men have the freedom to choose to care or not to care for their children. Black women should (1) press for birth control and abortion rights (2) exact sanctions against black men and women who desert and abandon their families (3) deny leadership roles to black men and women married to whites and (4) refuse legitimation to black leaders who are not accountable to the black poor.

Black women should begin an active search for new alternative institutions for child care and rearing to accommodate the needs of mothers. More cooperative models must be implemented for black women to work together. To be certain sisters now embracing the semi-purdah conditions of the Nation of Islam, the Spirit House Movers and the Republic of New Africa may be opposed, but, even so, the problems of motherhood and child care are universal and should transcend ideological differences.

Black women must unite to influence other black women in leadership positions to attend to the survival needs of the black community before those of other communities. Sisters must understand that they need the support of other black women in order to maintain their political clout. Sanctions applied against black leaders must work toward unity rather than permanent cleavage, understanding fully the dangers of divide and conquer and the benefit from such tactics to the white European man with money. Solutions to the problem of female oppression need not be made at the expense of black men nor in such a way as to be a threat.

But, black women must exact more accountability from black men in response to their problems by demanding parity at the decision-making table of organizations and associations designed to promote survival and achieve liberation, for black men must work toward liberation through means which do not oppress and exploit women. All black people are needed in the struggle. The struggle will define the role. Black women must be ready to accept the responsibility which parity grants. If soldiers are needed in the struggle, black women must be ready and willing to serve.

Fanon describes this phenomenon as it manifested itself in the liberation of the Algerian woman. He said:

The women in Algeria, from 1955, began to have models. In Algerian society stories were told of women who in even greater number suffered death and imprisonment in order that an independent Algeria might be born. It was these militant women who constituted the points of reference around which the imagination of Algerian feminine society was to be stirred to the boiling point. The women-for-marriage progressively disappeared, and gave way to the woman-for-action. The young girl was replaced by the militant, the woman by the sister.[15]

The new militancy should be shared with men in the struggle and a new socialization process should develop for child rearing.

Job opportunities and alternative institutions must be designed for teenage youth, both male and female. Men must be recruited into the black community as surrogate fathers; maybe randomly assigned to female-headed households to induct young men into manhood through *rites de passage* and to offer them protection and guidance during the crucial years of adolescence so needed now because of the increase in the drug traffic in the black community.

Capitalistic models should be pursued only from promotively interdependent cooperative approaches which assure benefits for everyone in the black community. The contriently interdepen-

[15]Frantz Fanon, *A Dying Colonialism,* N.Y.: Grove Press, Inc., 1965, pp. 107–08.

dent competitive model assures losers and promotes ''divide and conquer.''

Frederick Douglass, long ago, said that power concedes nothing without a demand. Black women must remember that the largest single group in support of male superiority is women. Therefore, the fight must begin there . . . with ourselves.

But Where Are the Men?

Jacquelyne Jackson

There is a significant shortage of Black males in relation to Black females in our society. The author is concerned with the social implications of this trend for Black male/female relationships, and especially for the Black family. She points out that while the shortage is increasing, there are a number of regions where Black males outnumber Black females. She suggests ways to counteract this shortage.

The question ''But where are the males?'' refers inevitably to that of the sex ratio (i.e., the number of males per every one hundred females). One highly significant gap in almost all contemporary scientific, pseudo-scientific, and ideological concerns about black women—and especially about black female household heads—is that of the failure to consider the implications of the sex ratio itself. This gap can be attributed directly to the general tendency of social scientists and social policymakers to ignore the realities of the prevailing black sex ratios and concomitant factors, such as the aforenoted tendency of white females to seek black mates.

Such a gap is particularly deplorable in the social sciences, inasmuch as Oliver C. Cox[1]

focused specific attention upon sex ratios and their implications at least as early as 1940. For present purposes, it is imperative to note that Cox indicated quite clearly the following:

1. Differences in the marital status of persons in different areas and communities may be due to differences in the ratio of marriageable men to women;[2]

2. The racial sex ratio varies considerably in the different regional divisions of the United States;[3]

3. The percentage of Negro females married in cities is particularly sensitive to changes in the sex ratio, while the percentage of males married seems to respond almost not at all.[4]

Thus, as the black sex ratio rose, the percentage of black females who were married rose. As that sex ratio declined, so did the percentage of married black females.

Since 1940, the black sex ratio has actually worsened, if judged at least from the perspective of black females. Yet most contemporary literature is written as if there were one black male for each black female. That literature almost always fails to inquire about male availability levels for black

---

[1] Oliver C. Cox, "Sex Ratio and Marital Status Among Negroes," *American Sociological Review,* 5:937–947, 1940. Incidentally, no opportunity should be lost in pointing out anew that the significant contributions of Dr. Cox to American sociology, and particularly those valuable in knowing and understanding blacks, have been largely ignored by the white, male-dominated American sociological establishment. At the 1971 annual meeting of the American Sociological Association, however, largely through the efforts of the Caucus of Black Sociologists, and Dr. James E. Conyers especially, the first

DuBois-Johnson-Frazier Award was conferred upon Dr. Cox in recognition of such contributions. Earlier, the first annual DuBois Award established by the Association of Social and Behavioral Scientists (founded in 1935) was given to Dr. Cox in recognition of his distinguished achievements.

[2] *Ibid.,* p. 937.
[3] *Ibid.*
[4] *Ibid.,* p. 938.

Abridged from *The Black Scholar* 4 (December 1971), 34–41. © 1971 by the Black World Foundation. Reprinted by permission.   Footnotes have been renumbered.

females. Probably the most glaring example is *The Moynihan Report*.[5] Moynihan tended to assume that male unemployment was the critical factor affecting the proportion of female-headed households among blacks, but he failed miserably in dealing with the actual supply of black males for black females.

Census data clearly reveal that females have been excessive in the black population of the United States since at least 1850, or a period of more than 120 years. In 1850, the black sex ratio was 99.1, rising slightly to 99.6 in 1860, but declining to 96.2 in 1870. In 1880, it was 97.8; in 1890, 99.5; in 1900, 98.6; in 1910, 98.9; and in 1920, 99.2. Since 1920, the black sex ratio has decreased consistently, from 97.0 in 1930, to 95.0 in 1940, to 94.3 in 1950, to 93.3 in 1960, and, in 1970 to 90.8, or approximately 91 black males for every 100 black females. Thus, for the past 50 years, black men have been becoming scarcer and scarcer. It is not just the case that they are more likely to be missed in the Census counts, but that they are just not there.[6]

If no adjustment is made for age, at least 1,069,694 of the 11,885,595 black females in the population of the United States in 1970 would have been without available, monogamous mates. When age-adjusted and regional-adjusted data are presented, as shown in Table 1, the unadjusted pattern does not undergo any significant change. As can be seen in Table 1, in the United States as a whole, black females are not more numerous than black males only within one age group, that of 5 to 14 years. They are more numerous in all of the remaining age groupings, and especially so during female childbearing ages. The same is true of the geographical divisions, with one exception occurring in the West among the 15 to 24 year-old grouping.

It is relevant now to inquire about alternative familial forms developed in the absence of a sufficient supply of males. Two of those forms, unnecessarily and irrationally viewed as "deviant" by the American white subculture, are those of female-headed households and of illegitimacy. The nomenclature of "illegitimacy" is inappropriately applied to blacks, for any number of reasons, but the common usage of such a con-

Age (years)	U.S.	Northeast[2]	North Central[2]	South[2]	West[2]
Total, all ages	90.8	87.5	91.3	98.8	97.6
Under 5	99.3	100.7	100.0	90.8	97.6
5–14	100.4	100.7	99.8	100.5	100.3
15–24	93.0	87.1	90.1	94.5	105.6
25–34 primary	84.3	78.6	83.4	85.4	95.7
35–44	82.9	81.1	84.5	81.0	95.3
45–54	86.4	83.4	90.4	84.9	94.0
55–64	85.3	78.3	89.7	85.6	90.3
65 +	76.4	71.7	81.4	76.2	76.3

Table 1. Black Sex Ratios by Age and Geographical Location, 1970[1]

Geographical Location

1. Source of raw data: U.S. Department of Commerce/Bureau of the Census. *1970 Census of Population, Advance Report*, "General Population Characteristics, United States," PC(V2)-1. U.S. Department of Commerce, Washington, D.C., February, 1971.

2. Northwestern states include Maine, New Hampshire, Vermont, Massachusetts, Rhode Island, Connecticut, New York, New Jersey, and Pennsylvania; North Central includes Ohio, Indiana, Illinois, Michigan, Wisconsin, Minnesota, Iowa, Missouri, North Dakota, South Dakota, Nebraska, and Kansas; the South includes Delaware, Maryland, District of Columbia, Virginia, West Virginia, North Carolina, South Carolina, Georgia, Florida, Kentucky, Tennessee, Alabama, Mississippi, Arkansas, Louisiana, Oklahoma, and Texas; and the West encompasses Montana, Idaho, Wyoming, Colorado, New Mexico, Arizona, Utah, Nevada, Washington, Oregon, California, Alaska, and Hawaii.

(2) Northeastern

[5]Daniel P. Moynihan, *The Negro Family: A Case for National Action*, U.S. Government Printing Office, Washington, D.C.: 1965.

[6]It may be interesting to note that some discussions of this point have brought retorts that the males are there, but simply avoid being counted. The chief argument here is that

even if all of the black males throughout the United States were counted, the females would still remain excessive, due to a variety of reasons certainly warranting systematic investigation. Some, of course, are not there due to the unnecessarily high infant and childhood mortality rates especially affecting black males, while some others are dead, victimized by war and wanton killings.

cept does reflect a tendency of many whites to attempt to ''desexify'' blacks. It is quite important to add that the development of that term occurred at a time when white males exceeded white females in the United States as well. The application of the term was also grossly unfair to blacks who were already in the process of developing alternative familial forms in the absence of a sufficient supply of males, a condition not confronting whites until 1950.

The ''problem'' of female-headed households can only be perceived as a ''problem'' by those who act, again, as if there were identical supplies of males and females. When such is not the case, as it is clearly not in the case of blacks, then the phenomenon should be perceived as a rational alternative to an ineffective traditional system. It should be quite obvious that slavery is an insufficient factor to be used in explicating both illegitimacy and female-headed households, for, by the usual measures of family stability, as Frazier has noted, black family stability continued progressively throughout the latter half of the nineteenth century and up until about 1910.[7]

In fact, Census data show that in 1900 for persons 15+ years of age, there were no significant differences in marital statuses by race or by sex between black and white females and males. But, since then, as the black sex ratio has decreased, the marital statuses of black females, in particular, have also been affected, as Cox demonstrated.[8] The marital statuses of black females have been far more sensitive to that reducing sex ratio than have those of black males, which leads us into an exploration of one of the relationships which may exist between black sex ratios and familial patterns, specifically that of female-headed households.

As that sex ratio has decreased, the proportion of female-headed households among blacks has increased, suggesting thereby that a possible causative factor for the latter may be the former. If we examine available 1970 data on the black sex ratio and the proportion of female-headed households among blacks in each state and the District of Columbia, what will emerge will be a significant

inverse relationship between those two variables ($r = -.68$, $df = 49$, and $p > .001$). In other words, as shown in Table 2, there is a tendency for the proportion of female-headed households to increase as the supply of males decreases. Conversely, when the supply of males increases, the proportion of female-headed households decreases. For example, the excess of black males over black females is greatest in Hawaii, where the proportion of black female-headed households ranks quite low. In fact, only two states North Dakota and South Dakota rank lower than Hawaii in the proportion of female-headed households among blacks. On the other hand, the sex ratio is lowest in New York (85.9, or approximately 86 males per every 100 females), and 32.1 percent of black families within the state were headed by females in 1970, exceeded only by Massachusetts, where 34.3 percent of black families were female-headed.

Despite the fact that black females are excessive in the black population, that excessive phenomenon is not equitably distributed throughout the United States. In 19 states, black males outnumber females. Those states are Hawaii, Montana, North Dakota, Idaho, South Dakota, Utah, Alaska, Vermont, Maine, New Hampshire, Wyoming, Washington, Colorado, Rhode Island, Minnesota, Arizona, New Mexico, Nevada and Oregon—none are southern states. They are also states containing extremely minute proportions of aged (i.e., 65+ years) blacks, which suggests that they are probably less affected by the considerably shortened life expectancy rates of black males than is true of the remaining states. Thus, the proportion of widowed black females who may find it necessary to assume a status as household head is reduced.

This geographical disproportionment in the distribution of black females and males also has consequences for familial patterns in that, as indicated above and as evident in Table 2, black females are generally least likely to be heads of households where the sex ratio is the highest. Thus, it may be that black male geographical mobility has been significantly different from that of black females, suggesting thereby two different types of policy alternatives for those concerned about the proportion of black female-headed households. One implication may well be that greater geographical mobility could be encouraged among black females, especially those in

---

[7]E. Franklin Frazier, *The Negro Family in the United States*, University of Chicago Press, Chicago: 1939. Here, perhaps, it should be noted that, contrary to a number of interpretations of Frazier, Frazier did not characterize matriarchy as the *dominant* family type among blacks.

[8]Cox, *op. cit.*

State	Sex Ratio	% Female-Headed Families	Sex Ratio Rank[2]	% Female-Headed Families Rank[2]
Hawaii	192.6	7.1	1.0	3.0
Montana	169.2	24.2	2.0	16.0
North Dakota	160.3	2.9	3.0	1.0
Idaho	158.5	9.0	4.0	5.5
South Dakota	157.0	6.2	5.0	2.0
Utah	151.6	21.6	6.0	10.0
Alaska	147.3	7.8	7.0	4.0
Vermont	139.3	13.0	8.0	8.0
Maine	136.9	9.0	9.0	5.5
New Hampshire	130.4	9.9	10.0	7.0
Wyoming	114.2	13.2	11.0	9.0
Washington	113.0	23.1	12.0	12.0
Colorado	105.2	22.1	13.0	11.0
Rhode Island	102.5	31.7	14.0	49.0
Minnesota	102.4	28.5	15.0	36.5
Arizona	102.2	25.5	16.0	21.0
New Mexico	101.1	24.3	17.0	17.5
Nevada	100.8	23.6	18.0	13.0
Oregon	100.5	26.1	19.0	26.0
Kansas	97.9	27.2	20.0	29.0
Iowa	95.9	28.9	21.0	42.0
California	95.2	28.1	22.0	34.5
Virginia	94.7	23.7	23.0	14.0
Wisconsin	94.0	30.8	24.0	46.0
Michigan	93.6	25.7	25.5	22.5
Nebraska	93.6	30.5	25.5	45.0
Kentucky	93.0	27.9	27.0	33.0
Maryland	92.8	27.0	28.0	27.0
Indiana	92.7	24.7	29.5	19.0
Delaware	92.7	28.1	29.5	34.5
Texas	92.4	24.0	31.0	15.0
North Carolina	92.1	25.8	32.0	24.0
Florida	91.7	28.5	33.0	36.5
South Carolina	91.4	26.0	34.0	25.0
Ohio	90.6	27.1	35.0	28.0
Mississippi	90.1	25.7	36.0	22.5
Louisiana	90.0	27.6	37.0	32.0
Arkansas	89.8	24.3	38.0	17.5
Connecticut	89.7	30.4	39.0	43.5
New Jersey	89.5	30.4	40.0	43.5
Illinois	89.4	28.8	41.0	40.5
Oklahoma	89.3	31.1	42.0	47.0
Missouri	89.1	28.8	43.0	40.5
Massachusetts	88.6	34.3	45.0	51.0
Georgia	88.6	28.6	45.0	38.0
District of Columbia	88.6	28.7	45.0	39.0
Tennessee	88.3	27.9	47.5	30.0
Pennsylvania	88.3	31.3	47.0	48.0
Alabama	88.0	27.4	49.0	31.0
West Virginia	87.6	24.8	50.0	20.0
New York	85.9	32.1	51.0	50.0

1. Source of raw data: U.S. Department of Commerce/Bureau of the Census. *1970 Census of Population, Advance Report,* "General Population Characteristics, United States," PC(V2)-1. U.S. Department of Commerce, Washington, D.C., February, 1971.

2. Rank ordering for the sex ratio is from high to low. That is, the state with the highest sex ratio (Hawaii) is ranked 1.0, while that with the lowest (New York) is ranked 51.0. Rank ordering for the percentage of female-headed households is from low to high. That is, the state with the lowest proportion (North Dakota) is ranked 1.0, while Massachusetts, with the highest, is ranked 51.0.

such states as New York, Massachusetts, Pennsylvania, Oklahoma, New Jersey, and Connecticut, where such encouragement would include the lure of significant opportunities for receipt of higher education, professional occupation, and incomes approximating at least the median income of all individuals in the United States. That might help move the "girls" to "where the boys are."

A second, but different type of implication, might well be the continuing development of alternative familial forms, including that of polygyny, a system appropriate in the absence of a sufficient supply of males. Polygyny, of course, requires male participants with sufficient resources to maintain adequately several or more families. At the present time, almost no black males are economically equipped within the United States to participate in such a system, which forestalls any present concerns about the acceptability of such a system to black females. Nevertheless, as some keen observers have indicated in various private conversations with at least the writer, the legitimacy of polygyny could well benefit some females who are involved in "playing at polygyny," but who are denied legally any of the benefits to which they might otherwise be entitled.

For example, on a recent visit to Kampala, Uganda, the Vice-Chancellor of Makerere University noted that, in defense of polygyny, the women participating as spouses had a legal status of wife, not that of whore, slut, mistress, et cetera. Thus, not only did such wives not have illegitimate children, but both they and their children had legal protection under the law, which he regarded as a more "civilized" system than that existing in the "civilized" United States. He may have a point worth further investigation. In any case, it is quite clear that there is not one absolute system of marriage and family which must be adhered to at any cost and under any circumstance. Such is even the case among white Americans.

White Sex Ratios

It has already been established that females have been excessive in the black population since 1850. Table 3, which provides a comparison of the black and white sex ratios, 1850–1970, shows clearly evidence permitting the statement already made that blacks have had a "headstart" on whites in developing alternative familial patterns in the absence of a sufficient number of males. Blacks are at least 100 years ahead of whites in this respect. A cursory examination of such variables as those of marital statuses, illegitimacy rates, and intermarriage rates is invaluable in noting certain trends depicting whites as becoming more like blacks.

Table 3.   Black and White Sex Ratios, 1850–1970[1]

Year	Sex Ratios	
	Black	White
1850	99.1	105.2
1860	99.6	105.3
1870	96.2	102.8
1880	97.8	104.0
1890	99.5	105.4
1900	98.6	104.9
1910	98.9	106.6
1920	99.2	104.4
1930	97.0	102.9
1940	95.0	101.2
1950	94.3	99.1
1960	93.3	97.3
1970	90.8	95.3

[1]. For whites in 1970, the data include non-blacks. Sex ratios were obtained from *Census* reports for the specified years.

Table 4 provides some limited information on two of the three variables referred to above, namely marital statuses and illegitimacy. If we examine female marital statuses, by race, from 1900 through 1970, we see that in 1900, when the black sex ratio was 98.6 and the white 104.9, there were no significant differences by race in marital statuses. In fact, a slightly higher proportion of the black females were returned as *married,* while a slightly larger proportion of the whites were returned as *divorced,* but slightly fewer as *widowed.* By 1940, when the black sex ratio had declined to 95.0 while that of the whites remained above 100, it is evident that the divorce rates by race were identical, while the widowhood rate was higher among blacks than whites. In addition, data available for persons married with spouses present (not available in the 1900 Census) showed that the decreasing sex ratio had affected the proportion of black females likely to fall within that category, while the whites remained relatively unaffected.

Table 4. Selected Statistical Comparisons between Blacks and Whites[1]

Characteristic	Black	White
Female marital status		
1900, 15 + years of age		
% single	39.8	40.1
% married	55.5	55.4
% divorced	0.2	0.3
% widowed	4.3	4.0
1940, 15 + years of age		
% single	23.9	26.0
% married, spouse present	44.2	56.9
% divorced	1.7	1.7
% widowed	15.8	11.1
1960, 14 + years of age		
% single	22.3	18.7
% married, spouse present	51.8	65.2
% divorced	3.6	2.7
% widowed	14.0	12.0
1970, 14 + years of age		
% single	28.0	21.3
% married, spouse present	42.0	60.3
% divorced	4.3	3.4
% widowed	13.5	12.4
Percent of female-headed families		
1950	17.6	8.5
1955	20.7	9.0
1960	22.4	8.7
1966	23.7	8.9
1970	26.4	9.1
1971	28.9	9.4
Percent of own children living with both parents, as percent of all own children		
1960	75	92
1970	67	91
Percent change in estimated illegitimacy rates		
1940–1944 to 1955–1959	+ 166	+ 139
1955–1959 to 1968	–8	+ 53

[1] Sources of data: U.S. Census Office, *Census Reports*, Vol. 2, Part 2, "Population," U.S. Gov. Printing Office, Washington, D.C., 1902; U.S. Bureau of the Census, *Sixteenth Census of the United States: 1940*, Vol. 2, "Population, Characteristics of the Population," U.S. Govt. Printing Office, Washington, D.C., 1943; U.S. Bureau of the Census, *U.S. Census of Population, 1960*, Vol. 1, "Characteristics of the Population," Part 1, "United States Summary," U.S. Gov. Printing Office, Washington, D.C., 1964; *The Social and Economic Status of Negroes in the United States, 1970*, BLS Report No. 394, CPR, Series P-23, No. 38, Special Studies, U.S. Department of Commerce/Bureau of the Census, Washington, D.C., July, 1971; and *Social and Economic Characteristics of the Population in Metropolitan and Non-metropolitan Areas: 1970 and 1960*, Current Population Reports, Series P-23, No. 37, U.S. Govt. Printing Office, Washington, D.C., 1971.

In 1960, when the sex ratios among both blacks and whites had declined to 93.3 and 97.3 respectively, we actually find that a larger proportion of females in both racial groups were returned as *married, with spouse present*. By that year, their divorce rates were no longer identical, but both were rising, 3.6 among the blacks, and 2.7 among the whites, as compared with the 1940 rate of 1.7.

By 1970 with the sex ratios continuing to decline (90.8 among blacks, 95.3 among whites), it is clear that the proportion of females *married, with spouse present* had declined *both* among black and white females from the percentage given in 1960. In 1970, 9.8 percent fewer black females and 4.9 percent fewer white females were so classified. The major factor contributing to that change may, perhaps, be found in the increased proportion of those single, which is over twice as high among the black females, 1960–1970, than among the white females. In 1970, as it may be recalled, over nine black females out of every 100 would have been theoretically classified as being without monogamous mates, true of only about five out of every 100 white females.

Thus, a partial explication of the differences in the marital statuses by race should not be sought, as is quite commonly done, within black family disorganization, but within the effects of sex ratios upon marital statuses. While the divorce rate in 1970 continued to be higher among black than among white females, the rate among the latter also continued to increase from 1960 to 1970.

Data in Table 4 depicting the percent of female-headed families do reveal, as expected, that the proportion of such families is considerably higher among blacks than among whites. However, the proportionate increase among blacks was less from 1960 to 1970 (119.6%) than it was from 1950 to 1960 (127.3%), whereas the proportionate increase among whites was greater in 1960–1970 (104.6%) than between 1950–1960, when it was 102.4 percent. Consequently, although the sex ratios were continuing to decline among both groups, the rate of increase in female-headed families among whites continued to rise between 1950–1970 while it had begun to decrease somewhat among blacks over the same time period.

A similar pattern emerges upon examination of the percentage changes occurring over time in two other variables—the percent of own children living with both parents as the percent of all own children, and the percent change in estimated illegitimacy rates. In the case of the former variable, from 1960–1970, the percent of such children among both races declined, from 75 to 67 percent among blacks, and from 92 to 91 percent among whites, a decrease which may also be related to their decreasing sex ratios and increasing proportions of female-headed families.

While illegitimacy as usually defined remains higher among blacks than among whites, it is very interesting to note that illegitimacy rates have been declining among blacks, while increasing among whites, as also shown in Table 4. In other words, the rate of illegitimate births is rising among whites while their sex ratio is declining, which is a pattern not at all unlike that which transpired much earlier among blacks. Thus, it appears that as females become more excessive in the white population, the proportion seeking family forms deviating from the traditional is on the increase. In this sense—and a very important sense, to be sure—whites are following trends mapped out earlier by blacks.

Whites, of course, have not yet "caught up" with blacks in developing various alternative patterns for several different reasons, with the most important one probably being that black females are yet more excessive in the black population than are those in the white population, and particularly so during the childbearing years of 15–44, as can be seen by inspecting the data provided in Table 5. For the years 15–44 inclusive, the sex ratios are much lower among blacks than whites, and especially so for the years 25–44, as of 1970. Interestingly, however, for those 65+ years of age, the black sex ratio is actually higher than that of the whites, a finding readily explicable by the greater longevity of white females as compared with blacks and with white males. In passing, what may also be quite impressive about Table 5 is an inference that the significant differences in the sex ratios between blacks and whites are not reflected to the same extent in the differences in their illegitimacy rates. That is, given the fact again that white females are not as excessive in the white population as are black females within the black population, and considering also that white females have far greater access to black

males as marital partners than do black females to white males, one must wonder why the white illegitimacy rate is as high as it is among whites and as low as it is among blacks!

Table 5. Differences in the Black and White Sex Ratios, 15+ Years of Age, 1970[1]

Age Group	Black	White	Difference
15–24 years	93.0	98.8	5.8
25–34 years	84.2	97.8	13.6
35–44 years	82.8	96.2	13.4
45–54 years	86.3	93.8	7.5
55–64 years	85.1	90.2	5.1
65+ years	76.4	71.9	−4.5

1. Source of raw data: U.S. Department of Commerce/Bureau of the Census. *1970 Census of Population, Advance Report,* "General Population Characteristics, United States," PC(V2)-1. U.S. Department of Commerce, Washington, D.C., February, 1971.

Summary and Conclusions

By now it may be quite evident that there are at least three major and interrelated concerns running through this discourse about "But where are the men?", with the most important one being that there simply are not enough men available for black women to assure their conformity to traditional patterns of sex, marriage, and family living, as defined for them by the white American subculture. More important, as the white sex ratio becomes more like that of blacks (as measured by excessive females within the population and particularly within the age ranges of 15–44 years), it is quite clear that whites are increasingly utilizing patterns or models already developed by blacks, who have had a "headstart" of at least 100 years.

Ultimately, black women must be concerned with resolution of the issue of an insufficient supply of males, and aid in developing means of increasing that supply (which can take a variety of tactics, not the least of which is improving the life expectancies of black men) or, should that fail, providing viable alternatives to this "supply-and-demand" problem, one of which may be aiding in reducing the supply of black males available to white females, a practice, incidentally, which seems to affect an unduly high number of black coeds on major campuses throughout at least most of the northern and western parts of the United States.

In closing, then, the critical issues confronting many black women are not those of black matriarchy or black female emasculation of the male but merely that of, *"But where are the men?"*

6

Female Sex Roles

Double Jeopardy: To Be Black and Female

Frances Beale

This article deals with what the author sees as a dual problem facing Black women. She stresses the impact of economic exploitation and its relation to both sex and race. Attention is given to the physical abuse Black women must face because of their disadvantaged economic position in this society.

In attempting to analyze the situation of the Black woman in America, one crashes abruptly into a solid wall of grave misconceptions, outright distortions of fact, and defensive attitudes on the part of many. The system of capitalism (and its afterbirth—racism) under which we all live has attempted by many devious ways and means to destroy the humanity of all people, and particularly the humanity of Black people. This has meant an outrageous assault on every Black man, woman, and child who resides in the United States.

In keeping with its goal of destroying the Black race's will to resist its subjugation, capitalism found it necessary to create a situation where the Black man found it impossible to find meaningful or productive employment. More often than not, he couldn't find work of any kind. And the Black woman likewise was manipulated by the system, economically exploited and physically assaulted. She could often find work in the white man's kitchen, however, and sometimes became the sole breadwinner of the family. This predicament has led to many psychological problems on the part of both man and woman and has contributed to the turmoil that we find in the Black family structure.

Unfortunately, neither the Black man nor the Black woman understood the true nature of the forces working upon them. Many Black women tended to accept the capitalist evaluation of manhood and womanhood and believed, in fact, that Black men were shiftless and lazy, otherwise they would get a job and support their families as they ought to. Personal relationships between Black men and women were thus torn asunder and one result has been the separation of man from wife, mother from child, etc.

America has defined the roles to which each individual should subscribe. It has defined "manhood" in terms of its own interests and "femininity" likewise. Therefore, an individual who has a good job, makes a lot of money, and drives a Cadillac is a real "man," and conversely, an individual who is lacking in these "qualities" is less of a man. The advertising media in this country continuously inform the American male of his need for indispensable signs of his virility—the brand of cigarettes that cowboys prefer, the whiskey that has a masculine tang, or the label of the jock strap that athletes wear.

The ideal model that is projected for a woman is to be surrounded by hypocritical homage and estranged from all real work, spending idle hours primping and preening, obsessed with conspicuous consumption, and limiting life's functions to simply a sex role. We unqualitatively reject these respective models. A woman who stays at home caring for children and the house often leads an extremely sterile existence. She must lead her entire life as a satellite to her mate. He goes out into society and brings back a little piece of the world for her. His interests and his understanding of the world become her own and

---

Adridged from *New Generation* 51 (Fall 1969): 23–28. Reprinted by permission.

she cannot develop herself as an individual having been reduced to only a biological function. This kind of woman leads a parasitic existence that can aptly be described as legalized prostitution.

Furthermore it is idle dreaming to think of Black women simply caring for their homes and children like the middle-class white model. Most Black women have to work to help house, feed, and clothe their families. Black women make up a substantial percentage of the Black working force, and this is true for the poorest Black family as well as the so-called "middle-class" family.

Black women were never afforded any such phony luxuries. Though we have been browbeaten with this white image, the reality of the degrading and dehumanizing jobs that were relegated to us quickly dissipated this mirage of womanhood. The following excerpts from a speech that Sojourner Truth made at a Women's Rights Convention in the nineteenth century show us how misleading and incomplete a life this model represents for us:

Well, chilern, whar dar is so much racket dar must be something out o' kilter. I tink dat 'twixt de niggers of de Souf and de women at de Norf all a talkin' 'bout rights, de white men will be in a fix pretty soon. But what's all dis here talkin' 'bout? Dat man ober dar say dat women needs to be helped into carriages, and lifted ober ditches, and to have de best place every whar. Nobody ever help me into carriages, or ober mud puddles, or gives me any best places, . . . and ar'nt I a woman? Look at me! Look at my arm! . . . I have plowed, and planted, and gathered into barns, and no man could head me—and ar'nt I a woman? I could work as much as a man (when I could get it), and bear de lash as well—and ar'nt I a woman? I have borne five chilern and I seen 'em mos' all sold off into slavery, and when I cried out with a mother's grief, none but Jesus heard—and ar'nt I a woman?

Unfortunately, there seems to be some confusion in the Movement today as to who has been oppressing whom. Since the advent of Black power, the Black male has exerted a more prominent leadership role in our struggle for justice in this country. He sees the system for what it really is for the most part, but where he rejects its values

and mores on many issues, when it comes to women, he seems to take his guidelines from the pages of the *Ladies' Home Journal.* Certain Black men are maintaining that they have been castrated by society but that Black women somehow escaped this persecution and even contributed to this emasculation.

Let me state here and now that the Black woman in America can justly be described as a "slave of a slave." By reducing the Black man in America to such abject oppression, the Black woman had no protector and was used, and is still being used in some cases, as the scapegoat for the evils that this horrendous system has perpetrated on Black men. Her physical image has been maliciously maligned; she has been sexually molested and abused by the white colonizer; she has suffered the worse kind of economic exploitation, having been forced to serve as the white woman's maid and wet nurse for white offspring while her own children were more often than not starving and neglected. It is the depth of degradation to be socially manipulated, physically raped, used to undermine your own household, and to be powerless to reverse this syndrome.

It is true that our husbands, fathers, brothers, and sons have been emasculated, lynched, and brutalized. They have suffered from the cruelest assault on mankind that the world has ever known. However, it is a gross distortion of fact to state that Black women have oppressed Black men. The capitalist system found it expedient to enslave and oppress them and proceeded to do so without consultation or the signing of any agreements with Black women.

It must also be pointed out at this time that Black women are not resentful of the rise to power of Black men. We welcome it. We see in it the eventual liberation of all Black people from this corrupt system of capitalism. Nevertheless, this does not mean that you have to negate one for the other. This kind of thinking is a product of miseducation; that it's either X or it's Y. It is fallacious reasoning that in order for the Black man to be strong, the Black woman has to be weak.

Those who are exerting their "manhood" by telling Black women to step back into a domestic, submissive role are assuming a counter-revolutionary position. Black women likewise have been abused by the system and we must begin talking about the elimination of all kinds of oppression. If we are talking about building a strong nation, capable of throwing off the yoke of capitalist oppression, then we are talking about the total involvement of every man, woman, and child, each with a highly developed political consciousness. We need our whole army out there dealing with the enemy and not half an army.

There are also some Black women who feel that there is no more productive role in life than having and raising children. This attitude often reflects the conditioning of the society in which we live and is adopted from a bourgeois white model. Some young sisters who have never had to maintain a household and accept the confining role which this entails tend to romanticize (along with the help of a few brothers) this role of housewife and mother. Black women who have had to endure this kind of function are less apt to have these utopian visions.

Those who project in an intellectual manner how great and rewarding this role will be and who feel that the most important thing that they can contribute to the Black nation is children are doing themselves a great injustice. This line of reasoning completely negates the contributions that Black women have historically made to our struggle for liberation. These Black women include Sojourner Truth, Harriet Tubman, Mary McLeod Bethune, and Fannie Lou Hamer, to name but a few.

We live in a highly industrialized society and every member of the Black nation must be as academically and technologically developed as possible. To wage a revolution, we need competent teachers, doctors, nurses, electronics experts, chemists, biologists, physicists, political scientists, and so on and so forth. Black women sitting at home reading bedtime stories to their children are just not going to make it.

Economic Exploitation of Black Women

The economic system of capitalism finds it expedient to reduce women to a state of enslavement. They oftentimes serve as a scapegoat for the evils of this system. Much in the same way that the poor white cracker of the South, who is equally victimized, looks down upon Blacks and contributes to the oppression of Blacks, so, by giving to men a false feeling of superiority (at least in their own home or in their relationships with women), the oppression of women acts as an escape valve for capitalism. Men may be cruelly exploited and subjected to all sorts of dehumanizing tactics on the part of the ruling class, but they have someone who is below them—at least they're not women.

Women also represent a surplus labor supply, the control of which is absolutely necessary to the profitable functioning of capitalism. Women are systematically exploited by the system. They are paid less for the same work that men do, and jobs that are specifically relegated to women are low-paying and without the possibility of advancement. . . .

Those industries which employ mainly Black women are the most exploitive in the country. Domestic and hospital workers are good examples of this oppression; the garment workers in New York City provide us with another view of this economic slavery. The International Ladies Garment Workers Union (ILGWU), whose overwhelming membership consists of Black and Puerto Rican women, has a leadership that is nearly all lily-white and male. This leadership has been working in collusion with the ruling class and has completely sold its soul to the corporate structure.

To add insult to injury, the ILGWU has invested heavily in business enterprises in racist, apartheid South Africa—with union funds. Not only does this bought-off leadership contribute to our continued exploitation in this country by not truly representing the best interest of its membership, but it audaciously uses funds that Black and Puerto Rican women have provided to support the economy of a vicious government that is engaged in the economic rape and murder of our Black brothers and sisters in our Motherland, Africa.

The entire labor movement in the United States has suffered as a result of the superexploitation of Black workers and women. The unions have historically been racist and chauvinistic. They have upheld racism in this country and have failed to fight the white skin privileges of white workers. They have failed to fight or even make an issue against the inequities in the hiring and pay of women workers. There has been virtually no struggle against either the racism of the white worker or the economic exploitation of the working woman, two factors which have consistently impeded the advancement of the real struggle against the ruling class.

This racist, chauvinistic, and manipulative use of Black workers and women, especially Black women, has been a severe cancer on the American labor scene. It therefore becomes essential for those who understand the workings of capitalism and imperialism to realize that the exploitation of Black people and women works to everyone's disadvantage and that the liberation of these two groups is a steppingstone to the liberation of all oppressed people in this country and around the world.

Bedroom Politics

I have briefly discussed the economic and psychological manipulation of Black women, but perhaps the most outlandish act of oppression in modern times is the current campaign to promote sterilization of non-white women in an attempt to maintain the population and power imbalance between the white haves and the non-white have-nots.

These tactics are but another example of the many devious schemes that the ruling-class elite attempt to perpetrate on the Black population in order to keep itself in control. It has recently come to our attention that a massive campaign for so-called "birth control" is presently being promoted not only in the underdeveloped non-white areas of the world, but also in Black communities here in the United States. However, what the authorities in charge of these programs refer to as "birth control" is in fact nothing but a method of outright surgical genocide.

The United States have been sponsoring sterilization clinics in non-white countries, especially in India, where already some three million young men and boys in and around New Delhi have been sterilized in makeshift operating rooms set up by the American Peace Corps workers. Under these circumstances, it is understandable why certain countries view the Peace Corps not as a benevolent project, not as evidence of America's concern for underdeveloped areas, but rather as a threat to their very existence. This program could more aptly be named the Death Corps.

Vasectomy, which is performed on males and takes only six or seven minutes, is a relatively simple operation. The sterilization of a woman, on the other hand, is admittedly major surgery. This operation (salpingectomy)[1] must be performed in a hospital under general anesthesia. This method of "birth control" is a common procedure in Puerto Rico. Puerto Rico has long been used by the colonialist exploiter, the United States, as a huge experimental laboratory for medical research before allowing certain practices to be imported and used here. When the birth-control pill was first being perfected, it was tried out on Puerto Rican women and selected Black women (poor), using them as human guinea pigs, to evaluate its effect and its efficiency.

Salpingectomy has now become the commonest operation in Puerto Rico, commoner than an appendectomy or a tonsillectomy. It is so widespread that it is referred to simply as *la operacíon. On the island, 10 percent of the women between the ages of 15 and 45 have already been sterilized.*

And now, as previously occurred with the pill, this method has been imported into the United States. These sterilization clinics are cropping up around the country in the Black and Puerto Rican communities. These so-called "maternity clinics" specifically outfitted to purge Black women or men of their reproductive possibilities are appearing more and more in hospitals and clinics across the country.

A number of organizations have been formed to popularize the idea of sterilization, such as the Association for Voluntary Sterilization and the Human Betterment (!!!?) Association for Voluntary Sterilization, Inc., which has its headquarters in New York City.

Threatened with the cut-off of relief funds, some Black welfare women have been forced to accept this sterilization procedure in exchange for a continuation of welfare benefits. Black women are often afraid to permit any kind of necessary surgery because they know from bitter experience that they are more likely than not to come out of the hospital without their insides. (Both salpingectomies and hysterectomies are performed.)

We condemn this use of the Black woman as a medical testing ground for the white middle

---

[1]Salpingectomy: Through an abdominal incision, the surgeon cuts both fallopian tubes and ties off the separated ends, after which act there is no way for the egg to pass from the ovary to the womb.

class. Reports of the ill effects, including deaths, from the use of the birth control pill only started to come to light when the white privileged class began to be affected. These outrageous Nazi-like procedures on the part of medical researchers are but another manifestation of the totally amoral and dehumanizing brutality that the capitalist system perpetrates on Black women. The sterilization experiments carried on in concentration camps some twenty-five years ago have been denounced the world over, but no one seems to get upset by the repetition of these same racist tactics today in the United States of America—land of the free and home of the brave. This campaign is as nefarious a program as Germany's gas chambers, and in a long-term sense, as effective and with the same objective.

The rigid laws concerning abortions in this country are another vicious means of subjugation and, indirectly, of outright murder. Rich white women somehow manage to obtain these operations with little or no difficulty. It is the poor Black and Puerto Rican woman who is at the mercy of the local butcher. Statistics show us that the non-white death rate at the hands of the unqualified abortionist is substantially higher than for white women. Nearly half of the childbearing deaths in New York City are attributed to abortion alone and out of these, 79 percent are among non-whites and Puerto Rican women.

We are not saying that Black women should not practice birth control. *Black women have the right and the responsibility to determine when it is in the interest of the struggle to have children or not to have them, and this right must not be relinquished to anyone.* It is also her right and responsibility to determine when it is in her own best interest to have children, how many she will have, and how far apart. The lack of the availability of safe birth-control methods, the forced sterilization practices, and the inability to obtain legal abortions are all symptoms of a decadent society that jeopardizes the health of Black women (and thereby the entire Black race) in its attempts to control the very life processes of human beings. This is a symptom of a society that believes it has the right to bring political factors into the privacy of the bedchamber. The elimination of these horrendous conditions will free Black women for full participation in the revolution, and thereafter, in the building of the new society.

Relationship to White Movement

Much has been written recently about the white women's liberation movement in the United States, and the question arises whether there are any parallels between this struggle and the movement on the part of Black women for total emancipation. While there are certain comparisons that one can make, simply because we both live under the same exploitative system, there are certain differences, some of which are quite basic.

The white women's movement is far from being monolithic. Any white group that does not have an anti-imperialist and anti-racist ideology has absolutely nothing in common with the Black woman's struggle. In fact, some groups come to the incorrect conclusion that their oppression is due simply to male chauvinism. They therefore have an extremely anti-male tone to their dissertations. Black people are engaged in a life-and-death struggle and the main emphasis of Black women must be to combat the capitalist, racist exploitation of Black people. While it is true that male chauvinism has become institutionalized in American society, one must always look for the main enemy—the fundamental cause of the female condition.

Another major differentiation is that the white women's liberation movement is basically middle class. Very few of these women suffer the extreme economic exploitation that most Black women are subjected to day by day. This is the factor that is most crucial for us. It is not an intellectual persecution alone; it is not an intellectual outburst for us; it is quite real. We as Black women have got to deal with the problems that the Black masses deal with, for our problems in reality are one and the same.

If the white groups do not realize that they are in fact fighting capitalism and racism, we do not have common bonds. If they do not realize that the reasons for their condition lie in the system and not simply that men get a vicarious pleasure out of "consuming their bodies for exploitative reasons" (this kind of reasoning seems to be quite prevalent in certain white women's groups), then we cannot unite with them around common grievances or even discuss these groups in a serious manner because they're completely irrelevant to the Black struggle.

The New World

The Black community and Black women especially must begin raising questions about the kind of society we wish to see established. We must note the ways in which capitalism oppresses us and then move to create institutions that will eliminate these destructive influences.

The new world that we are attempting to create must destroy oppression of any type. The value of this new system will be determined by the status of the person who was low man on the totem pole. Unless women in any enslaved nation are completely liberated, the change cannot really be called a revolution. If the Black woman has to retreat to the position she occupied before the armed struggle, the whole movement and the whole struggle will have retreated in terms of truly freeing the colonized population.

A people's revolution that engages the participation of every member of the community, including man, woman, and child, brings about a certain transformation in the participants as a result of this participation. Once you have caught a glimpse of freedom or experienced a bit of self-determination, you can't go back to old routines that were established under a racist, capitalist regime. We must begin to understand that a revolution entails not only the willingness to lay our lives on the firing line and get killed. In some ways, this is an easy commitment to make. To die for the revolution is a one-shot deal; to live for the revolution means taking on the more difficult commitment of changing our day-to-day life patterns.

This will mean changing the traditional routines that we have established as a result of living in a totally corrupting society. It means changing how you relate to your wife, your husband, your parents, and your co-workers. If we are going to liberate ourselves as a people, it must be recognized that Black women have very specific problems that have to be spoken to. We must be liberated along with the rest of the population. We cannot wait to start working on those problems until that great day in the future when the revolution somehow miraculously is accomplished.

To assign women the role of housekeeper and mother while men go forth into battle is a highly questionable doctrine for a revolutionary to maintain. Each individual must develop a high political consciousness in order to understand how this system enslaves us all and what actions we must take to bring about its total destruction. Those who consider themselves to be revolutionary must begin to deal with other revolutionaries as equals. And so far as I know, revolutionaries are not determined by sex.

Old people, young people, men and women, must take part in the struggle. To relegate women to purely supportive roles or to purely cultural considerations is dangerous doctrine to project. Unless Black men who are preparing themselves for armed struggle understand that the society which we are trying to create is one in which the oppression of *all members* of that society is eliminated, then the revolution will have failed in its avowed purpose.

Given the mutual commitment of Black men and Black women alike to the liberation of our people and other oppressed peoples around the world, the total involvement of each individual is necessary. A revolutionary has the responsibility not only of toppling those that are now in a position of power, but of creating new institutions that will eliminate all forms of oppression. We must begin to rewrite our understanding of traditional personal relationships between man and woman.

All the resources that the Black community can muster up must be channeled into the struggle. Black women must take an active part in bringing about the kind of society where our children, our loved ones, and each citizen can grow up and live as decent human beings, free from the pressures of racism and capitalist exploitation.

Sex Roles and Survival Strategies in an Urban Black Community

Carol B. Stack

The existence of a viable network of relationships between the single Black parent and other persons is shown. The author finds that in spite of disruptive forces on the single-parent family, a variety of creative solutions are available to the parent. She shows how these survival strategies help maximize the lone parent's independence.

The power and authority ascribed to women in the Black ghettos of America, women whose families are locked into lifelong conditions of poverty and welfare, have their roots in the inexorable unemployment of Black males and the ensuing control of economic resources by females. These social-economic conditions have given rise to special features in the organization of family and kin networks in Black communities, features not unlike the patterns of domestic authority that emerge in matrilineal societies, or in cultures where men are away from home in wage labor (Gonzalez, 1969, 1970). The poor in Black urban communities have evolved, as the basic unit of their society, a core of kinsmen and non-kin who cooperate on a daily basis and who live near one another or co-reside. This core, or nucleus, has been characterized as the basis of the consanguineal household (Gonzalez, 1965) and of matrifocality (Abrahams, 1963; Moynihan, 1965; Rainwater, 1966).

The concept of "matrifocality," however, has been criticized as inaccurate and inadequate. Recent studies (Ladner, 1971; Smith, 1970; Stack, 1970; Valentine, 1970) show convincingly that many of the negative features attributed to matrifocal families—that they are fatherless, unstable, and produce offspring that are "illegitimate" in the eyes of the folk culture—are not general characteristics of low-income Black families in urban America. Rather than imposing widely accepted definitions of the family, the nuclear family, or the matrifocal family on the ways in which the urban poor describe and order their world, we must seek a more appropriate theoretical framework. Elsewhere I have proposed an analysis based on the notion of a domestic network (Stack, 1974). In this view, the basis of familial structure and cooperation is not the nuclear family of the middle class, but an extended cluster of kinsmen related chiefly through children but also through marriage and friendship, who align to provide domestic functions. This cluster, or domestic network, is diffused over several kin-based households, and fluctuations in individual household composition do not significantly affect cooperative arrangements.

In this paper I shall analyze the domestic network and the relationships within it from a woman's perspective—from the perspective that the women in this study provided and from my own interpretations of the domestic and social scene. Many previous studies of the Black family (e.g., Liebow, 1967, and Hannerz, 1969) have taken a male perspective emphasizing the street-corner life of Black men and viewing men as peripheral to familial concerns. Though correctly stressing the economic difficulties that Black males face in a racist society, these and other studies (Moynihan, 1965; Bernard, 1966) have fostered a stereotype of Black families as fatherless and subject to a domineering woman's matriarchal rule. From such simplistic accounts it is all too easy to come to blame juvenile delinquency, divorce, illegitimacy, and other social ills on the Black family, while ignoring the oppressive reality of our political and economic system and the adaptive resiliency and strength that Black families have shown.

From *Woman, Culture, and Society*, ed. Michelle Z. Rosaldo and Louise Lamphere (Stanford University Press, 1974). Adapted from *All Our Kin: Strategies for Survival in a Black Community* by Carol B. Stack (Harper and Row, 1974). Copyright 1974 by Carol B. Stack. Reprinted by permission.

My analysis will draw on life-history material as well as on personal comments from women in The Flats, the poorest section of a Black community in the Midwestern city of Jackson Harbor.[1] I shall view women as strategists—active agents who use resources to achieve goals and cope with the problems of everyday life. This framework has several advantages. First, because the focus is on women rather than men, women's views of family relations, often ignored or slighted, are given prominence. Second, since households form around women because of their role in child care, ties between women (including paternal aunts, cousins, etc.) often constitute the core of a network; data from women's lives, then, crucially illuminate the continuity in these networks. Finally, the life-history material, taken chiefly from women, also demonstrates the positive role that a man plays in Black family life, both as the father of a woman's children and as a contributor of valuable resources to her network and to the network of his own kin.

I shall begin by analyzing the history of residential arrangements during one woman's life, and the residential arrangements of this woman's kin network at two points in time, demonstrating that although household composition changes, members are selected or self-selected largely from a single network that has continuity over time. Women and men, in response to joblessness, the possibility of welfare payments, the breakup of relationships, or the whims of a landlord, may move often. But the very calamities and crises that contribute to the constant shifts in residence tend to bring men, women, and children back into the households of close kin. Newly formed households are successive recombinations of the same domestic network of adults and children, quite often in the same dwellings. Residence histories, then, are an important reflection of the strategy of relying on and strengthening the domestic kin network, and also reveal the adaptiveness of households with "elastic boundaries." (It may be worth noting that middle-class whites are beginning to perceive certain values, for their own lives, in such households.)

In the remainder of the paper, the importance of maximizing network strength will be reemphasized and additional strategies will be isolated by examining two sets of relationships within kin networks—those between mothers and fathers and those between fathers and children. Women's own accounts of their situations show how they have developed a strong sense of independence from men, evolved social controls against the formation of conjugal relationships, and limited the role of the husband-father within the mother's domestic group. All of these strategies serve to strengthen the domestic network, often at the expense of any particular male-female tie. Kin regard any marriage as a risk to the woman and her children, and the loss of either male or female kin as a threat to the durability of the kin network. These two factors continually augment each other and dictate, as well, the range of socially accepted relationships between fathers and children.

Residence and the Domestic Network

In The Flats, the material and cultural support needed to sustain and socialize community members is provided by cooperating kinsmen. The individual can draw upon a broad domestic web of kin and friends—some who reside together, others who do not. Residents in The Flats characterize household composition according to where people sleep, eat, and spend their time. Those who eat together may be considered part of a domestic unit. But an individual may eat in one household, sleep in another, contribute resources and services to yet another, and consider himself or herself a member of all three households. Children may fall asleep and remain through the night wherever the late-evening visiting patterns of the adult females take them, and they may remain in these households and share meals perhaps a week at a time. As R.T. Smith suggests in an article on Afro-American kinship (1970), it is sometimes difficult "to determine just which household a given individual belongs to at any particular moment." These facts of ghetto life are, of course, often disguised in the statistical reports of census takers, who record simply sleeping arrangements.

Households in The Flats, then, have shifting memberships, but they maintain for the most part

[1]This work is based on a recent urban anthropological study of poverty and domestic life of urban-born Black Americans who were raised on public welfare and whose parents had migrated from the South to a single community in the urban North (Stack, 1972). Now adults in their twenties to forties, they are raising their own children on welfare in The Flats. All personal and place names in this paper are fictitious.

a steady state of three generations of kin: males and females beyond child-bearing age; a middle generation of mothers raising their own children or children of close kin; and the children. This observation is supported in a recent study by Ladner (1971: 60), who writes, "Many children normally grow up in a three-generation household and they absorb the influences of a grandmother and grandfather as well as a mother and father." A survey of eighty-three residence changes among welfare families, whereby adult females who are heads of their own households merged households with other kin, shows that the majority of moves created three-generation households. Consequently, it is difficult to pinpoint structural beginning or end to household cycles in poor Black urban communities (Buchler and Selby, 1968; Fortes, 1958; Otterbein, 1970). But it is clear that authority patterns within a kin network change with birth and death; with the death of the oldest member in a household, the next generation assumes authority.

Residence changes themselves are brought on by many factors, most related to the economic conditions in which poor families live. Women who have children have access to welfare, and thus more economic security than women who do not, and more than all men. Welfare regulations encourage mothers to set up separate households, and women actively seek independence, privacy, and improvement in their lives. But these ventures do not last long. Life histories of adults show that the attempts by women to set up separate households with their children are short-lived: houses are condemned; landlords evict tenants; and needs for services among kin arise. Household composition also expands or contracts with the loss of a job, the death of a relative, the beginning or end of a sexual partnership, or the end of a friendship. But fluctuations in household composition rarely affect the exchanges and daily dependencies of participants. The following chronology of residence changes made by Ruby Banks graphically illuminates these points:

Age	Household Composition and Context of Household Formation
Birth	Ruby lived with her mother, Magnolia, and her maternal grandparents.
4	To be eligible for welfare, Ruby and Magnolia were required to move out of Ruby's grandparents' house. They moved into a separate residence two houses away, but ate all meals at the grandparents' house.
5	Ruby and Magnolia returned to the grandparents' house and Magnolia gave birth to a son. Magnolia worked and the grandmother cared for her children.
6	Ruby's maternal grandparents separated. Magnolia remained living with her father and her (now) two sons. Ruby and her grandmother moved up the street and lived with her maternal aunt Augusta and maternal uncle. Ruby's grandmother took care of Ruby and her brothers, and Magnolia worked and cooked and cleaned for her father.
7–16	The household was now composed of Ruby, her grandmother, her grandmother's new husband, Augusta and her boyfriend, and Ruby's maternal uncle. At age sixteen Ruby gave birth to a daughter.
17	Ruby's grandmother died and Ruby had a second child, by Otis, the younger brother of Ruby's best friend, Willa Mae. Ruby remained living with Augusta, Augusta's boyfriend, Ruby's maternal uncle, and her daughters.
18	Ruby fought with Augusta and she and Otis moved into an apartment with her two daughters. Ruby's first daughter's father died. Otis stayed with Ruby and her daughters in the apartment.
19	Ruby broke up with Otis. Ruby and her two daughters joined Magnolia, Magnolia's "husband," and her ten half-siblings. Ruby had a miscarriage.
19½	Ruby left town and moved out of state with her new boyfriend, Earl. She left her daughters with Magnolia and remained out of state for a year. Magnolia then insisted she return home and take care of her children.
20½	Ruby and her daughters moved into a large house rented by Augusta and her mother's brother. It was located next door to Magnolia's house, where Ruby and her children ate. Ruby cleaned for her aunt and uncle, and gave birth to another child, by Otis, who had returned to the household.
21	Ruby and Otis broke up once again. She found a house and moved there with her daughters, Augusta, and Augusta's boyfriend. Ruby did the cleaning, and Augusta cooked. Ruby and Magnolia, who now lived across town, shared child care, and Ruby's cousin's daughter stayed with Ruby.
21½	Augusta and her boyfriend have moved out because they were all fighting, and the two of them wanted to get away from the noise of the children. Ruby has a new boyfriend.

Ruby's residential changes, and the residences of her own children and kin, reveal that the same factors contributing to the high frequency of moving also bring men, women, and children back into the households of close kin. That one can repeatedly do so is a great source of security and dependence for those living in poverty.

A look in detail at the domestic network of Ruby's parents, Magnolia and Calvin Waters, illustrates the complexity of the typical network and also shows kin constructs at work both in the recruitment of individuals to the network and in the changing composition of households within the network, over less than three months:

These examples do indeed indicate the important role of the Black woman in the domestic structure. But the cooperation between male and female siblings who share the same household or live near one another has been underestimated by those who have isolated the female-headed household as the most significant domestic unit among the urban Black poor. The close cooperation of adult siblings arises from the residential

patterns typical of young adults (Stack, 1970). Owing to poverty, young women with or without children do not perceive any choice but to remain living at home with their mothers or other adult female relatives. Even when young women are collecting welfare for their children, they say that their resources go further when they share food and exchange goods and services daily. Likewise, the jobless man, or the man working at a part-time or seasonal job, often remains living at home with his mother—or, if she is dead, with his sisters and brothers. This pattern continues long after such a man becomes a father and establishes a series of sexual partnerships with women, who are in turn living with their own kin or friends or are alone with their children. A result of this pattern is the striking fact that households almost always have men around: male relatives, affines, and boyfriends. These men are often intermittent members of the households, boarders, or friends who come and go—men who usually eat, and sometimes sleep, in these households. Children have constant and close contact with these men, and

Household	Domestic Arrangements, April 1969	Domestic Arrangements, June 1969
1	Magnolia, her husband Calvin, their eight children (4–18).	Unchanged.
2	Magnolia's sister Augusta, Augusta's boyfriend, Ruby, Ruby's children, Ruby's boyfriend Otis.	Augusta and boyfriend have moved to #3 after a quarrel with Ruby. Ruby and Otis remain in #2.
3	Billy (Augusta's closest friend), Billy's children, Lazar (Magnolia's sister Carrie's husband, living in the basement), Carrie (from time to time—she is an alcoholic).	Augusta and boyfriend have moved to a small, one-room apartment upstairs from Billy.
4	Magnolia's sister Lydia, Lydia's daughters Georgia and Lottie, Lydia's boyfriend, Lottie's daughter.	Lottie and her daughter have moved to an apartment down the street, joining Lottie's girl friend and child. Georgia has moved in with her boyfriend. Lydia's son has moved back into Lydia's home #4.
5	Ruby's friend Willa Mae, her husband and son, her sister, and her brother James (father of Ruby's daughter).	James has moved in with his girl friend, who lives with her sister; James keeps most of his clothes in household #5. James's brother has returned from the army and moved into #5.
6	Eloise (Magnolia's first son's father's sister), her husband, their four young children, their daughter and her son, Eloise's friend Jessie's brother's daughter and her child.	Unchanged.
7	Violet (wife of Calvin's closest friend Cecil, now dead several years), her two sons, her daughter Odessa, and Odessa's four children.	Odessa's son Raymond has fathered Clover's baby. Clover and baby have joined household #7.

especially in the case of male relatives, these relationships last over the years. The most predictable residential pattern in The Flats is that individuals reside in the households of their natal kin, or the households of those who raised them, long into their adult years.

Welfare workers, researchers, and landlords in Black ghetto communities have long known that the residence patterns of the poor change frequently and that females play a dominant domestic role. What is much less understood is the relationship between household composition and domestic organization in these communities. Household boundaries are elastic, and no one model of a household, such as the nuclear family, extended family, or matrifocal family, is the norm. What is crucial and enduring is the strength of ties within a kin network; the maintenance of a strong network in turn has consequences for the relationships between the members themselves, as demonstrated in the following discussion of relationships between mothers and fathers and between fathers and their children.

Mothers and Fathers

Notwithstanding the emptiness and hopelessness of the job experience in the Black community, men and women fall in love and wager buoyant new relationships against the inexorable forces of poverty and racism. At the same time, in dealing with everyday life, Black women and men have developed a number of attitudes and strategies that appear to mitigate against the formation of long-term relationships. Even when a man and woman set up temporary housekeeping arrangements, they both maintain primary social ties with their kin. If other members of a kin network view a particular relationship as a drain on the network's resources, they will act in various and subtle ways to break up the relationship. This is what happened in the life of Julia Ambrose, another resident of The Flats.

When I first met Julia, she was living with her baby, her cousin Teresa, and Teresa's "old man." After several fierce battles with Teresa over the bills, and because of Teresa's hostility toward Julia's boyfriends, Julia decided to move out. She told me she was head over heels in love with Elliot,

her child's father, and they had decided to live together.

For several months Julia and Elliot shared a small apartment, and their relationship was strong. Elliot was very proud of his baby. On weekends he would spend an entire day carrying the baby around to his sister's home, where he would show it to his friends on the street. Julia, exhilarated by her independence in having her own place, took great care of the house and her baby. She told me, "Before Elliot came home from work I would have his dinner fixed and the house and kid clean. When he came home he would take his shower and then I'd bring his food to the bed. I'd put the kid to sleep and then get into bed with him. It was fine. We would get a little piece and then go to sleep. In the morning we'd do the same thing."

After five months, Elliot was laid off from his job at a factory that hires seasonal help. He couldn't find another job, except part-time work for a cab company. Elliot began spending more time away from the house with his friends at the local tavern, and less time with Julia and the baby. Julia finally had to get back "on aid" and Elliot put more of his things back in his sister's home so the social worker wouldn't know he was staying with Julia. Julia noticed changes in Elliot. "If you start necking and doing the same thing that you've been doing with your man, and he don't want it, you know for sure that he is messing with someone else, or don't want you anymore. Maybe Elliot didn't want me in the first place, but maybe he did 'cause he chased me a lot. He wanted me and he didn't want me. I really loved him, but I'm not in love with him now. My feelings just changed. I'm not in love with no man, really. Just out for what I can get from them."

Julia and Elliot stayed together, but she began to hear rumors about him. Her cousin, a woman who had often expressed jealousy toward Julia, followed Elliot in a car and told her that Elliot parked late at night outside the apartment house of his previous girl friend. Julia told me that her cousin was "nothing but a gossip, a newspaper who carried news back and forth," and that her cousin was envious of her having an "old man." Nevertheless, Julia believed the gossip.

After hearing other rumors and gossip about Elliot, Julia said, "I still really liked him, but I wasn't going to let him get the upper hand on me. After I found out that he was messing with someone else, I said to myself, I was doing it too, so what's the help in making a fuss. But after that, I made him pay for being with me!

"I was getting a check every month for rent from welfare and I would take the money and buy me clothes. I bought my own wardrobe and I gave my mother money for keeping the baby while I was working. I worked here and there while I was on aid and they were paying my rent. I didn't really need Elliot, but that was extra money for me. When he asked me what happened to my check I told him I got off and couldn't get back on. My mother knew. She didn't care what I did so long as I didn't let Elliot make an ass out of me. The point is a woman has to have her own pride. She can't let a man rule her. You can't let a man kick you in the tail and tell you what to do. Anytime I can make an ass out of a man, I'm going to do it. If he's doing the same to me, then I'll quit him and leave him alone."

After Elliot lost his job, and kin continued to bring gossip to Julia about how he was playing around with other women, Julia became embittered toward Elliot and was anxious to hurt him. There had been a young Black man making deliveries for a local store who would pass her house every day, and flirt with her. Charles would slow down his truck and honk for Julia when he passed the house. Soon she started running out to talk to him in his truck and decided to "go" with him. Charles liked Julia and brought nice things for her child.

"I put Elliot in a trick," Julia told me soon after she stopped going with Charles. "I knew that Elliot didn't care nothing for me, so I made him jealous. He was nice to the kids, both of them, but he didn't do nothing to show me he was still in love with me. Me and Elliot fought a lot. One night Charles and me went to a motel room and stayed there all night. Mama had the babies. She got mad. But I was trying to hurt Elliot. When I got home, me and Elliot got into it. He called me all kinds of names. I said he might as well leave. But Elliot said he wasn't going nowhere. So he stayed and we'd sleep together, but we didn't do nothing. Then one night something happened. I got pregnant again by Elliot. After I got pregnant, me and Charles quit, and I moved in with a girl friend for a

while. Elliot chased after me and we started going back together, but we stayed separate. In my sixth month I moved back in my mother's home with her husband and the kids."

Many young women like Julia feel strongly that they cannot let a man make a fool out of them, and they react quickly and boldly to rumor, gossip, and talk that hurts them. The power that gossip and information have in constraining the duration of sexual relationships is an important cultural phenomenon. But the most important single factor affecting interpersonal relationships between men and women in The Flats is unemployment. The futility of the job experience for street-corner men in a Black community is sensitively portrayed by Elliot Liebow in *Tally's Corner*. As Liebow (1967: 63) writes, "The job fails the man and the man fails the job." Liebow's discussion (p. 142) of men and jobs leads directly to his analysis of the street-corner male's exploitive relationships with women: "Men not only present themselves as economic expoiters of women but they expect other men to do the same." Ghetto-specific male roles that men try to live up to at home and on the street, and their alleged round-the-clock involvement in peer groups, are interpreted in *Soulside* (Hannerz, 1969) as a threat to marital stability.

Losing a job, then, or being unemployed month after month debilitates one's self-importance and independence and, for men, necessitates sacrificing a role in the economic support of their families. Faced with these familiar patterns in the behavior and status of men, women call upon life experiences in The Flats to guide them. When a man loses his job, that is the time he is most likely to begin "messing around."

And so that no man appears to have made a fool of them, women respond with vengeance, out of pride and self-defense. Another young woman in The Flats, Ivy Rodgers, told me about the time she left her two children in The Flats with her mother and took off for Indiana with Jimmy River, a young man she had fallen in love with "the first sight I seen." Jimmy asked Ivy to go to Gary, Indiana, where his family lived. "I just left the kids with my mama. I didn't even tell her I was going. My checks kept coming so she had food for the kids, but I didn't know he let his people tell him what to do. While he was in Gary, Jimmy started messing with another woman. He said he wasn't, but I caught him. I quit him, but when he told me he wasn't messing, I loved him so much I took him back. Then I got to thinking about it. I had slipped somewhere. I had let myself go. Seems like I forgot that I wasn't going to let Jimmy or any man make an ass out of me. But he sure was doing it. I told Jimmy that if he loved me, he would go and see my people, take them things, and tell them we were getting married. Jimmy didn't want to go back to The Flats, but I tricked him and told him I really wanted to visit. I picked out my ring and Jimmy paid thirty dollars on it and I had him buy my outfit that we was getting married in. He went along with it. What's so funny was when we come here and he said to me, 'You ready to go back?' and I told him, 'No, I'm not going back. I never will marry you.' ''

Forms of social control in the larger society also work against successful marriages in The Flats. In fact, couples rarely chance marriage unless a man has a job; often the job is temporary, low-paying, and insecure, and the worker is arbitrarily laid off whenever he is not needed. Women come to realize that welfare benefits and ties within kin networks provide greater security for them and their children. In addition, caretaker agencies such as public welfare are insensitive to individual attempts for social mobility. A woman may be immediately cut off the welfare rolls when a husband returns home from prison or the army, or if she gets married. Unless there is either a significant change in employment opportunities for the urban poor or a livable guaranteed minimum income, it is unlikely that urban low-income Blacks will form lasting conjugal units.

Marriage and its accompanying expectations of a home, a job, and a family built around the husband and wife have come to stand for an individual's desire to break out of poverty. It implies the willingness of an individual to remove himself from the daily obligations of his kin network. People in The Flats recognize that one cannot simultaneously meet kin expectations and the expectations of a spouse. Cooperating kinsmen continually attempt to draw new people into their personal network; but at the same time they fear the loss of a central, resourceful member in the network. The following passages are taken from the detailed residence life history of Ruby Banks. Details of her story were substantiated by discussions with her mother, her aunt, her daughter's father, and her sister.

''Me and Otis could be married, but they all ruined that. Aunt Augusta told Magnolia that he was no good. Magnolia was the fault of it, too. They don't want to see me married! Magnolia knows that it be money getting away from her. I couldn't spend the time with her and the kids and be giving her the money that I do now. I'd have my husband to look after. I couldn't go where she want me to go. I couldn't come every time she call me, like if Calvin took sick or the kids took sick, or if she took sick. That's all the running I do now. I couldn't do that. You think a man would put up with as many times as I go over her house in a cab, giving half my money to her all the time? That's the reason they don't want me married. You think a man would let Aunt Augusta come into the house and take food out of the icebox from his kids? They thought that way ever since I came up.

''They broke me and Otis up. They kept telling me that he didn't want me, and that he didn't want the responsibility. I put him out and I cried all night long. And I really did love him. But Aunt Augusta and others kept fussing and arguing so I went and quit him. I would have got married a long time ago to my first baby's daddy, but Aunt Augusta was the cause of that, telling Magnolia that he was too old for me. She's been jealous of me since the day I was born.

''Three years after Otis I met Earl. Earl said he was going to help pay for the utilities. He was going to get me some curtains and pay on my couch. While Earl was working he was so good to me and my children that Magnolia and them started worrying all over again. They sure don't want me married. The same thing that happened to Otis happened to many of my boyfriends. And I ain't had that many men. I'm tired of them bothering me with their problems when I'm trying to solve my own problems. They tell me that Earl's doing this and that, seeing some girl.

''They look for trouble to tell me every single day. If I ever marry, I ain't listening to what nobody say. I just listen to what he say. You have to get along the best way you know how, and forget about your people. If I got married they would talk, like they are doing now, saying, 'He ain't no good, he's been creeping on you. I told you once not to marry him. You'll end up right back on aid.' If I ever get married, I'm leaving town!''

Ruby's account reveals the strong conflict between kin-based domestic units and lasting ties between husbands and wives. When a mother in

The Flats has a relationship with an economically nonproductive man, the relationship saps the resources of others in her domestic network. Participants in the network act to break up such relationships, to maintain kin-based household groupings over the life cycle, in order to maximize potential resources and the services they hope to exchange. Similarly, a man's participation is expected in his kin network, and it is understood that he should not dissipate his services and finances to a sexual or marital relationship. These forms of social control made Ruby afraid to take the risks necessary to break out of the cycle of poverty. Instead, she chose the security and stability of her kin group. Ruby, recognizing that to make a marriage last she would have to move far away from her kin, exclaimed, "If I ever get married, I'm leaving town!" While this study was in progress, Ruby did get married, and she left the state with her husband and her youngest child that very evening.

Fathers and Children

People in The Flats show pride in all their kin, and particularly new babies born into their kinship networks. Mothers encourage sons to have babies, and even more important, men coax their "old ladies" to have their babies. The value placed on children, the love, attention, and affection children receive from women and men, and the web of social relationships spun from the birth of a child are all basic to the high birthrate among the poor.

The pride that kinsmen take in the children of their sons and brothers is seen best in the pleasure that the mothers and sisters of these men express. Such pride was apparent during a visit I made to Alberta Cox's home. She introduced me to her nineteen-year-old son Nate and added immediately, "He's a daddy and his baby is four months old." Then she pointed to her twenty-two-year-old son Mac and said, "He's a daddy three times over." Mac smiled and said, "I'm no daddy," and his friend in the kitchen said, "Maybe going on four times, Mac." Alberta said, "Yes you are. Admit it, boy!" At that point Mac's grandmother rolled back in her rocker and said, "I'm a grandmother many times over, and it make me proud." A friend of Alberta's told me later that Alberta wants her sons to have babies because she thinks it will make them more responsible.

Although she usually dislikes the women her sons go with, claiming they are "no-good trash," Alberta accepts the babies and asks to care for them whenever she has a chance.

Although Blacks, like most Americans, acquire kin through their mothers and fathers, the economic insecurity of the Black male and the availability of welfare to the mother–child unit make it very difficult for an unemployed Black husband-father to compete with a woman's kin for authority and control over her children. As we have seen women seek to be independent, but also, in order to meet everyday needs, they act to strengthen their ties with their kin and within their domestic network. Though these two strategies, especially in the context of male joblessness, may lead to the breakup of a young couple, a father will maintain his ties with his children. The husband-father role may be limited, but, contrary to the stereotype of Black family life, it is not only viable but culturally significant.

Very few young couples enter into a legal marriage in The Flats, but a father and his kin can sustain a continuing relationship with the father's children if the father has acknowledged paternity, if his kin have activated their claims on the child, and if the mother has drawn these people into her personal network. Widely popularized and highly misleading statistics on female-headed households have contributed to the assumption that Black children derive nothing of sociological importance from their fathers. To the contrary, in my recent study of domestic life among the poor in a Black community in the Midwest (Stack, 1972), I found that 70 percent of the fathers of 1,000 children on welfare recognized their children and provided them with kinship affiliations. But because many of these men have little or no access to steady and productive employment, out of the 699 who acknowledged paternity, only 84 (12 percent) gave any substantial financial support to their children. People in The Flats believe a father should help his child, but they know that the mother cannot count on his help. Community expectations of fathers do not generally include the father's *duties* in relation to a child; they do, however, assume the responsibilities of the father's kin. Kinship through males in The Flats is reckoned through a chain of acknowledged genitors, but social fatherhood is shared by the genitor with his kin, and with the mother's husband or with her boyfriends.

Although the authority of a father over his genealogical children or his wife's other children is limited, neither the father's interest in his child nor the desire of his kin to help raise the child strains the stability of the domestic network. Otis's kin were drawn into Ruby's personal network through his claims on her children, and through the long, close friendship between Ruby and Otis's sister, Willa Mae. Like many fathers in The Flats, Otis maintained close contact with his children, and provided goods and care for them even when he and Ruby were not on speaking terms. One time when Otis and Ruby separated, Otis stayed in a room in Ruby's uncle's house next door to Ruby's mother's house. At that time Ruby's children were being kept by Magnolia each day while Ruby went to school to finish working toward her high school diploma. Otis was out of work, and he stayed with Ruby's uncle over six months helping Magnolia care for his children. Otis's kin were proud of the daddy he was, and at times suggested they should take over the raising of Otis and Ruby's children. Ruby and other mothers know well that those people you count on to share in the care and nurturing of your children are also those who are rightfully in a position to judge and check upon how you carry out the duties of a mother. Shared responsibilities of motherhood in The Flats imply both a help and a check on how one assumes the parental role.

Fathers like Otis, dedicated to maintaining ties with their children, learn that the relationship they create with their child's mother largely determines the role they may assume in their child's life. Jealousy between men makes it extremely difficult for fathers to spend time with their children if the mother has a boyfriend, but as Otis said to me, "When Ruby doesn't have any old man then she starts calling on me, asking for help, and telling me to do something for my kids." Between such times, when a man or a woman does not have an ongoing sexual relationship, some mothers call upon the fathers of their children and temporarily "choke" these men with their personal needs and the needs of the children. At these times, men and women reinforce their fragile but continuing relationship, and find themselves empathetic friends who can be helpful to one another.

A mother generally regards her children's father as a friend of the family whom she can recruit for help, rather than as a father failing his parental duties. Although fathers voluntarily help out with their children, many fathers cannot be depended upon as a steady source of help. Claudia Williams talked to me about Harold, the father of her two children. "Some days he be coming over at night saying, 'I'll see to the babies and you can lay down and rest, honey,' treating me real nice. Then maybe I don't even see him for two or three months. There's no sense nagging Harold. I just treat him as some kind of friend even if he is the father of my babies." Since Claudia gave birth to Harold's children, both of them have been involved in other relationships. When either of them is involved with someone else, this effectively cuts Harold off from his children. Claudia says, "My kids don't need their daddy's help, but if he helps out then I help him out, too. My kids are well behaved, and I know they make Harold's kinfolk proud."

Conclusions

The view of Black women as represented in their own words and life histories coincides with that presented by Joyce Ladner: "One of the chief characteristics defining the Black woman is her [realistic approach] to her [own] resources. Instead of becoming resigned to her fate, she has always sought creative solutions to her problems. The ability to utilize her existing resources and yet maintain a forthright determination to struggle against the racist society in whatever overt and subtle ways necessary is one of her major attributes" (Ladner, 1971: 276–77).

I have particularly emphasized those strategies that women can employ to maximize their independence, acquire and maintain domestic authority, limit (but positively evaluate) the role of husband and father, and strengthen ties with kin. The last of these—maximizing relationships in the domestic network—helps to account for patterns of Black family life among the urban poor more adequately than the concepts of nuclear or matrifocal family. When economic resources are greatly limited, people need help from as many others as possible. This requires expanding their kin networks—increasing the number of people they hope to be able to count on. On the one hand, female members of a network may act to break up a relationship that has become a drain on their resources. On the other, a man is expected to contribute to his own kin network, and it is assumed that he should not dissipate his services and finances to a marital relationship. At the same time, a woman will continue to seek aid from the man who has fathered her children, thus building up her own network's resources. She also expects something of his kin, especially his mother and sisters. Women continually activate these lines to bring kin and friends into the network of exchange and obligation. Most often, the biological father's female relatives are also poor and also try to expand their network and increase the number of people they can depend on.

Clearly, economic pressures among cooperating kinsmen in the Black community work against the loss of either males or females— through marriage or other long-term relationships—from the kin network. The kin-based cooperative network represents the collective adaptations to poverty of the men, women, and children within the Black community. Loyalties and dependencies toward kinsmen offset the ordeal of unemployment and racism. To cope with the everyday demands of ghetto life, these networks have evolved patterns of co-residence, elastic household boundaries; lifelong, if intermittent, bonds to three-generation households; social constraints on the role of the husband-father within the mother's domestic group; and the domestic authority of women.

References

Abrahams, Roger. 1963. *Deep Down in the Jungle*. Hatboro, Pa.

Bernard, Jessie. 1966. *Marriage and Family Among Negroes*. Englewood Cliffs, N.J.

Buchler, Ira R., and Henry A. Selby. 1968. *Kinship and Social Organization: An Introduction to Theory and Method*. New York.

Fortes, Meyer. 1958. "Introduction," in Jack Goody, ed., *The Developmental Cycle in Domestic Groups*. Cambridge, Eng.

Gonzalez, Nancie. 1965. "The Consanguineal Household and Matrifocality," *American Anthropologist*, 67: 1541–49.

———1969. *Black Carib Household Structure: A Study of Migration and Modernization*. Seattle.

———1970. "Toward a Definition of Matrifocality," in N. E. Whitten and J. F. Szwed, eds., *Afro-American Anthropology: Contemporary Perspectives*. New York.

Hannerz, Ulf. 1969. *Soulside: Inquiries into Ghetto Culture and Community*. New York.

Ladner, Joyce. 1971. *Tomorrow's Tomorrow: The Black Woman*. Garden City, N.Y.

Liebow, Elliot. 1967. *Tally's Corner*. Boston.

Moynihan, Daniel Patrick. 1965. *The Negro Family: The Case for National Action*. Prepared for the Office of Policy Planning and Research of the Department of Labor, Washington, D.C.

Otterbein, Keith F. 1970. "The Development Cycle of the Andros Household: A Diachronic Analysis," *American Anthropologist*, 72: 1412–19.

Rainwater, Lee. 1966. "Crucible of Identity: The Negro Lower-Class Family," *Daedalus*, 95 (2): 172–216.

Smith, Raymond. 1970. "The Nuclear Family in Afro-American Kinship," *Journal of Comparative Family Studies*, 1 (1): 55–70.

Stack, Carol B. 1970. "The Kindred of Viola Jackson: Residence and Family Organization of an Urban Black American Family," in N. E. Whitten and J. F. Szwed, eds., *Afro-American Anthropology: Contemporary Perspectives*. New York.

———1972. "Black Kindreds: Parenthood and Personal Kindreds Among Blacks Supported by Welfare," *Journal of Comparative Family Studies*, 3 (2): 194–206.

———1974. *All Our Kin: Strategies for Survival in a Black Community*. New York.

Valentine, Charles. 1970. "Blackston: Progress Report on a Community Study in Urban Afro-America." Mimeo. Washington University, St. Louis.

Black Liberation, Women's Liberation
Andrew E. Slaby and Joan R. Sealy

The authors interviewed 74 randomly selected college students in an attempt to determine reasons for black women's lack of involvement in the women's liberation movement. Black female students showed a great concern with blackness and its implications but less concern than their white counterparts about integrating vocational interests with their concept of their sex role. It was noted that the black students' fathers were often of lower occupational, educational, and social status than their mothers. The possible implications of these findings are discussed.

There has been a conspicuous absence of any significant involvement by black women in the women's liberation movement. This seems somewhat ironic since the rhetoric of the movement often includes allusions to the concept of the "woman as nigger," suggesting that a woman's plight in America is somewhat similar to that of blacks. The question of liberation as women somehow does not appear to be relevant to black women now or, if it is relevant, seems of less importance than their liberation as blacks.

At first glance the lack of affiliation between the two ostensible minority groups might seem incongruent with the observations of some (e.g., some women liberationists) that the two are sister victims of a predominantly white patriarchal social system. Yet comparisons between the two movements are increasingly coming under criticism. It is true that blacks and women not infrequently encounter comparable employment difficulties when presenting credentials, skills, and experience equivalent to or greater than those of white male applicants. However, American women are generally not segregated from the so-called oppressive male subculture while growing up, and in addition, women form approximately 51 percent of the population, while blacks constitute only 11 percent.[1]

Other clear differences between the two subcultures often overlooked by overzealous advocates of a union between the two movements have been discussed by women such as Anne Osborne of the Southern Christian Leadership Conference in Atlanta, Ga. Reflecting on the apparent reluctance of black women to participate in the liberation movement, she explained that black women are "just beginning to get the kind of good treatment as women that white women have always had. They don't want to give it up too fast. Black men have just gotten enough money to take them to nice places, and women like it.[2]

The literature on the women's liberation movement provides other suggestions for a basis of distinction between the two egalitarian movements. Kate Millett has contended that, given a patriarchal society, women are taken less seriously than men intellectually, are seen primarily as sexual objects, and are deemed less powerful in the marital contract.[3] However, it is not clear that these points are as applicable to the black subculture as to the white. Billingsley, for instance, has said that there is a stronger tendency toward mutual aid in black family life as a consequence of the black subculture's subordinate position in the largely white American society.[4] If this indeed is so, then it would not seem surprising that most black women reject a major concern for liberation as women at present and instead devote

[1]Brine, R. "Women's lib: beyond sexual politics." *Time*, July 26, 1971. pp 36–37.

[2]"Who's come a long way, baby?" *Time*, August 31, 1970, pp 16–21.

[3]Millett, K. *Sexual Politics* (Boston, Doubleday & Co, 1967).

[4]Billingsley, A. *Black Families in White America* (Englewood Cliffs, N.J., Prentice-Hall, 1968).

From the *American Journal of Psychiatry* 130 (February 1973): 196–200. Copyright 1973 the American Psychiatric Association.

their energies to the more general liberation of the black people.

Other factors possibly contributing to the general absence of blacks in the rank and file of the women's liberation movement emerged during interviews of 74 students who entered Yale College in September 1970. These students have been interviewed serially during their freshman year and again during their sophomore year in an attempt to identify psychosocial origins of student commitment and alienation in the early 1970s. All of these randomly chosen students consented to be in the study and have remained in it. There are 32 blacks and 29 women in the group.

Black Identity

It is striking that, when talking with black women, one repeatedly hears allusions to blackness, but none to involvement with women's liberation. Interviews are replete with references to the subjects' own blackness and their concern for their black "sisters" and "brothers." For instance, one black woman, when asked what she expected to be doing 20 years from now, stated, "I'd like to be involved in the black community and feel 20 years from now I will be." The sincerity of her response was evidenced by her present involvement as an officer in a black organization on campus. Another black student, when asked about the role of politics in her life, expressed concern for black youths looking for easy solutions to racial problems. "I'd like to be an activist, but I'm disgusted with the way things are. I think it is the height of arrogance for college kids to call Americans this and that and racist and all. I'm more concerned with the black people."

Many felt that the concern with blackness contributed to the formation of all-black groups that interacted little with white students. Commenting on this phenomenon, one black student said, "Three-fourths of blacks will just stick around with blacks. Although they may occasionally be with white friends, they eat with blacks and also party with blacks, and if they take gut courses, they try to take them with blacks." Another black woman student gave a rationale for the formation of a separate subculture and also for the choice of Yale as a college by some black students. She said, "My friends are from the same

ethnic background; it's less complicated . . . especially since not everyone believes in U.N.-type relationships. Some black students came to Yale explicitly to meet other black students who are achieving academically at the same level."

It would be misrepresentative to state that these young women were not concerned with the issues of womanhood, but they had no major concerns about the oppression of women. Attitudes toward women's liberation among black coeds ranged from that put forth by one who, when asked how she saw the concern for the environment and ecology, commented, "It's really a serious problem, but I think at the present people are jumping on the wagon because they have nothing better to do . . . and I think the same of women's liberation." Another was asked what she saw herself doing 20 years hence; in an open acknowledgment of "male chauvinism," she replied, "Living in New York or Paris . . . married, with two children . . . a free-lance architect . . . [and married to] someone with a formal education . . . through college at least . . . a male chauvinist who would let me work at home as long as I take care of the house and kids."

In addition to their relatively greater concern for blackness than for their role as women or "liberationists," these students generally were not overtly struggling with questions about the style of life they wanted to lead or with religious or philosophical issues. Major discussions centering around career choice were not found in the interviews of the black students as they were in many of the white students' interviews. In addition, the black students did not tend to define their primary goal in college as "vocational," as did many of the black students entering college in 1966 who were studied by Hedegard and Brown.[5] The interviews with black students, when compared to those with white students, contained less reflection about the most appropriate role for a young intellectual in contemporary society and about the difficulty in formulating a consistent philosophy of life when many of the major premises on which much of their parents' lives were based were being queried.

In some ways it seemed, in fact, that the black students were made so acutely aware of

[5]Hedegard, J. M., Brown, D. R. "Encounters of some Negro and white freshman with a public multiversity." *Journal of Social Issues* 25:131–144, 1969.

their blackness that it could not help but be a major issue in their lives, for others would not have it less. One black woman, asked whether black students were confronted with any particular problems at Yale, stated that indeed they were:

But it is hard to articulate them. That's all people talk about and some of the reasons given for problems with black students I don't agree with. Black students are more pressed by their peers to conform to a certain type. It is all outlined and you have no choice. Some teachers just love "niggers" and some grad students . . . very liberal students . . . who have read all the books on blacks. If you're not like they think you should be, you're a "Tom" or "white." And there are black students who want you to be like them. They go on like "you owe it to us, you're black and we're black." It's hard to be yourself.

She continued to elaborate on how many black students had never been in a predominantly white setting before and therefore did not "know how to act." She also spoke of classroom pressures: "If you're a black student, you don't speak for yourself but for all black students and what they are."

Occupational Status of Parents

These vignettes and others too numerous to recount document the concern among these students with black issues, but they do not explain the absence of references to concern with their oppression as women. For a possible explanation of this we must look beyond their days at Yale to what they told us about their homelife. When one closely examines the childhood experiences of these young people, one finds that most of the white male and female students come from families in which there is a clear disparity between the

occupational status of their fathers and mothers. While both parents may be seen as intelligent, sensitive, and well educated, the father clearly has attained a greater occupational status than the mother. Frequently their fathers are businessmen, lawyers, academicians, or physicians; their mothers often do not work outside the home, and if they do, they are usually employed in such traditional female positions, as social workers, teachers, and nurses.

This disparity in occupational status and/or academic achievement is highlighted again and again. One student's father was described as:

The son of Jewish Russian immigrants. They lived in Philadelphia and were very poor . . . and he had to work. He's probably the brightest person I know. I make the distinction because I don't think he's only smart. He went to high school there and then to Princeton and graduated Phi Beta Kappa and magna cum laude. He got an M.A. and Ph.D. in history at Harvard. He planned to teach history but then went to B.U. law school and now is a lawyer.

The same student's mother was described as: "From an upper-middle-class Jewish background. She went to Smith and back to Sarah Lawrence for teaching credits."

Although not all discrepancies in education are quite so remarkable, other students alluded to analogous situations. One coed whose father was an engineer-turned-teacher said, "My mother didn't go to college, but is going now. But without a college education she is one of the most brilliant people I have met."

Some white coeds seemed to associate certain types of achievement with their fathers. One girl, whose father had attended a prestigious college and had gone on to be a Rhodes Scholar at Oxford and whose mother had switched col-

Table 1.   Comparison of Mother's and Father's Occupational Status for Black and White Students

Relative Occupational Status of Mother[1]	Black Students (N = 32)	White Students (N = 42)
Greater than father's	8	1
Equal to father's	9	13
Less than father's	15	28

[1]. Occupations were ranked according to the seven positions on the modified scale used to calculate the occupational status for Hollingshead's Two-Factor Index of Social Position in Meyer's, J.K., and L.L. Bean, *A Decade Later: A Follow-up of Social Class and Mental Illness* (New York: Wiley, 1968).

leges to be with her future husband, reflected: "Part of my problem is that I am probably more like my mother . . . but I have certain traits of my father, too. My parents are very different, yet they come off quite well. My father is more practical and scientific; my mother is flamboyant."

Such perceptions of mothers as "flamboyant" or less practical than fathers were generally not found in interviews with black students, nor was there such a discrepancy in occupational status ($\chi^2 = 8.70$, p < .025) (see table 1).

In black families the occupational status of the mothers is not infrequently on a par with or greater than that of her husband. Mothers often work as teachers, nurses, and office clerks, while fathers frequently are mail carriers or servicemen or hold positions of comparable status. One black girl who never knew her laborer father, but whose mother holds a master's degree, described her parents thus:

My mother and father were divorced when I was very small, and I grew up with mom and grandmom. Mother knows what she wants and how to get it; I admire her determination . . . the fact that she is a strong person. I have the feeling she would do anything for her kids if she had to. She is unselfish when it comes to us. My stepfather has been married to mom for ten years. I really don't know him; I never wanted to know him. He's not interested in other people. Mom is a social worker. She got her bachelor's degree from Howard and her master's degree from Atlanta University. My stepfather is a mail carrier who went to school in Memphis and had no college. My real father and mother divorced when I was two. He also grew up in Memphis.

Regardless of the relative status of their parents' occupations, the black students usually described their mothers in terms suggesting a more practical and less flamboyant status than did their white counterparts. One whose father was a physician and whose mother was a social worker described her father as "very quiet . . . fairly easygoing but underneath always thinking . . . he's not one to initiate an argument . . . not heavy-handed. He loves his kids and out-of-doors. Inwardly my father has many aspirations for me because my brother didn't finish college and my father is hurt."

But she described her mother as "very dominant and outwardly strong . . . she can't hold anything in. She has fantastic wishes and hopes for both her kids . . . she's dominant!"

Another student, whose parents had not lived together since she was six years old, had a father who was a mail carrier and a mother who was employed as an executive secretary. Her description of her parents was nearly the reverse of that given by the girl whose father had been a Rhodes Scholar:

My father is really intelligent but also uneducated. He gives me all the luxury items; my mother gives me all the necessities. My mother paid for private school. I'm like my mother in my academic orientation. And I'm easygoing like my father . . . money is a thing to spend. My mother has a bachelor's degree and further credits; my father finished fourth or fifth grade.

Social Status of Parents

Although there were some families in which a black woman's father was a professional and her mother a housewife, we encountered this much less frequently than among the white coeds. In fact, not only was there a significant difference between the relative occupational status of black and white students' parents, but, in addition, if the social class of the fathers and those mothers who are employed is calculated, one discovers by comparison a statistically significant difference in the distribution in the two groups ($\chi^2 = 7.13$, p < .05) (see table 2). Black students' mothers, more frequently than their white counterparts', hold occupations of greater status than those of their husbands. Also, and not surprisingly, when calculating their social class (which combines both education and occupation), we find that they occupy positions that are more often equal to or greater than those of their husbands.

Is it any wonder, then, that the black coeds were less concerned with being emancipated from subservient occupations when they grew up in a culture in which the female identity models and predominant social ethic were such that a woman would work, and, moreover, work in occupations with status, in the eyes of the black

Table 2.   Comparison of Mother's and Father's Social Class for Black and White Students

Social Class of Mother[1]	Black Students (N = 24)	White Students (N = 28)
Greater than father's	9	2
Equal to father's	7	12
Less than father's	8	14

[1]   Social class was measured by Hollinghead's Two-Factor Index of Social Position (in Myers, J.K., and L.L. Bean, *A Decade Later: A Follow-up of Social Class* [New York: Wiley, 1968]), in which occupation and number of years of school completed are scored on the appropriate occupational and educational scales.

subculture (or white subculture for that matter), equal to or greater than their husbands'? It cannot be definitely stated from this study that roots of such female achievement lie in the fact that black women sought careers such as teaching to give them economic freedom and protection from the sexual exploitation that they might have suffered as domestics for whites, as Grier and Cobbs [6] have suggested. However, our study does confirm their observation that black women have sought careers in such areas.

The stereotypical Jewish immigrant families often encouraged their sons to pursue careers in medicine or law for economic security in the New World. Unlike them, black families forced into a status somewhat resembling that of immigrants in the dominant white subculture have often encouraged their women, either overtly or covertly, to pursue careers that could afford economic security in their adult years in a society in which educational and employment opportunities were greater for black women than for black men.

Discussion

Given, then, the fact that black female students are unlike their white counterparts, who as adults may be pursuing roles discordant with the predominant cultural ethic of their youth and in some ways antithetical to that of their predomi-nant identity models (their mothers), one would anticipate that this would be less of a concern in adolescence and early adulthood for an intel-ligent black woman than her blackness. Most of these students are upwardly mobile and aspire to high-status occupations. Yet they cannot dis-count the fact that for years most of them grew up in a subculture predominantly consisting of peo-ple relegated by limited educational and occupa-tional opportunities to a Class V or at best Class IV position. The same black female models who were on a par with their husbands occupationally were generally perceived as somewhat inferior by the predominant white subculture because of their blackness.

One could postulate—and, indeed, it would seem worthy of study—that blacks in some African nations who grew up in a predominantly black culture would be as unlikely to mention "black-ness" in such interviews as whites are to mention "whiteness" or concerns for the "white commu-nity" or "white power." Furthermore, should such an all-black society be of a patriarchal nature with greater educational and occupational oppor-tunities for men than for women and with a discre-pancy between men and women in occupational status, as in the white American culture, one could postulate that someday in its history, too, cries of sexism would arise and a movement would form to liberate the women of that society.

[6]Grier, W. H., Cobbs, P. M. *Black Rage* (New York, Basic Books, 1968).

7

Husbands and Wives

Ordinary Black Husbands:
The Truly Hidden Men

Jacquelyne Jackson

On the basis of research findings, the author presents some interesting ideas to contradict accepted stereotypes about Black men in Black families and about Black husband–wife relationships. There seems to be a definite role separation in household activities, with joint decision making on more significant family responsibilities. Some differences exist between older and younger Black husband–wife families and the Black husband figure shows signs of having a definite role and significant power.

The apparent voluminousness of and persisting myths in most literature about black families have generally been effective in masking its actually sparse, fragmentary, and inconclusive status. For example, any serious search for concrete data and generalizations about ordinary blacks functioning effectively or normally as spouses, parents, and grandparents is almost in vain. The present paucity of much of that literature has been generated primarily by the "culture of investigative poverty." That is, most of its contributors have been unduly possessed by a homogeneous view of blacks; an overconcentration upon abnormality (and especially upon by-products of sexual intercourse or, indeed, upon the sexual act itself); an apathetic lack of interest in interdisciplinary research; a short attention span; an exaggerated masculinity in defense of their adolescent knowledge; and an inability to defer gratification, as evidenced by their relatively frequent utilization of inappropriate racial comparisons and insufficient data which, of course, usually produce invalid conclusions.

Such traits, analogous in many respects to those commonly ascribed to the "culture of poverty," must be reduced to facilitate acquisition of realistic knowledge about black families in particular and families in general. One step in that direction is very simple: it is merely a description and uncomplicated statistical analysis of ordinary black family members. It recognizes the diversity of blacks, permits intragroup comparisons of blacks, and can eventually produce a baseline of normality from which deviations can be evaluated to determine if they are only "different strokes for different folks" or if they are inherently, structurally, or functionally deficient for their owners and those whose lives they affect.

This presentation is a humble step in that direction. It is merely a description and simple analysis of ordinary black husbands who, while numerically larger among black men, represent the truly hidden men from the perpetrators of the "culture of investigative poverty." It is so ordinary, so routine, so humdrum until you may well be bored by the absence of titillation about school drop-outs, streetcorner winos, drug addicts, muggers, absent fathers, and revolutionaries.

More specifically, this exploratory comparison of instrumental and affective relationships between spouses as reported by two sub-sample sets (i.e., nonmanually and manually employed husbands, and employed and nonemployed or largely retired husbands) from a larger study of roles and resources of older blacks in a southern

From the *Journal of Social and Behavioral Sciences* 20 (Spring 1974):19–27. © 1974 by the Association of Social and Behavioral Scientists. Reprinted by permission.

Presented orally at the 1973 annual meeting of the American Orthopsychiatric Association, New York, this research was partially supported by NIMH Grant # MH16554.

urban residentially segregated environment was particularly concerned about role allocations for ordinary household maintenance activities and about spouse unilaterality (i.e., decision-making by one spouse).

Following Adams' (1968) definition, *instrumental relationships* consisted of shared activities and mutual assistance patterns between subjects and spouses during the year immediately preceding the interview, with emphasis upon activity type and frequency of occurrence, while *affective relationships* were measured by *agreement* (i.e., responses to ''Would you say you and your spouse agree about things you really consider important in life?'' of no, very little, to some extent, to a great extent, or completely).

According to Blood and Wolfe (1963), *instrumental relationships* were also measured by ascertaining spouse dominance (i.e., husband only, husband more often than wife, husband and wife about equally, wife more often than husband, and wife only) in specific decision-making situations.

In the larger study, black interviewers, utilizing a modified Kinship Interview Schedule, modeled upon Adams (1968) and Blood and Wolfe (1963), collected data in 1968 and 1969 from approximately 73 percent of all male household heads or all males 21 or more years of age in an urban renewal area, as listed by the local Housing Relocation Office, and from 79 percent of adult male subjects randomly selected from designated blocks in areas peripheral to the urban renewal area, and produced a total of 170 male subjects married and living with spouse and included in this report.

Nonmanually (i.e., white-collar or salaried) and manually (i.e., blue-collar or wage-earning) employed subjects were similar in age (about 40 and 46 years respectively) and long-term or indigenous residence in the city. But, whereas well over two-thirds of the nonmanuals had completed or gone beyond high school, only about one-third of the manuals had achieved equivalent education. They also differed at the .05 level of confidence in that nonmanuals were less likely to be fathers (38 percent of the nonmanuals and 19 percent of the manuals were childless) and the manuals were somewhat more likely to be both fathers and grandfathers (true of approximately 35 percent of the manuals and 9 percent of the nonmanuals).

The mean age of nonemployed or largely retired subjects (about 61 years) was significantly higher than that of the employed subjects (about 45 years). Other significant differences at or beyond the .05 level of confidence also distinguished these two sub-groups: nonemployed subjects with less average education had longer community residence and more children and grandchildren, but they were more likely to be living only with spouse than were the employed subjects. All of these significant differences were, of course, expected, and they are normal.

Interview items, grouped under four major categories of (a) *household maintenance activities* (such as grocery shopping and breakfast preparation), (b) *household decision-making activities* (such as grocery budgeting and disciplining children), (c) *spouse interactive activities* (such as church attendance and family and commercial recreation), (d) *spouse affect* (i.e., agreement between spouses about major life values), were tabulated by response frequencies by (1) nonmanually and manually employed, and (2) employed and nonemployed or largely retired husbands, and chi-square analyses were utilized to test for significant differences.

Findings

Nonmanually and
Manually Employed Husbands

Among the 23 nonmanually employed husbands, about 70 percent had received more and 22 percent as much education as their wives, whereas approximately 52 percent of the manually employed husbands had received somewhat less education than their wives. Nevertheless both sets of husbands were not significantly different in their responses about *household maintenance activities*. Approximately three-fourths or more of both groups reported the wife as usually preparing her husband's breakfast, and washing, ironing, dishwashing, and housecleaning for the family, whereas 90 percent or more of the husbands usually performed the yardwork and household repairs. About 59 percent of the manually employed husbands reported that they most often performed grocery shopping as a couple, whereas about 57 percent of the wives of the nonmanually employed spouses were reported as usually doing the grocery shopping. About 61 percent of the nonmanually and 52 percent of the manually employed couples usually paid bills jointly.

Less role segregation was apparent in *household decision-making activities*. The majority of nonmanually and manually employed husbands reported husband-and-wife joint decisions in deciding about grocery budgets, insurance purchases, physician selections, and residential locations. About 61 percent of the nonmanually and 57 percent of the manually employed husbands also reported joint disciplining of children, but where joint discipline was generally absent, then husbands—and not mothers—most often served as disciplinarians for their offspring.

Whereas approximately 70 percent of the nonmanually and 76 percent of the manually employed husbands reported that they determined for themselves whether or not they would accept particular employment initially, a much smaller proportion (47.8 percent and 58.6 percent respectively) determined without spouse assistance if they would continue in that employment. A slightly higher percentage of the nonmanually (65.2 percent) than the manually (55.2 percent) employed husbands indicated that their wives only decided if and when they should work.

Among spouse interactive activities, where the activity had to have been engaged in jointly at least once during the year preceding the interview, nonmanually and manually employed husbands were indistinguishable only by church attendance with spouse. They differed, at or beyond the .05 level of confidence, in that nonmanually employed couples were much more likely to have shopped (other than grocery) or vacationed together, engaged in family or commercial recreation, visited relatives jointly, or engaged in other activities.

Manually employed husbands were also significantly more likely to report their wives as usually doing the family letter-writing (72.4 percent) than were nonmanually employed husbands (34.8 percent), and partial factors accounting for that difference may well include differential levels of education and employment statuses among the involved spouses. Although manually employed subjects reported their wives as those most likely to perform family letter-writing, they were not reported as those who usually telephoned relatives. Only about 45 percent of the spouses fell in that category. Among the nonmanually employed

spouses, a slightly higher percentage (39.1 percent) were reported as those who usually telephoned relatives than those who usually engaged in family letter-writing.

About 57 percent of the manually and 49 percent of the nonmanually employed husbands reported themselves and their spouses in complete agreement about the most important things in life.

Employed and Nonemployed or Retired Husbands

Among the 52 employed subjects (which includes both nonmanually and manually employed subjects compared above), about 46 percent had received more education than wives, as had about 30 percent of the nonemployed or retired husbands. In almost all of the remaining cases, husbands and wives had received equal education. Although educational levels of spouses among the employed group were higher than those among the nonemployed, the two groups were indistinguishable by differences in educational level between husbands and wives in each group.

The typical patterns of *household maintenance activities* reported for nonmanually and manually employed subjects also characterized those employed and not employed. Obviously, similarities would appear for the employed subjects, but what is most interesting is that they also tended to appear for the largely retired group who were older, had less education, and were most often no longer active in the labor force, as compared with employed subjects. Wives were most often reported as usually preparing their husbands' breakfasts and performing the family's laundry, dishwashing, and household cleaning chores. But two significant differences at or beyond the .01 level of confidence did emerge between the two groups: employed subjects were less likely to report their wives as usually performing household cleaning tasks and more likely to report them as dishwashers. Whereas almost all of the employed husbands reported themselves as the usual person responsible for yardwork and household repairs, a smaller percentage (but still a hefty majority) of the largely retired subjects fell within those categories. About 53 percent of the largely retired subjects reported their wives as the usual grocery shoppers, but the modal response

(46 percent) to this inquiry from employed subjects was husband and wife, a difference significant at the .01 level of confidence. About 40 percent of the largely retired subjects indicated that they most often paid bills, whereas the corresponding modal response from employed subjects (55.8 percent) was husband and wife. Although these two groups were statistically indistinguishable in their reports of the spouse most often paying bills (irrespective of the source of monies), greater spouse unilaterality was present among the largely retired.

For household *decision-making activities*, employed and nonemployed subjects resembled each other in spouse responsibility for grocery budgeting, deciding where to live, disciplining children, and physician selection. Joint decisions were most frequent among both groups for living locality and choice of physician. Those about grocery budgeting were much more characteristic of employed (56 percent) than the nonemployed (35 percent), which again reveals some greater spouse unilaterality among the latter.

These two sets of husbands differed critically by employment and insurance decisions. Nonemployed husbands reported greater unilateral power in decisions about their employment choices, and they also reported identical patterns for their wives. They also differed in spouse power regarding purchase of life and burial insurance. About 65 percent of the employed and 52 percent of the nonemployed reported joint decisions, while about 35 percent of the former and 30 percent of the latter reported husband only or husband mostly. None of the employed husbands reported wife only or wife mostly, but almost 18 percent of the nonemployed husbands placed their wives in that category.

Statistically significant differences were most apparent in a comparison of *spouse interactive activities*. Employed subjects were much more likely to report attending church, shopping, vacationing, family and commercial recreation, and other activities with their spouses. Although not statistically significant, they also visited relatives more frequently with their spouses. Their wives were usually more responsible for family letter-writing (53 percent) and somewhat less responsible for telephoning relatives (42 percent), with the reverse pattern typifying nonemployed husbands, where about 47 percent of their wives were usually

responsible for family letter-writing, and about 56 percent for telephoning relatives.

Modal *spouse affect* responses were complete agreement for employed (53 percent) and great agreement for nonemployed (58 percent) husbands. Fewer than four percent of both employed and nonemployed husbands indicated less than great agreement with spouses about the most important things in life.

Discussion

In general, this description of instrumental activities and perceived spouse agreement revealed the expected conjugal role segregation in household maintenance activities performed within or around the home. Wives engaged in traditional "women's work," and husbands in "men's work." Wives of nonmanually employed and of largely retired husbands were more likely to shop for groceries without their husbands than were their respective counterparts. Spouses were most often jointly involved in paying bills except among the largely retired group.

The reported pattern of household decision-making activities most often indicated joint spouse participation, particularly in activities directly affecting all family members. Data collected about parental responsibility for disciplining children suggested that fathers—and not mothers—in older black husband–wife families most often performed that function. Among younger families, there appeared to be a greater shift toward joint parental responsibility. Such data contradict the usual stereotype of the relative insignificance of the father in black families, and, perhaps more important, the extent of his power within his family. Undue emphasis upon matriarchal black families, e.g., has overshadowed patriarchal black families. In a recent comparison of selected research studies about black and white families between 1966 and 1970, it was noted that

When the concept of matriarchy is restricted to wife dominance in husband–wife families, existing evidence suggests strongly that matriarchy is most characteristic of white, professional families with unemployed wives. Lower-class, intact black families appear to be even more patriarchal (i.e., male dominated) than their white counterparts. That is, black males tend to exercise stronger power within their families than do white males. Clearly, among working-class and middle-class families, black or white, equalitarianism tends to be the dominant pattern, or at least there appears to be a shift towards that pattern (Jackson 1973:437–438).

Greater spouse unilaterality about employment statuses for husbands and wives was also more common among older than younger husbands.

With the exception of family letter-writing and telephoning relatives, the data clearly followed expected patterns of greater or more frequent spouse involvement in interactive activities among those in nonmanual than manual employment, as well as among those employed than those not employed. Such differences, of course, are functions of socioeconomic and health variables.

Perhaps most interesting was the striking amount of agreement reported by these husbands between themselves and their wives on the most important things in life. While these subjects were not asked specifically if they loved their wives, many of them volunteered sentimental comments about their wives to the field interviewers. My impressionistic judgments of many married black couples lead me to believe that love is valued. If so, we must question the validity of such assumptions about love and black couples as that given by Bell (1971:250).

There have been a number of studies indicating that husband–wife roles and patterns of interaction in the lower class are quite different from those of the middle class. In the Black lower class the notion of love as a prerequisite to marriage and as a condition for its successful maintenance is not a strong value. There is also strong evidence that companionship in marriage is not a strong value or behavior pattern in the lower class. Lack of marital companionship is reflected in the general patterns of sex-segregated activities. For example, lower-class partners tend to maintain old friendship and kinship ties rather than reorganize ties after marriage to make the spouse a part of one social network.

Bell (1971:250) further indicated that "Recent research indicates that the lower-class husband is not only tangential to family functioning but that very often his wife prefers it that way." These exploratory data about ordinary husbands, as well as data collected from many of their wives, but not reported herein, contradict Bell. But they also underscore the problems involved in generalizing about blacks from data unrepresentative of blacks.

Thus, in addition to this description of ordinary black husbands constituting the truly hidden men, obscured, as it were, by the "culture of investigative poverty," perhaps the primary purpose of this presentation could well have been that of calling attention anew to the critical need to accumulate meaningful and valid data about the diversities of black families. Except for purposes of demonstrating clearly racial discrimination and its consequences, the current paucity of our knowledge about black families mandates greater concentration upon comparisons of black families with black families, and not with white families.

In any case, these findings, while applicable only to the sample, could well be taken as hypotheses for future investigations of patterns of interaction between black husbands and wives.

References

Adams, Bert N.
1968 *Kinship in an Urban Setting*. Chicago: Markham.

Bell, Robert R.
1971 "The Related Importance of Mother and Wife Roles among Black Lower-Class Women." In *The Black Family, Essays and Studies*, ed. by Robert Staples. Belmont, California: Wadsworth, 248–255.

Blood, Robert, and Donald M. Wolfe
1963 *Husbands and Wives: The Dynamics of Married Living*. New York: Free Press.

Jackson, Jacquelyne J.
1973 "Family Organization and Ideology." In *Comparative Studies of Blacks and Whites in the United States*, ed. by Kent S. Miller and Ralph Dreger. New York: Seminar Press, 405–445.

The Power Relationship in
Black Families and White Families

Delores E. Mack

Eighty couples (forty Black, forty white) from the middle and working classes were investigated to examine the existing power relationship. Results showed that more differences existed between economic classes than across racial lines. Blacks and whites of similar classes exhibited the same decision-making power in the family unit. Dominance in the marital relationship was not unilateral but fluctuated as different situations arose.

Research on the black family in the United States has been dominated by the hypothesis that it is a matriarchal one, or one in which the husband is subordinated to the wife. This is in contrast to the white family that is viewed as having either an equalitarian family structure or one in which the wife is subordinated to the husband (Davis, Gardner, and Gardner, 1941). In the black family, however, the female rather than the male is viewed as the powerful, controlling figure. Sociologists contend that the black male plays only a peripheral role in family life. Drake and Cayton (1945) spoke of dependent men and forceful women. They described how both husband and child look to the female for steady support. Clark (1965) also contended that female job support leads to an unfortunate female dominance in the black family. Bernard (1966) went so far as to discuss the issue under the title "The unnatural superiority of the Negro woman." She did argue, however, that a more important factor than the wife's working to contribute to family support is the context in which this support occurs. She noted that in the Eastern European ghetto, a wife's supporting her scholar husband did not diminish his masculinity.

The existence of the black matriarchy has been attributed to the historical condition of slav-ery (Frazier, 1948) and to the present condition of a caste society. Sociologists (Bernard, 1966; Herzog, 1966) argue that slavery was an institution that had greater impact on the male than on the female; that is submissiveness was more expected of females than of males. Slavery kept black men in a permanent childhood, allowing them no responsibility for their "wives," their "children," or even for themselves. Slavery, in effect, was the castration of the black male.

Since the end of slavery, white fear of black males has succeeded in keeping the black female in her superior economic position and the black male in his inferior one. The black female is better educated than the black male, both at the elementary and the college level (Bernard, 1966; U.S. Department of Labor, 1965). Black women also have better employment opportunities (Bernard, 1966; Clark, 1965; U.S. Department of Labor, 1965).

Psychologists contend that this economic superiority has disastrous effects upon the male ego. Proshansky and Newton (1968) reported that the black female has a more positive self-concept than the black male. Herzog (1966) noted that the failure of the black male to hold a job lowers his self-esteem. It is hypothesized that the lack of economic achievement in the white world, coupled with the presumed critical, derogatory attitude of the female, intensifies the male's feelings of failure and inadequacy.

This analysis of the black family applies primarily to the working class. Sociologists suggest that the smaller black middle class has a family configuration that is quite different. Bernard (1966) reported that a stable family and conventional behavior were for many decades the criteria of social class among blacks. Drake and

Abridged from the *Journal of Personality and Social Psychology* 30 (September 1974): 409–413. © 1974 by the American Psychological Association. Reprinted by permission.

This study is based on a doctoral dissertation in psychology completed at Stanford University in 1969. The advice and support of the author's adviser, P. James Geiwitz, and other members of her committee, Leonard M. Horowitz and John W. Meyer, are gratefully acknowledged. This research was supported by National Science Foundation Grant GS 1680, principal investigator, P. James Geiwitz.

Cayton (1945) argued that this was a function of a long-time desire to be respectable, that is, white. Respectable to the black middle class meant imitating the white middle class. Thus, if the ideal white middle-class family is equalitarian, the ideal black middle-class family strives to be more so.

Although there is much consensus of opinion among sociologists and psychologists concerning female dominance in the black family, the research conducted in this area has failed to yield consistent results. This has been due partly to differences in indices used to measure power and partly to a failure to deal adequately with the class factor. Thus, a survey study conducted by Blood and Wolfe (1960) indicated that black females were more dominant in their families than white females. However, in a laboratory study conducted by Middleton and Putney (1960), in which husbands and wives were asked to fill out a questionnaire individually, then jointly, neither class nor racial differences were found. Another study cited by Bernard (1966) indicated that black families were more patriarchal than white families. This study, however, failed to indicate the social status of the families.

In the present study, the power relationship of black families and white families in both the middle and working classes was examined using several different indices of power.

Method

Subjects

The experimental units were 80 married couples between the ages of 20 and 50. The 80 couples were selected to form four experimental groups with 20 couples in each group: black middle class, white middle class, black working class, and white working class. All couples who participated were native Americans who had been married to each other for at least one year. The couples were recruited via local churches, schools, and businesses. The recruitment was selective, since the local residential area could be roughly divided into three zones: both middle- and working-class blacks lived in one zone; white middle-class couples lived in a second zone; and white working-class couples in a third zone. Recruitment of volunteers within a given zone was thus likely to select couples from a certain class and ethnic group. Similarly, the businesses ap-

proached employed either professionals (an engineering firm) or unskilled laborers (a janitorial service). The schools, on the other hand, employed both professionals and unskilled workers. Recruitment in a given residential area or business continued until the required number of couples had been reached. In this way, most couples who volunteered to participate met the criteria established for class; data from couples who did not meet the criteria were not included in the analysis.

In the recruitment procedure, couples were asked to participate in an experiment on husband–wife interaction and were not informed that the experiment focused on marital power. Each couple was paid $3.50 for approximately one hour of participation.

The criteria used for determining class were identical in both the black and white communities. The 40 couples categorized as middle class were those in which the husband had a professional or white-collar occupation, a bachelor's or higher degree, and the wife had at least a high school education. Couples categorized as working class were those in which the husband had a skilled or unskilled job and neither the husband nor the wife had more than a high school education.

Experimental Procedure

The sole experimenter was a black female. Each couple was tested in their own home. It was felt that couples would be both more willing to participate and more relaxed if the study was conducted in their own homes. The experimental procedure consisted of five tasks which are discussed below in the chronological order in which they were presented to the subjects.

Background information The first task presented to the subjects was the completion of a form used to classify couples as either middle class or working class. After the couples had completed these forms, they were presented with the second task.

Questionnaire In this task, each spouse was first asked to fill out a questionnaire individually with no consultation. Each couple was then asked to complete a second identical questionnaire jointly. There were a total of 18 questions in the areas of recreation, family purchases, and household tasks. The respondent was asked who usually made the final decision on a 5-point scale ranging from husband always (1) to wife always (5). Couples were not aware that they would be asked to fill out the same questionnaire. Most couples became quite involved in this situation, using the task of completing the questionnaire as a unique opportunity to examine their marriage relationship in greater depth. After couples completed the second questionnaire, they proceeded to the discussion task.

Discussion task   In the discussion situation, there were two questions with a five-minute discussion for each question. One question concerned child training and discipline, while the second question focused on President Nixon. Each spouse was asked to write an individual answer to the question. After completing the individual statement, each couple was asked to discuss the question, attempting to arrive at a joint statement within a five-minute discussion period. The experimenter recorded the amount of time the husband and the wife each talked. After the second joint statement was completed, the couples were presented with the bargaining situation.

Bargaining task   In this situation the husband and wife were asked to role play a customer and a salesman in an African boutique. They were given instruction sheets that asked them to bargain over four items imported from Africa: a ring, a dress, a wood carving, and a gourd. The four items were actually presented to the couples to use in the role playing.

The salesman instruction sheet given to the husband informed him that the total cost of the four items was $73. He was instructed to get as high a price as possible for the four items and not to inform the customer of the cost of the items to him. The customer instructions given to the wife told her that she had $150 to spend but that she should spend as little as possible. She was also instructed not to tell the salesman how much money she had to spend. The husband was informed that the best salesman (highest selling price) would receive a gift, while the wife was informed that the best customer (lowest selling price) would receive a gift.

There was no time limit on the amount of time spent in the bargaining situation. The experimenter recorded the total selling price of the four items agreed upon by the husband and wife. When the couples terminated the bargaining situation, they were given the postinquiry to complete.

Postinquiry   The postinquiry consisted of three sections. However, only the third section is discussed here. In this section each spouse was asked to rate who was the dominant partner in his marriage on a 7-point scale ranging from self to spouse. The experimental procedure terminated with the completion of the postinquiry.

Results

Questionnaire

The data obtained in the questionnaire situation were analyzed in a number of different ways. First, the index of power was defined as the percentage of resolutions decided in favor of the

Table 1.   Proportion of Resolutions on Questionnaire Increasing Husband Power: Means and Analysis of Variance

	Means	
Race	Middle Class	Working Class
Black	44.27	50.59
White	41.40	56.43

	Analysis of Variance		
Source	df	MS	F
Total	79		
Race (A)	1	44.11	.11
Class (B)	1	2,279.12	5.58[1]
A × B	1	379.31	.93
Error	76	408.66	

[1] $p < .025$.

Table 2.   Total Selling Price in Dollars: Means and Analysis of Variance

Race	Means	
	Middle Class	Working Class
Black	101.65	86.73
White	101.76	94.97

Source	Analysis of Variance		
	df	MS	F
Total	79		
Race (A)	1	349.07	.44
Class (B)	1	2,357.59	2.99[1]
A × B	1	330.86	.41
Error	76	788.32	

[1] $p < .10$.

husband. This index focused upon the way in which discrepancies between the individual statements of the husbands and wives were resolved by them on the joint questionnaire. The data (see Table 1) indicated a clear class difference . . . in which working-class husbands were more powerful than middle-class husbands. No racial differences were found.

The analysis above was concerned with the immediate interaction occurring in the experimental situation, while a second type of analysis focused on the perceptions or images that couples had of decision-making power in the family unit. In this type of analysis, a total score was obtained for each questionnaire by summing the responses to the 18 questions: the higher the score obtained, the greater the decision-making power attributed to the wife. The perceptions were analyzed separately for the husband, wife, and joint questionnaires. The data indicated that neither husbands nor wives differed in their perceptions of decision-making power. Similar results were also obtained for the joint statements.

Discussion Task

In the discussion task, the index of power was the proportion of time the husband talked. The data were analyzed separately for each of the two topics. Both the analysis of variance for the child-training topic and that for the Nixon topic revealed no significant difference by either race or class.

Bargaining Task

In the bargaining situation, the index of marital power was the total selling price that the husband and wife finally agreed upon. It was clear (see Table 2) that there was some tendency for middle-class husbands to obtain a higher price than working-class husbands. . . . However, the higher selling price reached by middle-class husbands may merely be an indicator of the acknowledged ability (and experience) of this class to pay more for their goods and services, rather than a function of the husband's power in the family relationship. Thus the important information obtained from this task is not that there were class differences but that there were no racial differences.

Postinquiry

The data obtained from the postinquiry on who was perceived as the dominant partner in the marriage were quite similar to those obtained in the questionnaire situation concerning the perception of decision making; that is, there were no significant differences among the husbands as to who was perceived as the dominant partner in the marriage. Moreover, husbands, tended to perceive themselves as only slightly more dominant than their wives. . . .

An examination of the data on wives (see Table 3), however, indicated that black working-class wives perceived themselves as more dominant in the marital situation than wives in the other three experimental groups. . . . However, all wives

Table 3.   Wife's Perception of Dominance: Means and Analysis of Variance

Race	Means[1]	
	Middle Class	Working Class
Black	5.30	4.30
White	5.10	5.45

	Analysis of Variance		
Source	df	MS	F
Total	79		
Race (A)	1	4.52	3.20[2]
Class (B)	1	2.12	1.50
A × B	1	9.10	6.45[3]
Error	76	1.41	

[1].   Maximum score for one subject $= 7$; higher score indicates the husband is more dominant.
[2]. $p < .10$.
[3]. $p < .025$.

saw the husband as slightly more dominant than the wife. . . . Thus, both husbands and wives subscribed to a rather equalitarian view of marriage, only slightly favoring the dominance of the husband.

Discussion

The results of this study indicate that complexity of the husband–wife power relationship. A comparison of the results obtained in the three experimental situations indicates the need for specification of the context to which one is referring. This is not surprising, since dominance in the three situations may require different skills. In the discussion situation, word volume was important. It did not matter what one said or even how one said it. In the bargaining situation, however, a more subtle type of manipulation occurred; that is, word volume was only one of the factors involved. In this situation, the experimenter observed husband–wife interaction in which several different strategies were used; for example, on several occasions, a rather nonverbal partner succeeded in besting his mate by simply repeating the word "No," thus forcing his mate to capitulate and change bids. The bargaining task also involved an element of deception. Situations were observed in which husbands started with selling prices in excess of $l,000, while in other cases, wives informed their husbands that they had only $50 to spend, "in all honesty." In a similar manner, the joint decision-making task was also one that

involved more than sheer word volume; that is, verbal manipulation and forcefulness in presenting one's side of an argument were important elements in this situation. This task, however, did not involve the element of deception that characterized the bargaining situation.

The results suggest that couple interaction in the three experimental situations may be a good index of power relationships in a marriage, and, moreover, that marital dominance is not a trait but a context-dependent function of the relationship between two marriage partners. Future studies of marital power must recognize and treat this complexity.

The perceptual data indicate that black and white working- and middle-class couples have very similar ideas about decision-making power and dominance in the family. These data indicate that the notion of equality or near equality between the husband and wife is a pervasive one in American society. On the other hand, the contradiction between the experimental and perceptual data highlights the problem of asking people what they do and assuming that the belief thus expressed is an accurate index of actual behavior in a given situation. Specificity, therefore, is required at two levels: both in the discussion of a couple's interaction in different situations, and in the comparison of their actual interaction with their declared intentions or perceptions.

The most important finding of this study is that class differences far outweigh any racial differences. Class differences were found in two out of the three situations examined; no comparable racial differences were found. The absence of racial differences and the importance of class suggest that a more careful analysis of these factors as determinants of various aspects of the marital relationship is needed.

References

Bernard J. *Marriage and family among Negroes.* Englewood Cliffs, N.J.: Prentice-Hall, 1966.

Blood, R., and Wolfe, D. *Husbands and wives: The dynamics of married living.* New York: Free Press of Glencoe, 1960.

Clark, K. *Dark ghetto: Dilemmas of social power.* New York: Harper & Row, 1965.

Davis, A., Gardner, B., and Gardner, M. *Deep south: A social anthropological study of caste and class.* Chicago: University of Chicago Press, 1941.

Drake, S., and Cayton, H. *Black metropolis: A study of Negro life in a northern city.* New York: Harcourt, Brace, 1945.

Frazier, E. F. *The Negro family in the United States.* (Rev. ed.) Chicago: University of Chicago Press, 1948.

Herzog, E. "Is there a 'breakdown' of the Negro family?" *Social Work*, 1966, 11(1), 3–10.

Middleton, R., and Putney, S. "Dominance in decisions in the family: Race and class differences." *American Journal of Sociology*, 1960, 65, 610–615.

Proshansky, M., and Newton, P. "The nature and meaning of Negro self-identity." In M. Deutsch, I. Katz, and A. R. Jensen (eds.), *Social class, race, and psychological development.* New York: Holt, Rinehart & Winston, 1968.

U. S. Department of Labor. *The Negro family: The case for national action.* Washington, D.C.: Office of Planning and Research, 1965.

8

Black and White: Sex and Marriage

Interracial Sex Relations

Robert Staples

In this article the author provides an explanation for the currently low frequency of Black female–white male relationships. He emphasizes both historical determinents and present factors.

. . . One thing should be stated about interracial sex relations from the outset. As far as black women and white men are concerned, there is considerable opposition to any sexual liaison between them, and the frequency of such sexual contacts—unlike past years—is much less than black male–white female relationships. In order to understand how this situation has evolved, two factors have to be examined: The historical relationship of white men and black women, and the different function and meaning of interracial sexual contacts for black women vis-à-vis black men.

. . . Black women have been raped by white men and subject to all sorts of other sexual abuses from them. They have served as sexual objects, concubines, and prostitutes to white men of all classes and racial philosophies. But they have rarely been accorded the protection and legal rights of white women. White men have seldom elevated them to the status of a wife with all the privileges attached to that position.

Even today when black women have more freedom from the wanton desires of the white male, [they are] the subject of annoying, obscene approaches of white men, both on the street and at social gatherings.[1] Black women report that they are insulted by white men daily. White men slam or close doors in their faces after holding them open for white women. Others complain of losing their jobs after refusing to acquiesce to white male requests for sexual favors.[2]

Because of the black woman's historical vulnerability to white male sexual overtures, whites stereotype her as a "slut," a woman who will go to bed with anyone, especially a white man. One of the results of this myth is a hatred of white men by some black women and a resolve to avoid any sexual contact with them.

Also, because their relationship with white men, historically, has been on a sexual basis, many black women assume that any white man who wishes to date them is interested only in sex. When Petroni asked a black girl how she would react if a white boy asked her out, she replied, "For a Negro boy to have a white girl is some sort of status symbol, but if a white asked me out, it would be a step down for him. I would think he wants something I'm not about to give him."[3]

One study comparing the interracial dating patterns of black and white male college students found some large differences. While 90 percent of the 80 black men reported experiences in interracial dating, only 12 percent of the 140 white men reported such experiences. Interracial dates without any sexual intimacy are in the minority in the case of black men. More than 50 percent of the white men report no intercourse associated with

[1]Poussaint, A. "Blacks and the Sexual Revolution." *Ebony*, Oct. 1971, p. 114.

[2]Hare, N., and Hare, J. "Black Women 1970." *Transaction*, Nov. 1970, p. 7.
[3]Petroni, F. A. "Teen-age Interracial Dating." *Transaction*, Sept. 1971, p. 54.

Abridged from "The Sexuality of Black Women," *Sexual Behavior* 3 (June 1972): pp. 11, 14–15. © 1972 by Robert Staples.

Footnotes renumbered.

interracial dating while only 9 percent of blacks so report. None of the white men had ever entered into a steady relationship with a black woman, while 45 percent of the black males had "gone steady" with one or more white females.[4]

Not only are black women less permissive with white dating partners, but their motivation for dating them is often different from that [for] dating black men. When we asked the women in our study about their feelings on interracial dating and sex, very few (less than 20%) approved of it or would participate in it. Some of them mentioned that they were not physically attracted to white men, others listed the historical abuse they had suffered from white people. Those who approved of interracial dating said they would do it but only for financial reasons. One said: "If a white man was good enough to satisfy me plus put money in my pockets, then it's alright."[5]

The economic motive along with the white male's higher status is cited by Clark as a primary reason for interracial sex relations.

Certain Negro women of status who have married white men report that their choice was related to their discovery that the Negro men they knew were inferior in status, interests and sophistication and hence unsuitable as partners. Many problems of race and sex seem to follow this principle of the self-fulfilling prophecy. The Negro woman of status may see the Negro male as an undesirable sexual partner precisely because of his low status in the eyes of whites. Unlike a white female who may reassure herself that the lower the status of the male, the more satisfying he is as a sexual partner, the upper-class Negro female tends to tie sexual desirability to status and exclude

many Negro males as undesirable just because their status is inferior.[6]

One other reason why few black women date white men is that they are rarely asked; in the interracial dating study, 77 percent of the white men expressed a preference for dating females of their own race. And [the black woman] is hardly in a position to do the asking herself. In this society women are expected to be passive while the men are aggressive and demanding. Thus, while black men have rapped their way into the heart of some white female, the black woman must wait to be approached by the white male who is often not as aggressive or as interested as his black counterpart.

Black women also have to cope with the attitudes of black men. One study tells of many black girls who will not date white boys because of pressures from black men who would object.[7] This situation has led one sociologist to assert that some black men are trying to imitate those white men who have had sexual access to both black and white women. She describes instances on white college campuses where black males date white coeds, reducing the number of dating partners for black coeds. Then, when some black coeds dated white men, a few black male students have castigated and threatened them.[8] Such black males seem to have acquired general male chauvinist values. They have a double standard of interracial dating which allows them a freedom to date white women while simultaneously restricting the freedom of black women to date white men. As one black woman stated: "While our [black] men seem thoroughly abreast of the times on every other subject, when they strike the woman question they drop back into sixteenth-century logic.[9] . . .

[4]Sebald, H. "Patterns of Interracial Dating and Sexual Liaison of White and Black College Men." Unpublished manuscript. Tempe, Ariz.: Arizona State University, 1971, pp. 7–8.
[5]Staples, R. "Sex and Games in the Black Community." Unpublished manuscript, 1971.
[6]Clark, K. *Dark Ghetto* (New York: Harper & Row, 1965), p. 68.
[7]Jackson, J. "Black Women in a Racist Society," in Willie, C., et al., eds., *Racism and Mental Health* (Pittsburgh: University of Pittsburgh Press), 1973, p. 195.
[8]Ibid.
[9]Cooper, A. J., quoted in Flexner, E., *Century of Struggle: The Women's Rights Movement in the United States* (Cambridge: Harvard University Press, 1959), p. 128.

The Prevalence of Black–White Marriage in the United States, 1960 and 1970

David M. Heer

The fear of marriage between Blacks and whites has been a standard feature of race relations in this country since the time of slavery. This author's research reveals a number of trends in Black–white marriages during the past decade. He points out, for example, that geography is related to the number of interracial unions. Emphasis is given to the amount of impact interracial marriages have had on reducing racial status differences.

Although marriages between blacks and whites are relatively infrequent in number, they are sociologically important because they serve as an indicator of the relationship between the two races. Moreover, it may be hypothesized that a low frequency of black–white marriages serves to reinforce the pattern of socioeconomic inequality between the two races. Several reasons for this may be advanced. First of all, on a per-capita basis white persons hold a far higher share of the nation's wealth than do blacks and a low frequency of racial intermarriage makes it unlikely for a black to inherit wealth from a white. Secondly, blacks are by and large excluded from the many unionized manual jobs to which entrance is strongly determined by kin connections because existing jobs of this type are usually held by whites and black persons rarely have white kin. Thirdly, the lack of close relatives among whites affects the socialization of black youth. In particular, they cannot obtain an easy familiarity with the social world of whites and hence are inhibited from applying for jobs demanding such familiarity even when their technical qualifications are completely satisfactory. Finally, over the long run it may be surmised that prejudice against blacks on the part of white persons would be diminished if the pro-

portion of whites with black relatives were substantial rather than negligible, as at present.

Only a very few states in the United States publish data on the incidence of newly contracted marriages by the race of each spouse. In a previous article (Heer, 1966) I presented data on the incidence of black–white marriage in four states—California, Hawaii, Michigan, and Nebraska in the late 1950's and early 1960's. Currently, however, neither Michigan nor California publish data on the incidence of black–white marriages and, furthermore, the annual number of black–white marriages in Hawaii and Nebraska is very small. More recently, Monahan (1970a, 1970b, and 1971) has presented data for recent years on the incidence of black–white marriage for Iowa, the city of Philadelphia, and New York State excluding New York City. My previous study and the various papers by Monahan all revealed a general upward tendency in black–white marriage for the period beginning in the 1950's with increase in marriages involving black husbands and white wives most pronounced. Additionally, an estimate of the total incidence of black–white marriage for the United States in 1967 has been presented by McDowell (1971) based on data from an unpublished tabulation of the number of such marriages for those states of the Marriage Registration Area reporting on race of bride and groom and an extrapolation to the remainder of the United States. However, since she presented data for only one year, no inference as to trends can be made.

In contrast to the paucity of data on the incidence of black–white marriage, a substantial set of data on the prevalence of such marriage has been available from the Decennial Census of the United States, first in 1960 and again in 1970. These data, based on a five per cent sample of the total United States population, show the number

From the *Journal of Marriage and the Family* 36 (May 1974): 246–258. © 1974 by National Council on Family Relations. Reprinted by permission.

The author wishes to acknowledge his indebtedness to Dr. Paul C. Glick, Mr. Robert Parke, Jr., and Mr. Arthur Norton, who were in charge of preparing the 1960 and 1970 Census tabulations upon which this paper is based.

of such marriages in existence at the time of the Census. Thus the data exclude interracial marriages dissolved by divorce, separation, or death prior to the date of the Census, and include any interracial marriages contracted outside the United States and still in existence at the time of the Census. Moreover, it is important to remember that the census data include consensual or common-law unions as well as those legally contracted. Analysis of the 1960 Census data on black–white marriage appears in Bernard (1966) and Carter and Glick (1970). The data upon which the present paper is based are contained in U.S. Bureau of the Census (1966), U.S. Bureau of the Census (1972), and U.S. Bureau of the Census (1973).

The number of existing black–white marriages by type and region in the United States as reported by the Censuses of 1960 and 1970 is shown in Table 1. The total number of such marriages increased 26.0 per cent between 1960 and 1970. This increase was considerably larger than the increase in the total number of married couples in the United States during the same time period, which was only 10.1 per cent. The total increase in the number of black–white marriages masks an important difference by type of marriage; there was a 61.7 per cent increase in the number of married couples in which the husband was black and the wife was white and a 9.1 per cent decrease in the number of married couples in which the husband was white and the wife black. The total increase in black–white marriages also hides an important difference by region; in the North and West black–white mar-

riages increased by 66.0 per cent whereas in the South they declined by 34.6 per cent. One may speculate that a large proportion of the black–white marriages existing in the South in 1960 and 1970 were consensual unions since the contracting of interracial marriages was illegal in every Southern state until the Supreme Court declared state miscegenation laws unconstitutional in June 1967. However, it would also have been possible for black–white couples to have moved to the South after having contracted a legal marriage in a Northern or Western state.

Before proceeding further, we should consider the validity of these data on interracial marriage reported by the Censuses. Although there is no direct measure of the validity of these Census statistics, data do exist concerning the validity of marriage certificates reporting black–white marriage. Monahan (1970b) compared the records of 485 black–white marriage certificates in Philadelphia with the corresponding marriage licenses. These licenses contained additional information on the race of the parents of both bride and groom. On the basis of this information, Monahan concluded that among these 485 cases of supposed black–white marriage, 32 per cent were erroneous and that 51 cases represented marriages between two whites and 105 cases represented marriages between two blacks. In a similar study in Washington, D.C., Lynn (1953) concluded that 10 out of 36 reported black–white marriages were actually racially homogeneous. In contrast to this over-reporting, it is also possible that some interracial marriages may not be recorded as such, particularly when the black part-

Table 1.   Number of Black–White Marriages by Type and Region, United States, 1960 and 1970

	1960	1970	Percentage Change Since 1960
United States: Total	51,409	64,789	+ 26.0
Husband black, wife white	25,496	41,223	+ 61.7
Husband white, wife black	25,913	23,566	−9.1
North and West: Total	30,977	51,420	+ 66.0
Husband black, wife white	16,872	34,937	+ 107.1
Husband white, wife black	14,105	16,483	+ 16.9
South: Total	20,432	13,369	−34.6
Husband black, wife white	8,624	6,286	−27.1
Husband white, wife black	11,808	7,083	−40.0

ner can pass as white. However, no data exist concerning the frequency of this type of error.

In line with the apparent over-reporting of black–white marriage from certificate data, it is also well known that the reported number of cases in census categories for which the true frequency is very small may include a substantial number for which the classification is in error (Truesdell, 1938; Coale and Stephan, 1962). Thus an over-reporting of black–white marriages in Census tabulations may occur simply because the race of a very few of the husbands or wives in the very large number of racially homogeneous marriages was inaccurately recorded. On the other hand, Census data-processing procedure has a tendency to reduce somewhat the reported number of interracial marriages since whenever the race of one spouse was not reported on the Census schedule it was assumed that it was identical to that of the other spouse.

If the great preponderance of reported black–white marriages represented nothing more than error in classification, it would follow that there would be few differences in black–white marriages by type, by region, or by any other characteristic, and that over time the number of black–white marriages would show a trend similar to that of all married couples. The data shown in Table 1, which show such marked differentials by type within each region, and such sharply diverging trends in number of such marriages by type and region, make it impossible to sustain the hypothesis that the great majority of reported black–white marriages represent nothing more than erroneous classification. We shall therefore proceed to a further discussion of the data to be

Table 2.   Percentage of Married Persons, Spouse Present, in Black–White Marriages by Sex, Race, Region, and Type of Residence, United States, 1960 and 1970

	Black Males		Black Females		White Males		White Females	
	1960	1970	1960	1970	1960	1970	1960	1970
United States:	0.8	1.2	0.8	0.7	0.07	0.06	0.07	0.10
In urbanized areas	0.8	1.4	0.7	0.6	0.07	0.07	0.08	0.14
Central city	0.8	1.3	0.7	0.6	0.10	0.10	0.11	0.23
Urban fringe	0.9	2.0	1.0	1.1	0.03	0.04	0.03	0.07
Outside urbanized areas	0.9	0.8	1.1	0.8	0.07	0.05	0.06	0.05
Northeast:	1.5	1.9	1.3	1.3	0.07	0.08	0.08	0.13
In urbanized areas	1.3	1.7	1.2	1.1	0.08	0.10	0.09	0.15
Central city	1.2	1.6	1.2	1.0	0.13	0.17	0.14	0.27
Urban fringe	1.6	2.2	1.1	1.7	0.03	0.05	0.04	0.07
Outside urbanized areas	3.8	5.4	2.8	3.5	0.04	0.04	0.05	0.06
North Central:	0.9	1.5	0.8	0.6	0.04	0.04	0.05	0.09
In urbanized areas	0.8	1.3	0.6	0.5	0.06	0.05	0.08	0.14
Central city	0.8	1.3	0.5	0.4	0.08	0.08	0.12	0.25
Urban fringe	0.7	1.9	1.4	0.9	0.03	0.02	0.02	0.05
Outside urbanized areas	2.5	3.9	2.9	3.0	0.03	0.03	0.02	0.03
South:	0.5	0.4	0.7	0.4	0.12	0.06	0.08	0.05
In urbanized areas	0.2	0.4	0.4	0.3	0.07	0.05	0.04	0.07
Central city	0.2	0.4	0.4	0.2	0.10	0.06	0.06	0.09
Urban fringe	0.2	0.6	0.4	0.4	0.03	0.03	0.02	0.04
Outside urbanized areas	0.7	0.3	0.9	0.5	0.14	0.07	0.11	0.04
West:	2.0	4.5	1.5	1.5	0.05	0.06	0.06	0.17
In urbanized areas	1.7	4.2	1.3	1.3	0.06	0.07	0.08	0.22
Central cities	1.7	4.0	1.1	1.3	0.08	0.10	0.12	0.33
Urban fringe	1.4	4.7	1.7	1.4	0.04	0.04	0.03	0.12
Outside urbanized areas	4.5	8.0	3.5	4.0	0.03	0.03	0.05	0.07

found from the two Censuses on the assumption that we are dealing with mostly valid cases.

Table 2 presents the proportion of persons by race and sex in black–white marriages by region and by type of residence for the United States in 1960 and 1970. For the United States, the proportion of black males married to white females increased from 0.8 per cent in 1960 to 1.2 per cent in 1970, and there was an increase of similar magnitude in the proportion of white females married to black males. On the other hand there was a slight decline in the proportion of black females married to white males (from 0.8 to 0.7 per cent) and of white males married to black females.

Substantial differences in the prevalence of black–white marriage by region existed both in 1960 and 1970. Let us consider first the data for blacks. In both years and for persons of each sex, the proportion of all black persons with a white spouse was highest in the West and lowest in the South. For example, in 1970 in the West as many as 4.5 per cent of all married black males, wife present, were married to white women and only 0.4 in the South. For blacks, the proportions married to a white spouse were generally highest outside urbanized areas and lowest in the central cities. An exception to this rule was the low proportion of black males married to white females in the South outside of urbanized areas in 1970. From 1960 to 1970 the proportion of black males with a white wife increased in all region-residence categories except for the South outside of an urbanized area. During the same time period the proportion of black females with a white husband increased in only 4 of the 12 region-residence categories.

The data for white persons, married and spouse present, present fewer uniformities than the data for blacks. For example, the proportion of white males married to black wives in 1960 was higher in the South than in any other region, but in 1970 was the same as the average for the United States. Moreover, in 1960 the proportion of white females married to black husbands in the South was as high as in any other region, but in 1970 the proportion of white females with black husbands was lower than in any other region.

In previous studies of racial intermarriage (Heer, 1966; Carter and Glick, 1970), it has been found useful to examine the ratio of actual number of persons intermarrying to the number which would be expected to intermarry if all marriages took place at random. This ratio allows one to examine the effect of factors affecting the choice of spouse other than sheer availability of potential partners. For example, one might argue that the relatively high proportion of Southern whites married to blacks in 1960 was due to the relatively higher proportion of blacks in the total population of the South compared to the remainder of the United States. Table 3 presents the ratios of actual to expected black–white marriage for husbands and wives by race and region for 1960 and 1970. In this table the expected proportion of black–white marriages for black males in each region was defined as the proportion of all wives in that region who were white. Analogous definitions were used for the expected proportions of black–white marriage among black females, white males, and white females. Table 3 shows, as we hypothesized, that the relatively higher proportion of blacks in the South can explain the relatively large proportion of Southern whites married to blacks in 1960. Indeed the ratios of actual to expected black–white marriage for the South are as low or lower than those of any region for each of the eight possible comparisons. Moreover, according

Table 3.   Ratio of Actual to Expected Black–White Marriage of Married Persons, Spouse Present, by Sex and by Race for the United States and Each Region, 1960 and 1970

	Black Males		Black Females		White Males		White Females	
	1960	1970	1960	1970	1960	1970	1960	1970
United States	.009	.013	.009	.008	.009	.008	.009	.013
Northeast	.016	.020	.014	.014	.014	.013	.016	.021
North Central	.009	.016	.008	.006	.008	.007	.010	.016
South	.006	.005	.008	.005	.008	.005	.005	.004
West	.021	.049	.016	.016	.017	.018	.020	.050

Table 4.   Proportion of Marriages in Which Both Husband and Wife Married Only Once, by Race of Husband, by Race of Wife, United States, 1970

Husband Black, Wife White	Husband White, Wife Black	Husband Black, Wife Black	Husband White, Wife White
%	%	%	%
61.1	67.4	72.7	80.7

to Table 3, from 1960 to 1970 the ratio of actual to expected black–white marriages for black males and for white females increased for the United States and for every region except the South, where it fell slightly. On the other hand, the ratio of actual to expected black–white marriages for white males and black females remained almost constant from 1960 to 1970 for the United States and the three regions in the North and West but declined substantially in the South.

Some Characteristics of Black–White Marriages by Type

Table 4 presents data on the proportion of marriages in which both husband and wife had been married only once among marriages with: (1) black husband and white wife, (2) white husband and black wife, (3) both husband and wife black, and (4) both husband and wife white. The highest proportion of marriages in which both husband and wife had been married only once occurred in marriages in which each spouse was white (80.7 per cent), the next highest (72.7 per cent) in marriages in which each was black, the next to lowest (67.4 per cent) in marriages with white husband and black wife, and the lowest proportion (61.1 per cent) in marriages with black husband and white wife.

racial marriages is their durability over time relative to racially homogeneous marriage. Monahan (1970a) studied this question for Iowa by examining the ratios of divorces in 1955–67 per 100 marriages in 1948–60 by race of husband and by race of wife. With both partners white he found a ratio of 19.4, with both black a ratio of 39.1, with white husband and black wife a ratio of 35.1, and with black husband and white wife a ratio of 16.8. Unfortunately, in such a study there can be no control for migratory divorce. Furthermore, not all divorces in 1955–67 pertained to the marriages of 1948–60. In view of the existing paucity of data on the relative stability of black–white marriage it is important that the 1960 and 1970 Census data can throw considerable light on this topic. Table 5 presents data concerning the ten-year attrition in the number of marriages by type among married couples where each spouse had been married only once and was first married in 1950–60. Attrition in these marriages could have resulted either by divorce or separation or as a result of death of spouse; however, the greater part is probably due to divorce or separation. A small amount of error is introduced because the tabulations for 1970 are for marriages which took place in 1950 through 1959 whereas the tabulations for 1960 are for marriages which took place in the period from 1950 through March 1960. Furthermore, a few married couples in 1970 whose marriage took place in 1950 through 1959 may have married

Table 5.   Number of Married Couples by Race of Husband and by Race of Wife, Both Spouses Married Only Once and First Married in 1950–60, United States, 1960 and 1970

	1960	1970	Number in 1970 as Percentage of Number in 1960
			%
Husband black, wife white	7,534	4,780	63.4
Husband white, wife black	6,082	2,842	46.7
Husband black, wife black	780,239	607,089	77.8
Husband white, wife white	8,430,979	7,571,614	89.8

outside of the United States and only entered the nation after the 1960 Census, and an additional small number of couples who were living apart in 1960 may have joined together in 1970. However, these small errors are no doubt negligible compared to the magnitude of the differences in attrition according to marriage type. After ten years, the proportions of marriages still in existence were as follows: (1) with black husband and white wife, 63.4 per cent, (2) with white husband and black wife, 46.7 per cent, (3) with both husband and wife black, 77.8 per cent, and (4) with both husband and wife white, 89.8 per cent. Clearly, the black–white marriages are shown to be less stable than the racially homogeneous marriages, and marriages involving white husbands and black wives more unstable than those of black husbands and white wives.

Another set of characteristics which may be examined from the 1970 Census relates to fertility. Table 6 shows the average number of children ever born, and the percentage childless, by age of wife for the four types of marriages considered previously. For wives younger than 55, the average number of children ever born was fewer in marriages of a white husband with a black wife than in marriages of a black husband with a white wife. On the other hand, an opposite situation obtained when the wife was 55 years of age or older. In all age groups the proportion childless was higher for married couples with white husband and black wife than for married couples with black husband and white wife; however, the difference was greatest when the wife's age was less than 55 years.

In both types of interracial marriages the average number of children ever born was fewer than in homogeneous black marriages, and, on the whole, was similar to that among couples where both husband and wife were white. Nevertheless, the proportion childless among wives in the two types of interracial marriages was in every age group greater than among homogeneous white couples and also greater than among homogeneous black couples provided the wife was younger than 45 years.

It should be noted that it is impossible to provide exact data from the 1970 Census on the number of children born with racially-mixed parentage. This is because we cannot be sure that the children born to women in a racially heterogeneous marriage in 1970 were necessarily born during their mother's then current marriage. As was shown in Table 4, in a substantial number of the racially mixed marriages either husband or wife had been married more than once and thus it is plausible to assume that some of the wives in a racially heterogeneous marriage in 1970 may have born some or all of their children in a previous racially homogeneous marriage. Apparently the only data concerning the number of children actually born within black–white marriage comes from Golden (1954). He noted the relatively small number of offspring. However, generalization from this sample would be risky because the number of

Table 6.   Average Number of Children Ever Born to Wife and Proportion of Wives Childless by Age of Wife and by Race of Husband, by Race of Wife, United States, 1970

Average Number of Children Ever Born	Husband Black, Wife White	Husband White, Wife Black	Husband Black, Wife Black	Husband White, Wife White
Age of wife:				
15 to 24 years	.999	.847	1.491	.941
25 to 34 years	2.107	1.923	2.923	2.325
35 to 44 years	2.801	2.583	3.881	3.082
45 to 54 years	2.775	2.216	3.338	2.703
55 years and over	2.474	2.538	2.936	2.436
Proportion Childless				
Age of wife:				
15 to 24 years	37.6	48.4	23.0	39.7
25 to 34 years	21.8	25.4	11.4	11.7
35 to 44 years	16.7	19.0	11.2	7.0
45 to 54 years	19.1	26.5	20.0	10.6
55 years and over	24.5	26.3	28.0	17.8

Table 7. Percentage of Persons in Black–White Marriage, by Sex, Race, and Decade in Which Husband and Wife First Married When Both Married Once, United States, 1970

Couple First Married	Black Males	Black Females	White Males	White Females
1960–70	1.8	0.8	0.08	0.18
1950–59	0.8	0.5	0.04	0.06
1940–49	0.5	0.5	0.03	0.03

Table 8. Percentage of Persons in Black–White Marriages by Sex, Race, and Decade in Which Husband First Married, United States, 1960

Husband First Married	Black Males	Black Females	White Males	White Females
1950–60	1.0	0.8	0.08	0.10
1940–49	0.8	0.8	0.06	0.06
Before 1940	0.7	0.9	0.07	0.06

couples studied, 50, was so small and, moreover, the sample was not randomly drawn.

Proportion of All Married Persons with Given Characteristics Involved in Black–White Marriage

Table 7 presents data from the 1970 Census concerning the proportions of married persons, spouse present, married only once and with spouse married only once, involved in a black–white marriage by race and by sex and by the decade in which the couple first married. Table 8 presents similar data from the 1960 Census except that the table refers to all married persons, spouse present, subdivided by decade in which the husband first married. The 1970 data show for each race and sex group a substantially higher proportion involved in a black–white marriage if the couple were first married in the decade just preceding the Census. The results are particularly striking for black males and white females. The

data for 1960 do not reveal substantial differences by decade in which the husband was first married.

Table 9 presents data from the 1970 Census concerning the proportions of married persons, spouse present (with both husband and wife married only once and first married in 1960–70), who were involved in black–white intermarriage according to race, sex, and own income in 1969. For black males and white females there is a substantial positive relationship between income in 1969 and proportion involved in black–white marriage. No strong relationship is evident for white males or black females. Table 10 presents data from the 1970 Census concerning the proportions involved in black–white intermarriage for married persons, spouse present (with both husband and wife married once and first married in 1960–70), by race, by sex, and by educational attainment. For both black males and black females, the proportion involved in a black–white marriage is substantially higher if educational attainment was 13 years or more. In contrast, for white males and females, the proportion in a black–white marriage was

Table 9. Percentage of Persons in Black–White Marriages by Sex, Race, and Income in 1969 When Both Husband and Wife Married Once and First Married 1960–70, United States, 1970

	Black Males	Black Females	White Males	White Females
Total	1.8	0.8	0.08	0.18
Less than $3,000	1.6	0.8	0.09	0.16
$3,000 to 6,999	1.7	0.9	0.11	0.24
$7,000 to 9,999	1.9	1.2	0.07	0.25
$10,000 +	2.9	0.9	0.05	0.36

Table 10.   Percentage of Persons in Black–White Marriages by Sex, Race, and Educational Attainment When Both Husband and Wife Married Once and First Married in 1960–70, United States, 1970

	Black Males	Black Females	White Males	White Females
Total	1.8	0.8	0.08	0.18
0 to 8 school years	1.1	0.6	0.13	0.22
9 to 12 school years	1.6	0.5	0.07	0.20
13 or more school years	3.5	2.1	0.09	0.15

substantially higher if the educational attainment was eight years or less.

Relation Between Racial-Caste Hypogamy and Class Hypergamy

Racial-caste hypogamy is defined as a situation where a female from a higher racial caste marries a man from a lower racial caste. In the United States, assuming that the white population were defined as the higher racial caste, racial-caste hypogamy would predominate in those situations where the number of marriages involving a black male and a white female was substantially larger than the number of marriages involving a white male and a black female. Racial-caste hypergamy might be said to predominate when the opposite was true. Available data concerning the incidence of legal marriages in selected Northern and Western states (Heer, 1966; Monahan, 1970a, 1970b, 1971) indicates a definite pattern of racial-caste hypogamy. Census data on the prevalence of black–white intermarriage (shown in Table 1) reveal a definite predominance of racial-caste hypogamy for the North and West in 1970 and a similar but less definite predominance in 1960. On the other hand, the Census data reveal a clear predominance of racial-caste hypergamy in the South in 1960 and a less definite tendency toward predominance of racial-caste hypergamy in the South in 1970.

Both Kingsley Davis (1941) and Robert Merton (1941) attempted to explain racial-caste hypogamy by advancing the theory that such marriages tended to be class hypergamous (defined as a situation where a female from a lower social class married a man from a higher social class). Thus Davis and Merton predicted that for a

white female the excess of her husband's educational attainment over her own would be greater if her husband were black than if he were white. Similarly, for a black male, the excess of his own educational attainment over that of his wife would be greater if his wife were white rather than if she were black. According to this theory, the black man who wished to marry a white wife had to compensate for his black skin by rewarding her with an additional resource, namely, a higher educational attainment than she could expect to find from a husband of her own race. Presumably also the black husband's higher educational attainment would translate itself into higher monetary earnings than the earnings of the potential white spouse of lower educational attainment.

The Davis-Merton theory did not consider the case of racial-caste hypergamy. For legal marriages of this type one might conclude from their assumptions that a black woman would generally have a relatively greater educational advantage over her husband if he were white than if he were black, and that a white man would generally have a relatively lesser educational advantage over his wife if she were black than if she were white. However, these assumptions might not hold for consensual unions, particularly those where the white man was legally married to a white wife, also had a consensual relationship to a black female, and was double-counted in the Census as husband to both of these women.

Empirical testing of the Davis-Merton hypothesis with data from the 1960 Census did not confirm its veracity. Bernard (1966) showed no substantial tendency for wives of black males to be of relatively lower education attainment if white than if black. Nor did her analysis show any tendency for black females to have a husband with relatively lower educational attainment if white than if black.

Table 11.   Number of Married Couples by Education and Race of Husband and by Education and Race of Wife Among Couples Where Each Spouse Was Either White or Black, and Where Both Spouses Had Been Married Only Once and Were First Married in 1960–70, United States, 1970

Husband's Race and Educational Attainment	Wife's Race and Educational Attainment					
	White			Black		
	13 +	9–12	0–8	13 +	9–12	0–8
White, 13 +	2,096,927	1,407,467	31,307	1,868	1,173	62
White, 9–12	548,294	4,030,133	252,724	409	2,442	402
White, 0–8	37,118	459,291	279,555	18	612	366
Black, 13 +	3,421	1,694	161	77,491	64,954	3,052
Black, 9–12	1,262	7,358	796	62,658	487,027	48,014
Black, 0–8	112	973	642	6,730	90,876	60,271

Tables 11 and 12 use 1970 Census data to test the Davis-Merton theory and its extension to consider racial-caste hypergamy. Table 11 presents the distribution of married couples by education and race of husband by education and race of wife. Parts A and B of Table 12 convert the data of Table 11 into index form. The derivation of the indices in Table 12 may be illustrated by considering how the indices for white females with 13 or more years of completed schooling were computed. The number of such women (2,096,927) whose husband was white and had completed the same years of schooling as his wife, i.e., 13 or more years, was given an index value of 100; likewise the number of such women (3,421) whose husband was black and had completed 13 or more years of schooling was given an index value of 100. Then the number of such women (548,294) whose husband was white and had completed 9–12 years of schooling was divided by the number (2,096,927) of such women whose husband was white and had completed 13 or more years of schooling to give the index number (26) for such women married to white men with 9–12 years of schooling; similarly, the number (1,262) with a black husband having 9–12 years of schooling

Table 12.   Index Numbers for Data in Table 11 Designed to Test Hypothesis That Racial Caste Hypogamy Is Associated with Educational Hypergamy and Racial Caste Hypergamy with Educational Hypogamy, with Indices for Husbands and Wives Shown, Each to Be Read Horizontally

Husband's Race and Educational Attainment	Wife's Race and Educational Attainment						Number of Predictions	
	White			Black			Correct	Incorrect
	13 +	9–12	0–8	13 +	9–12	0–8		
White, 13 +	100	67	1	100	63	3	1	1
White, 9–12	14	100	6	17	100	16	1	1
White, 0–8	13	164	100	5	167	100	1	1
Black, 13 +	100	50	5	100	84	4	1	1
Black, 9–12	17	100	11	13	100	10	1	1
Black, 0–8	17	152	100	11	151	100	0	2

Wife's Race and Educational Attainment	Husband's Race and Educational Attainment						Number of Predictions	
	White			Black			Correct	Incorrect
	13 +	9–12	0–8	13 +	9–12	0–8		
White, 13 +	100	26	2	100	37	3	0	2
White, 9–12	35	100	11	23	100	13	0	2
White, 0–8	11	90	100	25	124	100	2	0
Black, 13 +	100	22	1	100	81	9	0	2
Black, 9–12	48	100	25	13	100	19	1	1
Black, 0–8	17	110	100	5	80	100	0	2

was divided by the number (3,421) with a black husband having 13 or more years of schooling to give the index number (37) for such females married to black males with 9–12 years of schooling. Finally, the number (37,118) in which the husband was white and had completed 0–8 years of schooling was divided by the number (2,096,927) in which the husband was white and had completed 13 or more years of schooling to give the index number (2) for such females married to white males with 0–8 years of schooling; additionally, the number (112) in which the husband was black with 0–8 years of schooling was divided by the number (3,421) where the husband was black with 13 or more years of schooling to provide the index number (3) for such females married to black males with 0–8 years of schooling. According to the Davis-Merton theory we should expect that white females with 13 or more years of schooling would be less likely to be married to a husband of lower educational attainment if he were black than if he were white. We test this hypothesis by comparing the index numbers for the white husbands of these women with the index numbers for the black husbands. In this particular case, the theory incorrectly predicts that the index value for black husbands with 9–12 years of schooling, which is 37, will be less than the index value of 26 for white husbands with 9–12 years schooling. Furthermore, the theory incorrectly predicts that the index number for black husbands with 0–8 years of schooling, which is 3, will be less than the index number for white husbands with 0–8 years of schooling, which is 2.

In total, for the case of racial-caste hypogamy (marriages involving black husbands and white wives) 12 predictions are possible. Of these only 4 are correct and 8 incorrect. For the case of racial-caste hypergamy, there are likewise only 4 correct predictions and 8 incorrect ones.

However, it would be unwise to give up the Davis-Merton theory too easily. The theory is congruent with the assumptions of exchange theory—a theory which for familial behavior has attained rather wide support from many empirical studies (Edwards, 1969; Heer, 1963). It is possible, therefore, that the Davis-Merton theory is not wrong per se but that we have tested it without adequately controlling for an important variable which distorts the relationship we wish to test. The obvious variable which we have failed to control is the availability of mates of various educational-

attainment categories within each separate racial group. Consider the case of black males with 0–8 years of schooling, for which both the predictions are incorrect. The theory predicts that the white wives of these men should have lower education attainment than the black wives. However, the simple fact is that the median years of schooling completed by all white wives is considerably higher than that completed by all black wives. Therefore, sheer lack of availability makes it unlikely that the black wives of black men with 0–8 years of schooling could have higher educational attainment than the white wives of these men.

To test the Davis-Merton theory with a control for the availability of spouses at each educational-attainment level we can deal with ratios of actual intermarriage to intermarriage expected if marriage were to take place randomly without regard either to race or educational attainment. Table 13 presents the ratio of actual to expected intermarriage by sex, race, and educational attainment in urbanized areas outside of the South. The narrower geographic focus than was employed in Table 11 is used to maximize the accuracy of the expected proportions intermarried as a measure of actual availability of spouses of each type in the local area from which each spouse might have sought a marriage partner. The expected proportions for females are obtained simply by computing the proportions of all black and white males in each of the six categories which cross-classify race by educational attainment. Similarly, the expected proportions for males are the proportions of all black and white females in each of the six racial-educational categories.

Table 14 presents the index numbers for these ratios of actual to expected intermarriage calculated in the same manner as the index numbers presented in Table 12. Also in Table 14 is the number of correct and incorrect predications from the revised test of the theory. For the situation of racial-caste hypogamy we find eight correct predictions and four incorrect ones. For the situation of racial-caste hypergamy we likewise have eight correct and four incorrect predictions. It is evident that the predictive power of the theory has been very much improved. Out of 24 possible predictions, 16 are now correct whereas in the original testing out of 24 possible predictions only 8 were correct. However, even under the modified testing, the theory cannot be said to be a very successful

Table 13.   Ratio of Actual to Expected Intermarriage by Education and Race of Husband and by Education and Race of Wife among Couples Where Each Spouse Was Either White or Black and Where Both Spouses Had Been Married Only Once and Were First Married in 1960–70, for Urbanized Areas in the United States Outside of the South, 1970 (Actual Number of Marriages Is Indicated in Parentheses under Each Ratio)

Husband's Race and Educational Attainment	Wife's Race and Educational Attainment					
	White			Black		
	13 +	9–12	0–8	13 +	9–12	0–8
White, 13 +	2.040 (1,058,040)	.705 (700,714)	.185 (16,971)	.0378 (1,142)	.00590 (748)	.00396 (62)
White, 9–12	.407 (236,455)	1.486 (1,653,269)	.944 (97,060)	.00801 (270)	.00983 (1,396)	.0162 (284)
White, 0–8	.191 (16,346)	.967 (158,669)	7.762 (117,716)	0.0 (—)	.0190 (400)	.0831 (215)
Black, 13 +	.113 (2,755)	.0261 (1,222)	.0306 (132)	27.57 (39,138)	6.52 (38,936)	2.01 (1,477)
Black, 9–12	.0106 (941)	.0318 (5,434)	.0298 (472)	6.305 (32,690)	11.28 (246,245)	7.358 (19,846)
Black, 0–8	.00415 (68)	.0200 (631)	.201 (588)	3.37 (3,222)	8.45 (33,972)	35.93 (17,850)

predictor. Nor is its lack of good predictability likely to be mostly a matter of sampling error. A major reason for the lack of successful prediction may be that we still have not attained sufficient control on the availability of spouses by race at each educational-attainment level. For example, prediction is still entirely unsuccessful for black females with 13 or more years of schooling. Ac-

cording to the extension of the Davis-Merton theory, husbands of these women should be of lower educational attainment if white than if black, after control for the total availability of potential mates by race and by education. However, it is likely that these black women of high educational attainment would not have had the chance to meet many white men with less educational at-

Table 14.   Index Numbers for Data in Table 13 Designed to Test Hypothesis That Racial Caste Hypogamy Is Associated with Educational Hypergamy and Racial Caste Hypergamy with Educational Hypogamy, with Indices for Husbands and Indices for Wives Shown, Each to Be Read Horizontally

Husband's Race and Educational Attainment	Wife's Race and Educational Attainment						Number of Predictions	
	White			Black			Correct	Incorrect
	13 +	9–12	0–8	13 +	9–12	0–8		
White, 13 +	100	35	9	100	16	16	1	1
White, 9–12	27	100	64	81	100	165	1	1
White, 0–8	2	12	100	0	23	100	1	1
Black, 13 +	100	23	27	100	24	7	1	1
Black, 9–12	33	100	94	56	100	65	2	0
Black, 0–8	2	10	100	9	24	100	2	0

Wife's Race and Educational Attainment	Husband's Race and Educational Attainment						Number of Predictions	
	White			Black			Correct	Incorrect
	13 +	9–12	0–8	13 +	9–12	0–8		
White, 13 +	100	20	9	100	9	4	2	0
White, 9–12	47	100	65	82	100	63	2	0
White, 0–8	2	12	100	15	15	100	2	0
Black, 13 +	100	21	0	100	23	12	0	2
Black, 9–12	60	100	19	58	100	75	0	2
Black, 0–8	5	19	100	6	20	100	2	0

tainment than themselves. Probably most of the white men they ever had a chance to meet were met in college or were college alumni met in a professional or managerial job. In contrast, these black women would have become acquainted during their elementary and high school years with many black men who ended up with less than a college education. Thus there is good reason to believe that the testing of the Davis-Merton theory (and its extension to racial-caste hypergamy) still suffers from inadequate control on the real availability of spouses by race at each educational-attainment level. However, with the present data no more adequate control on availability is obtainable.

Implications of the Findings Concerning Black–White Marriage for Future Changes in the Relative Status of the Two Races

During the decade of the 1960's there was a 26 per cent increase in the number of black–white marriages. The 66 per cent increase of such marriages in the North and West was countered by a 35 per cent decline in the South. Moreover, the 62 per cent rise in marriages involving a black husband and a white wife was accompanied by a 9 per cent decline in the number involving a white husband and a black wife. During the decade existing black–white marriages suffered a high rate of attrition. Of marriages involving a white husband and a black wife contracted in the ten years prior to the 1960 Census only 47 per cent were still in existence in 1970 and of those involving a black husband and a white wife only 63 per cent. What are the implications of these various findings for the further reduction of status differences between white and black populations in the United States?

It is obvious that a definitive answer to this question requires more information than we have at hand. First of all, we still do not have exact information concerning the total number of children ever born to intermarried couples as distinguished from the number of children ever born to women currently intermarried. However, from the information we do possess, one can safely state that fertility in black–white marriages is less than in homogeneous black marriages. Accordingly, the total number of children born to black–white couples would form a smaller proportion of the total number of all or partially black children than would have been the case if the fertility of such marriages were as high as that among homogeneous black couples. This fact would then tend to dilute somewhat the importance of interracial marriage as a factor in reducing the status differences between blacks and whites in the United States.

Is it important that marriages involving a black husband and a white wife have greatly increased whereas those involving a white husband and a black wife have declined? One might presume that the combination of a white father and a black mother, other things being equal, might be a better springboard to a child's upward mobility than the combination of a black father and a white mother. This would follow if we supposed that the role of the father was more important than that of the mother in facilitating access to jobs obtainable through kin connections and if we further supposed that white mothers provided no advantage over white fathers with respect to inheritance and instruction concerning the social world of white persons. However, other things may not be equal. In particular, it is possible that marriages involving a white husband and a black wife may more often be consensual unions and that the consensually married white husband may display relatively less interest in his children.

It would appear that the shifting locus of black–white marriages from South to North and West should enhance the effect of such marriages on the reduction of status differences between blacks and whites. This would ensue if we assumed that the social discrimination meted to children of such marriages is greater in the South than elsewhere.

However, it is clear that before we can evaluate the impact of shifts from caste-hypergamous to caste-hypogamous marriages and in the geographic locus of interracial marriages, we must have direct measurement concerning the intergenerational mobility of children from the various types of interracial marriage and comparative data concerning the children from racially homogeneous marriages. So far no such information has been gathered from a large and representative sample.

At the beginning of this paper we also speculated that an increase in the proportion of white persons with black relatives would serve to reduce the magnitude of white prejudice towards blacks.

Although in-depth interviews with black–white couples indicate clearly the shock that many white parents experience when they discover their child is entering an interracial marriage (Gordon, 1964), there is apparently no direct information on how the experience of having a close relative marry interracially affects the attitude of a white individual to blacks. Ideally, one should have measurement of the white person's racial attitudes both before and after the marriage of a close relative to a black person. In default of this, it would be desirable at least to have retrospective data following such a marriage.

References

Bernard, Jessie
1966   "Note on educational homogamy in Negro–white and white–Negro marriages, 1960." *Journal of Marriage and the Family* 28:274–276.

Carter, Hugh, and Paul C. Glick
1970   *Marriage and Divorce: A Social and Economic Study.* Cambridge, Mass.: Harvard University Press.

Coale, Ansley, and Frederick F. Stephan
1962   "The case of the Indians and the teenage widows." *Journal of the American Statistical Association* 57:338–347.

Davis, Kingsley
1941   "Intermarriage in caste societies." *American Anthropologist* 43:376–395.

Edwards, John N.
1969   "Familial behavior as social exchange." *Journal of Marriage and the Family* 31:518–526.

Golden, Joseph
1954   "Patterns of Negro–white intermarriage." *American Sociological Review* 19:144–147.

Gordon, Albert I.
1964   *Intermarriage.* Boston: Beacon Press.

Heer, David M.
1963   "The measurement and bases of family power: an overview." *Journal of Marriage and the Family* 25:133–139.

1966   "Negro–white marriage in the United States." *Journal of Marriage and the Family* 28:262–273.

Lynn, Anne Q.
1953   *Interracial Marriages in Washington,D.C., 1940–47.* Washington: Catholic University of America Press.

McDowell, Sophia F.
1971   "Black–white intermarriage in the United States." *International Journal of Sociology of the Family* 1 (Special Issue):49–58.

Merton, Robert K.
1941   "Intermarriage and the social structure: fact and theory." *Psychiatry* 4:361–374.

Monahan, Thomas P.
1970a   "Are interracial marriages really less stable?" *Social Forces* 48:461–473.

1970b   "Interracial marriages in Pennsylvania and Philadelphia." *Demography* 7:287–299.

1971   "Interracial marriage in the United States: some data on upstate New York." *International Journal of Sociology of the Family* 1:94–105.

Truesdell, Leon E.
1938   "Residual relationships and velocity of change as pitfalls in the field of statistical reporting." *Journal of the American Statistical Association* 33:373–379.

United States Bureau of the Census
1966   U.S. Census of Population: 1960. Subject Reports. Marital Status. Final Report PC(2)–4E. Washington, D.C.: U.S. Government Printing Office.

1972   Census of Population: 1970. Marital Status. Final Report PC(2)–4C. Washington, D.C.: U.S. Government Printing Office.

1973   Census of Population: 1970. Women by Number of Children Ever Born. Final Report PC(2)–3A. Washington, D.C.: U.S. Government Printing Office.

Part Three
The Family

Child Bearing

The bearing of children has traditionally been considered a very important function in the Black community. The sacrifices of Black mothers for their children have been legendary for hundreds of years. Although children are still highly valued by Blacks, attitudes toward having large numbers of them have changed dramatically in the past ten years. Many Black women believe that the responsibility of rearing large numbers of children limits too severely their personal freedom and their job mobility. In addition, they face new problems raising children in urban centers where there has been a decline in the number of two-parent households, forcing many to raise children alone. In 1976, single women between 18 and 24—Black *and* white—expected to have fewer than two children in their lifetime.[1]

These figures, however, are the expected, not the actual fertility rates for Black women. In 1973, the actual fertility rate was 2.44 children per Black woman and 1.80 per white woman. And in urban areas in the period between 1960 and 1970, Black fertility actually declined at a faster rate (37%) than white fertility (27%).[2] The birth rate among college-educated Black women has been unusually low for a number of years, and is so low now that they are no longer replacing themselves. In fact their birth rate is about the lowest in the United States. A major factor in this class difference in Black fertility patterns is the long period of the wife's employment, which delays the age at which college-educated Black women bear children.[3]

Even the Black woman without a college education has obviously made a conscious decision to limit the size of her family. Greater access to contraceptives and abortion have helped her to achieve her desired family size. The increase in number of abortions is somewhat surprising, considering the traditional Black hostility to this practice. There may still be some residual resistance to it, but the ineffectiveness of some contraceptives has probably forced many Black women to resort to abortion as a way of preventing unwanted births. In some cities the number of hospital abortions performed on Black women is proportionally greater than for white women.[4] Some of this birth control and abortion among Black women may not be entirely voluntary, for many of the poor are forced to reduce family size in order to get welfare or other government assistance. There have also been numerous cases reported of Black women being sterilized without their knowledge or consent.[5]

The article by Darity and Turner is a survey of Black attitudes toward family planning and its relation to level of racial consciousness and fears of race genocide. They found that a significant number of Blacks rejected certain forms of birth

---

[1]U.S. Department of Commerce, Newsletter (November 26, 1976).

[2]U.S. Bureau of the Census, *The Social and Economic Status of the Black Population in the United States, 1974* (Washington, D.C.; U.S. Government Printing Office, 1975).

[3]Clyde Kaiser and Myrna Frank, "Factors Associated with the Low Fertility of Non-White Women of College Attainment," *Milbank Memorial Fund Quarterly,* October 1967, p. 428.

[4]Robert Staples, *The Black Woman in America: Sex, Marriage and the Family* (Chicago: Nelson-Hall, 1973), p. 146.

[5]Naomi T. Gray, *Sterilization and the Black Female: An Historical Perspective in Mental and Physical Health Problems of Black Women* (Washington, D.C., Black Women's Community Development Foundation, 1975), pp. 80–90.

control, such as abortion and sterilization. Suspicions were particularly prevalent where family planning programs were controlled by non-Blacks. The selection by McKay provides valuable information on sex ratios at birth. In her study of Black families in a major city, with incomes between $13,000 and $17,000, she learned that two thirds of them had only one child. Even more interesting was the secondary sex ratio: 83 males to every 100 females at birth. The obvious implication of her study, if generalized to the rest of the middle-class Black population, is that the critical shortage of Black males will continue.

Parental Roles and Socialization Processes

Raising a Black child has never been an easy task. Black parents have done a more than adequate job, despite the obstacles they face. Usually they have more children to rear, with fewer resources, than white parents. They must also socialize their children into the values of the mainstream culture if the offspring are to adapt successfully to majority group requirements and institutions. At the same time they must teach the folkways of Black culture and what it means to be Black in a racist society. Given the adverse social conditions under which most Black children are raised, it is not surprising that some fail. It is even more surprising that so many succeed.

Child rearing practices do not differ significantly by race. Variations in socialization techniques are more a function of class membership. Middle-class parents, Black and white, are more likely to use verbal punishment than physical punishment to discipline a child.[6] Lower-class Black mothers are often regarded as ineffective parents because they use physical punishment to control their children. That assessment does not consider the tendency of many Black mothers to combine physical measures with emotional nurturance. The combination of spanking and affection may be more beneficial to a child's development than the middle-class threat of withdrawal of love for bad behavior. Many observers of the Black family have noted that children in the lower-class Black community are well treated and emotionally and psychologically healthy.

The attitudes and behavior of many Black parents are changing. Fewer children are born per family and there are indications that these children are not as well treated. This is also indicated in the white community and could be related to the recent tendency of mothers to put their own wishes first. Social tensions, particularly in urban areas, also affect children; for instance, there is an increase in child abuse in Black families and a decline in the respect of Black children for their elders. Changes in the Black fertility pattern are responsible for some of this. While there has been an overall decline in the Black birth rate, there has also been a significant increase in out-of-wedlock pregnancies, primarily involving teenagers. With the decline in the Black extended family system, immature mothers and one-parent households have fostered an arrogance and negativism among many Black youth.

While there may be problems stemming from the one-parent household, Rubin's study of fatherless Black families found that boys in these homes do not see themselves as less worthwhile than boys who live with their fathers. One reason for this high self-esteem, he suggests, is that male role models are available outside the home; other significant adult males also are present in the family. Scanzoni's investigation of intact working-class Black families describes the importance of the mother and father to a child's development. The parents provide aid, values, and encouragement for their children's mobility aspirations. In their survey of female-headed households, Peters and Ford note that it is not easy to raise children alone but that mothers were coping well with their circumstances and created a viable family.

The Extended Family

Kinship bonds have always been important to Blacks. In African societies, kinship was and is the basis of social organization. During the period of slavery, many bondsmen were organized into an extended family system based on both biological and non-biological factors. Most studies of Black kinship networks indicate that they are more extensive and more significant than in the white community.[7] There is some disagreement as to the reasons for the racial variations in kinship bonds

[6]Robert Hess and Virginia Shipman, "Early Experience and the Socialization of Cognitive Modes in Children," *Child Development* 36 (1965): 869–886.

[7]Bert Adams, "Isolation, Function and Beyond: American Kinship in the 1960's," *Journal of Marriage and the Family* 32 (1970): 575–598.

and interactions. Some contend that it is a carry-over from African traditions;[8] others suggest that minority status strengthens kin ties because of a need for mutual aid and survival in a hostile environment.[9] Whatever the reason, there is little doubt that kinsfolk play an important role in the Black family system.

Among the valuable services they provide are the sharing of economic resources, child care, advice, and other forms of aid. While these are acknowledged functions of a kinship network, members of the extended family also serve to liberate children from the confines of the nuclear family unit. Children have someone other than a mother or father to relate to and from whom to receive emotional nurturance. The extended family also helps to socialize children more effectively into the values that rural and Southern Blacks held. The function of kinship groups to Blacks is so important that many non-blood relatives are regarded as kinsfolk. Usually, these are special friendships in which the normal claims, obligations, and loyalties of kin relationship are operative, such as with godmothers or play brothers.[10]

Today there is a decline in the Black extended family system, largely as a result of Black mobility patterns. Many Blacks have moved to large cities, where they have few, if any, kinsfolk. Large numbers of Blacks are moving to suburban areas, where they often lack friends or relatives in their immediate neighborhood. Changes in the attitudes of Black youth toward their elders have also weakened the role of some older kinsfolk. Young Blacks are developing anti-authority attitudes and they are less responsive to the wisdom and guidance of their older kin.

In the first article in this section, Hill and Shackleford look at the contemporary extended family pattern among Blacks. They find that the characteristics of Black families remain the same over the years and that the informal adoption of children is an important and overlooked function of the extended family, one which has been a source of strength and resilience in the Black community for generations. Jackson details more closely the role of Black grandparents in the urban setting. She finds they are needed because they provide affectional closeness, value consensus, and role identification.

Personality Development

Adolescence has been regarded as a time of identity formation and liberation from parental control. For Black youth the problems of transition from adolescence to adulthood have been compounded by their unique status in society. Many, for example, do not have a carefree period in which to form an identity, as do middle-class white youth. Many must find jobs to help support their families, but without special skills and with little education, the majority of Black youth have no regular employment of any kind. In America's inner cities as many as 65% of Black teenagers are unemployed.[11]

Because of high unemployment, Black youth are overrepresented in crime statistics, in the volunteer army, among drug addicts, and in other negative social indexes. There has been a tendency to place the responsibility for the problems of Black youth on their disorganized family system. Although nearly a majority of Black youth are now living in one-parent homes, it is questionable that such homes necessarily produce uneducable and delinquent children. One-parent households generally have a low income and it is the relationship between poverty and youth behavior that warrants analysis. Elsewhere in this section are studies that show that many female-headed households are functional units.

Diane Lewis's paper focuses on socialization in the Black family. She finds that sex role differences in Black culture exist but have a cultural basis that makes them different from the Euro-American model, particularly early in a child's life. In later life, socialization reflects more closely the structure and expectations of the dominant society. Taylor's article investigates the general socio-historical context of the psycho-social development of Black youth. He was looking for role model identifications and their function in molding psycho-social identity. He found that these youth had a rich variety of social and psychological supports, as well as a fund of experience on which to rely for the formation of identity.

[8]Gloria Marshall, "An Exposition of the Valid Premises Underlying Black Families," in *The Black Family: Fact or Fantasy*, Alyce Gullattee, ed. (Washington, D.C.: National Medical Association, 1972), pp. 12–15.

[9]Adams, "American Kinship."

[10]Elliot Liebow, *Tally's Corner* (Boston: Little, Brown & Co., 1966), p.169.

[11]"Black Teens Unemployed," *Los Angeles Sentinel*, April 10, 1975, p. A-2.

Socioeconomic Characteristics

It is necessary to recognize the effect of economics on Black family life in order to understand the conditions under which the Black family functions—or fails to function—as a viable system. Ever since Blacks were released from slavery, economic deprivation has been a fact of life. Over the past forty years the rate of unemployment among Blacks has remained twice that of whites. The National Urban League's index of hidden unemployment shows the current unemployment rate of Black men to be around 25%.[12] A man who cannot find work not only has trouble maintaining a stable marital and family life, but often cannot find a woman willing to marry him in the first place. Only 55% of Black men with annual incomes under $1000 marry, in comparison with 80% of those earning between $3000 and $5000. The number of Black men who marry rises with income.[13]

Intact Black families have a median income of $8779 per year, compared to $14,000 a year for white families.[14] Black family income today is 60% as high as white family income, a drop from 61% in 1969. If adjustments for inflation are made, Black families are slightly worse off than they were in 1973.[15] This does not consider that more Black families than white derive their income from multiple earners (two thirds against one half).[16] The implications are obvious when we observe that the higher the income of a Black family, the more likely it is to be a two-parent family. Black families headed by women have an average income of only $4898 a year, approximately 40% of the earnings of intact Black families.[17]

Charles Willie's article examines Black family life styles at three different class levels. He finds that styles of life vary by social class but that, in general, Black and white families still share a common value system. The article by Harwood and Hodge examines the stereotype that Black women enjoy an economic advantage over Black men in access to employment opportunities. The analysis indicates that for the last four decades the Black woman has in fact faced handicaps in the labor market.

---

[12]National Urban League Research Department, *Quarterly Economic Report on the Black Worker* 2 (1975):1.

[13]Paul Glick and Karen Mills, "Black Families: Marriage Patterns and Living Arrangements" (Paper presented at the W.E.B. DuBois Conference on American Blacks, Atlanta, Ga. October 1974), p. 18.

[14]"Blacks on a New Plateau," *Newsweek,* October 4, 1976, p. 73.

[15]National Urban League Research Department, *Inflation and the Black Consumer* (Washington, D.C.: 1974), p. 25.

[16]U.S. Bureau of the Census, *Social and Economic Status of the Black Population,* p. 24.

[17]"Blacks on a New Plateau." op. cit.

9

Child Bearing

Family Planning, Race Consciousness and the Fear of Race Genocide

William Darity and Castellano Turner

The issue of family planning takes on a special meaning among many Blacks, according to the authors of this article. Blacks, in general, are involved in family planning programs that are controlled by non-Blacks and they perceive these programs as potential means of genocide. The authors point out that this fear is based, in part, on historical events that have had adverse effects on Blacks. Family planning and its related agencies have become symbolic of the oppression that many Blacks believe exists in this society.

Introduction

One of the current and abiding issues facing family planning educators is the perception of the objectives of family planning among black Americans (as well as other minority groups). There have recently been expressions from many sources suggesting strong feelings that family planning programs (in some or all of their methods) are forms of black genocide. Our purpose in this paper is to provide some preliminary answers to several of the broad and important questions that are generated by the reported expressions: First, to what extent are fears of race genocide held in the black community? Second, to what extent can one attribute the use (or nonuse) of family planning methods to such fears of race genocide? We will attempt to answer these questions, as well as several more specific questions, in two ways: First, by means of a review of historical and anecdotal material; second, by discussing some preliminary findings in a research

project attempting to answer these and similar questions.

An Historical and General Survey

Contemporary proponents of the black genocide notion are able to cite historical as well as contemporary factors which provide evidence of a black genocide conspiracy. These include both general factors and factors which are more specific to the question of family planning (or birth control). They include such historical factors as slavery and the long-lived residual slave economy; they include direct physical violence perpetrated against blacks such as lynchings, bombings, and demasculation of many black males; they include social-economic pressures which make life difficult to maintain such as poor housing, job discrimination, and lack of access to educational opportunities leading to marketable skills; they include social-psychological pressures which make life less bearable such as social discrimination, segregation, and intimidation of every kind; they include the very direct evidence of excessive hysterectomies among black women in the past and many proposals to increase hysterectomies for black women in the future.

In 1933 the late E. Franklin Frazier discussed concerns about birth control and whether it would have a eugenic or dysgenic effect on black people.[1] According to Frazier:

[1]Frazier, E. Franklin. "The Negro and Birth Control." *Birth Control Review*, Vol. XVII, 8, 68–70 (March, 1933).

From the *American Journal of Public Health* 62 (November 1972): 1454–1459. Reprinted by permission.

As the knowledge of contraception spreads, so runs the argument, the process will become eugenic; the economically incompetent and mentally deficient will have fewer or no children and the race will be improved.[2]

Frazier studied census data and analyzed his personal observations; he remained unconvinced that birth control practice among blacks would have an eugenic effect. On the contrary, he observed decreasing numbers of better educated blacks. Also, on the other hand, he reasoned that natural forces such as disease would cause a similar decrease in the number of low-income blacks.[3]

W. E. B. DuBois in an article published in 1938, "Black Folk and Birth Control," stated:

There comes, therefore, the difficult and insistent problem of spreading among Negroes an intelligent and clearly recognized concept of birth control, so that the young can marry, have companionship and natural health, and yet not have children until they are able to take care of them.[4]

DuBois also pointed out that black people, like most people at that time who followed middle-class standards of morality, considered birth control inherently immoral. However, his own position is made quite clear in his criticism of those who opposed the use of birth control methods among blacks:

. . . they are quite led away by the fallacy of numbers. They want the black race to survive. They are cheered by a census return of increasing numbers and a higher rate of increase.[5]

The brief review above simply suggests that the issue of family planning in the black community is by no means a new one. Obviously, it was not meant to be exhaustive, but it indicates that important black scholars have regarded the use of birth control as an important issue for black people in America.

Contemporary Thought

Contemporary proponents of the black genocide notion maintain that the black man's security in the United States lies in "strength of numbers." It is noteworthy that even black physicians are among those who support such a position. For instance, a black physician in Pittsburgh a few years ago was quoted as saying, in essence, that all the strength black people have is in their numbers. Moreover, he went on to enumerate four aspects of what he referred to as the "genocide plot." These were: (a) the idea, perpetuated by a majority of the white community, that the black man is "no good" and inferior because he is black. This is a psychological factor which develops a real *sense* of inferiority and consequent inability to compete; (b) the destruction of the moral code within the black community. This process is so long-standing and powerful that the black man is himself convinced that the white man's moral code, whatever that may be, is superior to his own; (c) the systematic method by which whites keep the black man broke and hungry, keep black children in disadvantaged circumstances, and keep black women on relief or "on the block." This situation leaves blacks essentially at the mercy of whites and with no control over their own destiny; and (d) the procedure of herding black people into ghettos and into limited areas and subsequently withdrawing ordinary municipal services, ceasing to enforce building codes, and removing preventive policing.[6] This same physician has also noted that, in addition to the above, "population control" is a euphemism for limiting the American black population. He maintains that any effort in the direction of birth control is basically an effort to eliminate all black people or all nonwhite people.[7]

The late Malcolm X, in an interview in 1962, simply objected to the term "birth control." He felt that blacks did not need to be controlled. He preferred the term "family planning," which used in the broader sense suggests the importance of self-determination for black people. Planning, he

[2]*Ibid.*

[3]*Ibid.*

[4]DuBois, W. E. B. "Black Folk and Birth Control." *Birth Control Review,* Vol. XVII, 8, 90 (May, 1938).

[5]*Ibid.*

[6]Extracted and paraphrased from a speech entitled "Black Genocide," delivered by Charles E. Greenlee, M.D., at Lincoln University, Pennsylvania, March 10, 1969.

[7]Smith, Mary. "Birth Control and the Negro Woman." *Ebony,* March, 1968.

felt, was something that black people had to be concerned about.[8]

On the other hand, in contrast to Malcolm X's moderate approach, there has recently been increasing evidence developing of strong opposition to family planning as well as birth control programs. Several moderate black civil rights organizations as well as more militant black organizations have provided the context for strong criticism of family planning programs and organizations. For instance, during a meeting of the Southern Christian Leadership Conference having to do with *Family Planning in South Carolina,* opposition to family planning programs was voiced in such spontaneous statements from participants as:

Birth control is a plot just as segregation was a plot to keep the Negro down . . .

Let's just have more and more Negroes and we'll overcome them in sheer numbers alone; we'll take what's ours.

It (birth control) is a plot rather than a solution; instead of working to give us our rights, reduce us in numbers, therefore not have to give us anything.[9]

Such statements, though expressed only by individuals, seem to crystallize the general meaning of race consciousness and race genocide as bases of opposition to family planning. In another instance in Cleveland at the *Conference on Human Values in Family Planning,* similar statements were made which suggest how widespread such feelings are. The following comments also suggest the depth of feelings that is involved in this issue:

Birth control is compared to "stopping the germ (black people) before it starts" and "weeding out impurities."

It's a genocidal program set up by whites who are playing with murder.

Population is our strength in this country . . . the black man must realize this (birth control) is a form of genocide . . . history tells us that the white man is capable of genocide.

The idea is expressed that "birth control pills" could make the second generation sterile. This might be the whole thing a process of extermination.[10]

At this conference there were other reasons (aside from notions of genocide) presented to explain the rejection of family planning programs by the black community. These included: general rejection of white American values; fears regarding health; lives of poverty; and rejection of "tampering" with the normal body functions.[11] However, the connection between the notion of race genocide and rejection of family planning programs seems to have been substantial.

An example of the position of more militant black organizations has been presented by Walter Thompson, head of EROS (Endeavor to Raise Our Size). In a 1966 conference with two staff members of the Planned Parenthood Federation of America, Mr. Thompson indicated that his organization was vehemently opposed to the Planned Parenthood Federation and considered it to be an immoral organization. He stated that his organization had two major purposes, namely (a) to increase the voting power of black people, and (b) to improve the life and conditions of black families.[12]

Newspaper and Magazine Articles

To some extent reports in newspapers and magazines, as well as other types of mass com-

[8]Cowles, Wylda, B. Summary of Interview with Malcolm X, Black Muslim Leader in Harlem, May, 1962. The information was extracted from the subject document which was a memorandum from Mrs. Wylda B. Cowles, Field Consultant with Planned Parenthood Federation of America, to Alan F. Guttmacher, President of Planned Parenthood Federation of America.

[9]Information extracted from a memorandum from Mrs. Elsie Jackson, Planned Parenthood Federation of America Consultant, to Alan Guttmacher. Subject, The Southern Christian Leadership Conference Workshop on Family Planning, April 4, 1966.

[10]Extracted from tapes and notes of the Conference on Human Values in Family Planning, November 7–8, 1968, Cleveland.

[11]*Ibid.*

[12]Cowles, Wylda, and Hamilton, Madrid. Meeting with EROS—February 23, 1966. A memorandum from Mrs. Cowles and Mrs. Hamilton to Alan F. Guttmacher, President of Planned Parenthood Federation of America. Mrs. Cowles and Mrs. Hamilton were Field Consultants to Planned Parenthood Federation of America.

munication media, reflect the importance of ideas; they also function to stimulate and spread ideas. In the case of the former, we wish here merely to point out that newspaper and magazine articles, which raise the question of a relationship between race genocide and family planning programs, appear to be increasing. We would assume that this might mean that more black people have begun to be concerned about this issue and are acting on their concerns—i.e., not using family planning methods. Approaching this issue from a different direction, we would assume that the increasing expressions of concern will themselves increase awareness and concern in the larger black community.

The late Langston Hughes[13] in his syndicated column in the *New York Post* in 1965 indicated that concepts "birth control" and "population explosion" were unacceptable to black people. He pointed out the considerable support given to the practices of sterilization and abortion by some well-known conservative organizations, particularly the American Medical Association. The general conservative stance of such organizations might well cause blacks to be suspicious both of the motives underlying such practices and of the motives of the organizations supporting them. Hughes, whose articles were read by a large proportion of the black population, pursued this point through his mythical character *Simple,* who expresses the fear all too clearly:

They got all kinds of Health Wagons going up and down the streets of Harlem now, free x-rays, free vaccine shots, and things. But nobody has to take them. Suppose, though, they passed a birth control law and the Supreme Court upheld the right of the city to cut down by law on the uptown population explosion and then sent a Sterilization Wagon to Harlem. Naturally . . . they would try it out on the colored folks first, calling themselves being helpful to poor underprivileged Harlem, curbing the population explosion.[14]

Other newspapers have carried articles (editorial, serials, or statements from leading black spokesmen) concerning birth control and black

genocide.[15] These include articles and serials in *Muhammad Speaks* (the major publication of the Muslim religion), which are vehemently opposed to the use of birth control methods by black Americans.

Summary

If one will accept the idea that general written expressions of concerns and reported oral expressions of concerns reflect something real in the population, several things follow. On the basis of the above review, one must conclude that concerns exist among black Americans concerning the meaning of family planning programs. One must conclude that this concern has been a long-abiding one, which has recently become intensified. Finally, one must conclude that the concern has not existed within any narrowly defined part of the black community, but can be found among very different groups.

The Research Project

The preliminary report here is based on pilot work done as part of a larger project. One major purpose of this study (as well as the larger research project) was to determine the relationship between family planning practices and belief in a race genocide conspiracy against black Americans. A second major purpose of this study was to determine the relationship between family plan-

[13]Hughes, Langston. "Population Explosion." *New York Post,* December 10, 1965, p. 44.

[14]*Ibid.*

[15]For examples of articles dealing with family planning objectives and discussions of genocide see the following articles:

"White Drive on to Hold Down Black Births." *Muhammad Speaks,* September 1, 1967.

"Doctor Exposes Plot to Block Black Births." *Muhammad Speaks,* January 5, 1968.

Bryant, Hilda. "Family Planning Center Here Wages Grim Social Struggle." *Seattle Post-Intelligencer,* December 15, 1968.

Greenlee, Charles. "Death in a Douche Bag." *Thrust,* July 12, 1968.

Woodford, John. "Birth Control: White Man's Heaven?" *Muhammad Speaks,* January 24, 1969.

Hawkins, Frank N., Jr. "India's Birth Rate is Getting Out of Control." *Long Island Press,* November 19, 1969.

Anspacher, Carolyn. "Why Birth Control Frightens Blacks." *San Francisco Chronicle,* April 10, 1969.

"Julian Bond Fears Genocide of Poor, Black." *The Springfield Sunday Republican,* Springfield, Massachusetts, June 7, 1970.

Kashif, Lonnie. "Why Don't Black Women Like Population Control Plot?" *Muhammad Speaks,* July 31, 1970.

ning practices and race consciousness. In addition to these general purposes we also simply wished to determine the extent to which fears of genocide were present in the black community, the extent of rejection by blacks of various family planning methods (especially sterilization and abortion), and the extent to which blacks feel that black community control of family planning programs would make a difference in the degree of receptiveness to them.

In addition to answers for the above general questions concerning prevalence of certain ideas, we are attempting to test two hypotheses:

1. Race consciousness will be significantly related to rejection of family planning methods.

2. Fears of race (black) genocide will be significantly related to rejection of family planning methods.

Definitions

Race (black) consciousness is generally defined as positive identification with physical features of and cultural aspects related to the black race. In the present study we are using an indirect putative measure of race consciousness, in which the respondent simply designates the preferred racial identifying term from among these: Colored, Negro, Afro-American, and Black. A survey of contemporary thought and popular literature suggests to us that the degree of racial consciousness increases as one moves from "Colored" to "Black."

Race (black) genocide fear is the fear that there is a general plan or conspiracy aimed at the elimination of the black race.

Family planning (birth control) is defined as any method or technique used to limit live births.

Sample

A medium-sized New England city was chosen for this pilot project. Several black communities within this urban area were identified with the help of local black citizens. By means of census data and street lists it was possible to classify several black neighborhoods in terms of income level. The classification system was very simple: low-income neighborhoods and middle-

to-upper income neighborhoods. In those neighborhoods which had been classified as middle-to-upper income a 40% sample of households was initially designated; in those neighborhoods classified as lower income a 60% sample of households was initially designated. From this total designated group of households a 2.5% random sample was drawn. This procedure provided an approximately stratified sample of the black community in that city. The total sample was 160 households.

Procedure

After sampling procedures were complete, the interviewing began. When the interviewers found households empty or potential interviewees were inaccessible, a new household was randomly selected. Ten interviewers were employed to interview the head of the household or a female member of the household in the reproductive age range. Every attempt was made to balance the group in terms of age.

An interview schedule was used which contained items seeking information concerning: general demographic characteristics, attitudes toward family planning methods, attitudes toward family planning agencies, racial consciousness, racial genocide, and general attitude items.

Results

Some general characteristics of the population sample should be noted. Females made up 66% of the sample. The median age for the females was 27; the median age for the males was 30. The median educational attainment was high school graduation.

The first hypothesis was tested by means of cross-tabulations and Chi-square analyses. As an indirect index of attitudes toward family planning we used the number of additional children the respondent wished to have. The index of race consciousness was the preferred racial identifying term (as discussed above). Table 1 shows the cross tabulation for those two variables. As is clear, the number of children desired was collapsed into two categories. Although there appears to be some tendency for the higher race consciousness group to report wanting more children, the Chi-square value was not statistically

Table 1.   Frequencies and Percentages of Respondents by Race Consciousness Level and Desired Number of Children

| Desired Number of Children | Ethnic or Color Designation Preference | | Total |
	Negro, Colored or No Preference	Black or Afro-American	
0–2	21 (60%)	40 (49%)	61 (52%)
3 or more	14 (40%)	42 (51%)	56 (48%)
Total	35	82	117

Table 2.   Frequencies and Percentages of Respondents by Race Consciousness Level and Attitude Toward Family Size Limitation

	No Preference, Negro or Colored	Black or Afro-American	Total
Agree	8 (26%)	29 (29%)	37
Disagree	23 (74%)	72 (71%)	95
Total	31	101	142

significant. Moreover, if one relates race consciousness to a more general item concerning family planning ("Black Americans should not limit their family size.") no significant Chi-square value is found (Table 2).

A much more indirect measure of attitude toward family planning was this item: "Birth control clinics operated by blacks will be more acceptable to blacks than if operated by whites." This may be considered an item aimed at attitude toward family planning in the sense that the respondent who endorses it is saying that he or she sees a connection between race and the acceptability of family planning organizations. The respondent is also saying that family planning programs are not acceptable without this condition. Table 3 is a presentation of frequencies and percentages agreeing and disagreeing with the statement by race consciousness level. As can be noted in that table, there is considerable indication that the more race conscious respondents tended to agree (Chi-square = 9.38, df = 1, $p < 01$).

In testing the second hypothesis a different statistical method was used. Here the relationship between reported actual use of any birth control method was correlated with endorsement of the various items directly asking about genocide. A tetracheric correlation coefficient was computed. This statistical technique is conceptually related to non-parametric tests such as the Chi-square technique. It is particularly appropriate in situations in which test items are being correlated and the responses have been dichotomized. It assumes, as is the case here, that there is underlying

Table 3.   Comparison by Race Consciousness Level on Statement: Birth Control Clinics in Black Neighborhoods Should Be Controlled and Operated by Blacks*

	No Preference, Negro or Colored	Black or Afro-American	Total
Agree	15 (47%)	80 (75%)	95 (68%)
Disagree	17 (53%)	26 (27%)	43 (32%)
Total	32	106	138

*   Chi-square = 9.38, df = 1, $p < .01$

Table 4. Tetrachoric Correlation Coefficients Relating Reported Use of Family Planning Methods and Belief in the Notion of Racial Genocide ($N = 159$)

Item (Agree/Disagree)	r
1. As the need for cheap labor goes down there will be an effort to reduce the number of black Americans.	.67*
2. As black Americans increase their demands for civil rights there will be an effort to rid the country of American blacks.	.04
3. The assassination of black leaders is an indication of the white effort to eliminate blacks.	.34*
4. Encouraging American blacks to use birth control is comparable to trying to eliminate this group from society.	.38*
5. Abortions are a part of a white plot to eliminate blacks.	.52*
6. Sterilization is a white plot to eliminate blacks.	.36*
7. All forms of birth control methods are designed to eliminate black Americans.	.41*

* $p < .01$

continuity in each of the variables in spite of the dichotomous scoring. Table 4 presents each item and its correlation with the reported use of birth control methods. As can be seen in that table all of the correlation coefficients are statistically significant except for one. One possible explanation for lack of significance with that item may be that the item is made complex by the inclusion of the very salient (but unrelated) notion of "civil rights." In summary, it can be said that support has been found for the second hypothesis.

Some additional findings are worthy of note. It should be recalled that, in addition to the two hypotheses, several general questions were raised at the beginning of our discussion of the research project. One question had to do with the simple extent to which fears of genocide were present in such a sample; another was the extent of rejection by blacks of various family planning methods; and the extent to which blacks feel that black community control over family planning programs would make a difference in the degree of acceptability of such programs. Several items which bear on the question concerning extent of fear of genocide are listed in Table 5 with the percentage endorsing responses keyed for fear of genocide. In an attempt to assess the statistical

significance of these percentages, K values were computed. This statistical test, which was developed by McCall and Simon[16] simply determines the degree to which unpopular views are held in a particular population. The K value ranges from 0 (no strength in a minority view) to 1 (the highest degree of group division). The minus signs indicate that the unpopular response was the agreement response in each case. Neither the percentages nor the K values are large. This suggests, especially when one considers the findings discussed above, that it is a small but consistent group of the respondents who are making the difference. This does not, of course, detract from the importance of the findings already reported. Indeed, it is remarkable that the relationships between the variables are as consistent as they are.

Next, the question of the extent of rejection of various family planning methods. Note that this is not necessarily a direct function of fear of genocide; other reasons may exist for rejecting various methods. Table 6 lists four questions concerning the acceptability of birth control methods.

[16]McCall, George J., and Simmons, J. L. "A New Measure of Attitudinal Opposition." *National Opinion Quarterly,* Vol. 30, No. 2 (Summer, 1966), pp. 271–278.

Table 5. Percentage Endorsement on Items Dealing with Race Genocide

Item	Percent Agree	K
1. Birth control methods are designed to eliminate the black population.	13	−.079
2. Abortion is a plot to eliminate black Americans.	29	−.243

Table 6.   Percentage Respondents Rejecting Certain Birth Control Methods

Item	Percent Rejecting
1. If you had the desired number of children, would you have an abortion (female) or encourage your partner to have an abortion (male).	71%
2. If you had all the children you wanted, would you allow yourself to be sterilized.	79%
3. Sterilization is an acceptable method of family planning.	90%
4. There are acceptable methods of birth control.	37%

Table 7.   Comparison by Sex: Birth Control Clinics in Black Neighborhoods Should Be Controlled and Operated by Blacks

	Male	Female	Total
Agree	32 (67%)	50 (58%)	82 (61%)
Disagree	16 (33%)	36 (42%)	52 (39%)
Total	48	86	134

The fact that all methods are rejected by only 37% and the percentage rejecting abortion and sterilization ranges from 71% to 90%, clearly suggests that these two latter methods are considered especially objectionable. Sterilization, because it is a method which has finality, is reasonably less acceptable to most individuals. There may be both religious and moral restrictions which cause individuals to reject abortion as a method of birth control.

Finally, we should attempt to determine from these data the extent of feeling in the sample that black control of the family planning programs in black communities would be more acceptable. The respondents were asked whether they agreed or disagreed with the following statement: "Birth control clinics operated by blacks will be more acceptable to blacks than if operated by whites." The per cent agreeing was 62%; 28% disagreed; 10% did not answer. On another item—"Birth control clinics in black neighborhoods should be

controlled and operated by blacks"—received the following responses: 59% agreed; 37% disagreed; 4% did not answer. Although these percentages speak for themselves, it is worth pointing out that the 62% agreement is considerably higher than the 37% who considered no family planning method acceptable. That is, this large percentage cannot be attributed only to the responses of those who hold extremely negative feelings about family planning.

Conclusions and Implications

If one considers both the general survey which was presented early in this paper as well as these preliminary findings, one must conclude that there is a significant group of black Americans who are wary of family planning programs, especially if those programs involve certain types

Table 8.   Comparison by Sex: Birth Control Clinics Operated by Blacks Will Be More Acceptable to Blacks Than if Operated by Whites

	Male	Female	Total
Agree	36 (75%)	59 (66%)	95 (69%)
Disagree	12 (25%)	31 (34%)	43 (31%)
Total	48	90	138

of family planning methods, and especially if the programs are run by non-blacks.

One rather striking conclusion which we must come to on the basis of these data is that there is a relationship between fears of racial genocide and the use of family planning methods. One immediate implication of this finding is that those individuals who have interpreted various historical and current events as a conspiracy to eliminate black people are responding in a direct way to counter the effects of the assumed conspiracy. One might think that a person might well allow that whites have done many things contrary to the well-being of black people (including systematic attempts to reduce their numbers), and yet not find that the response is the one which would potentially counter the effects of such a situation.

The limitations of these conclusions are obvious. As we implied early in this paper, one might well take issue with a brief historical survey, a few references to conference statements, and newspaper articles as the basis for inferring that there is widespread belief in something among the black people of America. However, when we have added some evidence based on a randomly selected group of black people, then one must consider the trend as more than trivial.

It is our general feeling about the data as analyzed so far that there are groups who feel estranged from the larger society in more ways than in birth control. Their feelings are based on a great deal more than the notion of family planning as a method for eliminating black people. Their response is to a great deal more than information about family planning agencies. They are responding to a long history of every possible type of oppression which has been perpetrated against blacks. The resistance to family planning and to family planning agencies run by whites is merely a symptom of the deep sense of historical and life-long estrangement.

One-Child Families and Atypical Sex Ratios in an Elite Black Community

Ruth McKay

The author provides several explanations for the large number of one-child families among a sample of Blacks who are solidly upper-middle class. Attention is also given to the significant number of female offspring in comparison to male offspring in this setting.

My original intention in writing this paper had been to discuss some of the cultural factors affecting family size in the Black Elite and Ghetto communities I had studied between 1960 and 1967. In the course of examining the Elite data recently for numbers and ratios of children, which had not been done when the material was analyzed previously for socialization trends, a number of surprising relationships involving disproportionate numbers of one-child families and female children came to light. Today's presentation will focus exclusively on the Elite material.

The Elite Black community data was collected in Border City[1] during a two-year field study of socialization practices, six months of which were devoted to a definition of the social class structure as it was perceived by the members of the Black community. The criteria for determining social class placement most frequently mentioned by my informants were: education, occupation, income, and "old family" affiliation. The best perspective on the distribution of Elite status characteristics within the Black community can be gained by looking at some 1960 U.S. census findings for Border City. In that year, it had a total

[1]A fictitious name for a city on the mid-Atlantic coast.

Reprinted by permission. Footnotes have been renumbered.

population approaching one million (939,024), of which two thirds were classed as "White" (610, 608), and one third were classed as "Non-White" (328,416). All but 2,800,[2] or more than 99% of the "Non-Whites" were Negro. (The 1960 Census Report figures do not differentiate Negroes from other "Non-Whites.")

Six per cent, or 3,900 "Non-White" families had an annual income of $10,000 or more. Three per cent, or 5,929 "Non-White" individuals had completed four or more years of college. (In our community survey, more Negro females than males had completed college.) 7,760 "Non-Whites" were engaged in occupations falling in the two highest occupational categories of "Professional and Technical"; and "Managerial and Proprietary." Of the "Non-Whites" engaged in high status occupations, 47% (3,685) were male, 53% (4,075) were female. Given the fact that more Black women than men possessed high status educational and professional credentials, some Elite status Black women married Black men with less education and less prestigious occupations than they themselves possessed.

The Elite Black Border City family in the early 1960's typically consisted of parents who were college educated. The family income typically ranged from $13,000 to $17,000 in families in which both husband and wife worked (81%), although incomes over $50,000 were reported. In descending order, the occupations represented in the Elite Black community sample studied were: elementary school teacher, secondary school teacher; social worker; physician; college professor; clerical worker; postal clerk; judge; junior high school principal; clergyman; engineer; build-

[2]Other "Non-White" races included American Indian, Japanese, Chinese, Filipino, Korean, Asian Indian, and Malayan.

ing contractor; newspaper reporter; investment broker; business manager; chemist; nurse; policeman; pharmacist; and college dean. Although some of the families had achieved Elite status in their own lifetimes, many of the Elite adults were themselves children of Elite parents whose names could be found in the first edition of "Who's Who in Colored America," published in the 1920's.

In the course of conducting the study of socialization practices, the author experienced extreme difficulty in locating families with at least one young child of each sex. At the end of the two-year study, the Intensive Study Sample of twenty-five families included seven one-child families because no other families with young children of opposite sex could be found. In attempting to get greater breadth to the observations derived from the twenty-five family sample, the author was fortunate in being given access to the membership roster of a mothers' and children's organization with which all but a handful of the Elite Black families were associated. In the course of two years of attending parties, barbecues, dances, club meetings, and other social and community events, I encountered only two Elite women who did not belong to this organization. I shall call this elite club the "Lads and Lassies."

Excluding a few families with adopted children, and mothers who were not natives of the United States, the "Lads and Lassies" provided a sample of 162 mothers and 249 children. In looking at family size in this larger sample, I was surprised to learn that almost two thirds of the Elite Black families consisted of families with one child. Of a total of 162 families, 102 (63%) had one child, 39 (24%) had two children, 16 (10%) had three children, 4 (2.4%) had four children, and 1 family (0.6%) had five children. (See Table 1.)

The great proportion of one-child families in this generation is in sharp contrast to the family size of the Elite mother's own family of orientation. In the Intensive Study Sample, the mothers reported up to eleven siblings, and an average family size of 5.2 children. The average family size for the 162 families in our "Lads and Lassies" sample was 1.54 children.

The findings of a majority of one-child families in the Elite Negro community also contrasts strongly with numbers of children born to Non-White married women in the Border City Standard Metropolitan Area. For a population of 6,686 Non-

Table 1.   Family Size, Elite Black Community Sample

Children per Family	Number of Families	% of Total
1	102	63
2	39	24
3	16	10
4	4	2.4
5	1	0.6
Total	162	100

White married women, ages 45–49, 1,877 (28%) had borne one child, 1,333 (20%) had borne two children, 949 (14%) had borne three children, 721 (11%) had borne four children, 830 (12%) had borne either five or six children, and 966 (15%) had borne seven or more children. Although the "Lads and Lassies" mothers ranged in age from early thirties to late forties, we may still infer that few of the children in the one-child families would acquire younger siblings at some future time. Seventy of the 102 children in the one-child families were over ten years of age.

A closer look at the seven one-child families in the twenty-five Intensive Study Sample revealed that five of the seven children in these one-child families were girls. In turning to the larger "Lads and Lassies" sample, I expected that the children in the 102 one-child families would be about evenly divided between boys and girls. I was startled to learn that there were almost twice as many girls as boys in this group of one-child families. The Elite Black population appeared to be a community in which girls and one-child families predominated. Both of these characteristics run counter to population trends for the United States and the world at large.

The secondary sex ratio, or the sex ratio at birth, is approximately 106 males to 100 females for United States Whites and 102.6 males for every 100 females among United States Negroes.[3] Urban sex ratios tend to run lower than rural ratios and national averages. The secondary sex ratio of White babies born in Border City in 1960 was 104.3; the secondary sex ratio of Negro infants born in that city in 1960 was 100.7. The sex ratio for Border City White youth, ages 3 to 19 years, in 1960 was 100.2; for Non-White youth, ages 3 to 19

years, was 95.7. The sex ratio in our "Lads and Lassies" sample of 249 children, ages 3 to 19, was 83.0 males to every 100 females. The sex ratio for the 102 children in the one-child families in the "Lads and Lassies" sample was 61.9.[4]

The "United Nations Report on the Role of Women," issued in November 1974, indicates a world trend in the direction of a growing increase of men over women which is expected to continue until the end of the century.[5] A community in which children run on the order of five girls for every four boys is, therefore, contrary to the expected ratio.

My first explanation for the preponderance of girls in the one-child families was that there must have been some sort of matrifocal influence at work. Once a mother had borne a female, she had the child of the desired sex and there was no need to bear additional children. If this were the case, in looking at the multi-child families, one would expect to find a greater number with an oldest male child, leading the parents to try again for the desired female child. Actually, the sex of the first child in the multi-child families was evenly divided between the sexes. Twenty-eight of the multi-child families had had a son first; twenty-eight of these families had had a daughter first. Since there did not seem to be any greater inclination for the families with an only son to try for additional children in the hope of attaining the

[3]Curt Stern, *Principles of Human Genetics* (San Francisco, W. H. Freeman, 1973) pp. 529–530.

[4]Human geneticist Curt Stern has stated that the "observed [secondary] sex ratios are empirical values which are subject to chance variation. . . . [In] a population of one hundred, the probability of observing a deviation from 106 as large as 158.1 or 71.4 or larger would be 5%" (Ibid., p. 530). The only Black Elite population on which I could derive the secondary sex ratio, or the sex ratio at birth, was the sixty-child sample in the Intensive Study Sample of families. Their secondary sex ratio was 68.5. If there had been one hundred children in this sample, the sex ratio of 68.5 would probably border on the 5% probability range (see Ibid., chapter 20).

[5]*Washington Post,* November 19, 1974, B3.

Table 2.   Sex Ratios

	White	Negro
U.S. secondary sex ratio, 1960	106.0	102.6
Border City secondary sex ratio, 1960	104.3	100.7
Border City youth, ages 3–19 years	100.2	95.7*
Lads and Lassies (Total of 249 children, 3–19		83.0
Lads and Lassies (102 "only" children, 3–19)		61.9

* A figure for Negro youth alone was not available. This ratio is based on total "non-white" youth in this age category in Border City, 1960.

desired female child, another explanation would have to be found.

I am grateful to my physical anthropological colleagues for information about recent work in the field of Human Reproductive Biology which helps to explain the unusual sex ratio among the children in this community. We shall see how *a culture pattern has interacted with a biological trend to produce a situation in which the expected sex ratio of children is reversed.*

The culture pattern is an Elite social structure in which the full-time income of the wife is necessary for the maintenance of the desired standard of living. Typically, she interrupts her professional career just once, in order to bear one child, and then returns to full-time earning power for the balance of her professional life.

Studies of human reproduction have revealed that although the sex ratio of males to females is greater at conception and birth, there tends to be a reduction in the disparity of males over females as the age of the father increases and as the rank order of birth increases. "In nearly all populations, the ratio of males is highest for the first birth and decreases with successive births. Such a correlation . . . may be directly related to the birth order itself; or to the ages of the parents, which obviously increase with increasing birth order. . . . Analysis has shown that the age of the mother is not correlated with the sex ratio, but, curiously enough, the age of the father may be."[6]

Since the population with the atypical sex ratio is predominantly a population of one-child families, we may discount birth order as a likely explanation for the over-representation of girls. In turning to a more careful look at the timing of conception of the child or children in the Elite Black family, we see that child-bearing, which interferes with the wife's earning capacity, is usually postponed for several years after marriage until the couple have completed professional training, acquired a home, furnishings, automobile, and other necessary accoutrements of elite life-style. For the small number of Elite families in which the age of the fathers at the time of the birth of the child is known, we learn that the mean age of the fathers was 32.66 years, with a range from 24 to 50 years of age. Thus, while the delay in child-bearing was caused by the women's

wish to contribute to the families' nesteggs, the husbands had, perforce, aged along with their wives during the waiting period. Fathers moderately to well-advanced in their reproductive cycle might well tend to produce fewer male than female children in the first conception.

In the concluding section of this paper, I would like to consider some of the possible social structural implications our findings of large numbers of one-child families and of girls over boys may hold for the future of the Elite Black community. For a woman beginning her child-bearing career in 1960, Thompson[7] reckoned that an average of 2.38 children would be necessary to maintain the population at a stationary level. Although the greater number of females borne by Elite Black women may mean that a slightly lower number of children per mother would be required to maintain the population at a stationary level, the average of 1.54 children borne by mothers in our sample may not be high enough to replace the Elite population. We will look at replacement of population by recruitment a little later.

The greater ratio of males to females at birth for most human populations means that the higher attrition rate for males through life will lead to parity in the sex ratio somewhere in the middle adult years. A population in which numbers of girls exceeds numbers of boys at birth is one in which there will be an increasing surplus of females or, stated differently, an increasing deficit of males, as the generation grows to maturity. We may foresee a future Elite adult population which is proportionately higher in females than was true for the generation of parents we studied in 1960. Recall that the Elite adult community of 1960, coming from good-sized families in which there was no marked over-representation of females, was one in which more women than men had completed college and more women than men occupied positions in the highest two occupational categories.

"No matter," some may say. "A community replaces itself not only by births within but through recruitment of individuals from outside of the community." This indeed happens. Every generation witnesses the ascent of some individuals from lower- to middle- and upper-class standing.

---

[6]Stern, op. cit., p. 538.

[7]Warner S. Thompson and Donald T. Lewis, *Population Problems* (New York: McGraw Hill, 1965), pp. 270–271.

The dilemma this process of recruitment poses for the Elite Black community is that, traditionally, more women than men have made the transition to Elite status. For a variety of historical and cultural reasons, ranging from differential patterns of discrimination within educational and occupational systems to differential expectations and socialization pressures for boys and girls within lower-class Black families, social mobility has been easier for the Black woman to achieve.

Until the social and psychological structures which serve to block the Black man's mobility are dismantled, a disproportionately female endogenous Elite of the future will be joined by a similar population of mobile newcomers to their community. All of which might very well lead the upper-class Black Border Citian of the 1980's to query, "Where did all these girls come from?"

10

Parental Roles and Socialization Processes

Adult Male Absence and the Self-Attitudes of Black Children

Roger H. Rubin

The lack of a male head of household and its effect on the identity of male offspring has been the focus of a number of controversial studies. The author of this study challenges the assumption that the absence of a visible male head of household results in negative self-esteem among young Black males. He discusses prime alternatives that such Black youth have for developing positive self-esteem.

An examination of literature on black family structure indicates frequent absence of adult males from the households of the lower-class with claims of a resultant lack of male role models for young boys to identify with and subsequent sex-role confusion (Frazier, 1950; Ausubel and Ausubel, 1963; Pettigrew, 1964; Clark, 1965; Rosen, 1969; Willie, 1970; TenHouten, 1970; Staples, 1971; Bracey, Meier, and Rudwick, 1971). Female dominance in such households can further create psychological inadequacies in the developing male through the espousing of negative attitudes toward men. In its extreme, males may be viewed with contempt, degraded, and treated with antagonism and hostility (Rohrer and Edmonson, 1960). Such attitudes developed out of a history and tradition of female self-reliance emergent within an American society which severely limited black males (King, 1945; Frumkin, 1954; Blue, 1959). These factors reportedly culminate in a boy's greater tendency to perceive himself as an unworthwhile person (Rohrer and Edmonson, 1960; Clark, 1965).

On the other hand, the girl is psychologically encouraged and supported in this situation as well as having an available same sex-role model (Pettigrew, 1964). Solidarity against men and a strong bond of mutual female dependency has been reported (Rohrer and Edmonson, 1960).

Children of both sexes from complete homes, although they may be affected by many variables influencing self-attitudes, should still view themselves more positively than boys from homes with no adult males.

If this is the situation then numerous lower-class black males are socialized in a family system which produces little sense of value in their own worth (Dai, 1953; Cavan, 1959). Kardiner and Ovesey (1951) maintained that poor self-esteem was a major psychological handicap among blacks. Evidence supports the contention that one's conception of who and what he is is markedly influenced by interpersonal dynamics within the family constellation (Jersild, 1952; Jourard, 1957; Wylie, 1961; Smith and Suinn, 1965). Child development research indicates that how an individual feels about himself is of central significance to the manner in which he will behave (Kuhn and McPartland, 1954; Cavan, 1959; Kvaraceus, 1964). The implications for interpersonal relations among blacks, as well as interracial contacts, should not be underestimated.

Thus, the major hypothesis of this study was that black boys from homes having no adult male figures would have significantly poorer self-attitudes than girls from this type home, and boys and girls from homes with adult males and females.

In addition, three other hypotheses using the independent variables of sex, class standing,

Abridged from *Child Study Journal* 4 (1974): 33–45. Reprinted by permission. Tables have been deleted.

and family interaction were examined. The hypotheses were (a) that females will have more positive self-attitudes than males at this age level, (b) children from bright classes will have more positive self-attitudes than those from slower classes, and (c) the more family interaction the more positive the self-attitudes. The employment of these variables was based upon the possibility that they may be even more important factors in self-attitude formation, especially in childhood, than type of family structure, per se.

Method

Self-attitude is an inclusive term encompassing both self-concept and self-esteem. This was done because a paper and pencil questionnaire was developed from several previous studies which utilized different terminology. Part of an instrument developed by Piers and Harris (1964) for measuring self-concept in children was used. It contained questions concerning behavior, general and academic status, physical appearance and attributes, anxiety, popularity, and happiness and satisfaction. Self-esteem questions were drawn from the work of Rosenberg (1965) and Lipsett's (1958) self-concept scale was also utilized. These constituted the eight dependent variables. Additional questions obtained data on sex, family interaction, ability level of school class, and presence or absence of adult males. These were the independent variables.

Participants were placed in four categories. These were boys having adult males living at home, boys not having adult males living at home, girls having adult males living at home, and girls not having adult males living at home. The sample consisted of 280 fifth and sixth grade children in two public elementary schools in a black, ghetto area of north Philadelphia, Pennsylvania. The age range was nine to eleven. Forty-three boys and thirty girls claimed no adult male was residing in their home. Siblings 18 and older were considered adults. . . .

Results

No significant differences were found in any self-attitude measure when comparing boys from homes having no adult males with girls from such homes and boys and girls from homes with adult male figures.

Only very minor support was found for the hypothesis that girls at this age level have more positive self-attitudes than boys. Girls rated themselves higher than boys in general and academic status. Methodologically, this was probably the only meaningful finding. This was significant at $p < .05$, df = 2, $\chi^2 = 6.372$. At the $p < .01$ level of significance boys scored higher on the physical appearance and attributes scale, df = 3, $\chi^2 = 19.600$. Girls were more anxious than boys, $p < .05$, df = 2; $\chi^2 = 7.010$. No other significant findings appeared.

Children from bright classes scaled higher on self-attitudes concerning general and academic status than those in average and slow classes. Significance was at the $p < .01$ level, df = 4, $\chi^2 = 16.804$. Anxiety was found to increase as one's class position decreased. This was significant at the $p < .01$, df = 4, $\chi^2 = 14.210$. Other measures showed no significant differences.

A curvilinear relationship was found at the $p < .05$ level of significance, df = 6, $\chi^2 = 14.673$ when the independent variable of family interaction was examined against the self-concept rating. It indicated that low family interaction concerning interest in school achievement and the poorest self-concepts appeared concurrently. In the intermediate range both increased together. However, self-concept began tapering off again at the highest level of family interaction. Significant at the $p < .05$ level, df = 6, $\chi^2 = 7.444$ was a slight relationship between family interaction and general and academic status. Other measures of self-attitudes were not significant at the $p < .05$ level. Therefore, only some positive support was found for the hypothesis that increased family interaction results in better self-attitudes. . . .

Discussion

Two possible factors may contribute to cancelling out differences between the self-attitudes of boys from homes without adult males and those from homes with male adults. The former may find models for identification and role learning on the streets, in the classroom, or even from one's own mother (Tennyson, 1967; Hartnagel, 1970). On the other hand, the adult male living with the latter may be a poor model due to his own demoralized state. Also, female hostility toward males, whether they are present or absent, may effectively lower a boy's self-attitudes. Derbyshire et al. (1963) noted that adult, black male mental patients often perceived their fathers as ineffective and emasculated and the mother as a major decision maker and upholder of middle-class values.

These explanations may also help to account for the lack of self-attitude difference between boys without adult males at home and girls from homes with and without male adults. One may contend that the lower-class black male may demoralize the girls as well as the boys. Then again, street models, particularly "gang" members, may raise the boy's self-attitudes to the girl's level. This may reflect chauvinistic male values developed partly as a response to extensive female dominance (Rohrer and Edmonson, 1960; Tennyson, 1967; Rosen, 1969). Finally, some studies on female dominance claim girls are favored (Rohrer and Edmonson, 1960; Ausubel and Ausubel, 1963). Perhaps this has been given undue emphasis.

In regard to the sex variable girls may have tended to give more positive self-attitudes on general and academic status because of the unmasculine cultural connotations school achievement may carry for boys. However, girls may genuinely be more adept at school work because of their greater maturity at this age. Adult female encouragement of the girls may also be a factor, at least on this variable.

The greater vanity among boys and the higher showing of anxiety among girls may have reflected the male "gang" philosophy with its emphasis on overt signs of masculinity. However, the questions used may have contributed to a discrimination along sexual lines. For example, crying, worrying, fear, and nervousness were the traits listed under anxiety. These are usually considered more feminine behaviors than masculine by the general society. Therefore, it is not surprising for males to deny that they have these traits, especially when "gang" acceptance is important.

Thus, only very minor support was found for the hypothesis that girls have more positive self-attitudes than boys at this age level.

The concomitant rise in class standing and self-attitude concerning general and academic status may indicate awareness of school achievement and position. Its prime value, however, seems to be that of a validity check.

Anxiety, in the form of worry, fear, and nervousness seems to increase with decreased class level. Frustration at one's inabilities, or peer disfavor, may help to account for this. Perhaps these emotions preceded poorer academic achievement.

Therefore, only slight support was found for the hypothesis that children in bright classes would be more positive in self-attitudes.

The formation of a curvilinear relationship between family interaction and self-concept ratings may be accounted for in the following manner. As interaction in the form of relying upon and talking to one's family increases so does self-concept. However, there seems to come a point where the possibility of too much interaction, perhaps due to too many family members, results in a competition and comparison with siblings which can damage self-concept.

Increased interaction yielding praise and reward may have resulted in the positive relating of this variable to general and academic status.

Again, however, only vague support was found for the hypothesis which states the more the family interaction the more positive the self-attitudes.

Summary

Support was not found for the major hypothesis that black boys from homes having no adult males would have significantly lower self-attitudes than girls from such homes and boys and girls from homes with adult male figures. The physical presence or absence of adult males in the home says little about the availability of other male role models. Neither does it provide insight into the personal adequacy of an available adult male nor how he is perceived by others. Future research should concern itself with these issues.

References

Ausubel, D. P., and Ausubel, P. Ego development among segregated Negro children. In H. A. Passow (Ed.), *Education in Depressed Areas.* New York: Teachers College, Columbia University, 1963, pp. 109–134.

Bledsoe, J. C. Sex differences in mental health analysis scores of elementary pupils. *Jour-

nal of Consulting Psychology, 1961, 25, 364–365.

Blue, J. T., Jr. An empirical study of child–parent relations: matricentrism in the southern family. *Dissertation Abstracts,* 1959, 19, No. 2178.

Bracey, J. H., Jr., Meier, A., and Rudwick, E. *Black matriarchy: myth or reality?* Belmont, California: Wadsworth Publishing Company, 1971.

Cavan, R. S. Negro family disorganization and juvenile delinquency. *Journal of Negro Education,* 1959, 28, 230–239.

Clark, K. B. *Dark ghetto.* New York: Harper & Row, 1965.

Dai, B. Problems of personality development among Negro children. In C. Kluckholn and H. A. Murray (Eds.), *Personality in Nature, Society, and Culture.* New York: A. Knopf, 1953, pp. 437–458.

Derbyshire, R. L., Brody, E. B., and Schleifer, C. Family structure of young adult Negro male mental patients: preliminary observations from urban Baltimore. *Journal of Nervous Mental Disease,* 1963, 136, 245–251.

Frazier, E. F. Problems and needs of Negro children and youth resulting from family disorganization. *Journal of Negro Education,* 1950, 19, 269–277.

Frumkin, R. Attitudes of Negro college students toward intra-family leadership and control. *Journal of Marriage and Family Living,* 1954, 16, 252–253.

Hartnagel, T. F. Father absence and self conception among lower class white and Negro boys. *Social Problems,* 1970, 18, 152–163.

Jersild, A. *In search of self.* New York: Teachers College, Columbia University, 1952.

Jourard, S. M. Identification, parent-cathexis, and self-esteem. *Journal of Consulting Psychology,* 1957, 21, 375–380.

Kardiner, A., and Ovesey, L. *The mark of oppression.* New York: W. W. Norton, 1951.

King, C. E. The Negro maternal family: the product of an economic and culture system. *Social Forces,* 1945, 24, 100–104.

Kuhn, M. H., and McPartland, T. S. An empirical investigation of self-attitudes. *American Sociological Review,* 1954, 19, 68–78.

Kvaraceus, W. C., Gibson, J. S., Patterson, F., Seasholes, B., and Grambs, J. D. *Negro self-concept.* Lincoln Filene Center for Citizenship and Public Affairs. Medford, Massachusetts: Tufts University, 1964.

Lipsett, L. P. A self-concept scale for children and its relationship to the children's form of the Manifest Anxiety Scale. *Child Development,* 1958, 29, 463–472.

Pettigrew, T. F. *A profile of the Negro American.* New York: Van Nostrand, 1964.

Piers, E. V., and Harris, D. B. Age and other correlates of self-concept in children. *Journal of Educational Psychology,* 1964, 55, 91–95.

Rohrer, J. H., and Edmonson, M. S. *The eighth generation: cultures and personalities of New Orleans Negroes.* New York: Harper, 1960.

Rosen, L., Matriarchy and lower class Negro male delinquency. *Social Problems,* 1969, 17, 175–189.

Rosenberg, M. *Society and the adolescent self-image.* Princeton, New Jersey: Princeton University Press, 1965.

Smith, T. L., and Suinn, R. M. A note on identification, self-esteem, anxiety, and conformity. *Journal of Clinical Psychology,* 1965, 21, 286.

Staples, R. (Ed.) *The black family: essays and studies.* Belmont, California: Wadsworth Publishing Company, 1971.

TenHouten, W. D. The black family: myth and reality. *Psychiatry,* 1970, 33, 145–173.

Tennyson, R. A. Family structure and delinquent behavior. In M. W. Klein (Ed.), *Juvenile Gangs in Context.* Englewood Cliffs, New Jersey: Prentice-Hall, 1967, pp. 57–69.

Willie, C. V. (Ed.) *The family life of black people.* Columbus, Ohio: Charles E. Merrill Publishing Company, 1970.

Wylie, R. C. *The self-concept.* Nebraska: University of Nebraska Press, 1961.

Parental Functionality

John Scanzoni

The research presented in this article pertains to the values Black families have towards education and achievement. The author contends that there is a strong value orientation to acquiring an education, and that the roles of father/mother are important in providing the support needed for the attainment of these educational goals.

[This study does not] cover the full range of parental socialization. . . . But it does focus on the perceptions of these respondents regarding particular values that their parents transmitted *to* them, and also particular behaviors that their parents performed *for* them. These parental values and behaviors may be described as being "functional" or useful in terms of later economic and conjugal role performance by those in the sample. They are resources transmitted by parents to children that can be effectively utilized by the latter.

Educational Values

To apprehend these values and behaviors, we first asked respondents to identify their "natural" father or else their father-substitute. . . . The same applied to their "natural" mother or mother-substitute. We then asked questions designed to measure the ways in which they perceived these particular parents (parent-substitutes) had prepared them to function effectively in the larger society. One such question was: "Did your father (father-substitute) ever say that it was especially important for you to get as much education as you could because you are a Negro?" (A separate

question probed the same matter in terms of the mother.). . .

[Two] themes are in fact present among our respondents' families of orientation: on the one hand the belief that education is *especially* crucial to blacks; on the other, the feeling that it is *equally* important to blacks and whites. In terms of actual proportions, the latter theme seems to have been favored by *fathers* of our respondents (see Table 1). Sixty-one percent of husbands and also sixty-one percent of wives replied "no" to this question in connection with their fathers; only thirty-nine percent in each case responded "yes."[1] Although their fathers evidently urged our respondents to get as much education as possible, it was not couched in a specific context of racial need. Yet this was less true of respondents' mothers. Forty-eight percent of males in the sample report "yes," their mothers did urge education within a racial context. And 52 percent of females report the same. Consequently, the "push" from mothers toward increased educational efforts due to "relative black deprivation" is greater than that from fathers.

Why this difference should exist is not completely certain. The literature on the black family makes a great deal, of course, about the traditional dominance of the female and especially her greater involvement with the children—particularly female children. If indeed it is true that education is terribly vital to blacks because they are denied access to job opportunities that are open to whites with less training, then of course it is in the best interests of the black child to be aware of this. If these mothers tended to expose

[1]The total N in the tables includes those who identify a parent or parent figure and who also respond to the question.

Adapted from *The Black Family in Modern Society* (Chicago: University of Chicago Press, 1977), pp. 64–81. Reprinted by permission. Most footnotes have been deleted.

Table 1.   Perceived Parental Stress on Education

Did Parent Urge Educa-tion Because of Race?	Male Respondents		Female Respondents	
	Fathers	Mothers	Fathers	Mothers
Yes	39.0	48.0	39.0	52.0
No	61.0	52.0	61.0	48.0
T	100%	100%	100%	100%
N	(169)	(188)	(179)	(195)

$\chi^2 = 5.0$

n.s. $p < .05$; 1 df

their children to this notion more than fathers did, they were perhaps being highly sensitive to the need for sustained educational efforts. It is not that these fathers did not have the best interests of their children in mind; they simply seem to have felt that a marked emphasis on education per se (irrespective of skin color) would serve their children's interests best.

The major point that emerges from Table 1, as well as from Tables 2 and 3, is *that most of these blacks grew up in homes where education was strongly stressed and encouraged in one fashion or the other by both parents. . . .*

Educational Help

While studies of the black lower class suggest this kind of value orientation is missing or else muted through lack of appropriate role models, this was not the case among these blacks who presumably represent the majority of American blacks above the underclass. Furthermore, their parents not only talked about the importance of education, but also actually behaved in such a fashion as to implement the value. *Behavior of this kind is clearly other than a lower-class pattern.* Specifically, each respondent was asked: "Do you

feel that your father (father-substitute) actually helped you in getting your education, or that he may have hindered you?" The same question was asked separately regarding mothers. Possible responses in each item were "helped," "hindered," "neither" (see Table 2). Among males in the sample, 72 percent said that their fathers had been a help to them in getting their education; 77 percent of females responded similarly. Once again, however, both males and females were *more* likely to view their mothers as being a "help" than their fathers. Seventy-nine percent of males and 85 percent of females reported that their mothers had helped them in this particular fashion.

Those respondents who said that their fathers or mothers had helped were asked *how* they had done so. These replies fell into two general categories of help: *intangible* and *tangible* (see Table 3). More specifically, within the "intangible" category were "interpersonal pressures" involving encouragement, or goading, or continual reinforcement to go to school and to remain there as long as possible. . . .

Many adolescents in American society become discouraged with school and perhaps entertain the notion of leaving it at the earliest possible time. This notion was undoubtedly more

Table 2.   Perceived Parental Help in Getting Education

Did Parent Help in Getting Education?	Male Respondents		Female Respondents	
	Fathers	Mothers	Fathers	Mothers
Helped	72.0	79.3	77.0	85.4
Other	28.0	20.7	23.0	14.6
T	100%	100%	100%	100%
N	(168)	(188)	(178)	(192)

n.s.   n.s.

Table 3.   Type of Parental Help Provided in Obtaining Education

	Male Respondents		Female Respondents	
	Fathers	Mothers	Fathers	Mothers
Intangible help	31.7	54.1	47.1	42.0
Tangible help	68.3	45.9	52.9	58.0
T	100%	100%	100%	100%
N	(123)	(148)	(138)	(162)

$$X^2 = 13.59$$
$$p < .001; 1 \text{ df} \qquad \text{n.s.}$$

true during the years when these respondents were young, and it surely varies with socioeconomic position. Black children, more so than white, may have genuine difficulty in perceiving what difference an education will actually make in terms of achievement and success in society. For instance, . . . the black with *some* college earns less than the white with only eight years of school. . . .

Blacks in our sample appear to have been amply "imbued with this basic value." The interpersonal pressures described here—the continual goading and encouragement—would seem to be especially vital in black families. These pressures appear to be a necessity if the black child is to resist the counter-societal pressures to "give up" in school. The fact that rewards from years of education are so dimly perceived stands a good chance of being outweighed through continual parental reinforcement as to the worthwhileness of school. To point out the advantages of education is indeed a crucial parental "function."

Under the "tangible" category, there was one main theme and two subthemes. The main theme was "material aid" (what Blau and Duncan call "economic resources"). In the case of the father, several different respondents answered in these terms: "He provided for us, sent us to high school, and so we didn't have to get out and work." "He went without clothes so I could go to school." "By supporting me he kept me in school or else I might have had to drop out." "He helped me by financing the things I needed for school." The two minor (in terms of proportion of responses), but related, tangible help forms were "help with homework and lessons," and "keeping clothes clean and neat." (This last behavior, when it was cited, applied equally to fathers and mothers.)

In terms of material aid, the comments

above suggest that the father's role was to provide a financial base on which the child could rely in order to continue his schooling. Within the dominant society, this familial behavior pattern is taken for granted and its significance is hardly recognized. But among many black ("disadvantaged") families, where there is often constant struggle for survival or to "get by," parental behavior of this sort takes on major proportions. Its consistency during the adolescent period makes substantial difference whether or not the child can actually remain in school. Note, incidentally, the kind of role model that these fathers were able to be, in contrast with what Schulz described earlier in terms of the lower-class father even when he was present.

Yet material aid by the father was not the whole story in many of these cases. Forty-five percent (N = 178) of the total sample report that their mothers worked outside the home during their adolescent years. Over the decades of the 20's, 30's, and 40's, when compared to women in general with children 12–18, this is a high figure. But as Ginzberg and Heistand note, "the proportion of Negro women who work has always tended to be higher than among white women." At least one reason for this may perhaps be found in the comments of several respondents regarding their mothers' material help: "She washed and ironed for white folks and helped out so I could go to school." "She worked to get money for my clothes." "She helped pay expenses." "She supplied spending money." The need for black women to work when the father is absent is obvious. But even when he is present and employed, his limited income (relative to whites at the same occupational level) may simply not stretch far enough to keep teenagers in school. Thus, the mother's added income is often a necessity if this valued goal is to be attained.

Goode notes that sometimes the less advantaged husband may resent such an intrusion into his traditional male "bread-winner" or provider role. He may feel that his wife's working undercuts his already limited prestige and power, since this definition of her employment underscores his inability to meet fully the family needs. Yet there is no indication that, as adolescents, these respondents perceived any such strain between their parents. . . . [T]his absence of strain may be owing to the different definitions of wife employment in black compared with white society. In black society, her employment is perhaps more likely to be defined as a "right" rather than an "option" as it often is in white society. So defined by blacks themselves, it consequently introduces less tension into husband-wife relations than is true for whites. In any case, these respondents perceived their mothers' working as a "necessary" means to attain valued ends, and as such is "acceptable." Hence, when respondents report their mothers helped them materially in receiving education, her role was not merely peripheral. It was very likely an essential element in attainment of that goal.

With regard to intangible and tangible forms of educational help, respondents continue to indicate certain differences in the ways their fathers and mothers behaved toward them. Wives report the greater similarity in how their parents helped them in that both fathers and mothers were more apt to have helped them in material or tangible fashion than by interpersonal pressure (see Table 3). On the other hand, although two thirds of husbands also report that their fathers helped them *tangibly*, a majority of them indicate that their mothers were active in the *other* direction, i.e., encouraging them to "keep at it," to stay in school. And these latter differences are markedly significant.

Given the conclusions of many earlier studies regarding the emotional and economic deprivations experienced by black lower-class males, this pattern may have great import. Although as youths these males generally perceived no significant differences between their mothers and fathers as to the *sheer fact* of being helped by them, meaningful differences do emerge as to the specific *nature* of this help. At the economic level, the deprivation of these young males was being alleviated by a father (or other male) active in the occupational system, while the mother played a

crucial role in encouraging the youth to remain in school. Together these efforts were complementary—the *economic* means supplied chiefly by the father, and the *social-psychological* motivation supplied chiefly by the mother. It is obviously not the case that the father provided no encouragement, nor that the mother did not often work. But in terms of role emphasis, these males perceived these particular kinds of differences in their parents. . . .

In response to the question regarding whether the parent "helped," "hindered," or did "neither," some 16.5 percent (N = 66) of our respondents indicated the father did "neither," and 14.3 percent (N = 57) said the same about the mother. We did not probe these particular kinds of replies, but it may be assumed that those respondents could not perceive or identify their parents as having been particularly helpful in gaining an education. By the same token, they did not perceive parents as having actually stood in the way of this goal. The parents had been neutral, and neutrality in this realm is actually a *positive* gain when compared to those situations where the parent was reported to have *hindered* the child in getting to school.

Although the numbers are small in the remaining category (fathers who hindered, 6.5 percent, N = 26; mothers, 4.5 percent, N = 18), the kind of hindrance reported when we probed was instructive. In almost all cases the complaint was of a combined twofold nature. (1) The parent had *made* the child quit school either to care for younger siblings at home or else to work outside the home to help support the family. (2) There were attitudes of indifference, apathy, and even antipathy on the part of the parent toward school. As one male put it regarding his father: "He hindered us because he wanted us to quit school and go to work; he did not allow us to participate in school activities." And one female said this about her mother being a hindrance: "Because I had to do all the housework, she didn't care if I went to school or not."

As suggested earlier, the effort to keep the child in school required, among black families particularly some years ago, determined and sustained effort. The great majority of these respondents' parents made those efforts at both economic (often with sacrifice) and interpersonal levels. In so doing, they operated as a source of *positive* functionality for their children. At the same time, a small number of these parents behaved in a "dysfunctional" manner as far as their children's education was concerned. By making them leave school and go to work, or by even putting pressure on the child to do so, they obviously had a negative impact on this kind of goal attainment.

Achievement Values

In exploring the positive rewards or benefits provided for these respondents as children by their parents, it is necessary to look at [one other kind] of functionality: . . . values and behavior pertinent to achievement and success. . . . The actual extensiveness and intensiveness within American society of what has been variously described as the "Protestant work and success ethic," is a matter of debate. Some social observers argue that the ethos of achievement and success is held only weakly, if at all, by those segments of society (many blacks, for instance) that have been excluded from the opportunity structure. Others contend that these values are distributed rather uniformly throughout the class structure, but that expectations concerning their attainment vary directly with degree of opportunity. . . .

In spite of the general tendency in Table 4 of the respondents to see both parents conveying these kinds of values, only husbands report a meaningful difference between parents. Husbands saw their mothers clearly more active toward them in this regard than their fathers were. This pattern complements the one observed in connection with parental emphasis on education. There we saw that mothers stressed the "double

value" of education for blacks more than fathers did. Aside from the possibility of greater involvement of black mothers than fathers with their children, the explanation for this may lie also with the frustration of the certain proportion of black adult males. Although the majority may hold to the American Dream, a minority (of respondents' fathers) may have been so discriminated against and so deprived that they no longer had much faith in it. As a result they did not (unconsciously perhaps) bother seeking to communicate it to their sons.

However, the overriding consideration to keep in mind as we examine Tables 4, 5, and 6, is that the great majority of respondents' mothers *and* fathers were highly beneficial in providing the kinds of resources and rewards that would enable their children to achieve and succeed and thereby raise the likelihood of their marital stability. . . .

Achievement Aid

These respondents defined their parents, not only as verbally urging success, but also as *behaving* in such a way toward their children so as to increase the probability of its attainment. From Table 5, we may conclude that the majority of respondents did indeed perceive their parents to behave toward them in this positive fashion—their parents did *help* them to try to get ahead. As with education, however, mothers once again seem to play more of a role in this process for both sexes than do fathers. When we probed to find exactly *how* the respondents' parents helped them get ahead, the responses fell into two different, but, as we shall see, not totally unrelated categories.

The majority of respondents indicated their

Table 4.   Perceived Parental Stress on Getting Ahead

Did Parent Stress Getting Ahead?	Male Respondents		Female Respondents	
	Fathers	Mothers	Fathers	Mothers
Yes	77.3	87.8	82.0	88.3
No	22.6	12.2	18.0	11.7
T	100%	100%	100%	100%
N	(168)	(188)	(179)	(196)
	$X^2 = 6.41$			
	$p < .05$; 1 df		n.s.	

Table 5.   Perceived Parental Help in Getting Ahead

Did Parent Help in Getting Ahead?	Male Respondents		Female Respondents	
	Fathers	Mothers	Fathers	Mothers
Helped	68.8	78.4	67.0	79.7
Other	31.1	21.6	33.0	20.2
T	100%	100%	100%	100%
N	(167)	(185)	(173)	(188)

$X^2 = 6.82$

n.s. $p < .01$; 1 df

Table 6.   Type of Parental Help in Getting Ahead

	Male Respondents		Female Respondents	
	Fathers	Mothers	Fathers	Mothers
Material help	25.6	24.0	34.8	21.2
Counsel and example	74.4	76.0	65.2	78.8
T	100%	100%	100%	100%
N	(113)	(142)	(112)	(146)

$X^2 = 6.44$

n.s. $p < .05$; 1 df

parents helped them get ahead by means of "counsel and example" (see Table 6). The nature of this counsel and example can be described as a kind of "anticipatory socialization," i.e., respondents' parents behaved and communicated ideas that were designed, probably consciously, to try to move the respondents *from* a position of relative disadvantage in the total society *to* a position of greater advantage at sometime in the future. These behaviors differ from those under educational interpersonal pressures and goading since they are much broader and generalized. In the former, the objective was simple and straight-forward—"stay in school." In the latter, it is more complex and amorphous, yet equally if not more urgent because it is after all (in the minds of most Americans) the chief goal that education is directed toward. . . .

It seems that respondents' parents were conscious of the relative deprivation of blacks in society, yet, felt, nonetheless that their children could somehow share in the "Dream." To do so however, the children would have to conform to dominant norms in terms of work, consumption patterns, and general life-style. Their parents communicated these kinds of norms and sought

themselves to conform (i.e., as role models) inso-far as possible. The other category of "help" perceived by respondents has been labeled (Table 6) "material." All those replying here indicated in one fashion or another that money expended by their parents to send them to school had been the prime factor in their "getting ahead." In about half these cases, however, the school in view was not on the elementary or secondary level as had been true when we looked at tangible educational help. Here it refers to schooling beyond high school, i.e., business or trade school, or college. For example: "She sent me to John Herron Art Institute." "He got me into a trade school." "She had connections with white folks who helped me get into college."

With regard to "getting ahead," parents of these respondents appear to have exhibited a good deal of "functionality" on their behalf. Although this functionality was predominantly in terms of "mobility-type" counsel, it was also in terms of material aid designed to attain education essential to improved social and economic advantage. We learn from Table 6 that while males show virtually no differences in behavior of fathers and mothers, females do. Fathers of females gave substantially *more material* help to them than their mothers did, and more than either parent did for males. Females also received less counsel from fathers than from mothers.

This finding may be due to two related factors: (1) As girls, they may have needed more material help than boys, because it was more difficult to obtain part-time work that would pay enough to help defray school expenses. (2) Black females are less prevented than black males from identifying with the middle-class school system and general middle-class values. They may simply have needed less counsel than males regarding the desirability and necessity of adopting particular means to effectively manipulate the world "out

there." Instead, their fathers concentrated on providing for them.

As was true for education, when the parent is perceived as *neither* a help nor hindrance, this neutral stance would seem to facilitate the success goal more than when (he-she) is defined as a *hindrance.* Respondents who indicated "parental hindrance" made two kinds of observations: (1) Their parents seemed to be indifferent to the notion of getting ahead. They never counseled nor gave "advice" to their children on how this goal might best be attained. (2) Their parents failed to provide adequate material aid to keep them (as children) in school. . . .

The Solo Mother

Marie Peters and Cecile de Ford

The recent growth of single-parent, female-headed families is a well-documented phenomenon of American society as a whole. Its existence among Blacks has been the subject of a number of controversial studies. The authors of this study focus on the viability of the Black mother-headed family and the mother's strategies for coping with this situation. Attention is given to the values and support of the larger Black community.

Introduction

It is usually assumed that the "biological parent team" of mother and father is the appropriate descriptive model for contemporary American families and a departure from that norm has been typically viewed as deviant. In an earlier day, the female who had no husband was referred to as a "poor widow" to be viewed with "sympathy and understanding." More recently, mother-headed families have been generally viewed as "indicative of breakdown and failure" and Black broken mar-

riages have been officially considered to be pathological (Moynihan, 1965).

However, female-headed families in this country are growing at double the rate of husband–wife families and, as will be shown, there is beginning to be some recognition that the mother-and-children unit may be a viable family form.

How Many?

In 1973 there were over 6.6 million families who were headed by a woman. In over half (57.5%) of these families the mother had children under 18 years of age. Twenty-three percent of the families had children under age 6 (U.S. Bureau of Census, *The Social and Economic Status of the Black Population in the U.S., 1973*).

Four million, three hundred and twenty-six thousand (4,326,000) female-headed families with children under 18 years of age cannot be ignored; nor can 9,627,000 children under 18 years of age or 2,153,000 children under 6 years of age who live with their mothers be studied only

Revised and reprinted by permission. Updated and condensed version of paper presented at the 1974 annual meeting of the

National Council on Family Relations, St. Louis, Mo.

from the perspective of some presumed patholog-ical effects resulting from living in a household without a father. Brandwein *et al.* (1974:498-515) in a recent review of studies of divorced mothers and their families noted the "paucity of studies on mothers" and "the assumption throughout the literature that the female single-parent family is deviant and pathological." In fact, as they found, much of the literature on single-parent families focuses not on the mother at all, but on the effect of father absence on the children.

Several years ago, Herzog and Sudia (1968:181) made a similar observation. They wrote,

The fatherless home in the United States . . . deserves study as a family form in itself, rather than a mutilated version of some other form. It would be useful to give clearer recognition to the one-parent family as a family form in its own right . . . one that exists and functions.

The purpose of this study, then, is to exam-ine solo-parent family as a viable family form, not to document pathology, but to learn about family functioning, patterns of living, and techniques for coping with problems. We will look for the strengths and diversity, as well as the stresses and strains. We will consider first the attitudes and values the Black community generally hold con-cerning the family roles of Black women. Then we will report the findings of interviews with solo female parents who through divorce, widowhood or by choice are raising families without hus-bands.

Understanding Black Female-Headed Families

Black women have been raising families successfully in this country for three hundred years, the result of having been snatched from their families in Africa and transported to America where for generations they were forced to propa-gate, but not always allowed to have husbands. (During slavery, the men were sold away from families. More recently, men were legislated out of their families when government-funded welfare programs routinely denied financial assistance to the families of unemployed fathers.)

The Black single female parent is part of a culture which understands that a woman may be either co-head of family as wife/mother, or head-of-family as solo mother. Each or both statuses is possible for female adults, and Black children are socialized accordingly.

Black families, then, unlike most families in the dominant culture, have subscribed to atti-tudes and values which include (1) commitment to employment in the labor force for women as well as men (Scanzoni, 1971; Jackson, 1973, Peters, 1974); (2) egalitarian relationship between hus-band and wife within the marriage (TenHouten, 1970; Mack, 1971; Hyman and Reed, 1969; Yancey, 1972); and (3) recognition that women who marry and bear children can not necessarily expect to raise children to adulthood in an intact family (although, of course, some do) and there-fore there is acceptance within the Black commu-nity of single-parent status, whether by choice or by chance, as will be discussed below.

Divorce and Separation: Logical Adjustment When Marriages Flounder

The divorce rates in this country are rising steadily. We are approaching the ratio of one divorce per two marriages. Although marital breakup has been traditionally viewed as un-desirable and many clergymen and marriage counselors in the traditional mold still counsel toward keeping marriage intact, there is [an] in-creasing acceptance of divorce in our society, especially if there are no children. There is also [an] increasing acceptance of divorce when there are children.

Nye and Hoffman (1963) concluded from their research that an unhappy "unbroken" family is psychologically more damaging to children than a happy "broken" family. Robert Bell (1971) also pointed out that research has shown that two parents are not necessarily better than one. LeMasters (1970:168) concluded in a review of the literature on the one-parent family that the one-parent family is not "inherently dysfunctional or pathological." He wrote,

It is obvious to any clinician that the two-parent system has its own pathology—the two parents may be in serious conflict as to how their parental roles should be performed; one parent may be competent but have his (or her) efforts undermined by the incompetent partner;

the children may be caught in a "double bind" or crossfire between the two parents; both parents may be competent but simply unable to work together as an effective team in rearing their children; one parent may be more competent than the other but be inhibited in using this competence by the team pattern inherent in the two-parent system.

LeMasters suggests that there are problems inherent in the two-parent family system that will be absent in a one-parent family. For these and many other reasons, then, divorce, with or without remarriage, may then be viewed positively as a logical and sometimes necessary way to resolve family difficulties in a complex culture. If divorce has greater beneficial consequences to children as well as to parents than does continuing an unhappy family, then it may be functional to socialize both male and female children into a self-sufficiency which allows disruptions and changes in marital status to occur without demoralization or dependency, as is done in Black families.

Some time ago, J. Bernard suggested the startling idea that perhaps an intact home is not the norm for American families, as researchers had so long assumed. Many families exist (during some part of their life cycle) as a one-parent

family. According to Bernard (1966:41), "Recently it [has] become clear that for a considerable proportion of the population, Negro or white, the female-headed family is a standard phenomenon—culturally acceptable, if not prescribed or preferred."

Many families will exist during some part of their life cycle as a one-parent family. They may be both one-parent and two-parent during the growing up years of the children.

An examination of the Census data confirms this. In 1974, over half the Black families with incomes under the poverty line were female-headed and more than one third (35%) of all Black families were female-headed (U.S. Bureau of Census, 1975). As Figure 1 shows, the number of Black female-headed families has been increasing rather rapidly over the past twenty years—the percentage, in fact, has doubled. . . .

Family Stability: A Matter of Definition

If the single parent family has historically been an adaptive life style within the Black subculture, one wonders why it has been widely viewed so negatively. Part of the problem is due, as J. Jackson (1973) has correctly observed, to the way social scientists measure family stability. Family stability is determined not from rating the quality of parent–child or family relationships, but from demographic data such as (1) proportion of female-headed households, coupled with data concerning (2) illegitimacy rates, (3) percentage of minor children residing with only one parent, and/or (4) separation and divorce rates. This is misleading. It is solving a social "problem" via teleology.

Sixty-five percent of single mothers require no welfare support. However, a working mother who is fully supporting her own child (and perhaps her own mother as well) but chose not to marry her children's father would be a statistic of instability because the family is female-headed, her child is illegitimate, and the child is residing with only one parent. Or, if she had married and divorced and is now working and self-sufficient (one third of divorced fathers make no payments and 80% are paying nothing by ten years later), she would be a statistic of instability because the family is female-headed, the child is residing with only one parent, and she is divorced. She be-

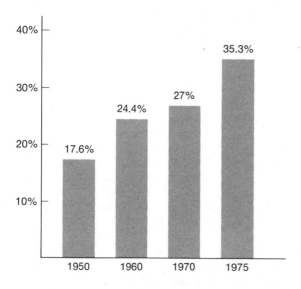

Figure 1.   Percentage of Black Families Headed by a Woman (Source: U.S. Bureau of the Census, 1973; 1975)

comes a statistic and placed into negative categories because of definitions used, although in fact the mother may be supporting and maintaining a "stable" home. As J. Jackson (1973) pointed out, the presence or absence of a male head is insufficient criterion for family stability.

In spite of the teleology involved, however, female-headed families continue to be viewed as unstable. There are several reasons for this. First, female-headed families are associated in the public mind with poverty (Jackson, 1973). Because women face discrimination in employment and in income when they are heads of families, they are often poorer.

As LeMasters (1970) points out, the one-parent family is more likely to be poor, Black, and over-represented on the public welfare rolls. This, perhaps, is to be expected in a society which has, through the years, discriminated against women and Blacks in the job world. Because solo-parent families are more likely than two-parent families to be poor, LeMasters (1970:168) suggests, does not demonstrate inadequacy. He maintains that poverty in single parent families "merely proves that our economic, political, and social welfare systems are not properly organized to provide adequate standard of living for the one-parent family."

However, in spite of discrimination against women and Blacks in the labor market, almost two thirds of single mothers are not on welfare (Helco et al., 1973). However, it is commonly assumed that female-headed families are dependent and on public assistance.

A second reason for instability to continue to be associated with the female-headed family, especially the Black female-headed family, is the associations which the term *matriarchy* brings to mind. Matriarchy connotes deviance in a society that values traditional patriarchy or male dominance in the family. Female-headed families are almost by definition assumed to be pathological. So, in the "deviant" matriarchal family, sons are presumed to be inadequately socialized; they are expected to fall into juvenile delinquency. Daughters are presumed to perpetuate the cycle of intergenerational desertion of wives.

But this, too, is a myth. In Duncan and Duncan's (1969) national sample no relationship was found between the current marital status of the mother and the marital stability of her family of origin. Kriesberg's (1970) research reported a similar finding. Those low-income mothers who grew up in intact families were as likely to be separated or divorced as those who grew up in one-parent families. Most of the solo mothers came from complete families. Duncan and Duncan also found that sons (Black or white) who grew up in female-headed families were no more likely to be separated or divorced than sons from intact homes.

Finally, there is the factor of visibility (Jackson, 1973). Most poor female-headed families live in metropolitan areas (62%) and are therefore more visible and more involved with society's institutions (courts, welfare agencies, school social workers). Most poor male-headed families, on the other hand, live in rural (non-metropolitan) areas (U.S. Census, 1969).

One-Parent Families Do Survive

At any one time most Black families are managing pretty well: they are intact; they are self-supporting. At the same time there are other Black families that are also managing to survive pretty well: most are self-supporting;[1] but many are not intact. Not only do we need to know more about the functionings of Black families, but we need to know about the Black single-parent family, a variant form of the Black family. We need to understand its durability, in spite of its association with poverty and neglect. We need to study its survival and coping practices, its emotional maintenance, the social control and patterns of enculturation of children.

It has been suggested here that Black females are socialized to expect to be employed throughout a lifetime. If they marry they typically maintain an egalitarian relationship with their husbands. They are able to adjust competently to separation and/or divorce. Most seem to be able to consider solo parenthood without guilt or a lifetime of welfare dependency.

In the section that follows, a study of Black solo mothers who are raising children in stable one-parent families will be reported. In this study

[1]According to the Bureau of Census, 1971, 75% of Black and other races are self-supporting. Only 25% of all persons of Negro and other races received public assistance or welfare income.

Black female-headed families are viewed as a viable form of the Black family.

The Study

Eleven solo Black mothers who are heads of families participated in this study. The mothers lived in a medium-size New England city. They represented a socio-economic status from working class to middle class, as determined by their income, education, occupation, and life-style—ranging from welfare recipient to professional worker. The women spanned a generation: from 25 to 56. All shared, however, the double disadvantaged status in our society of being not only husbandless but also Black.

The sample was obtained in two ways: the middle-class mothers were secured by contacting eligibles within the researchers' personal acquaintances. The working-class mothers were those whose children attended Get Set for School,[2] a half-day pre-school program sponsored by the city Board of Education.

The mothers were interviewed in their own homes by one of the two interviewers, both of whom were Black. The interviews were informal, but at the same time they were structured. (An interview schedule was followed.) The interviews were also lengthy, taking from two to four hours, with the interviewers taking notes.

Sometimes family members (usually children) were present or on the periphery during most of the interview. In one case the respondent's mother was present during the entire interview (which stimulated general family discussion).

A special effort was made at the beginning of the interview to explain that the purpose of the study is to discover how women who are heads of families manage their families and their lives. We attempted to demonstrate our interest in them as individuals and, in turn, elicit their interest in our study. We also explained that we were interested in the positives as well as the negatives of single parenthood status, that we wanted to know about the good things, the advantages and the pleasures of single parenthood (if there were some) and the disadvantages, problems, and/or annoyances of single parenthood (if there were some).

All the women seemed to enjoy the interviews. In fact, for some it seemed to be therapeutic. They welcomed the chance to pause and view their lives from a different perspective.

The question occurs as to whether or not an individual's own statement about his/her attitudes or his/her values can be accepted as veridical. However, as Robin Williams (1951:378) observed:

No student of human conduct can accept uncritically, as final evidence, people's testimony as to their own values. Yet, actions may deceive as well as words, and there seems no reason for always giving one precedence over the other.

As Williams points out, direct observations of these mothers' interacting with their children may also be somewhat unreliable in terms of revealing the parents' true feelings.

Findings

As this is an exploratory study attempting to assess parental conceptions of their own situation, the findings will be reported in summary form.

Two types of women emerged from this sample:

1. An older, middle-class woman, working at a professional job and making an adequate salary to support herself and three or four children, and

2. A younger, working-class woman managing with the financial support of public assistance and through her own resourcefulness (and support of family and friends) a family of three or four children.

Two types of housing patterns emerged:

1. Own or rented house in a good Black or integrated neighborhood (women who have been single for over five years), and

2. Good-sized rented apartment in a transitional neighborhood (women who have been single for less than five years).

[2] This is a pseudonym.

Reaction to Divorced Status

The typical reaction of the families of the women in this study to divorce was to give emotional support (especially in the situation where the mother's parents had originally exerted pressure for the couple to marry because the girl was pregnant). Other families were noncommital, expecting the mother to make her own decisions in this matter without family interference.

Typically the children accepted the marital breakup, if they were old enough to understand, because it was the resolution of an unhappy, difficult, and tense situation.

The community typically was unconcerned or disinterested in the marital status of the mother. Her relationships with her friends continued pretty much as before. The loneliness some divorcees have reported because their social world is made up of couples did not appear to be a problem for these mothers.

Social life for the younger mother was hampered only if she had baby-sitting problems. Moreover, the children (especially as they became older) typically not only did not object to their mother's going out, they encouraged it. However, the older women encountered the problem described by J. Jackson—no men.

The modal woman in this study indicated that she did not feel overwhelmed when she assumed single parenthood and solo head-of-household status. The women typically recalled that, as adults, they always felt autonomous, rather than dependent. They felt competent as workers and believed that they had adequate resources within themselves to manage alone. Some mothers took on a second regular job. Others used public assistance for a while, until, as one mother expressed it, "I could get on my feet." Others picked up extra employment here and there.

Although most of the mothers felt independent and capable of raising a family, the unpleasant reality of having your children welfare recipients or the awesome responsibility of being dependent solely upon oneself was sometimes more than some mothers wanted. Half of them indicated that at times they felt resentful or drained, and would have preferred having someone share their responsibilities with them—especially when there were important decisions to be made. However, some of the women had families they could talk to at critical times.

Single parenthood is not an easy job. Some of the mothers indicated that they were adapting somewhat reluctantly to the stresses of solo head-of-family. Others were more satisfied with their solo status.

Problems Solo Mothers Faced and How They Solved Them

Money, however, was always a problem in these families. Nevertheless, the children were adequately clothed, housed, fed, and generally were well-cared for. As employed workers in the labor force, the mothers of young children had to make substitute child-care arrangements. These mothers, typically did not use day care facilities, nor did they find community agencies in general very helpful (except for the financial support some of the mothers received through AFDC).

Concerning child-care arrangements, most mothers stayed home while they had a young baby at home or had two or more pre-schoolers at home. If and when they returned to work, they used their own mothers, other relatives, or neighbors to baby-sit until their youngest children were of school age. By then, older children were expected to supervise their younger siblings. Emergencies were taken care of as they came along, knowing family and friends were available as a last resort.

In general, any problems the mothers had with the school authorities developed out of racial discrimination or prejudice, rather than over the issue of the absent father. The school personnel seemed comfortable dealing with mothers if a child presented a problem.

For the occasional mother whose child came in contact with the police, however, it was a different situation. Mothers would note a change in a policeman's treatment of a boy once he learned there was no father present in the home. Not only did the police become more harsh, but the mothers felt a "what-else-can-you-expect-from-a-boy-with-no-father" attitude. All the mothers, except one, reported that there were important male figures in the lives of these children, although they lived in a fatherless household. Sometimes it was the child's own father. Other important male figures reported were the child's uncle, cousin, or other male relatives, or the mother's boyfriend. Most of the children saw other people (grandparents or aunts or uncles or mother's boyfriend) in addition to their mother as an authority figure.

In the area of discipline, some mothers responded that one or more children were problems; more of the mothers reported no special discipline problems (beyond the youngest child being spoiled). Typically, the mothers reported that misbehavior is punished immediately by spanking. As children get older mothers do more talking, punishing by denial or restriction. Some mothers also emphasized the importance of verbalization about an offense and made a special point of explaining to a child why punishment was necessary.

Credit was a problem only during the time a mother was receiving public assistance and, according to these mothers, the credit problems they had were due to the fact of their welfare status, not their sex. These employed women had no trouble getting credit, nor did their single parenthood status affect their ability to obtain decent housing. Here, the problem was the number of children in the family. Landlords did not welcome "large" families with more than two children.

Single-Parent Families Versus Two-Parent Families

When the mothers were asked about the advantages in their present situation compared to life with a husband (if they had been previously married) or the life of their married friends, all but one felt that there are actually a number of advantages. Most mothers said that their children were more independent and responsible. Most were happy that now the children no longer see their parents in constant conflict. (One mother observed that now the children don't see the father drunk.)

Some also expressed the strong feeling that their family now was closer, worked as a cooperative unit, and that family life was more flexible and more reflective of what the mother or the children want to do.

Each mother was asked about her plans for the future. Would she work? Would she marry? Mothers still home with pre-schoolers expected to take a job as soon as possible. Mothers in the labor force expected to continue to work. When asked if she expected to marry most mothers said

no, although four answered with a tentative maybe. Only one responded yes.

Response to Questionnaire

A questionnaire was administered to the mothers at the end of the interview which contained seven questions about the children's response to father absence. Answers were varied and individualistic. About half the children were described as missing their father; half as not. Some children were too young to know their father. Similarly, when asked if they thought father absence affected their children's development, here again answers were diverse—some "not at all," some "very much," some "somewhat."

These mothers considered their sons to be somewhat more aggressive than their peers. They also felt that their sons were higher academic achievers and more mature than their age mates. Most daughters were also viewed as more aggressive than their peers.

It is of interest to note that when asked how the behavior problems they had with their children compared to the behavior problems they noticed in children in intact families, these mothers either felt that they had more behavior problems or that they had fewer behavior problems than other families. Only one mother indicated that she thought her children were just about like other children in this respect.

Summary

In this study Black female-headed families were viewed as a viable form of the Black family, a flexible pattern of functioning that has developed within the Black community where there is (1) expectation of egalitarian relationships between competent females and males and (2) where there is a preponderance of females over males of marriageable age.

The life styles of eleven solo Black parents who are heads of families were examined. These parents were seen, in general, to be coping competently with their individual circumstances.

This study of solo Black mothers was exploratory. There needs to be continued research on the divorced, widowed, or single Black working-class and middle-class mother in order to find how they cope with the exigencies of single parenthood and head-of-family status. This would provide information which may be of use to other American female-headed families, which are becoming increasingly prevalent in American society. It could, perhaps, inform how communities can more effectively be supportive of single parents who are neither pathological nor dependent.

References

Bell, Robert, *Marriage and Family Interaction,* Third Edition. Homewood, Illinois: Dorsey Press, 1971.

Bernard, Jessie, *Marriage and Family Among Negroes.* Englewood Cliffs, N.J.: Prentice-Hall, 1966.

Billingsley, Andrew, "Black Family Structure: Myths and Realities," in Studies in Public Welfare, Paper No. 12 (II), *The Family, Poverty, and Welfare Programs: Household Patterns and Government Policies.* Washington, D.C.; December 3, 1973.

Brandwein, Ruth; Brown, Carol; Fox, Elizabeth, "Women and Children Last: The Social Situation of Divorced Mothers and Their Families," *Journal of Marriage and the Family,* August, 1974, 498–515.

Duncan, Beverly, and Duncan, Otis Dudley, "Family Stability and Occupational Success," *Social Problems* (1969) 16: 273–285.

Frazier, E. Franklin, *Black Bourgeoisie.* New York: Collier Books, 1962.

Green, Lorenzo, *The Negro in Colonial New England.* New York: Atheneum, 1968.

Helco, Hugh; Rainwater, Lee; Reiss, Martin; Weiss, Robert, "Single-Parent Families: Issues and Policies," O.C.D. Working Paper. Washington, D.C.; October, 1973.

Herzog, Elizabeth, and Sudia, Celia, "Fatherless Homes: A Review of Research," *Children,* Sept.–Oct., 1968, 177–182.

Hyman, Herbert, and Reed, John, "Black Matriarchy Reconsidered: Evidence from Secondary Analysis of Sample Surveys," *Public Opinion Quarterly* 33 (Fall 1969): 346–354.

Jackson, Jacquelyne J., "Black Women in a Racist Society," in Willie, Charles: Kramer, Bernard; and Brown, Bertram (eds.), *Racism and Mental Health.* Pittsburgh, Pa.: University of Pittsburgh Press, 1973.

Jackson, Jacquelyne J., "But Where Are the Men?" *The Black Scholar* 3:4 (December 1971): 30–41.

Kriesberg, Louis, *Mothers in Poverty.* Chicago: Aldine, 1970.

LeMasters, E. E., "Parents Without Partners," in *Parents in Modern America.* Homewood, Ill.: Dorsey, 1970, pp. 157–174.

Lewis, Hylan, and Herzog, Elizabeth, "The Family: Resources or Change," in Bracy, John; Meier, August; Rudwick, Elliott (eds.), *Black Matriarchy; Myth or Reality.* Belmont, Ca.: Wadsworth Publ. Co., 1970, pp. 160–184.

Mack, Delores W., "Where the Black Matriarchy Theorists Went Wrong," *Psychology Today,* 1971, 4:24ff.

McMillan, Sylvia, "Aspirations of Low-Income Mothers," *Journal of Marriage and the Family* 29:2 (May 1967): 282–287.

Middleton, Russell, and Putney, Snell, "Dominance in Decisions in the Family, Race and Class Differences," in Willie, Charles, *The Family Life of Black People.* Columbus, Ohio: Charles E. Merrill, 1970, pp. 16–22.

Moynihan, Daniel P., *The Negro Family: The Case for National Action,* Washington, D.C., U.S. Department of Labor, Office of Policy, Planning and Research, 1965.

Nye, Ivan, quoted in Schulz, David, *The Changing Family.* Englewood Cliffs, N.J.: Prentice-Hall, 1972, p. 415.

Nye, Ivan F., and Hoffman, Lois, *Employed Mothers in America.* Chicago: Rand McNally, 1963.

Parker, S., and Kleiner, R., "Characteristics of Negro Mothers in Single-Headed Households," *Journal of Marriage and the Family* 28 (1966): 507–513.

Peters, Donna-Marie, "A Study of the Sex Role Attitudes and Future Plans of Black and White Middlebury College Students." Unpublished Senior Thesis, Middlebury College, 1975.

Peters, Marie F., "The Black Family—Perpetuating the Myths: An Analysis of Family Sociology Textbook Treatment of Black Families," *The Family Coordinator,* October, 1974, 349–357.

Ross, Heather, and MacIntosh, Anita, "The Emergence of Households Headed by Women," The Urban Institute, Washington, D. C., Working Paper: 776–01, June 1, 1973.

Scanzoni, John, *The Black Family in Modern Society.* Boston: Allyn and Bacon, 1971.

Staples, Robert, "The Myth of the Black Matriarchy," *The Black Scholar,* February 1970.

TenHouten, Warren, "The Black Family: Myth and Reality," *American Journal of Sociology,* Nov. 1970, 145–172.

U.S. Bureau of the Census, *Census of the Population's General Social and Economic Characteristics,* PC (1)-C1, Washington, D.C.: U.S. Government Printing Office. 1970.

U.S. Bureau of the Census, *Household and Family Characteristics,* March, 1973, Series P-20, No. 258, Dec. 1973, Washington, D. C.: U.S. Government Printing Office.

U.S. Bureau of the Census, *Negro Population, 1970,* Washington D.C.: U.S. Government Printing Office.

U.S. Bureau of the Census, *The Social and Economic Status of the Black Population in the U. S., 1971,* Washington, D.C.: U.S. Government Printing Office.

U.S. Bureau of the Census, *The Social and Economic Status of the Black Population in the U.S., 1973,* Washington, D.C.: U.S. Government Printing Office.

U.S. Bureau of the Census, *The Social and Economic Status of the Black Population in the U.S., 1975,* Washington, D.C.: U.S. Government Printing Office.

U.S. Bureau of the Census, "24 Million Americans: Poverty in the U.S. 1969," Washington, D.C.: U.S. Government Printing Office.

Williams, Robin, *American Society.* New York: Alfred Knopf, 1951.

Willie, Charles V., "The Black Family and Social Class," *American Journal of Orthopsychiatry* 44(1) (January 1974): 50–60.

Yancey, William L., "Going Down Home: Family Structure and the Urban Trap." *Social Science Quarterly* 52(4) (1972): 893–906.

11
The Extended Family

The Black Extended Family Revisited
Robert B. Hill and Lawrence Shackleford

The authors stress the importance of the extended Black family, in its variety of forms, as a stabilizer of otherwise fragmented urban families. They see the extended family pattern as a source of strength to the Black family.

One mechanism that has provided resilience to black families for generations has been the extended family—or the informal absorption of families and individuals by relatives. During slavery, for example, thousands of children of slave parents were often reared by elderly relatives, who served as a major source of cohesion and fortitude for many black families.[1]

The extended family pattern has also served historically as a means of pooling meager resources, particularly during periods of severe economic decline. For example, during the Great Depression of the 1930s, thousands of blacks moved in with other relatives until they were able to obtain a more secure economic position that permitted them to go out on their own. A disproportionate number of the families that were doubling up with relatives were female-headed families with dependent children. As a result of recent recessions, the proportion of black children living with only their mothers in subfamilies of households headed by relatives rose sharply from 22 to 33 percent between 1969 and 1974.[2]

The number of children being taken in by relatives is still exceedingly high. Today, about 3 million children under 18 years old are living in households headed by relatives and 45 percent (or 1.3 million) of these children are black.[3]

Despite the disproportionate number of blacks who have been reared by relatives throughout the history of blacks in America, it is surprising that there have been few systematic empirical studies of the distinctive characteristics of extended family arrangements, particularly those related to the informal adoption of children, and how they have adapted over time. Almost all the literature on black adoption relates to formal adoption, despite the fact that less than 10 percent of black children born out of wedlock each year are placed with formal adoption agencies.[4]

Extended Family Patterns

Although there have been few systematic studies that have focused solely or primarily on the black extended family, most of the classic studies on black families have underscored the significance of extended family patterns for the survival, stability and advancement of black families.[5]

[1]E. Franklin Frazier, *The Negro Family in the U.S.* (Chicago: University of Chicago Press, 1939); Charles S. Johnson, *Shadow of the Plantation* (Chicago: University of Chicago Press, 1934).

[2]Hortense Powdermaker, *After Freedom* (New York: Russell and Russell, 1939); National Urban League Research Department, *Black Families in the 1974–75 Depression* (Washington, D.C.: National Urban League, 1975); Committee

for Children in New York, *Children's Allowances and the Economic Welfare of Children.*

[3]U.S. Bureau of Census, "Marital Status and Living Arrangements: March 1974," *Current Population Reports: Population Characteristics* (Washington, D.C.: U.S. Government Printing Office, 1975).

[4]Robert B. Hill, *The Strengths of Black Families* (Washington, D.C., National Urban League Research Department, 1971).

[5]Frazier, *Negro Family;* Johnson, *Shadow of the Plantation;* Powdermaker, *After Freedom.*

From *The Urban League Review* 1 (Fall 1975): 18–24. Reprinted by permission.

Charles S. Johnson noted that the black extended family has the "semblance of a normal and natural family and functions as one, except that the members of the group are drawn into it by various circumstances rather than being a product of the original group."[6] Hortense Powdermaker also observes, ". . . stepchildren, illegitimate, adopted children, mingle with the children of the house. No matter how small or crowded the home is, there is always room for a stray child, an elderly grandmother, an indigent aunt."[7]

Some scholars, such as Herskovits, trace the origins of the black extended family to Africa: "The African immediate family, consisting of a father, his wives and their children, is but a part of a larger unit. This immediate family is generally recognized by Africanists as belonging to a local relationship group termed the "extended family."[8] Several anthropological studies of black families in the rural South have identified family patterns that closely correspond to those in patrilineal tribes of West Africa.[9]

Subfamilies

As Billingsley has noted, black extended families take many forms depending on the composition of the individuals and families that are absorbed by primary family units: subfamilies, families with secondary members and augmented families. Subfamilies, which consist of at least two or more related individuals, can be differentiated into the following extended family categories: (a) the "incipient" extended family, which consists of a husband–wife subfamily with no children of their own living in the household of relatives; (b) the "simple nuclear" extended family, which consists of a husband–wife subfamily with one or more own children living in the household of a relative's family; and (c) the "attenuated" extended family, which consists of a parent and child subfamily living in the household of a relative.[10]

[6]Johnson, *Shadow of the Plantation.*

[7]Powdermaker, *After Freedom.*

[8]Melville Herskovits, *The Myth of The Negro Past* (Boston: Beacon Press, 1958).

[9]M.J. Herskovits et al., "The Physical Form of Mississippi Negroes," *American Journal of Physical Anthropology* 16 (1931): 193–201.

[10]Andrew Billingsley, *Black Families in White America* (Englewood Cliffs, N.J.: Prentice-Hall, 1968).

Over the past decade, the proportion of black subfamilies has remained constant. Although the number of black subfamilies rose from 248,000 to 332,000 between 1965 and 1974, the proportion of black subfamilies of all black families remained unchanged at 6 percent. Basic characteristics of black subfamilies are essentially the same.

Black subfamilies are overwhelmingly attenuated families, i.e., they consist of one female parent and her children living in a relative's household. About three-fourths of black subfamilies are headed by women with at least one own child under 18. More than three-fourths of the women heading black subfamilies are living with one or both of their parents (or parents-in-law). About 10 percent of these women, however, are living in their sister's household.

The overwhelming majority of the women heads of black subfamilies were formerly married, but are currently separated, widowed or divorced. There is an average of 1.8 children per black subfamily headed by a female and about half (45 percent) of these subfamilies consist of only one own child.

Secondary Members

In addition to taking in already existing families, black extended families take in four classes of relatives, or secondary members, who come alone: (a) minor relatives, including grandchildren, nieces, nephews, cousins and young siblings under 18; (b) peers of the primary parents, including siblings, cousins and other adult relatives; (c) elders of the primary parents, particularly aunts and uncles; and (d) parents of the primary family.

Dependent children are much more likely than elderly persons to be taken into black families as secondary members. Half the black families headed by women 65 and over have children under 18 not their own living with them. On the other hand, only 4 percent of black husband–wife families and families headed by women have persons 65 years and over living with them.

Most dependent secondary members of black extended families are grandchildren. Two-thirds of the 800,000 black children under 18 living in families without either parent are being reared by their grandparents or great-grandparents. The rest are mostly being reared by their aunts and uncles.

Augmented Families

Although the overwhelming majority of children informally adopted are relatives of the heads of household, a disproportionate number are not related at all. About 100,000 (or 6 percent) of black children living in families without either parent are not relatives of the heads of household. Nonrelated children make up 8 percent of all other than own children in husband–wife families, but only 3 percent of those in female-headed black families.

Since Census Bureau data fail to distinguish foster care nonrelated children from informally placed nonrelated children, it is not possible to precisely determine the extent to which nonrelated children were placed through formal or informal channels. HEW data on child care arrangements indicate that a total of 243,000 children were in foster care families in 1969. Since this would account for only a little over half of all unrelated children in families without their parents, it is safe to say that almost half the nonrelated children in families are not in foster care.[11]

Dependent children under 18 do not constitute the majority of unrelated persons taken into augmented extended families. Most of these unrelated individuals are adults living as roomers, boarders, lodgers or other relatively long-term guests. Over half a million (522,000) black persons live with families with whom they were not related by marriage, ancestry or adoption. Eighty percent of these nonrelated individuals are 18 years of age and over, and 56 percent of these nonrelated adults in black households are men.

In sum, black extended families are primary family units that take in: (a) two or more related persons (i.e., subfamilies); (b) one related person (i.e., secondary members); and (c) nonrelatives (i.e., augmented families). But all of these extended family types, according to Census Bureau definition, presuppose the existence of a primary family unit consisting of at least two or more related persons that takes in other relatives or nonrelatives.

These typologies fail to incorporate an extended family pattern that is one of the most prevalent of all—the informal adoption of individuals or subfamilies by relatives who live alone (e.g., widowed grandmothers or aunts). Forty-five percent of the 1.3 million black children living with kin are in households headed by female relatives, while 9 percent are living with male relatives who are without spouses. Thus over half of the black children living with kin are being reared by relatives who are without mates. There are numerous accounts in the literature of black children being taken into one-parent households of relatives.[12]

Grandparents

Most of the "adopting" relatives in black extended families are either grandparents (many of whom are not necessarily elderly) or aunts and uncles. Two-thirds of black children under 18 living with relatives today are grandchildren of the heads of household, while one-fifth are primarily nieces and nephews. The historic fortitude and self-reliance of the black elderly is vividly reflected in the fact that they are more likely to take others into their households than to be taken into the households of younger relatives.[13]

Frazier, in particular, took special note of the role of the grandmother in his classic work on black families in the United States in a chapter entitled "Granny: the Guardian of the Generations."[14] Some contemporary social scientists have distorted Frazier's original meaning of the matriarch and have incorrectly applied it to young black women with dependent children who "castrate" their husbands. But the "matriarch," according to Frazier, referred to a warm, compassionate, but resolute grandmother who inspired her children and grandchildren to achieve, and not to a domineering wife who continually competed with and ridiculed her husband.[15]

[11]U.S. Department of Health, Education and Welfare, Social and Rehabilitation Service, National Center for Social Statistics, *Child Welfare Statistics: 1969,* NCSS Report CW-1(69).

[12]Frazier, *Negro Family;* Johnson, *Shadow of the Plantation.*

[13]U.S. Bureau of the Census, *1970 Census of Population: Persons by Family Characteristics,* Subject Report PC(2)–4, table 1; U.S. Bureau of the Census, "Marital Status"; Hill, *Strengths of Black Families.*

[14]Frazier, *Negro Family,* esp. chap. 8

[15]Frazier, *Negro Family,* chap. 7; Daniel P. Moynihan, *The Negro Family: The Call for National Action* (Washington, D.C.: U.S. Department of Labor, 1965).

Many outstanding blacks have been reared by their grandparents or see them as having been major influences in their lives. Frederick Douglass, for example, wrote in his autobiography with deep affection of the impact that his grandmother had in the early stages of his life in slave quarters.[16]

As Frazier observed, "Granny" served many roles in black families, as nurse, midwife, mother, educator, minister, disciplinarian, and transmitter of the family heritage. Some grandparents were held in such high esteem by plantation owners that they often received favorable treatment, such as in Frederick Douglass's grandmother's case, receiving a special plot of land on which to live out their lives and to pass on to kin.[17]

Who Are Adopted?

What are the social characteristics of black children who are informally adopted? Are they more likely to be preschoolers or school-age? Were most of them born out of wedlock? Sixty percent of black children living with neither parent in the household of relatives today are 6 years and over, while 41 percent of them are 10 years and over. One-fourth of these informally adopted children are less than 3 years old.

As a result of declining birth rates among blacks, the proportion of informally adopted children under 3 has been steadily decreasing. In 1969, 35 percent of black children living with kin without their parents were under 3 years old, but by 1974 only 26 percent were under 3.

This does not mean that children who are informally adopted are more likely to be adopted when they are school-age than preschool. On the contrary, most studies of informal adoption patterns indicate that children are most likely to be taken in at very early ages. According to the Tuskegee Institute study of informal adoption patterns in rural counties of Alabama, 70 percent of the families reported that informally adopted children were less than 2 years old when taken in and 31 percent said that the children had been born there.[18]

Although a majority of informally adopted children were born in wedlock, a sizable minority was not. About two-fifths of black children living with relatives in 1970 had parents who were never married. This was particularly the case for children who lived in one-parent subfamilies in the household of relatives.

In a study of the six-year experience of unwed mothers, the Community Council of Greater New York found that 10 percent of 136 black mothers interviewed had placed their out-of-wedlock, first-born child in an informal adoption arrangement. Most of these children were being reared by one or both grandparents.[19] Similarly, in her study of kinship patterns of blacks in the Midwest, Carol Stack reported several instances of out-of-wedlock children being reared by grandparents, great-grandparents and great-aunts and -uncles.[20]

Reasons for Adoption

Why are these children taken in? There are a variety of circumstances that lead to informal adoption of children. One frequent factor is death or illness of the child's parents. Frazier gives an account of such a case by an elderly female who was a former slave:

I was 77 years old this last gone February. The two little orphan children. I raised them here with me. These little orphan children mother dead and father dead too. I'm they great aunt. Me being the oldest one and me being they mother's auntie and the oldest head, that's how I come by them. So me and my husband raised them children from little bit a things.[21]

Another factor often leading to informal adoption is separation or divorce of parents. Johnson describes such a situation with regard to the adoption of an older black child:

When Hesekie was 13 years old his mother and father separated. He does not know

[16]Frederick Douglass, *My Bondage and My Freedom* (New York and Auburn, 1855).

[17]Ibid.

[18]Lewis W. Jones, *Informal Adoption in Black Families in Lowndes and Wilcox Counties, Alabama* (Alabama: Tuskegee Institute, 1975).

[19]Community Council of Greater New York, *The Six-Year Experience of Unwed Mothers* (New York: Community Council of Greater New York, Research Department, 1970).

[20]Carol B. Stack, *All Our Kin: Strategies for Survival in a Black Community* (New York: Harper & Row, 1974).

[21]Frazier, *Negro Family.*

why. They never told him and he did not inquire. One day his mother just went off and did not come back. Later his father left for Illinois. Now both have remarried and Hesekie is living with his grandparents who, as tenants go in this section, are fairly well off.[22]

Many children who are born out of wedlock to young women are often informally adopted by older relatives because of the "immaturity" of an unwed mother.[23] A frequent reason for temporary or short-term informal adoption is to permit the parents to go to work or to attain a more secure economic footing:

Violet married and moved to another state with her husband and her two youngest children. She left her two older daughters with their grandmother. After about seven months Violet took the train back home in order to get her daughters and take them to a new home out of state.[24]

Proximity of a relative to a school is also a factor leading to informal adoptions. Shimkin described a case where a mother moved and wanted her son to continue at the same school he was attending. Since a great-aunt lived closer to the school, the child lived with her.[25] Johnson cites a case where a child was taken in by nonrelated family friends because they lived closer to the school that the parents wanted the child to attend.[26] Today, many children not only give the addresses of relatives who live within the boundaries of the schools that they would like to attend, but they often live with those relatives as well.

Many children are often taken in by relatives simply because they wanted a child to raise. In the Tuskegee study of informal adoptions, several respondents indicated: "I wanted a child and found out I could have this one; I needed company in the house; I needed someone to help me around the house, so I gave him a home."[27]

According to the Tuskegee study, most of the reasons for informally adopting children were for "parental convenience" (i.e., work, illness, schooling, etc.) and feelings of family responsibility. In most instances, the taking in of the child just happened without any formal agreement as to the length of time that the child would live with relatives. Although many informal adoptions began as temporary arrangements, they became long-term. Even among those with a more definite understanding of how long they expected to keep the child, 90 percent said "until grown" or "as long as I live."

Most informally adopted children are aware that their parent surrogates are not their biological parents, and in many cases have periodic contact with their natural parents, especially their mothers. In the Tuskegee study about two-thirds of the parent surrogates reported that the mothers of the children were in contact with the children monthly or more frequently.[28]

Although it is frequently believed that informal adoptions are primarily a result of irresponsible males abandoning mother and child, case studies of informal adoption reveal numerous instances where the father or relatives on the father's side assumed a major responsibility for rearing the child. Stack describes a situation in which a two-year-old child was adopted by the mother's ex-boyfriend and family because of their deep affection for the child. She also cites several instances of informal adoption by paternal aunts and grandparents.[29] The Community Council of Greater New York also cites several cases where out-of-wedlock children were reared by relatives of the father.[30]

Economic Status

What is the economic status of these families? How do they cope financially? Although three-fifths of black families with related children are above the poverty level, they tend to have a disproportionate number below the poverty level. Over half of the female-headed black families with informally adopted children are poor, compared

[22]Johnson, *Shadow of the Plantation.*

[23]Stack, *All Our Kin.*

[24]Ibid.

[25]Demitri B. Shimkin, Gloria J. Louie and Dennis A. Frate, "The Black Extended Family: A Basic Rural Institution and a Mechanism of Urban Adaptation" (University of Illinois at Urbana-Champaign, 1975). *The Extended Family in Black Societies* (The Hague: Mouton, *forthcoming*).

[26]Johnson, *Shadow of the Plantation.*

[27]Jones, *Informal Adoption.*

[28]Ibid.

[29]Stack, *All Our Kin.*

[30]Community Council of Greater New York, *Six-Year Experience.*

to only three out of ten husband–wife black families with other than own children.

The disproportionate poverty status of informally adopted children is most vividly reflected in the relatively low median income of their families. Although all black children under 18 lived in families with a median income of $4,256 in 1969, children under 18 living with kin were in families that had a median income of $2,592—only two-thirds of all black families. Moreover, although husband–wife black families with informally adopted children had a median income of $3,796, female-headed families with related children had a median income of only $1,632. Since almost half of these children live in female-headed families, it is clear that thousands of these children are being reared in economically disadvantaged settings.

Most financial support of informally adopted children comes from the adopting relatives. In the Tuskegee Institute study, the biological parents (primarily the mother) provided some support for the child in 43 percent of the families. The most frequent types of help provided by parents were money and clothes. Of those that reported specific amounts of money, over half gave less than $50 per month. Parent surrogates assumed the primary financial responsibility for rearing these children.

Despite their limited economic resources, most families with informally adopted children do not receive public assistance. Only one-third of the informally adoptive black families in the rural Alabama study indicated that they were receiving AFDC public assistance or food stamps. Over half of those who did receive AFDC received less than $80 a month. On the other hand, 62 percent of them said that the children were receiving free school lunches.

It is also surprising that while over half of the parent surrogates were 60 years and over, three-fourths of them did not receive any Social Security assistance. These findings of the Tuskegee study strongly suggest that many impoverished black families in rural areas are not receiving basic public benefits.

Despite the absence of some formal mechanisms of economic support, two-thirds of the respondents felt that they had enough clothes. The overwhelming majority reported that the children were in good health. Many of these parent surrogates are sufficiently resourceful to provide their informally adopted children with the basic necessities even at a low-income standard of living. There are mutual networks of assistance in many of these rural areas from churches, neighbors and other relatives.

The extended family has been a source of strength and resilience in the black community for generations. Much more research should be conducted on its patterns of adaptation in urban Southern and Northern areas as well as in rural settings. In-depth studies are also vitally needed to identify insensitive policies and programs at the national and local levels that have a negative impact on the functioning of kinship networks.

According to current federal income tax guidelines, child care deductions can only be made by working mothers whose children are cared for by nonrelatives or placed in a child care facility. But 40 percent of black women who work depend on responsible adult relatives to care for their children. Thus expenses made to those relatives (often an elderly grandmother or aunt of the child being cared for) are not tax deductible, despite the vital services being performed. What is needed are federal policies that reinforce and build on the strengths of extended families, not weaken them.

Black Grandparents in the South

Jacquelyne Jackson

The transition from a rural to an urban setting has had a strong impact on the traditional position of the elderly in the family. The author examines the living situations of older Blacks in urban areas and the impact on family relations, particularly between grandparents and grandchildren.

This [chapter] focuses specifically upon . . . grandparental roles in a contemporary urban Southern setting and certain implications of those roles relative to sociocultural conditions of aged blacks. . . .

Perhaps the most impressive finding about the black grandparental roles is their striking similarity to comparable findings about non-black grandparent–grandchild patterns. If so, the emphasis often placed upon the "peculiarity" of "Black Grannies" may be unwarranted or unduly exaggerated. These findings tend to be in general agreement, e.g., with those of Shanas, *et al.,*[1] Shanas and Streib,[2] Townsend,[3] and Young and Willmott[4] in such areas as (1) emphasis upon the usually vivid presence of grandmothers especially in kinship networks, with an important task being involvement in grandchild rearing; (2) more involvement of grandmothers than grandfathers in activities with grandchildren; (3) closer bonds among grandmothers, daughters, and grandchildren than among grandfathers, sons, and grandchildren; and (4) the presence of extended or three-generational families within urban areas.

Frazier's classic description of "Granny: The Guardian of the Generations" depicted an energetic, courageous, and devoted "Granny" whose prestige and importance were great during and after the Civil War. "Granny" continued watching "over the destiny of the Negro families as they have moved in ever increasing numbers to the cities during the present century," wrote Frazier, with the gradual increase in patriarchal authority in family relations and in female economic subordination, decreasing "Granny's" prestige and importance. Frazier made no explicit mention of grandfathers.[5] A majority of the grandmother subjects in this study still resemble Frazier's "Granny." Grandmothers are still generally more important than grandfathers, but the importance of the latter within black urban kinship systems is increasing, necessitating a reassessment of black families and a burial of extant myths.

Kahana and Kahana[6] noted that most grandparental studies focused only upon them rather than upon both them and their grandchildren. This section is traditional in focusing upon grandparental perceptions only, but atraditional in focusing upon black grandmothers and grandfathers. Specifically, analytical data about *interactional* and *subjective* roles between (a) grandparents residing in predominantly low-income, urban renewal areas and the grandchildren they see most often, and (b) selected comparisons of the grandparental subgroupings are presented.

The subgroupings of the sampled 68 black grandparents, whose ages, marital statuses, and subgroupings are detailed in Table 1, . . . were as

[1]Ethel Shanas, *et al., Old People in Three Industrial Societies* (Chicago, 1968).

[2]Ethel Shanas and Gordon Streib, *Social Structure and the Family: Generational Relations* (Englewood Cliffs, 1965).

[3]Peter Townsend, *The Family Life of Old People* (London, 1957).

[4]Michael Young and Peter Willmott, *Family and Kinship in East London* (London, 1957).

[5]E. Franklin Frazier, *The Negro Family in the United States* (Chicago, 1939), pp. 114–24.

[6]Boas Kahana and Eva Kahana, "Grandparenthood from the Perspective of the Developing Grandchild (Mimeographed, Washington University, St. Louis, Missouri, 1969).

Abridged from "Aged Blacks: A Potpourri in the Direction of the Reduction of Inequities," *Phylon* 32 (1971): 260–271. Reprinted by permission. Footnotes have been renumbered. This paper was partially supported by the Center for the Study of Aging and Human Development, Duke University Medical Center, Durham, North Carolina, Grant 5 T01 HD00164 of the National Institute of Child Health and Human Development, and by the U.S. Public Health Service Grant #MH 1655402.

Table 1.   Black Grandparental Subgroupings, by Age and Sample Size

Subgrouping	N	Age (in Years)	
		X	s
By sex:			
All grandmothers	54	59.4	13.6
Older, with spouse	6	66.7	7.5
Older, without spouse	33	66.5	7.6
Younger, with spouse	3	45.0	0.0
Younger, without spouse	12	40.0	6.7
Employed	9	49.4	12.4
Nonemployed	45	61.4	13.0
All grandfathers:[1]	14	69.3	7.8
Older, with spouse	5	73.0	4.5
Older, without spouse	9	67.2	8.3
Employed	4	62.5	9.6
Nonemployed	10	72.0	4.8
By living arrangements:			
All grandparents			
Living alone	26	64.2	11.6
Not living alone	38	59.7	13.7
By age:			
Younger grandparents	15	41.0	6.4
Older grandparents	53	67.2	7.7

[1]. No grandfathers were under 50 years of age.

follows: (1) by sex, grandmothers and grandfathers; (2) by age, younger (i.e., under 50 years) and older (i.e., 50+ years); and (3) by household composition, grandparents living alone and grandparents not living alone. No significant age differences characterized the latter subgroup. Using t, both the grandfathers and older grandparents were significantly older than their subgroup counterparts (p <.001). The subjects reported approximately (a few were imprecise) 391 grandchildren, about 5.8 grandchildren per subject. Almost 12 percent had no granddaughters; almost 15 percent no grandsons. Table 2 contains selected background information of these grandchildren.

A modified form of the Adams Kinship Schedule[7] was used to collect data in personal interview settings within the subject's homes. Following Adams (1968),[8] *interactional characteristics* referred to the "frequency of interaction and kinds of or occasions for interaction with" grandchildren, including telephone contacts and letter writing, or the non-face-to-face means of

keeping in touch. His eight "contact types" (i.e., home visiting, social activities, voluntary organizations, working together at the same occupation and location, rituals, communication, aid received from a specific relative, and aid given to a specific relative) were modified to seven: home visiting, social activities (including reading), church, luxury gifts, communication, aid received from grandchildren, and aid given to grandchildren. The subjective characteristics were affectional closeness, value consensus, identification, and obligation.

Determination of affectional closeness is in answer to the question: "How close would you say you feel to your . . . ?" Responses of "quite close" and "extremely close" are combined and designated as strong feelings of closeness. Value consensus is ascertained by the following question: "Do you and your . . . agree in your ideas and opinions about the things you consider really important in life?" Answers of "yes, completely," and "yes, to a great extent" appear to indicate substantial value consensus, as distinct from value divergence. Idealization of or identification with the relative is determined by responses to this

[7]Bert N. Adams, *Kinship in an Urban Setting* (Chicago, 1968), pp. 10–14.

[8]Ibid, pp. 13–15.

Table 2.   Background Data on Grandchildren, by Grandparental Subgroups

			Grandparental Subgroups			
				Grandparents Living		Grandparents
		Grandmothers	Grandfathers	Alone	Not Alone	
Characteristic[1]		(N = 54)[1]	(N = 14)[1]	(N = 26)[1]	(N = 38)[1]	Younger	Older
	Percent Base:	100.0	100.0	100.0	100.0	100.0	100.0

Characteristic[1]	Grandmothers	Grandfathers	Alone	Not Alone	Younger	Older
Number of grandsons						
None	14.3%	37.5%	13.0%	16.7%	23.1%	19.2%
One	16.3	0.0	8.7	13.3	30.8	7.7
Two	18.4	18.8	30.4	13.3	15.4	19.2
Three +	51.0	43.8	47.8	56.7	30.8	53.8
Number of granddaughters						
None	21.6	31.3	30.4	16.1	15.4	25.9
One	21.6	18.3	30.4	16.1	15.4	22.2
Two	9.8	6.3	8.7	12.9	15.4	7.4
Three +	47.1	43.8	30.4	54.8	53.8	44.4
Grandchildren's residence						
In same household as grandparent	30.4	0.0	0.0	34.5	46.2	16.7
In same city as grandparent	37.0	40.0	52.4	27.6	38.5	37.5
In northeastern states	19.6	40.0	38.1	20.7	15.4	14.6
Elsewhere	13.0	20.0	9.5	17.2	0.0	31.3
Ages of grandchildren						
Under 6 years	25.6	14.3	14.3	29.6	58.3	13.3
6–11 years	27.9	42.9	33.3	25.9	25.0	33.3
12–17 years	20.9	28.6	19.0	29.6	8.3	26.7
18 + years	25.6	14.3	33.3	14.8	8.3	26.7
Grandchildren's marital status						
Married	41.2	33.3	62.5	22.2	0.0	44.4

[1] Percentages were computed upon available responses, so N is sometimes less than given.

question: "Would you like to be the kind of person your . . . is?" Close identification is based upon the responses "yes, completely," and "in most ways." Feelings of obligation are ascertained . . . by asking . . . how important certain reasons for keeping in touch are in relation to a particular relative.[9]

Findings

In general, when the data were controlled for grandparents with at least one son with offspring and at least one daughter with offspring, who either both resided elsewhere (i.e., not within the same locality as the subject) or within the same location as did the subject, the grandchild seen most often was the daughter's, as opposed

to the son's, child, a finding consistent with Young and Willmott's observation that grandchildren usually interact more frequently with their mother's mother than with their father's mother.[10] Rare exceptions in this sample were among subjects whose son's offspring resided with them.

Interactional characteristics Possible responses for frequency of interaction between a grandparent and grandchild ranged from daily through "never during the past year." Percentage data in Table 3 depict frequency of interaction in five "contact types" for subjects interacting at least "once during the year" with the grandchild.

Grandparental subgroupings emerged Younger grandparents, grandparents living alone, and grandmothers were more likely to report home visiting than were their respective counterparts,

[9]Ibid., pp. 14–15.

[10]Young and Willmott, *op. cit.*

Table 3.   Responses to Interactional Items, by Grandparental Subgroups

Characteristic[1]	Grandparental Subgroups					
			Grandparents Living		Grandparents	
	Grandmothers	Grandfathers	Alone	Not Alone	Younger	Older
Percent Base:[1]	100.0	100.0	100.0	100.0	100.0	100.0
	Percentage	Percentage	Percentage	Percentage	Percentage	Percentage
Frequency of contact with grandchild						
Daily, same household	29.3	0.0	0.0	32.0	50.0	15.9
Monthly, or more often	43.9	53.8	60.0	36.0	40.0	47.7
At least once during past year	24.4	30.8	35.0	24.0	10.0	29.5
Not at all during past year	2.4	15.4	5.0	8.0	0.0	6.8
Home visiting						
Yes	31.3	27.3	42.1	11.8	60.0	26.3
No	68.8	72.7	57.9	88.2	40.0	73.7
Social activities						
Going to the park	22.0	15.4	10.0	20.0	36.4	16.3
Attending the movies	4.8	0.0	0.0	3.8	0.0	4.5
Grocery shopping	35.7	15.4	15.0	42.3	54.5	25.0
Shopping, other than grocery	45.2	15.4	30.0	46.2	63.6	31.8
Local or other trips/vacation	28.6	7.7	15.0	26.9	27.3	22.7
Reading	14.3	7.7	5.0	11.5	18.2	11.4
Church	45.2	23.1	35.0	42.3	72.7	31.8
Luxury gifts						
Yes	32.4	33.3	15.8	47.4	75.0	23.7
No	67.6	66.7	84.2	52.6	25.0	76.3
Communication						
S writes out of town grandchild	28.6	25.0	27.3	33.3	0.0	28.6
S written by out of town grandchild	53.3	33.3	58.3	30.0	0.0	47.8
No telephone communication on special occasions or emergencies	42.3	21.4	31.3	38.9	0.0	42.4
Telephone communications monthly or more frequently	15.4	28.6	25.0	16.7	14.3	21.2

1.   All percentages based upon interaction having occurred at least once during the past year.

true even when the data were controlled to exclude grandparents and grandchildren in the same household. Those living alone and those not living alone differed since the latter reported greater frequency of contact (p < .05).

The modal form of interaction in social activities was "shopping, exclusive of grocery shopping," with joint movie attendance especially rare. Reading was largely restricted to interaction with preschool grandchildren. Table 4 contains a rank ordering, in decreasing frequency, of these activities.

The data on church revealed that older grandparents, grandparents living alone, and grandfathers reported less frequent church activities (most often joint attendance at regular Sunday morning worship services) with grandchildren than their counterparts. Younger grandparents were far more likely to be accompanied by or to accompany a grandchild to church than were older grandparents (p < .05), attributable partially to greater shared residence among the former. Joint church activity decreased as the ages of the grandparents and grandchildren increased.

Excepting younger grandparents, subjects reported infrequent or no luxury gift-giving to their grandchildren, a finding explicable perhaps by

Table 4.   Rank Order of the Frequency of Social Activities between Grandparents and Grandchildren

| Social Activity | Rank Order[1] | | | | | |
| | | | Grandparents Living | | Grandparents | |
	Grandmothers	Grandfathers	Alone	Not Alone	Younger	Older
Shopping other than grocery shopping	1	2	1	1	1	1
Grocery shopping	2	2	2.5	2	2	2
Going to the park and/or walking	4	2	4	4	3	4
Movies	6	6	6	6	6	6
Trips/vacations	3	4.5	2.5	3	4	3
Reading	5	4.5	5	5	5	5

[1]. 1 = greatest frequency of occurrence; 6 = least occurring activity.

such variables as (a) a greater likelihood of younger grandparents being employed; and (b) greater likelihood of grandparents providing younger grandchildren with luxury gifts and older ones with practical gifts.

Non-face-to-face communication patterns investigated were (a) telephoning grandparent–grandchild contacts; and (b) written communication among grandparent–grandchild pairs not residing within the same city. No more than one third of any grandparent subgroup reported writing to a grandchild within the preceding year. More had received correspondence from their grandchildren. Grandfathers, as well as grandparents living with others, were less likely to have had telephonic communication with grandchildren than grandmothers and grandparents living alone, but the differences were insignificant. Older grandparents were significantly more likely than younger grandparents to have such interac-

Table 5. Mutual Aid Patterns between Grandchildren and Grandparents

| Characteristic[1] | Grandparental Subgroups | | | | | |
| | | | Grandparents Living | | Grandparents | |
	Grandmothers	Grandfathers	Alone	Not Alone	Younger	Older
Aid received from grandchildren						
Financial assistance	12.5%	0.0%	10.5%	11.8%	20.7%	7.9%
Feeling of usefulness	35.3	36.4	26.3	42.1	57.1	31.6
House or yard chores	27.8	18.2	5.3	35.0	55.6	18.4
Visiting	31.3	27.3	42.1	11.8	60.0	26.3
Transportation	6.5	0.0	5.3	6.3	0.0	5.3
Gifts	18.8	9.1	15.8	23.5	20.0	15.8
Advice	12.5	9.1	10.5	11.8	40.0	7.9
Writing letters, reading, etc.	3.1	0.0	0.0	5.9	0.0	2.6
"Not much help at all"	25.0	50.0	27.8	36.8	20.0	33.3
Aid given to grandchildren						
Indirect financial assistance	15.2	0.0	0.0	17.6	50.0	5.3
Direct financial assistance	30.6	18.2	15.8	40.0	75.0	17.9
Necessary gifts	33.3	9.1	10.5	89.5	66.7	18.4
Housing	36.8	27.3	15.0	42.9	66.7	27.5
Assistance with illness	11.8	9.1	0.0	16.7	16.7	10.3
Child care	43.6	9.1	5.3	56.5	81.8	23.1
Took grandchild on a special trip	6.3	10.0	0.0	5.9	20.0	5.4
Advice	52.8	33.3	42.1	42.9	75.0	42.5
Keeping after school until parent arrives	8.8	9.1	0.0	15.8	16.7	7.7
Other	14.3	0.0	16.7	10.5	0.0	14.8

[1]. All percentages based upon interaction having occurred at least once during the past year.

tion ($p < .05$), an artifact, perhaps of more grandchildren living with younger grandparents. While few subjects reported relatively frequent (i.e., monthly or more often) telephone contact, most reported at least one call (usually an emergency or a "special occasion" day) during the preceding year.

Table 5 contains responses concerning grandparent–grandchild aid patterns. A minority perceived their grandchildren as "not much help at all," a statement verbalized most often by grandfathers (50 percent), and less often by those who were not living alone (37 percent), older (33 percent), living alone (28 percent), grandmothers (25 percent), and younger (20 percent). But inquiry about specific aid revealed that a majority had received assistance from grandchildren during the preceding year. Their modal responses were not instrumentally, but affectively, oriented: disregarding the "not much help at all response," the modal response for younger grandparents and grandparents living alone was "visits"; for the remaining subgroups, "a feeling of usefulness." Those living alone received more visits from grandchildren than those not living alone ($p < .05$), while the latter received greater assistance with household and/or yard chores ($p < .05$) than the former. Younger grandparents also received more chore assistance than older grandparents ($p < .05$), and more advice from grandchildren as well ($p < .05$).

The modal form of grandparent–grandchild assistance was childcare; almost 44 percent of the grandmothers, 56 percent of grandparents living with others, and 82 percent of the younger grandmothers, had grandchildren residing with them. A smaller proportion of the subjects "babysat" with school-age children awaiting parental arrival at residences other than those of the grandparents. Younger, as contrasted with older, grandparents provided more direct financial assistance to a grandchild and/or his parents ($p < .01$); they were also more involved in patterns of luxury and practical gift-giving to grandchildren ($p < .01$), childcare ($p < .001$), and housing ($p < .05$). Grandmothers were more involved as childcare agents than grandfathers ($p < .05$), as were grandparents not living alone compared with those living alone ($p < .001$). Among the latter subgrouping, those not living alone tended to engage in greater luxury and necessary gift-giving as well ($p < .05$).

While impressionistic judgments suggested that the older grandparents had been far more active in grandchild rearing earlier, it was quite clear that grandparental involvement in childrearing is directly related to the grandchild's familial structure: grandparental involvement, as Frazier[11] indicated, increased with the absence of the grandchild's parent.

Subjective characteristics   Qualitative data on affectional closeness, value consensus, identification with grandchild, satisfaction of present contact with grandchild, and the primary initiant of grandparent–grandchild contacts were available for analysis. A majority of the subjects verbalized strong affectional closeness between themselves and their grandchildren. Only grandmothers considered themselves significantly closer to grandchildren than did grandfathers ($p < .05$), but grandparents living with others and younger grandparents tended to report greater closeness than their counterparts, suggesting probably the importance of considering more closely sex, age, and residential proximity in future grandparent–grandchild studies.

Value divergence was more typical than substantial value consensus, but the greatest congruence of value consensus between grandparents and grandchildren was found among grandfathers, which warrants an investigation of black generational transmission of political socialization and advocates for the aged. Older grandmothers displayed the most distance in grandchild–grandparent value consensus. In addition, less than five percent of the subjects closely identified with grandchildren. Almost 20 percent rejected any close identification (i.e., they would not like to resemble the grandchild in any way).

Obligatory kinship ties were apparent. Most subjects, and particularly younger grandparents and grandparents living with others, felt that the obligation of "keeping in touch" was very important. Excepting younger grandparents, all of the subjects placed greater emphasis upon the obligatory than upon the enjoyable aspect of "keeping in touch." Older grandparents and those living alone desired greater grandchild contact. Compared with their respective counterparts, they were significantly less likely to be satisfied with the

[11]Frazier, *op. cit.*

present contact levels (p < .05). A very small percentage of older grandparents (2 percent) and grandparents not living alone (4 percent), however, felt that less frequent grandchild contact would be desirable.

Most subjects felt that grandchildren should live near (but not necessarily with) their grandparents, and provided rationalizations categorized as unilateral and bilateral need-fits (e.g., "Grandchildren can be a lot of help to their grandparents," "Grandparents can help parents with children," and "Because we need each other") and kinship obligations (e.g., "Everyone should be close around their family"). Equally important, almost 15 percent of the subjects feeling that grandchildren should not live near grandparents cited the necessity for physical generational separation so as to reduce problems for the grandparent (e.g., "Do not want to be worried with them") and/or the grandchild (e.g., "It tends to spoil the child") and emphasized parental responsibility. Almost 25 percent of the subjects stressed the primary responsibility of parents for rearing their own children in neolocal residences. Most were specifically concerned about possible detrimental effects of extremely close grandparent–grandchild residential proximity upon development of independence in a maturing grandchild; and, to a less extent, childrearing roles constraining grandparents with "other fish to fry," as they develop or maintain new roles as they aged.

In general grandchildren were not considered the initiants of the grandparent–grandchild contacts. Grandfathers also did not perceive themselves in this role, but considered a parent of the grandchild as the primary contact agent for them. Younger grandparents and grandparents living alone rarely regarded themselves as prime contact agents either, inasmuch as those younger grandparents with spouses felt that the spouses actually initiated the contact most often, and both groups felt that their own children also served as links between themselves and grandchildren. Younger grandparents and grandfathers, however, were more likely to telephone a grandchild than the reverse, whereas grandchildren were more likely to contact grandmothers, older grandparents, and grandparents not living alone. The only significant subgroup distinction occurred in that grandfathers were more frequent initiators of telephone calls with grandchildren than were grandmothers (p < .05).

Discussion

Apparently these grandparents prefer children's children to live near, but not with, them, and younger to older grandchildren.[12] Very old grandparents appeared more concerned about proximity in the event grandchildren were needed for instrumental and affective support. Relationships among affectional closeness, value consensus, and identification were unclear, but they are probably related to such preferences as those mentioned above. Any postulation of a "generation gap" per se between black grandparents and their grandchildren is too vague. That is, far greater specificity and empirical data about those gaps which may exist are needed, with particular emphasis upon separation of spurious or superficial gaps (e.g., clothing or hairstyles) and substantial ones (e.g., divergence upon dominant values). Age is not a sufficient explication of generation gaps in dominant values.

The specific contact types investigated suggested relatively infrequent grandchild–grandparent interaction, due perhaps to an artifact of the study in focusing directly upon those rather than upon other contact types, and/or to such variables as inadequate income, transportation, and awareness of or free and friendly access to available resources. The general findings clearly point up some problem areas, a specific one being public housing.

In this connection, empirical data on relationships between housing and kinship patterns among blacks are clearly warranted. For example, grandparent–grandchild patterns may be affected positively and negatively by public housing policies for the aged. For blacks at least, alternative forms of housing (e.g., age-segregated and age-integrated) within the same locale are desirable. Telephone service should be available. Single blacks dependent upon public housing (and especially when such dependence is fostered through their involuntary relocation as a result of

[12]Cf., Kahana and Kahana, op. cit., and also Jacquelyne J. Jackson, "Kinship Relations Among Older Negro Americans" (Paper read at the Eighth International Congress of Gerontology, Washington, D.C., August, 1969); Jacquelyne J. Jackson, "Urban Negro Kinship Relations" (Paper read at the annual meeting, American Sociological Association, San Francisco, California, September, 1969); Jacquelyne J. Jackson, "Changing Kinship Roles and Patterns Among Older Persons in a Black Community" (Paper read at the annual meeting, American Psychological Association, Washington, D.C., September, 1969); Jacquelyne J. Jackson, "Kinship Relations Among Urban Blacks," Journal of Social and Behavioral Sciences, 16 (Winter, 1970), 1–13.

urban renewal and highway express programs) should not be forced (as is true in some localities) to accept one-room or efficiency apartments, but should be permitted to occupy at least one-bedroom apartments, if they prefer such an arrangement. Physical space permitting brief or extended visits from relatives should be available.

These findings about black grandparents and their grandchildren help to debunk myths of the deaths of the "Black Grannies"; the "powerful matriarchies" ruled by "Black Grannies"; and the disintegrating or ephemeral kinship ties between aged and aging blacks. They indicate that many black grandparents serve as a point of anchorage for grandchildren and provide kinds of supports for them unavailable from their own parents. In that sense, the grandparents take on the responsibilities of and function as individual departments of welfare. Many black families, in all probability, adhere to familial norms characteristic of the larger culture. Finally, these data are most significant in [pointing toward the] need for [more research about grandparental roles among Americans]. . . .

12

Personality Development

The Black Family:
Socialization and Sex Roles

Diane K. Lewis

In this selection the author examines what she sees as a neglected area in the study of the Black family: its function as a primary agent of socialization. She urges that more attention be given the African quality of Black cultural life and to its impact on the early stages of socialization.

This exploratory paper attempts a synthesis and reinterpretation of existing literature on socialization, in particular sex role socialization, in black families. Three main areas of consideration are: (a) the extent to which socialization patterns express a distinctive Afro-American culture; (b) whether Afro-American and Euro-American child rearing practices offer significantly contrasting bases for differentiating behavior; and (c) the role of cultural processes and macro-structural constraints in defining adult sex roles in black life. Hopefully this examination will raise some questions and point the way to much-needed further research.

Before proceeding, it is important to note methodological difficulties introduced by biases in the existing literature. A serious shortcoming is that the scanty data on black child rearing comes generally from working-class families while corresponding data on Euro-American families is primarily from middle-class families. Obviously, a valid comparative analysis should control for class in order to distinguish ethnic as opposed to class patterns in child rearing.

A further difficulty is the paucity of empirical evidence on sex role socialization in black families. Most recent anthropological and sociological studies focus more on conceptions of the ideal male and female or on generalized parent–child relations than on the actual process of socialization to adult roles. A notable exception to this is the excellent 1970 study by Virginia Heyer Young to which I shall return later.

Another problem is that the literature on the black family is mainly concerned with the matrifocal family, where there is either no husband/father present, or the man who occupies the position husband/father is largely ineffective in his role. This bias exists in spite of considerable research by anthropologists and sociologists which shows that "the most common family structure among blacks is one in which there are both a husband and a wife present in the home,"[1] and which stresses the egalitarian nature of black family relationships.[2]

The studies surveyed estimate the husbandless family as anywhere from 2 percent to 25 percent of the total numbers studied. However, it is this percentage, the atypical, rather than the typical, that forms the basis of generalization about the black family. In this paper, I am particularly interested in two-parent rather than single-parent families, in an effort to redirect attention to

[1]Warren D. TenHouten, "The Black Family: Myth and Reality," *Psychiatry*, XXXIII (May, 1970), p. 153. See also Ulf Hannerz, *Soulside* (New York, 1971), p. 71 and Daniel Moynihan, *The Negro Family: The Case for National Action* (Washington, 1965), pp. 6–8.

[2]Charles Johnson, *Shadow of the Plantation* (Chicago, 1969); Charles Valentine, "Blackston: Progress Report on a Community Study in Urban Afro-America" (unpublished manuscript, February, 1970); Hylan Lewis, *Blackways of Kent* (New Haven, 1964); Peter Kunkel and Sara Sue Kennard, *Spout Spring: A Black Community* (New York, 1971); Virginia Heyer Young, "Family and Childhood in a Southern Negro Community," *American Anthropologist*, LXXII (April, 1970), 269–88.

From *Phylon* 36 (Fall 1975): 221–237. © 1975 by Atlanta University. Reprinted by permission. Table numbers have been added.

the family experience of the majority of black people.

A major assumption of this paper is that Afro-Americans share a distinct sub-culture in American society and that "the hard Black core of America is African."[3] Just as there has been scant attention paid the typical black family, there has been little acknowledgment of Afro-American culture. The arguments are too well known to be more than briefly alluded to here. The major theses are either that Afro-Americans have a pathological version of mainstream culture;[4] or share a culture of poverty with other impoverished groups;[5] or are indistinguishable from the mainstream in terms of values, but differ in situational adaptations to wider structural constraints.[6] These approaches have been challenged since 1970 by recent work in anthropology, sociology, socio-linguistics and folklore,[7] and since the sixties by Afro-American commentators on the black condition.[8] It is significant that both essayists and social scientists touch repeatedly on the same themes. While a number of distinctive features of Afro-American culture are beginning to be identified, space permits the analysis of only a few which seem to have a critical bearing on childhood practices.

A high valuation for personal uniqueness is a significant configuration in black culture. Individualism, expectations of idiosyncratic behavior and non-conformance within bounds, are traits which have been well-documented in the recent research of sociologist Hylan Lewis, socio-linguist Tom Kochman, anthropologist Virginia Young and by folklorists.[9] They have also been discussed in

the more impressionistic works of Fanon, Lester, and Bennett.[10]

Hylan Lewis in his study of a Southern town in the late fifties notes that blacks, both males and females, display two contrasting personalities: one is the facade of conformity which is offered to the white world; the other is the highly developed sense of one's self as a distinct personality which is presented to the black world. The individual's sense of uniqueness is expressed in the terms he uses to define himself and by which he is known to others. Lewis writes:

. . . *everyone tends to be a "character." There is adaptation and conformity but with a distinctly individual twist marked by an organization of responses that often borders on the queer, the colorful, the whimsical, or the stubbornly "just different."*[11]

He further asserts that blacks in this town lack a class structure and that the individual is judged not in terms of his education or occupation, but according to his personality and his ability to get along with others.[12] This focus on the uniqueness of people, and on their essential equality is interpreted as a response to the status starved position of blacks in the wider society. Blacks who lack status and power in the wider society highlight personal traits and patterned non-conformity, as a means of obtaining individual recognition and respect.

Tom Kochman, in his socio-linguistic analysis of differences in black and white cultural personalities cites the importance of personal attributes rather than status or office in defining the individual in black life.[13] In white culture, personal interaction, deference and authority are dependent on the social position or office which an individual occupies, while in black culture, these factors are determined by the individual's personal attributes, such as his verbal ability, personality, wit, strength, intelligence, speed, etc. It is noted that the menial and marginal jobs blacks could obtain have offered less prestige, power and influence within their own group than

[3]LeRoi Jones, "The Changing Same (R & B and New Black Music)," in Addison Gayle, Jr., ed., *The Black Aesthetic* (New York, 1972), p. 116.

[4]Gunner Myrdal, *An American Dilemma: The Negro Problem and Modern Democracy* (New York, 1944); E. Franklin Frazier, *The Negro Family in the United States* (Chicago, 1966).

[5]Oscar Lewis, "The Culture of Poverty," *Scientific American*, CCXV (October, 1966), pp. 19–25.

[6]Hylan Lewis, op. cit.; Hannerz, op. cit.

[7]Valentine, op. cit.; Ivan Vansertima, "African Linguistic and Mythological Structures in the New World," in Rhoda L. Goldstein, ed., *Black Life and Culture in the United States* (New York, 1971), pp. 12–35; Thomas Kochman, "Cross-cultural Communication: Contrasting Perspectives, Conflicting Sensibilities," *The Florida FL Reporter*, IX (Spring/Fall, 1971), pp. 3–16, 53–54; Alan Dundes, *Mother Wit from the Laughing Barrel* (Englewood, 1973); Joyce Ladner, ed., *The Death of White Sociology* (New York, 1973).

[8]Ralph Ellison, *Shadow and Act* (New York, 1964); Lerone Bennett, *The Negro Mood* (Chicago, 1964); Julius Lester, *Look Out, Whitey, Black Power's Gon' Get Your Mama* (New York, 1968).

[9]Hylan Lewis, op. cit.; Kochman, op. cit.; Young, op. cit.; Dundes, op. cit.

[10]Frantz Fannon, *Black Skins, White Masks* (New York, 1967); Lester, op. cit.; Bennett, op. cit.

[11]Hylan Lewis, op. cit., p. 322.

[12]Ibid., pp. 221–23.

[13]Kochman, op. cit., pp. 9–11.

they could acquire themselves through development of personal attributes. Thus, Kochman, like Lewis, feels that the high valuation of the person, at least in part, is an adaptation to conditions of marginality and powerlessness.

On the other hand, anthropologist Virginia Young,[14] who did research in a Southern black community, discusses traits very similar to those analyzed by Lewis and Kochman above, but views them as representative of a distinct cultural heritage. Young focuses on parental behavior and child rearing practices, and finds highly individualized patterns of behavior among mothers and others in the family.[15] She notes the lack of routine and the broad range of idiosyncratic behavior in preparation of food, in eating, in feeding and in toilet training.

Lewis, Kochman, and Young all describe individualism, idiosyncratic behavior and focus on personal attributes as distinct characteristics of black adult life. To gauge the cultural significance of these traits we must consider child rearing practices and ask whether there is evidence that children are socialized to display these behaviors. Is there continuity between childhood experience and the manifestation of these traits in adult behavior?

Young's child rearing study provides rich data in this area. She shows that behavior in young infants which is defined as random and reflexive in mainstream culture is interpreted as a manifestation of a specific motive or personality trait in black culture.[16] Thus, infant exploration with hands, feet and mouth are viewed as hitting or biting. They are considered expressions of individual traits and the infant is said to be "mad" or "mean." For example, a "mother will duck the flying two month old fist and say: 'she sure is mad at me.'" The uniqueness of the infant is also emphasized through constantly inquiring about its wants and through viewing its movements as indicative of wanting a person or of wanting to go someplace.[17] Young[18] also describes common forms of interplay between adults and infants and adults and toddlers in which the children are encouraged to be assertive, initiating and defiant within bounds. She writes:

The baby is treated as though willful and assertive beyond his natural inclination and able beyond his natural abilities. He is highly stimulated and admired for his assertiveness, and his acceptance of authority is expected to be defiant.[19]

Defining the infant as having a highly developed character has consequences not only for the baby but for the other youngsters in the home who are socialized to view babies in this way. It seems richly suggestive that children brought up to attribute to infants well defined wills and unique personalities are, at a very early age, developing a conceptualization of the nature of the person as an independent, initiating being, which profoundly affects their own self-image and their expectations of others as they move into adulthood.

I think it is significant that Young views the socialization techniques she describes as leading specifically to a "cultivation of will and volition." Initial reading in some African philosophical systems suggests that the Afro-American conception of the person as willful and initiating may be paralleled by related views of man which have been described for a number of African cultures.

For example, Jahn[20] describes the primacy given the human being in several African philosophical systems. He attempts to show that man as intelligent force is viewed as controlling all energy through the Word, which when uttered gives being and essence to all things, including God.[21] Thus, he contrasts European culture, where God commands man who assumes a passive relationship to the deity, with African culture, where man evokes God and enters into an active relationship with Him.[22] Jahn's works place the human being as a central, creative, imperative force in the African universe. Furthermore, he finds this African mode clearly expressed in a number of New World African forms, particularly music and poetry.[23]

Similarly, contemporary Afro-American artists are now reevaluating past and present Afro-American writing, art and music in the context of a

[14]Young, op. cit., p. 286.
[15]Ibid., p. 277.
[16]Ibid., p. 278.
[17]Ibid., p. 279.
[18]Ibid., pp. 278, 281

[19]Ibid., p. 285.
[20]Janheinz Jahn, *Muntu* (New York, 1961).
[21]Ibid., pp. 121–36.
[22]Ibid., p. 158.
[23]Ibid., pp. 155–213.

serious study of African cultural form. They are beginning to identify a distinct black aesthetic in much of Afro-American writing and art which they conceptualize as strikingly similar, in its initiating and creative style, to African forms.[24]

The folklorists, too, have unearthed evidence from riddles that the "intrusive I" form is of African origin.[25] This form makes an African or Afro-American song or tale a subjective "personal account." It is quite unlike the Euro-American form where the "objective, third-person technique is used."

While these attempts to compare Afro-American and African conceptions of man are still exploratory, they indicate that there are African cosmologies to which one can look as a possible source for the Afro-American view of the person, even in infancy, as willful and initiating.

Young's data also highlight the individualism which is fostered in black child rearing. Obviously Euro-Americans, as well as Afro-Americans, display a high degree of individualism as adults. Yet the forms of expression are quite different in the two cultures. It is important to stress that Afro-American individualism is experienced in a context of great interpersonal involvement. Young repeatedly stresses this aspect of black child rearing when she shows the rich interpersonal involvement of infants, children and adults with one another. She writes:

Strong individuality, however, is paired with strong interpersonal connectedness, not absorption in a group or acceptance of group identity as higher than individual identity, but merely relatedness as distinguished from the isolation that characterizes individualism in the Western tradition.[26]

In describing the inseparability of "opposites," the way in which both individuality and immersion in group experience characterize black child rearing, Young is focusing on another important characteristic of Afro-American culture.

This Afro-American cultural orientation, the bringing together of polarities, stands in direct contrast to the Euro-American concern with dualism. Mainstream culture is understood in the setting up of linguistic, analytic, and moral dichotomies, such as subject/object; mind/body; good/bad; sacred/profane, etc. Afro-American culture, however, is characterized by unity and synthesis. Lerone Bennett notes that the black tradition affirms that good and bad, creative and destructive, wise and foolish, up and down, are inseparable facets of existence.[27] Therefore these polarities are not conceptualized as dichotomies. He finds that the existential unity expressed in "good *is* bad," is in conflict with the Euro-American dichotomy, "either good *or* bad."

Kochman in his discussion of linguistic and cultural codes discusses how the differences between mind/body synthesis and mind/body dichotomization creates linguistic and cultural interference between whites and blacks in this society.[28] Similarly, Jahn contrasts the unity of an African world view where all forces are thought to have both constructive and destructive potentialities with the European world view which perceives the world as a conflict between opposing forces.[29]

Euro-American dualism is most evident in the way sex roles are defined.[30] Jerome Kagan in an article, "Acquisition and Significance of Sex Typing and Sex Role Identity" writes that a sex role "dictates the adoption of different responses for boys and girls."[31] I found the following terms scattered throughout his article used to describe typical masculine and feminine standards of sex behavior. I have juxtaposed them for greater clarity in Table 1. Along many dimensions the traits listed are not merely contrasting but mutually exclusive. They represent a differentiation of polarities.

Many people feel that this dichotomous view of sex roles, while traditional, is not representative of rapidly changing standards. However, Kagan writing in the mid-sixties notes that children continue to internalize the traditional standards and to act in terms of them.[32] Perhaps the contradiction between adults who feel that sex

---

[24]Gayle, op. cit.

[25]Dundes, op. cit., p. 96.

[26]Young, op. cit., p. 285.

[27]Bennett, op. cit., pp. 50–52.

[28]Kochman, op. cit.

[29]Jahn, op. cit., p. 64.

[30]This idea was first suggested to me by Sandra Jardra.

[31]Jerome Kagan, "Acquisition and Significance of Sex Typing and Sex Role Identity," *Review of Child Development Research* I (1964), p. 138.

[32]Ibid., p. 143.

Table 1.

Males	Females
Aggressive	Passive
Independent	Dependent
Dominance	Nurturance
Self-confidence	Feelings of inadequacy
Independent of attitudes and opinions of others, *i.e.*, non-conformity	Conformity
Pragmatic attitude	Facilitative attitude, *i.e.*, focus on harmonious personal relationships
Controls emotions, suppresses fears	Expresses emotions, fears
Motor ability, mechanical skills	Ability to deal with people
Initiator sexually	Receptive sexually

role standards are changing rapidly and children who adhere to traditional standards can be explained by a gap between ideal and actual behavior; that is, between what parents say they believe and what they actually do in childrearing. The largely unconscious level at which differential behavior toward boys and girls operates among parents has been shown by Scandinavian researchers. For example, Brun-Gulbrandsen surveys research which shows that parents with an ideology of sex equality do in fact differentiate sharply between their sons and their daughters in terms of treatment and expectations of behavior.[33]

Kagan argues that the concept male and female and the attributes associated with maleness and femaleness are basic to the language and sex-role identity of Euro-Americans. He writes that by the time a child is four, he has already

. . . *dichotomized the world into male and female people and is concerned with boy–girl differences. By the time he is seven he is intensely committed to molding his behavior in concordance with cultural standards appropriate to his biological sex and he shows uneasiness, anxiety, and even anger when he is in danger of behaving in ways regarded as characteristic of the opposite sex.*[34]

An appropriate question to ask at this point is: What are the socialization processes that occur with Euro-American children which result in such highly differentiated sex role behaviors and expectations?

While child rearing research from Scandinavia and the United States provides material on differential treatment in areas such as emotional warmth, degree of control, length of breast feeding, type of punishment, and different processes of identification with role models,[35] a provocative review of recent research on the subject has been reported by Michael Lewis, a developmental psychologist.[36]

Lewis is acutely aware of the fact that sex largely determines parental response to infants and reviews a number of studies where parents were observed in interaction with infants.[37] He believes that attachment is a significant component in the parent's behavior to the child and notes that the mode of attachment varies according to the sex of the child. He distinguishes between two types of attachment behaviors: proximal and distal. Proximal behaviors are those involving physical contact such as touching, holding, rocking. Distal behaviors are those performed at a distance such as looking at, smiling and vocalizing to.

Lewis finds that for the first two years, children are trained to move from what is considered an infantile type of interaction, the proximal mode, to what is viewed as a more adult type of interaction, the distal mode.[38] However, there is a significant difference in the ages and rates at which this occurs for boys and girls. While girls are encouraged to spend more time near their mothers, are touched significantly more often than boys, and are trained much less severely and much more slowly to move from a proximal to a distal mode of interaction, boys are discouraged from close physical contact and encouraged at an early age to move into a more "adult" type of interaction. Lewis finds that for the first two years, girls receive both more proximal and more distal behavior than boys, while from the age of six months boys receive a marked reduction in proximal behavior.

[33]Sverre Brun-Gulbrandsen, "Sex Roles and the Socialization Process," in Edmund Dahlstrom, ed., *The Changing Roles of Men and Women* (London, 1967), pp. 59–78.

[34]Kagan, op. cit., p. 162.

[35]See especially Dahlstrom, op. cit.

[36]Michael Lewis, "Parents and Children: Sex-Role Development," *School Review* LXXX (February, 1972), 229–40.

[37]Ibid., pp. 232–34.

[38]Ibid., pp. 234–35

He feels that this differentiation in socialization is intended to deliberately stimulate autonomy and independence in boys at an early age and to encourage dependence in girls.[39] These differential expectations follow the child into adulthood. While women are permitted more proximal behavior with one another, it is not appropriate for men to have physical contact with other men. This is also true in adult interaction with children. Women are expected to have close physical contact with children, while "it is less appropriate and much less in the masculine ideal for men to do this."[40] This childhood training for boys is interpreted by Lewis as being congruent with adult expectations that males will be competitive and individualistic. From this viewpoint, proximal behaviors would be disadvantageous to a boy raised to fill a role in a competitive, individualistic society. Such a child would be group rather than individualistically oriented. It is interesting to note that this reflects a thoroughly dichotomous view of the world.

If the dualistic nature of Euro-American culture is reflected in a highly differentiated system of sex roles, then we might expect that the Afro-American insistence on the unity of opposites would be reflected in a quite different system of sex role expectations. Indeed, a careful examination of Young's findings reveals that black families handle sex role training and role expectations in ways which are compatible with the overall cultural handling of polarities.

The black child, to be sure, distinguishes between male and females, but unlike the white child he is not inculcated with standards which polarize behavioral expectations according to sex. Attributes other than sex prove more crucial in differentiating behavior. Many of the behaviors which whites see as appropriate to one sex or the other, blacks view as equally appropriate to both sexes, or equally inappropriate to both sexes; and the sex differences that do exist are more in the nature of contrasts than of mutually exclusive traits.

Earlier, recent ethnographic and sociological research on black families was noted which showed that neither spouse tends to be dominant over the other. For example, Kunkel and Kennard report on black marriages that

. . . both men and women are proud and have strong self-images. In most marriages, husband and wife achieve a kind of balance of role expectations, involving tacit mutual agreements about areas in which each will be dominant.[41]

Similarly, TenHouten in an empirical study of black and white families at the same class levels specifically tested the hypothesis that lower-class black wives were dominant and their husbands sub-dominant in comparison with lower-class white families. He found that black lower-class husbands were not "powerless in either their conjugal or their parental roles."[42]

These findings are supported by Young's study. In the community she studied there is, from a Euro-American perspective, a remarkable degree of overlap in the behavior considered appropriate for men and women.[43] Behavior which is associated with the male role in Euro-American culture is associated with both males and females in this community. For example, females as well as males are viewed as individualistic and non-conforming in their behavior. Both husband and wife have authority in the home; both are responsible for the economic support of the family; both take the initiative in forming and breaking up a marriage and both may find separation to their advantage. Young's material also shows that both men and women display confidence and a sense of worth, and that both are independent in sexual behavior.

Since differential standards as to sexual behavior have high salience in distinguishing males and females in Euro-American culture, it may be instructive to elaborate a bit. While in Euro-American culture the male is the aggressor and the female the passive receptor, in Afro-American culture, the woman is expected to take an active role in the male's attempt to establish a sexual encounter. That is, a great deal of assertiveness is expected on the part of the woman, whether she is agreeable to, or rejects the male's advances. Kochman, for example, describes an interesting case of cultural misunderstanding when a black man, a student, made a verbal pass

39Ibid., pp. 237–38.
40Ibid., p. 238.
41Kunkel and Kennard, op. cit., pp. 45–46.
42TenHouten, op. cit., p. 170.
43Young, op. cit., pp. 284–86.

at a young white woman, a teacher.[44] The woman was unable to deal with the situation, both because it violated her definition of proper status relationships (he was a student; she was a teacher) and because it conflicted with her expectations of how a "nice" woman should be approached. Consequently she adopted a pleading and placating demeanor which earned utter contempt from the student and the rest of the class. Had the young woman been a participant in the young man's culture, she could have rejected his approach in a way that recognized his worth as a person and at the same time reaffirmed her own worth as a confident and assertive individual.

Not only is behavior considered appropriate for males in white culture displayed by both women and men in black culture, but behavior which is associated with females in white culture is characteristic of both men and women in black culture. For example, in black families, both males and females display similar styles of child care: they are nurturing and highly interactive physically with children. Both men and women value personal relationships and are expressive emotionally. Both are more adept at handling the world of interpersonal relationships than the world of objects and the physical environment.[46] In Table 2 I have listed behavioral traits to which *both* males and females in Afro-American culture are socialized, but which are differentially assigned to the sexes in Euro-American culture.

An examination of socialization patterns in the families studied by Young reveals the process by which children learn not only that certain traits are equally important for males and females, but that factors other than sex are a crucial basis of differential treatment and expectations of behavior.

I have already noted that black child rearing techniques instill in both male and female infants similar traits of assertiveness, willfulness and independence. Both sexes are also trained to be extremely receptive to people, but are inhibited in early childhood in their attempts to learn about the physical environment.[46] The baby as Young shows has a rich human environment, not only because many people of all ages are constantly holding, fondling and playing with it, but also

Table 2.   Afro-American Behavioral Traits

Mainstream "Male" Behavior	Mainstream "Female" Behavior
Aggressiveness	Nurturance
Independence	Expressive emotionally
Self-confidence	Focus on personal relationships
Non-conformity	
Assertive sexually	

because the experience of being held, bathed, fed, weaned, toilet trained, etc., is of a highly intense personal nature.

In contrast to this rich personal environment, the baby has very little contact with the physical environment. Material objects associated with babies in black culture are few or lacking, and the baby's attempts to crawl and stand are actively inhibited. The encouragement of interpersonal experience, along with the inhibition of examination of objects and the physical environment results in a child who feels a great deal of self-confidence in dealings with people, but little familiarity and interest in the physical environment.

These socialization practices contrast sharply with those experienced by a white child, who has less involvement with the personal world but who may be intimately knowledgeable of the object world. Young compares the way white babies are usually held, looking impersonally over their mother's shoulder and the way a black baby is held, almost always face up on someone's lap.[47] We can also contrast the black baby, continually held and fondled, with the white baby content in a play pen piled with toys. The white child is also actively encouraged to crawl, stand and explore his physical environment. White children early develop a sense of mastery over the physical environment which is lacking in black children.

Robin Horton interestingly describes how the African mastery of the world of people and the European mastery of the world of objects, have resulted in different modes of explanation: the personalized which is African, and the impersonal which is Western science. In a statement unusual

44Kochman, op. cit., pp. 3, 6–7.
45Young, op, cit.
46Ibid., pp. 279–81.
47Ibid., p. 276.

for its candor, Horton describes his childhood when he felt most at ease, not with his family or friends, but with his Bunsen burners and chemicals: "Potassium hydroxide and nitric acid were my friends; sodium phosphate and calcium chloride my brothers and sister." He continues:

> . . . the image of the man happier with things than with people is common enough in modern Western literature (and) shows that what I am talking about here is the sickness of the times.[48]

Horton tried to explain to a group of Nigerian students how life in an urban industrial West differed from life in the students' own traditional communities by telling them of his childhood ease with objects and sense of alienation from people. He writes:

> What I was saying about a life in which things might seem a welcome haven from people was just so totally foreign to their experience that they could not begin to take it in. They just stared. Rarely have I felt more of an alien than in that discussion.[49]

Another characteristic which is deliberately fostered in black children, both males and females, is that of "mothering." It has already been noted that both fathers and mothers display similar styles of child care in black families: both nurture and have close physical contact with babies.[50] This was also found to be the case in the Kunkel and Kennard study of a black community in a Southern city.[51]

Young's study shows that one of the first and most important things a small black child learns is to care for and fondle a smaller child and that throughout one's life there is a high positive valuation of "mothering" in this culture. She writes: "The training that the one-year-old gets in kissing and holding the newborn is his training for all of childhood."[52] Thus individuals of all ages

and both sexes: young men as well as young women, teenage boys as well as teenage girls, one-year toddlers as well as older siblings, find babies pleasurable and display many public gestures of affection for them. This cultural expectation, as we have seen, is at variance with white norms where gentle, close physical contact with small babies is sex-linked behavior, the ideal for women, but considered inappropriate for men.[53]

While sex is relatively unimportant and few patterned differences of behavior are seen between little boys and little girls, age and relative birth order are crucial determinants of differential treatment and behavioral expectations in black families.

It has already been noted that the baby has a very close personal relationship with its parents and others, and that it is constantly being stimulated. This attention lasts for the first three years.[54] At about the age of three, however, an abrupt change occurs. Parental attention virtually stops and the child is pushed into the gang of older children and comes under the authority of the oldest child who is in charge of the gang. Age, rather than sex, elicits striking differences in the way the child is treated and the way he is expected to behave. While before he was a center of attention and a favorite, now he is expected to become a self-reliant member of a peer group.

Birth order, as well as age, are crucial in determining treatment. In this Southern black community where people, as Young notes, find in babies and young children "perhaps the greatest pleasure of their lives"[55] and where all babies receive a great deal of love, it is the first born who receives the greatest amount of "mothering" and stimulation.[56] The early attention given the first born, whether it is male or female, produces a child who is usually the most competent and self-assured of all the children in the family.

As this first child grows older he or she becomes nurse-child to those younger and takes on major responsibility for their care. He or she is in charge of the children's gang, a child-tending group. The frequency with which first born children, regardless of sex, displayed distinctive per-

[48]Robin Horton, "African Traditional Thought and Western Science," Africa, XXXVII (January, 1967), p. 64.

[49]Ibid., p. 65.

[50]Young, op. cit.

[51]Kunkel and Kennard, op. cit., p. 46.

[52]Young, op. cit., p. 284.

[53]Michael Lewis, op. cit., p. 238.

[54]Young, op. cit., p. 282.

[55]Ibid., p. 275.

[56]Ibid., p. 273.

sonality traits which set them apart from younger siblings leads to the conclusion that their treatment is highly differentiated and highly patterned. Young writes:

The nurse-children are bossy but gentle and protective and easy-going. The heightened attention that the nurse-girl or boy, as first baby, got, prepares him for his responsible position.[57]

It might be useful to look at the treatment of black children in terms of the conceptual framework provided by Lewis in his categories of proximal and distal behaviors.[58] This might also highlight the differences between dualism and synthesis in the Euro-American and Afro-American cultural models. In Euro-American culture, as Lewis has shown, proximal behavior is differentiated on the basis of sex, ceasing much earlier for boys than for girls. This is viewed as preparing boys for adult roles of independence and competitiveness and girls for adult roles of dependence and personal involvement. In Afro-American culture, on the other hand, it is seen that proximal behavior is differentiated on the basis of age, with both sexes receiving a great deal of physical and personal handling, along with independence training, until about the age of three, when the intense attention from others ceases abruptly, and the child is expected to form part of a cooperative children's gang. This treatment is associated with preparing both boys and girls for adult roles of independence and personal involvement.

It is important to emphasize that the concept of proximal behavior as Lewis defines it, i.e., "touching, holding," is apparently qualitatively different in the white and black cultural context. Reference has already been made to Young's evidence that infant care as shown in the manner of holding, feeding, etc., is intensely personalized in the black families she studied. Not only is the child constantly played with due to the abundance of people in the household, but "mothering" is an important cultural value. Furthermore, in the child's attempts to explore the physical environment "the personal is . . . often substituted for the impersonal"[59] and "babies' reachings to feel ob-

jects or surfaces are often redirected to feeling the holder's face."[60]

Another important difference is Lewis's implication that an infant's experience of or lack of proximal treatment prepares him to be either independent or dependent, competitive or cooperative. The data on black families show that these polarities do not exist; that the child is trained from infancy to be both independent, assertive and deeply responsive to interpersonal relationships.

It has been suggested that highly differential sex role socialization and adult role expectations may be viewed as reflections of an essential dualism in Euro-American culture. I have also hypothesized that sex role socialization which tends to synthesize rather than dichotomize the sexes may be an expression of the tendency to merge polarities in Afro-American culture.

Further research is needed to explore the extent to which the Afro-American unity of opposites is an important theme in some African philosophical systems, a thesis propounded by writers such as Jahn, and Dixon and Foster.[61] More information is also needed on African child rearing practices and patterns of sex-role training. Preliminary reading in some West African societies indicates that women in those societies, as well as men, are expected to be independent and self-sufficient when they marry. For example, among groups such as the Yoruba, women are expected to be self-confident and competent and it is rare for a woman to be dependent economically on her husband. A dependent woman, it is said, is treated with contempt.[62]

It has also been pointed out that African women are considered to have the same human needs, including sexual needs, as men, thus women are not sharply differentiated from men in this area, as in the West.[63] This is not to suggest that men do not hold ultimate authority in African societies, for they do. Thus, while African women are self-confident and independent, they also come under the authority of a man, either a father or a husband. Apparently, however, female inde-

[57]Ibid., p. 284.
[58]Michael Lewis, op. cit.
[59]Young, op. cit., p. 280.

[60]Ibid., p. 279.
[61]Jahn, op. cit.; Vernon Dixon and Badi Foster, *Beyond Black and White: An Alternative America* (Boston, 1971).
[62]Demse, Pauline, ed., *Women of Tropical Africa* (London, 1963); Elizabeth Wheeler, "SubSahara Africa," in Raphael Patai, ed., *Women in the Modern World* (New York, 1967), p. 334.
[63]Carolyn Clark, personal communication, 1972. Professor Clark recently conducted fieldwork among the Kikuyu.

pendence and recognition of male authority are not viewed as mutually exclusive situations.[64] This conception of sex role expectations appears to be compatible with an Afro-American stress on the unity of opposites rather than the Euro-American focus on mutually distinct polarities.

Obviously much more information is needed in this area. It is necessary to learn to what extent African child training, adult expectations and cultural values appear to be congruent. It is also important to determine whether African insistence on comparability of certain needs and behavior between the sexes seems to have contributed to Afro-American patterns.

The Afro-American material raises an important question. If behavioral expectations are comparable for males and females, and if age rather than sex is more important in differentiating behavior, then what factor does contribute to the development of a child's sexual identity?

The answer may lie in the different ways that sexuality is handled in Afro-American culture as opposed to Euro-American culture. In Euro-American culture, children are viewed as asexual. Benedict has written about the anxieties and other problems this presents for males.[65] Kagan has pointed out that the little boy acquires a sex role identity on the basis of how much he believes he possesses male-linked traits, i.e., behaviors, feelings, as well as physical attributes.[66] I suggest that in a society where there is discontinuity between the asexual child and the sexual adult, the only way a child can assure his masculinity is by displaying traits defined as masculine, that is, aggressiveness, independence, self-confidence, etc. Therefore, it is important that these traits lack ambiguity so that the child is assured of his proper sexual identification.

In Afro-American culture, on the other hand, children are considered sexual beings.[67] They learn about sex, menstruation and birth while very young, so that there is continuity between their lives as children and as adults. For the black child his sex identity is primarily tied to his definition of himself as a sexual being, rather than to behavior which has arbitrarily been defined as masculine. I

would submit that in a culture where independence, nurturing, assertiveness, etc., do not distinguish between males and females, and where sexuality is an expected attribute of the person from childhood on, a boy understands he is a male on the basis of his sexuality and success at seduction and a girl realizes her femaleness on the basis of her sexuality and her ability to procreate.

As Afro-American children grow up, they are subjected not only to the internal cultural practices which I have tried to describe, but also to pressures from the wider society. Both of these influence their behavior and in particular their role expectations as adults. The differential behavior cited by Young for late adolescence; the work done by Hannerz, Liebow and others in ghetto communities attest to the strength of macro-structural forces on black lifeways.[68] Thus, an attempt to analyze black family life as an expression of a unique black culture cannot ignore the forces of oppression and racism which also affect family practices. An attempt must also be made to distinguish between micro-structural and macro-structural factors and their influence on behavior.

It is instructive to apply a colonialist model and ask how the inculcating and learning of sex roles have been affected by conditions of subjugation and marginality.

Cross-cultural materials reveal that under normal conditions, in most societies, sex roles are played out in the domestic and the public spheres, with women usually primary in the domestic arena and men foremost in the public arena.

The impact of colonialism has a differential effect on role expectations in the oppressed group. While women continue their traditional functions, of childrearing and household care, the men find their public roles destroyed (e.g., it is in fact in the destruction of a meaningful and viable public life and the vast alteration of private life that one understands the meaning of slavery). Continuity in domestic roles is also assured since the oppressed woman can easily be exploited through an expansion of her traditional female occupations in the marketplace as she cares for the homes and children of the oppressors. This of course is not the case for men, for to allow them to

---

[64]Ibid.

[65]Ruth Benedict, "Continuities and Discontinuities in Cultural Conditioning," in Logan Wilson and William Kolb, eds., *Sociological Analysis* (New York, 1949), pp. 223–3l.

[66]Kagan, op. cit.

[67]Young, op. cit., p. 284.

[68]Ibid., pp. 284–85; Hannerz, op. cit.; Elliot Liebow, *Tally's Corner* (Boston, 1967).

function in the public sphere would put them in direct competition with men of the oppressor group. Thus oppressed men are either excluded from the marketplace or expected to function along with their women in low level service occupations. It is no accident, that the legal codes developed during and after slavery were primarily directed against black men and that the male is still seen as the major threat to the existing system of oppression.[69]

It is a well-known fact that the historical and structural factors of first slavery, and then colonialism, have molded differentially the expectations and opportunities for black men and women in the wider society. Hannerz, for example, gives one interpretation as to how differential expectations and opportunities have influenced internal life within the black neighborhood he studied.[70] While the degree to which these macro-structural factors have affected child rearing practices and sex role socialization in black families can only be touched on here, it is a subject which demands a great deal of careful research.

I would like to apply the colonialist model sketched above to the literature with which most of us are familiar. This literature points out that black children are differentially socialized during the growing up years: i.e., girls are reared to fulfill adult roles of responsibility, while boys lack the necessary training to fill mainstream adult roles; that is, to become providers, achievement oriented, etc. The mother is viewed as the crucial figure in making this distinction. Thus, much of this literature affirms that while mothers have high expectations for their daughters, they do not expect as much from their sons. Kunkel and Kennard report:

Mothers are apt to be strong disciplinarians, particularly toward daughters, from whom they expect more responsibility than from sons.[71]

Reid, who collected statements from almost 200 black women, noted that many spoke of the fact that their brothers received preferential treat-

ment in that they had greater freedom, got away with more and were in general "raised in a different way." One young woman stated:

The men got away with everything. The women did all the work for them. The guys could run the streets all the time. Mother would take up for my brothers because she was preparing the girls for our later life.[72]

The contradiction between Young's study on infant and early childhood training and the material from early adolescence which has been quoted above is, I feel, more apparent than real.

One way to unravel this contradiction is to distinguish between adaptive patterns of socialization which would stem directly from the situation of oppression as outlined in the colonialist model on the one hand, and the unique cultural patterns which define early childhood training and which have their probable source in African tradition, on the other.

I suggest that in early childhood socialization, when patterns are probably most unconscious, and at an age when the child is minimally influenced by dominant societal expectations, there is greater cultural influence; while in later socialization, particularly as the child reaches puberty, socialization reflects more closely the structure of expectations and opportunities provided for black men and women by the dominant society. At this later stage black socialization is adaptive to macro-structural constraints.

Thus, later socialization, depending on the conditions under which the families live, is more adaptive to particular situations of opportunity or exclusion as they operate for males and females. For example, in a matrifocal family in the inner city, where wider societal pressures are crucial, a mother's expectations for and consequent behavior toward her sons may be quite different than in a nuclear family in a small New England town.[73] These variations in role expectations would oper-

---

[69]Gerda Lerner, *Black Women in White America* (New York, 1972); Daniel Moynihan, op. cit., p. 62.

[70]Hannerz, op. cit.

[71]Kunkel and Kennard, op. cit., p. 46.

[72]Inez Smith Reid, *"Together" Black Women* (New York, 1972), p. 25.

[73]The question of whether differential expectations with regard to sons and daughters in adolescence may be related to family structure (i.e., matrifocal as opposed to nuclear) is currently under debate in the literature (see especially Hannerz, 1971). I am indebted to Marjorie Mbilinyi for pointing out that both external constraints and familial structures may generate differential training for males and females in black culture. This is obviously a subject which requires careful empirical research.

ate not only spatially, but temporally. Thus, in the past, when black women had better employment opportunities than men, the black family adapted by providing preferential educational opportunities for daughters.[74] Now, as wider educa-

tional and employment opportunities are opening for blacks of both sexes, this should begin to be reflected in family patterns of later childhood training and role expectations.

[74]Lerner, op. cit., pp. 220–2l.

Black Youth and Psychosocial Development: A Conceptual Framework

Ronald L. Taylor

This article discusses the importance of role models for Black youth in their psychosocial development. The author feels that commitment is important to the success of Black youth in pursuing long-range goals.

While there exists a massive literature on the characteristics and problems of black Americans, few studies exist which take as the main focus of attention the black adolescent or youth and the problem of psychosocial development. Moreover, while there has been considerable genuine interest and concern for the psychosocial developmental problems of black youth, there has been little actual systematic or theoretically guided research in this area (Pettigrew, 1964; Proshansky and Newton, 1968). Indeed, a perusal of that small corpus of research which does exist suggests that many of the more fundamental and significant questions have not even been broached, much less subjected to empirical investigation. For example, the way in which black youth "construct" or cultivate their identities through the use of others as models has been virtually ignored, despite evidence from psychological, clinical, and sociological studies on the significance of role models as sources of psychosocial development (Bandura and Walters, 1963).

The dearth of research on psychosocial development among black youth, in contrast to the wealth of data on early self-identity development among black children, is all the more surprising when seen against the background of recent social change (both within and without the black community), the substantial growth and visibility of a black professional leadership class sufficiently available as models of achievement, and the dramatic growth in the number of black youth currently enrolled in traditionally white and black colleges and universities. In view of these recent developments, together with new and expanded opportunities in employment and the apparent new level of self-awareness among black youth, it is reasonable to assume that these events have created new and unfamiliar developmental problems for not a few black youth.

The development of a relevant theoretical or conceptual framework is essential for a more thorough understanding and analysis of psychosocial identity development among black youth. The purpose here is to emphasize, through theoretical formulation and case study analysis, the utility of the role model approach as a conceptual framework for investigating the development of psychosocial identity among black youth. More specifically, this paper focuses upon the ways in which role models are selected and rendered useful by these youth in their various attempts to cultivate features of their personal and social

From *Journal of Black Studies* 6 (June 1976): 353–372. Reprinted by permission of the publisher, Sage Publications, Inc.

identities. Such a focus allows observation of how the youth shapes his own identity through his own actions, rather than being acted upon by his social environment. While such an approach is subject to certain limitations, it is clearly a useful strategy to explore the theoretical possibilities opened up by considering the function of role models in black psychosocial development.

Theoretical and Conceptual Orientation

Psychosocial development, of which identity formation is of prototypical significance, has been the subject of considerable discussion and investigation by behavioral scientists in recent years. Nowhere has this subject received fuller treatment than in the numerous works of Erikson (1950, 1964, 1968). While his perspective is dictated by psychoanalytic theory, he has systematically reorganized that theory to take greater account of the sociocultural environment. For Erikson, the quintessential task of youth is the establishment of a sense of one's own identity as a unique person. Identity represents an evolving configuration gradually established through successive synthesis and resynthesis of psychosocial components, involving the articulation of personal capacities, value, identifications, and fantasies with plans, ideals, expectations, and opportunities. Thus in Erikson's view, relative identity formation is not fully possible before late adolescence, when the body, "now fully grown, grows together into an individual appearance," when the fully developed cognitive structure enables the youth to envisage a career within an historical perspective, and when the emergence of the capacity for and interest in sustained heterosexual intimacy has been reached.

Most behavioral scientists are agreed that the youth stage of the life cycle is increasingly more problematic owing to social, psychological, and physical changes (Conger, 1973; Hauser, 1971). Youth find themselves in the position of having lost their former childhood status and yet not having acquired the full status of the adult. They are, as Hoffer (1965) suggests, in a traditional period between statuses and affiliations characterized by rootlessness and a high rate of

change. The experience of status discontinuity confronts the youth with few clearly defined expectations or norms to guide his behavior.[1] At the social level, youth are expected to become more seriously committed to the acquisition of values, skills, and patterns of behavior appropriate to the adult world of experience, to enlarge the range of potential reference groups and significant others, and to become much more sophisticated in relating to others. These relationships in turn bring new expectations, demands, and opportunities to which the youth is expected to respond. As a psychological phenomenon, the youth perhaps for the first time attempts consciously and deliberately to conceptualize himself, to reconcile the external and internal world of experience, i.e., to come to terms with himself and his society (Douvan and Adelson, 1966; Erikson, 1968). The growth in cognitive capacity and the development of intellectual skills permit new ways of learning and incorporating behavior while simultaneously serving as liberating and motivating forces impelling the youth toward more active participation in his own socialization. These unprecedented changes create perturbations if not severe stress. The normative identity crisis so often referred to in connection with this period is a result of these multiple transformations and social pressures.

There is little to indicate that black youth escape the tensions and turbulence of this period, as numerous autobiographical accounts and essays would seem to suggest (Malcolm X, 1965; Ellison, 1963; Brown, 1965; Cleaver, 1968). Moreover, problems precipitated by minority status, cultural conflict, and caste victimization may result in complications of a somewhat different order and may be seen to take different forms and find quite different solutions among these youth (Rainwater, 1966; Clark, 1965; Brody, 1964).

The issues of crucial significance for youth are questions of choice and commitment (Marcia, 1966; Erikson, 1968). The need to develop a sense of identity from among all past, current, and potential relations compels the youth to make a series of increasingly more circumscribed selec-

[1]While it is perhaps true that youth subcultures function as sources of interim status and social support, they are for most youth temporary solutions. It remains for the youth to come to grips with the adult world of experience where a mature (or more acceptable), permanent identity and status are to be found.

tions of personal, occupational, and ideological commitments. His choice and commitment to the performance of certain social roles aids in the establishment of his social identity, while his commitment to certain personally relevant values and beliefs permits membership in a larger community through which extensions of his identity are fostered and solidified. The variety of social roles and values as available options open to the youth are not, however, unlimited. With each choice the breadth and variety of alternatives narrow. Such variables as race, religion, level of education, and community have the effect of reducing the range of possibilities. Furthermore, there is some reason to believe that the specific ways in which the youth attempts to resolve these issues is determined in part by his position or the position of his parents in the hierarchy of social classes (Schonfeld, 1971; Musgrove, 1964). That is, the status differentials among youth are highly related to the ways in which they orient themselves to the society at large and have a decided influence on the content, duration, and stressfulness of the period. Hence, youth of various classes may be expected to differ in their modes of response to problems encountered during this period in their development and to move at differing paces toward relative identity formation.

With the prospect of choice and decision, the youth is likely to be shopping around for behavioral models and clarifying definitions that offer the possibility of relative permanence and stability in personal organization. Parents may only ambivalently serve as acceptable models during this period given the youth's early dependency on them. Furthermore, the inability of parents to confer extrinsic personal status is well recognized by the youth, as is the knowledge that a sense of identity and personal worth as an adult requires a degree of social recognition that transcends the family. How parents are displaced as role models is revealed in a study by Havighurst and his associates (1946) in their analysis of essays written by children and youth on the theme, "The Kind of Person I Want to Be." In childhood the persons most clearly idealized are parents, while during early adolescence parents are partially displaced by various glamorous "personalities" such as movie stars, athletes, or fictional characters. But in late adolescence, the most idealized individuals tend to be attractive and visible individuals who exemplify certain valued competences or skills, and who are generally admired by adults in the community. Yet parents are not altogether rejected by the youth. Their significance and function as models tend to vary depending upon socioeconomic status and the nature of early parent–child relationships.

Perhaps at no other time is the tendency to rely on models more open to observation than during the adolescent period of development. The literature abounds in examples of youth seeking desperately for someone to have faith in, to look up to, someone to serve as a reliable and trustworthy model for experimentation and guidance into their new identities (Goethals and Klos, 1970). "To such a person," Erikson (1956) writes, "the late adolescent wants to be an apprentice or disciple, a follower . . . a patient." The phrase "in search of identity" quite appropriately describes the youth's experimentation with different models and value systems to find the ones of best fit. Since identity is something to be cultivated and not merely a function of social inheritance, there is the necessity of experimenting and choosing, and the possibility of making incorrect and inappropriate choices. Nonetheless, how the youth relates himself and is related to his society is revealed through these crucial choices.

To the extent that identity formation involves the activity of relating oneself to persons, values, and institutions in one's society, it invariably involves the process of identification. As the massive literature and research reveals, the process of identification is one of the principal media through which behavior, values, skills, and other identity elements are learned—the essential means by which identity grows in ever more mature interplay with the identities of the individual's models. The cultivation of identity through the process of identification inevitably gives to the individual's identity features which are common to the identities of others. Thus the youth identifies with others and those others become extensions of his identity, i.e., features or symbols of its content.

The selection and identification with role models may be determined by several factors. As Bandura and Walters (1963) have shown, models must be perceived as having high utility value for the realization of personal aspirations and goals. In addition, such variables as age, sex, social class, and racial and ethnic status are all important determinants in role model selection. Equally important are the potential identifier's own characteristics that affect his preferences and determine the types of models who are selected for observation and emulation (Bandura and Walters, 1970). Most youth may be assumed to have some plans regarding their personal futures, the outlines of which are only roughly sketched in. Hence, the youth's anticipations and aspirations may be said to serve as the reference ground for present conduct and stylizations of his identity (Hauser, 1971). In his choice of models he is likely to choose attributes or qualities that fit him, become him, those things that go with his other qualities. Again, much depends on how the youth sees himself and his future, for appropriateness and fit are only meaningful in terms of the ideal identity for which the qualities of the model are chosen.

In considering the role of models as they function in the service of relative identity formation, attention should be focused on relevant psychosocial tasks to be resolved at this stage in the life cycle. Among the tasks encountered during this period are those of instrumental and interpersonal competence, i.e., the development of role skills and styles of performance related to particular social roles. For male youth, choosing and preparing for a vocational role takes precedence in awareness, since occupation plays a crucial defining role in his identity (Blau,1963). The dominant theme in his choice of models is therefore likely to be work relevant. An equally important task has to do with the establishment of a set of personal values and, more generally, the commitment to an ideological system. Lane (1969) and Smith et al. (1956), among others, have demonstrated the important function of ideological commitments in the search for a personal sense of identity. The values to which the youth commits himself are not simply carbon copies of parental values, nor are they the result of internalization of disembodied rules, principles, or other abstractions; rather they are the outcome of discovery through experience of these ideals and principles appropriate to his circumstances.

From the foregoing, two types of role models

can be conceptually distinguished. Models may be conceived as: (1) specific persons who serve as examples by means of which specific skills and behavior patterns are acquired, and (2) a set of attributes or ideal qualities which may or may not be linked directly with any one particular person as such, in which case the model is symbolic, representing a synthesis of diffuse and discrete phenomena. Hence, *exemplary* and *symbolic* models may be observed to serve different functions and to be invested with quite different meanings by the youth engaged in the process of cultivating various features of his social and personal identity.[2]

Exemplary models may be seen as persons who provide the technical knowledge, skills, or behavioral patterns which can be effectively utilized by the youth for developing certain competencies; in effect, they demonstrate for the youth how something is done (Kemper, 1968). A variety of exemplary models may be utilized for cultivating different features of identity and may reflect more clearly achievement strivings and identity goals. Symbolic models may be conceived as representing particular value orientations, ideal or ideological perspectives. We have in mind the tendency of cultures to embody abstract values, principles, and other "collective representations" in mythical, historical, and living figures (e.g., heroes), and the inclination of individuals to view certain figures as repositories of particular virtues, ideals, or esteemed attributes. As persons, symbolic models function as guides in the search for congenial ideology and values through their "personalization" of values and ideals. Through personal achievement, courage, or social activities, they serve to inspire adherence to certain ways of behaving and thinking.

The nature and extent of a given model's influence in the emerging psychosocial identity of youth may vary, and such a possibility must be taken into account. As a means of approach, the relationship between a given youth and his models may be conceptualized in terms of *type, content, and scope* of their relationship. *Type* refers to

[2]Orrin Klapp uses the term "symbolic leaders" to describe such persons as movie stars, politicians, and other celebrities; see his *Symbolic Leaders* (1967). Bandura and Walters (1963) have used the term symbolic and exemplary models to describe persons presented through films to children. As these terms are used here, both take on a largely different meaning than those assigned by Klapp or Bandura and Walters.

the quality or tone of the relationship and may be defined as *positive, negative, or neutral.* The quality of the relationship between the subject and the model can be established largely through an analysis of the content of the relationship. By *content* we refer to the nature of the model's influence as this is defined or described by the subject. Such influence may be described as having occurred on the level of overt behavior or conscious orientations, with respect to values, aspirations, beliefs, or goals. In addition, the influence of the model may be seen as general or specific, in which case we refer to the *scope* of the model's influence, that is, whether the youth is inclined toward appropriating specific behaviors or orientations of the model, or whether his desire is generally to ''be like'' the model in most respects. In those terms, the scope of the model's influence would indicate whether he functions in the capacity of exemplary or symbolic model.

This approach to psychosocial development attempts to remedy what Matza (1964) has termed the ''hard determinism'' perspective, which suffuses sociological and social psychological research at some levels with an emphasis on personal choice, commitment, and uniqueness as essential ingredients in identity formation. Hence, it seeks to focus attention on the interactional and constructive processes of psychosocial development in which the individual is an active participant. Its value lies in the potential for providing useful data on the content and character of black youths' evolving sense of identity as reflected in their choice of models. Its utility has already become apparent in a recent investigation carried out by the author (Taylor, 1973). Some of the more salient findings from that study are summarized below.

Black Youth and
Role Models Identification

Thirty black male youth made up the total sample for the investigation. They ranged in age from 18 to 21 and represented a wide range of

[3]Black females were not included in the sample because it was assumed on the basis of some empirical evidence that females are normally presented with a somewhat different set of psychosocial problems and thus would have made the task of analysis more difficult.

socioeconomic backgrounds and geographical locations. The sample is therefore a highly specific one. To begin with, it consists only of male college youths.[3] While this fact places an important limitation on the kinds of conclusions that can be drawn, the aim was to examine the lives of a certain segment of the youth population to discover the function of role models in their emerging psychosocial economies. The techniques of investigation consisted of the autobiography and the intensive interview. A number of topics empirically shown to be relevant to psychosocial development were explored, including the youth's early and more recent experiences in the family and community, his conceptions of the future as reflected in aspirations and plans, and his value orientations and self-definitions (Douvan and Adelson, 1968; Elder, 1968; Hauser, 1971). Data from these areas provided the basis upon which to establish the general sociohistorical context within which psychosocial development occurred, and it was within this context that role model identifications and their function in psychosocial identity were examined.

It is in the youth's striving to systematize and order the various and sundry influences on his life that his significant models can be observed to emerge. In fact, the clarity of self-concept can be seen to have been aided by the establishment of significant identifications; we found that such models could be isolated for most of these youth and that they were closely related to the quality of integration of their psychosocial organization.

Who are the figures that emerge in the imagery of these youth as they move toward engagement of identity-related issues and the task of evolving an identity ideal? When the data are analyzed for those models having a significant impact on the psychosocial identity of these youth, patterns of identification are centered primarily, though not exclusively, in the family. Parental models are observed to play powerfully active roles in the evolving sense of identity of these youth. To be sure, other models are also observed to have a significant impact on shaping their identities and tend to reflect certain styles of psychosocial development.

Most behavioral scientists seem to agree that the influence of one parent or the other tends to exceed the influence of any other one or two persons in our lives. Some students attribute the more formative and influential role to the mother whose early relationship with the child is assumed to be of crucial importance in subsequent development. In this connection, the role of the black mother has been given particular attention owing to her alleged dominant position in the family and the assumed consequences this seems to have for the child. A variety of empirical evidence would appear to support the view of the mother's influential role in the child's early development (Emmerich, 1956; Mussen, 1969; Winch, 1962). However, a somewhat different pattern of influence may emerge during later stages of development. For the male youth, the mother may continue to function as an object of moral and emotional support, while others, including the father, serve as models through whom he seeks to cultivate his social and personal identity. Indeed, this is precisely the pattern which emerges from the accounts of our subjects. The model who figures most prominently in their accounts of their more recent development is clearly the father or father surrogate.

From their various accounts it becomes clear that a considerable transformation has occurred over the years in their relationship with the father, growing stronger or weaker as the case may be, as each youth has gained in the capacity and knowledge to make critical judgments of the father's personal qualities, competences, and limitations. Changes at both the conceptual and perceptual levels have apparently resulted in changes in valuing and behaving toward the father as model, and more often than not these changes have revealed new and different aspects of his personal qualities previously overlooked or ignored. This may be seen to have important consequences for the father's role as model for his son.

At least several factors or conditions could be identified as having influenced the extent to which the father became a salient model for the youth. In general, the father's influence as a model stems from his ability to provide what may be called crucial resources, i.e., pertinent behavior patterns, general value orientations, and the like, which the youth has found, through experience, to be particularly effective in coping with certain developmental problems. Hence, the father's role as significant model was often contingent upon and expressed in terms of what he did or failed to do for the youth at various crucial periods in life. What emerges, then, is a general principle of "reciprocity," i.e., an exchange of resources for identification between father and son (compare Scanzoni, 1971).

For most youths the father functions generally as exemplary rather than as symbolic model. That is, few choose him as their identity ideal. Rather, a pattern emerges whereby the father, during various stages in the early life of the youth, functions as a powerful symbolic model, but growth and maturity lead to an apparent rejection of him at later stages, though he continues to serve the useful function of exemplary model. However, where appropriate opportunities for making critical judgments of the father's personal attributes or competences were not possible, or where such opportunities were severely limited, a transformation in this role frequently did not occur. This tendency was often observed in cases where the father was absent from the home through separation, divorce, or death, and where his place in the psychological economy of the youth became that of an unchanging figure whose personal characteristics and expectations were imagined to always be the same. Under these circumstances, the youth desired to become like this idealized image of the father (often encouraged by the mother and other relatives) and sought to cultivate his putative characteristics.

Just as the father may come to serve as a powerful object of positive identification, both admired and emulated by the youth, he was also observed to function in the capacity of "negative model," an evil prototype of identity features the youth should seek to avoid and of a potential future he should seek to prevent. This seeming rejection of the father as a relevant or useful model does not necessarily see the end of his influence, however. Indeed, he may "live on" in the shadows of the youth's consciousness, assuming the role of *rival,* and thus come to occupy a prominent place in the evolving identity. Implicit here, of course, is the notion that the perception and rejection of the father as appropriate model extends beyond simple nonacceptance of his modes of behavior, attitudes, or values, frequently encompassing the formation of counter-behavior and values. Hence, the father's role as negative model may often turn out to be just as influential in shaping the behavior, values, and identity aspirations of the youth as his function in a more positive sense.

In general, from these data it becomes clear that the father plays a highly significant role in the evolving identity of these youth. It seems that in one way or another, they are compelled to come to terms with the paternal figure. And since different motives may be seen to have driven the youth at different periods in life, the extent to which the father becomes a salient model may be governed by the relevance of certain of his personal attributes or qualities for coping with the central concerns of the youth during a given period, including the resolution of certain tasks related to identity formation. Thus our analysis suggests that the father's function as role model is never static or unchanging, except under conditions where he may be absent from the home during crucial periods in the life of the youth.

Other models are also observed to play active roles in the emergent identity of these youths. While these models are seen to come and go, to wax and wane in importance across the span of the youth's biographical career, they tend to fall roughly into two main categories: work relevant and value relevant models. Both are essential in the youth's ability to evolve an identity ideal, an interrelated set of images that have psychological significance for him. Almost all youth had strong work models, i.e., they had identified closely with someone in a vocational area in which they were interested. Although it is difficult to know whether the choice of an occupation preceded identification with a specific model, or whether the discovery of the model resulted in a strong interest in a given field, it is clear that the model often served to deepen vocational interests and inspire commitment of a significant nature. Indeed, the model was often said to have more clearly focused the interests and energies of the youth, a typical response being: "I became more serious about my studies and more concerned about really preparing myself for a career."

Value relevant models come into focus as the youth moves toward setting priorities among his interests and preferences, as he seeks to give a certain structure and meaning to his life. Such attempts reflect a growing awareness of the diversity of human values, the complexity of human experience, and the relationship between values and the achievement of social purpose. Such value relevant models were both living and dead, and were frequently selected on the basis of their convictions, courage, and achievements. They provided values and beliefs about what is worthwhile in life and inspired hope in the future and in one's individual chance.

Perhaps one of the most serious and recurring problems encountered by many of these youth in evolving an identity ideal—that is, in selecting appropriate models for inclusion in the evolving pattern—has to do with the impermanence of potentially useful models which, in turn, renders significant and lasting identifications difficult, if not impossible. In recent years numerous popular black figures have appeared, persons with whom these youth have become familiar and to whom many have become attracted. Yet the failure of many such persons to withstand the press of events and changing times has often resulted in their failure to hold the imagination of these youth. Indeed, the emergence and demise of once popular models has at times been so incessant as to leave many youth confused, frustrated and eventually unwilling to invest themselves, their admiration, and their trust in any and all models.

Here one may observe a strong skepticism toward popular and not so popular models. The attitude may be assumed that all models are constantly becoming out of date, beginning to decline even as they emerge, since things are in a state of flux. For some youth a solution is found in selecting as models more distant figures, those less vulnerable to change, e.g., the deceased. Thus it is not surprising that such figures as Martin Luther King, Malcolm X, Marcus Garvey, Frederick Douglass, or W. E. B. DuBois, all important black men of the past, are identified as the nearly most perfect models by these youth.

Since one's own fate may be thought to be linked with that of one's model in the sense that their failures and humiliations become one's own and, therefore, damaging to self-esteem, the selection of deceased figures may often be seen as "safer" investments, as less susceptible to the vicissitudes of contemporary life than are living models. In any case, one is less likely to be disappointed by such models in the future since their biographical careers have been terminated.

Summary and Conclusions

Although there are perhaps many ways of looking at the process of becoming an adult, that is, of achieving a mature and relatively stable sense of personal identity, we found it to be a useful strategy to see the process as one in which the youth gradually acquires a variety of commitments as revealed through his selections and identifications with certain role models who influence as well as constrain his psychosocial development. In effect, commitments create the conditions for stability in personal organization and thus permit the relative formation of identity. The extent to which a given youth was able to establish significant role model identifications was found to be intimately related to the character and quality of integration of his psychosocial organization. The notion of commitment allows us to focus upon the age at which it becomes possible to make serious choices of some lasting consequence. For example, it seems less likely that children are capable of making lasting commitments which more or less bind them to a future course of development than are youth about to enter upon a new and different status, youth who are not only encouraged to make serious commitments but who have at their disposal a rich variety of social and psychological supports as well as a fund of experience upon which to rely.

How the youth comes eventually to commit himself to achieving a certain identity requires a fuller analysis than we have given here. Investigations have only recently begun in this area of which the work of Hauser (1971) is a notable example. In his investigation of identity formation among black and white lower-class youth, he finds an identity foreclosure pattern to be most prevalent among black youth. He attributes this identity variant to "model deprivation," frequent failure, and to their perception of limited opportunities. Hence, their view of the future, together with absent role models, had a decided effect on their ability to make future commitments, i.e., to stake themselves on achieving certain identities with a fairly confident expectation that such identities would be realized in the future. But what of other youth? What antecedent conditions give rise to their permanence of choice and commitment? Does environmental stability, including such things as changes in family structure, frequent changes in social conditions, and the impermanence of popular and potentially useful models, affect the permanence with which they are able or willing to make more or less lasting commitments? While these data suggest that environmental stability is indeed an important aspect influencing personal commitments, only a more rigorous investigation can produce evidence that would either confirm or deny the validity of this observation.

There would appear to be heuristic value in conceptualizing psychosocial identity as a constructive process, a process mediated by the youth's conception of the future which he may render tractable by choices made in the present. Stated differently, the youth's anticipation of a certain future is the reference point for present conduct and stylizations of identity. His role model identifications would expose the changing meaning of the future. Youth lacking a clear conception of the future, having failed to develop a tentative life plan, were observed to have less instrumental and realistic notions of steps toward their goals, including the selection of appropriate models who might help to bring about their realization. Future investigations might focus more fully on the sequence of models as indications of the youth's changing perspectives, values, and identity goals. In addition, stability and change in role model identifications may offer important insights into the nature of the youth's conception of future possibilities in terms of identity construction.

A thorough developmental analysis of personal and social identity among black youth is a major task that goes beyond the present undertaking. What is required is a comprehensive longitudinal portrayal of development, including description and explanation of the evolving relations between the processes of construction, interaction, and enculturation. We have attempted to develop a tentative conceptual framework which, it is hoped, will facilitate analysis and interpretation in this area, one which will enable us to see the function of role models as integral parts of the developmental and maturational process.

References

Bandura, A., and R. H. Walters (1970) *Psychological Modeling*. Chicago: Aldine.

——(1963) *Social Learning and Personality Development*. New York: Holt.

Blau, P. (1963) "Occupational choice: a conceptual framework," in Neil Smelser and William T. Smelser (eds.), *Personality and Social Systems*. New York: John Wiley.

Brody, E. B. (1964) "Color and identity conflict in young boys." *Archives of Gen. Psychiatry* 10 (April): 354–360.

Brown, C. (1965) *Manchild in the Promised Land*. New York: Macmillan.

Clark, K. B. (1965) *Dark Ghetto: Dilemmas of Social Power*. New York: Harper.

Cleaver, E. (1968) *Soul on Ice*. New York: Delta.

Conger, J. J. (1973) *Adolescence and Youth*. New York: Harper.

Douvan, E., and J. Adelson (1968) *The Adolescent Experience*. New York: John Wiley.

Elder, G. H. (1968) *Adolescent Socialization and Personality Development*. Chicago: Rand McNally.

Ellison, R. (1963) *The Invisible Man*. Westminister, Md.: Modern Library.

Emmerich, W. (1956) "Parental identification in young children." *Genetic Psych. Monographs* 60: 257–308.

Erikson, E. (1968) *Identity: Youth and Crisis*. New York: Norton.

——(1964) "Memorandum on identity and Negro youth." *J. of Soc. Issues* 20: 29–42.

——(1956) "The problem of ego identity." *J. of the Amer. Psych. Association* 4: 58–121.

——(1950) *Childhood and Society*. New York: Norton.

Goethals, G., and D. S. Klos (eds.) (1970) *Experiencing Youth: First Person Accounts*. Boston: Little, Brown.

Hauser, S. T. (1971) *Black and White Identity Formation*. New York: John Wiley.

Havighurst, R., M. Robinson, and M. Dorr (1946) "The development of the ideal self in childhood and adolescence." *J. of Educ. Research* 40: 241–257.

Hoffer, E. (1965) "An age for juveniles." *Harper's* 6: 18–21.

Kemper, T. (1968) "Reference groups, socialization and achievement." *Amer. Soc. Rev.* 33 (February): 31–45.

Klapp, O. E. (1967) *Symbolic Leaders*. Homewood, Ill.: Dorsey.

Lane, R. (1969) *Political Thinking and Consciousness*. Chicago: Markham.

McKinley, D. G. (1964) *Social Class and Family Life*. New York: Free Press.

Malcom X (1965) *The Autobiography of Malcolm X*. New York: Grove.

Marcia, J. E. (1966) "Development and validation of ego identity status." *J. of Abnormal and Social Psychology* 3: 551–558.

Matza, D. (1964) *Delinquency and Drift*. New York: John Wiley.

Musgrove, F. (1964) *Youth and the Social Order*. London: Routledge & Kegan Paul.

Mussen, P. H. (1969) "Early sex-role development," in David A. Goslin (ed.), *Handbook of Socialization Theory and Research*. Chicago: Rand McNally.

Pettigrew, T. F. (1964) "Negro American personality: why isn't more known?" *J. of Social Issues* 20 (April): 4–23.

Proshansky, H., and P. Newton (1968) "The nature and meaning of Negro self-identity," in Martin Deutsch, Irwin Katz, and Arthur R. Jensen (eds.), *Social Class, Race, and Psychological Development*. New York: Holt.

Rainwater, L. (1966) "Crucible of identity: the Negro lower-class family." *Daedalus* 95 (Winter): 172–216.

Scanzoni, J. H. (1971) *The Black Family in Modern Society*. Boston: Allyn & Bacon.

Schonfeld, W. (1971) "Adolescent turmoil: socioeconomic affluence as a factor," in Ralf E. Muuss (ed.), *Adolescent Behavior and Society*. New York: Random House.

Smith, B. M., J. Bruner, and R. White (1956) *Opinions and Personality*. New York: John Wiley.

Taylor, R. L. (1973) "The Function of Role Models in Social Development: Explorations in Black Identity." Ph.D. dissertation, Boston University (unpublished).

Winch, R. (1962) *Identification and Its Familial Determinants.* New York: Bobbs-Merrill.

13

Socioeconomic Characteristics

The Black Family and Social Class
Charles V. Willie

Nine Black families representing three so-cioeconomic classes (middle class, working class and lower class) were investigated. Some values common to each class are examined and provide a prototype of each economic group. All three groups, though varied and unique, show a strong sense of survival.

. . . My interest in understanding the way of life of blacks independent of any reference to the way of life of whites is due to a desire 1) to extricate the social and behavioral sciences from a white ethnocentric perspective, and 2) to increase their contribution to the understanding of social change. Innovations in life-styles, including family life-styles, often develop among minority populations in the society before they are adopted by the majority. Such innovations may not be recognized when the way of life of the majority is looked upon as the "ideal type" and the behavior of others is considered deviant.

Method

During the past few years we have compiled approximately 200 case studies of black families, many southern migrants or descendants of southern migrants who now live in the northeastern region of the United States. The case studies were obtained as an assignment for students enrolled in a course on "The Black Family." The responsibility for locating a black family was that of each student. Many students interviewed families in their home towns scattered throughout the re-

gion. They interviewed families who were friends, referred to them by friends, referred by an agency, or selected at random by knocking on the door of a stranger. Students were provided with an interview schedule that requested specific information about economic, social and demographic characteristics, family customs, aspirations of parents for children, and patterns of authority within the family. Interviewers were black and white undergraduate students.

Out of the 200 or more case studies, nine were selected for detailed analysis in this paper as a composite representation of three income groups. Household income was the primary basis for more or less arbitrarily selecting three families each for middle-income, marginal-income, and lower-income groups. Utilized in this study were the student reports that contained the most complete and detailed descriptions. We cannot claim to have randomly selected the families for analysis. But we can say that the bias of the investigator was not the basic factor that determined whether or not a family was included among the nine for intensive study. The income groups studied ranged from $3000 to $6000 (low-income), $6000 to $10,000 (marginal-income), and $10,000 to $20,000 (middle-income). Essentially, this study is an example of inductive analysis. Two variables— race and economic status—were used. Since blacks often are referred to as if they were a homogeneous group, nine families of the same race but of different income groups were studied to determine if, in fact, their way of life, customs, and practices were similar. Probability sampling, of course, would be necessary if the goal had been to make generalizations about the frequency

Abridged from the *American Journal of Orthopsychiatry* 44 (January 1974): 50–60. © 1974 by the American Orthopsychiatric Association, Inc. Reprinted by permission. Footnotes have been renumbered.

of certain behavior forms within the total black population. This was not our goal. Thus, less rigor in the process of selecting the families for intensive analysis was possible.

Social class refers to style of life as well as economic resources. No operational definition of social class was developed for this study. The middle-class, working-class, and lower-class categories referred to later in this paper were derived from the analysis. The composite picture for the three families in each of the income groups was different from the style of life of black families in other income groups. Only the composite picture of the style of life for a social class is given. Detailed information on each of the nine families is presented elsewhere in a book-length manuscript.[1] The three social classes included in this study represent about 75% of all blacks. Not included are the upper middle class and the upper class, probably few in number, and at the other end of the stratification hierarchy, the under class—20% to 25% of all blacks.

Findings

Middle Class: The Affluent Conformists

Middle-class status for most black families is a function of dual employment of husband and wife. Black men and women have relied heavily on the public sector for employment at livable wages.

The public school has been an employment haven for black working wives. It has provided steady and continuous work and often has been the one occupational role in the family which has enabled it to lay claim to a professional style of life. Because of educational requirements, black female teachers of middle-class families are likely to be more highly educated than their male spouses. The length of employment of professional working wives is likely to be as long as that of their husbands, with only brief interruptions for childbearing. The numbers of children in black middle-class families tend to be small, ranging from one to three, but more often two or less. Thus, the black woman, in a public sector job with prescribed yearly increments and retirement benefits and with only a few interruptions in her labor

force status, tends to draw a decent income by the time she reaches middle age.

Continuity in employment also is a characteristic of black men in middle-class families. Public sector jobs, especially in the postal service, have been a source of support and security over the years. Some black men have, however, received financially rewarding professional positions in industry.

The economic foundation for middle-class black families is a product of the cooperation of the husband and wife. Their way of life is a genuine illustration of a team effort. Few, if any, family functions, including cooking, cleaning, and buying, are considered to be the exclusive prerogative of the husband or wife. Probably the best example of the liberated wife in American society is the wife in the black middle-class family. She and her husband have acted as partners out of necessity and thus have carved out an equalitarian pattern of interaction in which neither husband nor wife has ultimate authority. He or she alone could not achieve a comfortable style of life, because of racial discrimination and the resulting income limitations of the kinds of jobs available to most blacks. Together they are able to make it, and this they have done. In the 1970s middle-class black families earned $10,000 to $20,000 a year—the joint income of husband and wife.

Such income is lavishly spent on a home and on the education of children. Unless restricted by racial discrimination, middle-class black families tend to trade in older homes for new structures as their income and savings increase. Thus, families in the income range mentioned above are likely to be found in houses valued from $25,000 to $35,000. The real expense in housing, however, is in the up-to-date furnishings and modern appliances. For most middle-class black families, their home is their castle and it is outfitted as such.

Because work is so consuming for the husband and wife, little time is left for socializing. Most families have nearby relatives—usually the reason for migrating to a particular city. They visit relatives occasionally, may hold membership in a social organization, participate regularly in church activities, and spend the remainder of their free time in household upkeep and maintenance chores.

In most middle-class black families, one member almost always has attended college.

---

[1]Willie, C. 1976. *A New Look at Black Families* (Bayside, N.Y.: General Hall Publishers).

Often both have attended college. The husband and wife struggled and made great sacrifices to complete their formal education. Not infrequently, college and graduate school are completed on a part-time basis after adulthood and while the husband or wife, who also may be a parent, is employed full-time. Parents who have experienced these struggles and hardships know that their middle-class status, which usually is not achieved until middle age, is directly correlated with their increased education. New jobs, especially public school teaching, and salary increments can be traced directly to the added schooling. Education has been a major contributor to upward mobility for blacks.

Because education and, consequently, economic affluence are so closely tied together for middle-class black households, parents tend to go all out for their offspring. Particularly do they wish their children to go to college immediately after graduating from high school so that they will not have to struggle as long as did their parents whom middle-class status eluded during young-adult years. An ambition of most parents is to give to their children opportunities they did not have.

As a starter, almost all children in middle-class households are given music lessons. Daughters, in particular, are expected to learn to play a musical instrument, usually the piano. Recreational skills are developed, too. Most children in middle-class black families are expected to work around the house for an allowance. Families try to inculcate in their children positive attitudes toward work and thrift.

Active involvement in community affairs that take on the characteristics of a movement is not the cup of tea for most black middle-class, middle-aged adults. Their adolescent children may be deeply involved in various liberation movements but seldom are the parents.

Middle-class black families in America, probably more so than any other population group in this society, manifest the Puritan orientation toward work and success that is characteristic of our basic values. For them, work is a consuming experience. Little time is left for recreation and other kinds of community participation, except regular involvement in church affairs. The way of life of black middle-class Americans is a scenario patterned after Weber,[2] except that most blacks

[2]Weber, M. 1948. *The Protestant Ethic and the Spirit of Capitalism.* (London: George Allen and Unwin).

have little capital other than the house they own, which, of course, is their primary symbol of success.

Working Class: The Innovative Marginals

Family life in the black working class is a struggle for survival that requires the cooperative efforts of all—husband, wife, and children. Income for black working-class families ranged from $6000 to $10,000 during the 1970s. This is hardly enough for luxury living when the family size is considered. Black working-class families tend to be larger families, consisting of five or more children.

There is some indication that the size of the family is a source of pride for the parents, especially the father and maybe the mother too. The bearing and rearing of children are considered to be an important responsibility, so much so that black working-class parents make great personal sacrifices for their families. They tend to look upon children as their unique contribution to society, a contribution they are unable to make through their work roles, which at best are semiskilled. The family size of the black working-class also may be a function of age at marriage, usually before twenty-one for the wife and mother and often during the late teens. Husbands tend to assume parenthood responsibilities early too; often they are only one or two years older than their spouses.

The cohesion of the black working-class family results not so much from understanding and tenderness shown by one for the other as from the joint and heroic effort to stave off adversity. Without the income of either parent or the contributions of children from part-time employment, the family would topple back into poverty.

The parents in black working-class families are literate but of limited education. Most have completed elementary school but may be high school drop-outs. Seldom do any have more than a high school education. This is the educational level they wish their children to achieve, although some families hope that one or two of the smarter children in their brood will go on to college. The jobs they wish for their children also are those that require only a high school or junior college education, like work as a secretary, nurse, mechanic, or bank messenger.

Racial discrimination, on the one hand, and

insufficient education, on the other, have teamed up to delimit the employment opportunities for black working-class families. Their mobility from rural to urban areas and from the South to the North usually has been in search for a better life. Families tend to be attracted to a particular community because of the presence of other relatives who sometime provided temporary housing.

In general, the moves have opened up new opportunities and modest advancement such as from gas station attendant to truck driver, or from farm laborer to dairy tanker. The northern migration has resulted in some disappointments, too. On balance, new employment opportunities have resulted from the move from South to North, particularly for wives who have found work in institutional settings such as hospitals more profitable than private household work. Nursing aide and cooking jobs have been outlets for women and have enabled them to supplement the family income.

One sacrifice that the members of black working-class families have made so as to pull out of and stay beyond the clutches of poverty is to give up on doing things together as a family. Long working hours and sometimes two jobs leave little time for the father to interact with family members. In some households, the husband works during the daytime and the wife works during the evening hours. In other families, children work up to twenty hours a week after school and on weekends. These kinds of work schedules mean that the family as a unit is not able to share any meals together, except possibly on Sunday.

Despite the hardships, there is a constancy among the members of black working-class families that tends to pull them through. Some husbands and wives have been married more than two decades; they tend to have been residents of their neighborhoods for ten or more years and to have worked for the same employer over a long period of time. Though their earnings are modest, this continuity in area of residence and in other experiences has stabilized these families and enabled their members to accumulate the makings of a tolerable existence without the losses that come from frequent stops and starts.

Another stabilizing experience is the home that some black working-class families own. Rather than renting, many are paying mortgages. Their homes may range in value from $10,000 to $15,000, may be located in isolated rural or un-

sightly urban areas, and may be in a poor state of exterior repair but neat and clean on the inside. Home ownership for black working-class families is not so much a symbol of success as an indicator of respectability.

Black working-class parents boast of the fact that their children are good and have not been in trouble with the police. They also have a strong sense of morality, which emphasizes "clean living." The home they own is part of their claim to respectability. The owned home is one blessing that can be counted. It is a haven from the harsh and sometimes unfriendly world.

There is little time for community activities for black working-class families. Most spare time is devoted to associating with household members or with nearby relatives. Religion is important; but participation in church activities is limited to regular or occasional attendance at Sunday worship services. The mother in such families tries to maintain tenuous contacts with at least one community institution, such as the school. She even may be a member of the Parents–Teachers Association but is not deeply involved in organizational maintenance work as a volunteer.

Black working-class parents do well by their children if no special problems are presented. Their comprehension of psychological maladaption, however, is limited. These problems are dealt with by a series of intended remedial actions that seem to be of little assistance in solving the child's real problem and usually result in frustration both for the parent and for the offspring. Black working-class families have learned to endure, and so they bear with the afflictions of their members— those they do not understand as well as those with obvious sources of causation.

Cooperation for survival is so basic in black working-class families that relationships between the husband and wife take on an equalitarian character. Each knows that his or her destiny is dependent upon the actions of the other. Within the family, however, husbands and wives tend to have assigned roles, although in time of crisis, these roles can change. The husband tends to make decisions about financial expenditures, including the spending of money for furniture. He also has basic responsibility for household upkeep. The father is the chief advisor for the boys. The mother tends to be responsible for the cooking and cleaning, although she may delegate these chores to the children. She is the chief advisor for the girls. She also maintains a liaison relationship with the school and may be the adult link between the family and the church if the father is not inclined to participate.

We tend to think in terms of upward mobility in American society. Indeed, this is what many working-class families are—households moving out of poverty into respectability; households that emphasize mobility, goal, and purpose; households committed to making a contribution to society by raising and maintaining a family of good citizens. This, of course, involves a struggle. But the struggle may be a function of the ending of good times rather than the overcoming of adversity. A black working-class family may be of a lower-income household on its way up or a middle-income household on its way down. A middle-income family beset with illness, for example, could slip into the working-class status due to reduction in income and the requirement for change in style of living. How often this occurs, we do not know. It does occur often enough to keep the working class from becoming a homogeneous lot. For this and other reasons, one should not expect to find a common philosophical orientation within the working-class.

Lower Class: The Struggling Poor

The most important fact about black lower-class families is their low-income status; it forces them to make a number of clever, ingenious, and sometimes foolish arrangements to exist. These range from extended households consisting of several generations under one roof to taking in boarders or foster children for pay. Boyfriend-girlfriend relationships beween adults often assume some parental functions when children are involved, while the participants maintain their autonomy unfettered by marital bonds. Because every penny counts, poor households often do whatever they must do to bring money in. Conventional practices of morality may be set aside for expedient arrangements that offer the hope of a livable existence. The struggle among poor families is a struggle for existence. All else is secondary. Family income tends to vary from $3000 to $6000, and more often than not the household does not receive public welfare.

The struggle is severe and there is little margin for error. Black low-income families learn to live with contingency. They hope for little and expect less. Parents love their children but seldom understand them. Men and women become sexually involved but are afraid to entrust their futures to each other. There is much disappointment. The parents in broken families often have broken spirits—too broken to risk a new disappointment. For this reason, black lower-class parents often appear to be uncommitted to anyone or to anything when in actuality they are afraid to trust.

Movement is constant, as if one were afraid to stay put and settle down. Jobs, houses, and cities are changed; so are spouses and boyfriends and girlfriends. Unemployment is a constant specter. The womenfolk in the household usually find employment as maids or private household workers. The males are unskilled factory workers or maintenance men between periods of no work at all.

Marriage may occur at an early age, as early as sixteen years for some girls. The first child is sometimes born before the first marriage. Others tend to come in rapid succession. Some families have as many as eight or more children, while others are smaller. When the burdens of child care, illness, and unemployment strike at the same time, they often are overwhelming. Drinking, gambling, and other escape behavior may increase. A fragile love and capacity for endurance are shattered, and the man in the house moves out, no longer able to take it. One more failure is experienced.

The parents in black lower-class families are grade school or high school drop-outs. Neither spouse has more education than the other. Thus, parents in lower-class families sometimes hold themselves up to their children as failures, as negative images of what not to do. There is only limited ability to give guidance concerning what ought to be done. Thus, children are advised not to marry early, not to drop out of school, and not to do this and not to do that. There is admonition but little concrete effort at prevention.

Scapegoating is a common way of explaining deviant behavior in children. Juvenile delinquency may be attributed to the disreputable parent. The mother on location seldom knows what to do. Although little love may exist between parents, there is fierce loyalty between mothers and offspring, and between grandmothers, and children. The children come first. Mothers will extend every effort to take care of their sons and daughters, even into adulthood. Grandparents are excellent babysitters. They are expected to teach their grandchildren good manners and other fundamentals.

A strong custom of brothers and sisters helping each other exists in the lower class. The problem is that siblings are struggling too. About the most one can do for the other is share already overcrowded living quarters when a new member comes to town or when a two-parent family breaks down. The move from one city to another often is for the purpose of being near kinsmen. There is strong loyalty between siblings and a standing obligation to help.

Little participation in any community association is seen. Religion is important for some black lower-class families. But for others, it is no more than a delusion. Those who attend church regularly tend to engulf their lives with religion and especially with affirmations about its saving grace and reward system after death. Some shy away from the church as one more disappointing promise that has copped out on the poor without really helping. Black lower-class people are seldom lukewarm about religion. They are either all for it or all against it, although the latter are reluctant to deny their children religious experience, just in case there is more to it than was realized.

It is hard for a poor black family to overcome poverty; so much is lined up against it. If illness or unemployment do not drain away resources, there is a high probability that old age will.

Conclusion

We turn now to a theoretical discussion of the differences that have been observed. In his classical article, "Social Structure and Anomie," Robert Merton[3] identified five kinds of adaptations by individuals to social organizations: conformity, innovation, ritualism, retreatism, rebellion. We shall discuss three of the adaptations to explain the way of life of the three different social classes. The conformist acknowledges the legitimacy of societal values and goals and also accepts the means that are sanctioned and prescribed for achieving them. The innovationist believes in the socially sanctioned goals but must improvise new and different means. The retreatist gives up on the

socially sanctioned values and goals as well as the means and, therefore, is declared to be in a state of anomie or normlessness. This theoretical formulation provides a helpful way conceptually for approaching an understanding of the differences between middle-class, working-class, and lower-class black families.

Middle-class black families subscribe to the basic values and goals in American society and utilize appropriately prescribed means for their achievement. Its members are success-oriented, upwardly mobile, materialistic, and equalitarian. They consume themselves in work and leave little time for leisure. Education, hard work, and thrift are accepted as the means for the achievement of success. Property, especially residential property, is a major symbol of success. This is the American way and the prevailing way of life to which the middle-class black family in America conforms. Thus, its members may be called conformists.

Black working-class families also have internalized the basic values and goals of this nation. They too are success-oriented and upwardly mobile. However, their symbol of success differs from that of the black middle-class. The welfare of the total family is the principal measure of effective functioning. A black working-class family is successful if it is respectable. A family is respectable when its members are well-fed, well-clothed, and well-housed, and do not get into trouble with the police.

The location and value of a house is not so important. Home ownership is important but home value is something else. In the latter respect, the black working class differs from the black middle class, in which an expensive home is the symbol of success.

Almost everything that the black working-class parents do to achieve success and respectability is extraordinary, compared with the black middle class. Their education is limited; their occupations are unskilled; their income is modest; and their families are relatively larger. Yet they dream the impossible dreams about doing for their children what they could not do for themselves. By hook or crook, they—the parents—manage to do it when others said it couldn't be done. The members of the working class are the creative innovationists of our times. They strive to achieve the societal values and goals, are deficient in the possession of socially sanctioned means, but somehow overcome.

[3]Merton, R. 1949. *Social Structure and Social Theory* (New York: Free Press), p. 133.

The black lower class is fatalistic. No note of hope does it sing. Failure and disappointment recur repeatedly, as if they were a refrain. Unable to deal with the difficulties presented, black lower-class families withdraw. The parents appear to be uninvolved with anyone or anything. They have retreated from social organizations but not necessarily from all social relations for we know of their loyalty to their children.

The retreatist behavior of black lower-class families is sometimes described as being in opposition to the basic values and goals of social organization—a rejection of that which is socially sanctioned. This may not be the case, however, but only the way it appears. Presumably, lower-class households, like the working class, wish for family cohesion. The tie between mother and offspring is a residual family relationship indicative of this desire. Presumably, also, lower-class families, like the middle class, wish for material comforts and new experiences. Spending sprees and impulse traveling are indicative of these desires.

Because of inadequate resources, lower-class families dare not hope for the fulfillment of their wishes in a systematic and regularized way. To protect themselves from more disappointment, denial of the wish for improvement is one approach and poking fun at the struggle for social mobility is another.

A fuller explanation of the retreatist behavior of the lower class requires examination of the interaction between objective and subjective dimensions of social structure. Despite the rhetoric about self-reliance and self-sufficiency, the family members of the working class and the middle class did not make it on their own unassisted by the social system. They acknowledged their interdependence, and asked for and received help when they needed it. Upward social mobility involves giving and receiving from others. The poor are given precious little in our society and so their capacity to receive is underdeveloped. In the giving of help, we learn to love. In the receiving of assistance, we learn to trust. Because the poor have been given so little in society, the poor have not learned how to receive—which is to say, the poor have not learned how to trust.

We learn to trust before we learn to love. Love involves commitment to persons, social groups, and social organizations. The members of lower-class families can commit themselves to persons, especially the mothers to their offspring and the siblings to each other; but they cannot commit themselves to a society they have never learned to trust. Thus, the retreatist behavior of the lower-class may be a manifestation of the absence of trust rather than a rejection of social organization in favor of social disorganization.

This paper clearly demonstrates that it is inappropriate to say, "a black family is a black family is a black family." Styles of life do vary among blacks by social class. Recognition of this should serve as a corrective against stereotyping black ways of life.

The neat way in which the different black family life-styles by social class fit into the theoretical model developed by Robert Merton for explaining variation in adaptations to the social organization also suggests that all black families, including the middle-class, the working-class, and the lower-class, participate in a common system of values shared by all families, including blacks and whites in the United States.

Finally, there was evidence of limited opportunities available to blacks due largely to racial discrimination. This was a common experience of most black families of all social classes. A frequent manifestation of racial discrimination was the delimitation of economic opportunity. Inadequate financial resources frequently resulted in the joint participation of husband and wife in the labor force—a circumstance more or less pervasive among black families, especially those who were upwardly mobile.

On the basis of this analysis, one may conclude 1) that black and white families in America share a common value system, 2) that they adapt to the society and its values in different ways, largely because of racial discrimination, and 3) that the unique adaptation by blacks is further differentiated by variations in style of life by social class.

Our initial assumption that the way of life of blacks in America can be understood independent of their involvement with whites appears to be unwarranted. Moreover, the life-styles of different social classes cannot be understood apart from the rest of society.

Referring to the interdependence of blacks and whites in America, this paper ends with the statement of a modified version of the wisdom of Eliza Doolittle, created by George Bernard Shaw.

She said that she discovered the difference between a flower girl and a lady is not so much how she acts but how she is treated. Our revised version emphasizes *both* personal action *and* social reaction. We assert that the difference between the families of racial groups in the United States, and the difference between the families of various social classes within the racial groups are a result of how each family acts *as well as* how each family is treated.

Jobs and the Negro Family:
A Reappraisal

Edwin Harwood and Claire C. Hodge

In this article the authors challenge a number of stereotypes about the economic position of the Black male and female. They state that the economic position of the Black man, contrary to popular opinion, is superior to that of the Black woman, and that the economic hardship faced by Black women is of major concern to the Black family.

Louise Meriwether's recent novel, *Daddy Was a Number Runner,* deals with an adolescent Negro girl in Harlem at the depth of the Depression. Although the young heroine manages to fend off a variety of local predators—mostly whites who make sexual advances—she proves powerless to prevent the disintegration of her family, a process that becomes the dramatic anchor in the book's plot. When her father stumbles hard against New York's job-scarce labor market, her mother starts work as a domestic for a suburban housewife, at first for a few half-days a week, but, towards the end of the novel, on almost a full-time basis. She knows it wounds Dad's pride, but the children must eat. What little Dad does manage to earn, by running numbers slips for the racketeers, he squanders on bets. The conclusion is foregone. Bitter at his wife's taking relief and going to work as a domestic, he fades from the home and becomes "a streetcorner man."

None will deny that tragedies of this kind occurred. None will deny that economic recessions have posed serious problems for Negro city dwellers all along. Yet Meriwether's tale of woe relies heavily on a prevalent—and largely er- roneous—stereotype of the Negro's economic condition. This is to the effect that, relative to their menfolk, Negro women have enjoyed an advantage in the urban labor market, and that in this their situation has differed sharply from that of working-class whites. Recent fantasies about "internal colonialism" have sharpened this stereotype to the point where it is sometimes said that the black man has been kept down in order to keep him in line, and that black women have been allowed a freer economic adjustment as a part of this same strategy. These and other such notions have helped fuel the animosities of black militants during the past decade. What better justification could there be for the rage of angry young men if, as Richard Rubenstein claims in his thinly-veiled apology for black violence, *Rebels in Eden,* "young [Negro] men have been degraded by this lack of control over their lives—by their inability to get or keep jobs and the need to send their women out to clean Goldberg's floor."

This stereotype is so familiar, and so widely-accepted, that it is hard to believe it could be false. Yet false is what available evidence shows it to be. Today, even in the poorest urban neighborhoods, Negro men enjoy a clear economic superiority over Negro women, as the findings of the United States Bureau of Labor Statistics' 1968-9 Urban Employment Survey demonstrated. Moreover, and more surprising, all the evidence we have for past periods offers no significant support for the assumption that Negro women ever were advantaged in the search for jobs.

Since 1890, when separate tabulations for whites and Negroes first became available, every

From *The Public Interest* 23 (Spring 1971): 125–131. © 1971 by National Affairs, Inc. Reprinted by permission.

decennial census has revealed Negro men to have enjoyed a markedly greater diversification of jobs than Negro women. In the urban or non-agricultural labor force, this difference is particularly striking. While Negro men could be found in substantial numbers in jobs in every major industry, Negro women were concentrated in just a handful of the several hundred occupational classifications. As late as 1930, of 1.3 million Negro women in nonagricultural jobs, over one million (or roughly 85 per cent) were in domestic and personal service occupations. Over half were "laundresses not in laundries" and servants in private households. Of the Negro men outside agriculture, by contrast, less than 25 per cent (425,000 of over 2 million) were to be found in the domestic and personal service classification. When, after studying Harlem's working population at the turn of the century, George Edmund Haynes concluded that Negroes would, when given the opportunity, expand their job horizons, he could only have been referring to Negro men. For his statistics showed that over half of the men had moved into jobs in firms and businesses, whereas 90 per cent of all Negro female workers in his canvass were still confined to domestic and personal service jobs.

Taking economic dominance in its most literal sense, we might ask who held the supervisory and managerial jobs available to Negro workers then. Men did. With the exception of restaurants and boarding and lodging houses, Negro females in supervisory positions are rarely to be found at all in 1930. Second, and most contrary to popular belief, Negro men outnumbered women by heavy margins in white-collar clerical occupations (as did white men in relation to white women a generation ago). In 1930, Negro men in clerical occupations numbered almost 30,000 compared with 11,000 Negro women. In the single category, "Clerks" (except "clerks" in stores) the census located over 20,000 Negro males but only 5,000 Negro females in that year. In sum, *the historical pattern of occupational and earnings differences between the sexes reveals a striking similarity between whites and blacks, and not the reversal of roles or, as one writer phrased it, the "unnatural superiority" of women* that so many scholars have allowed themselves to believe without a careful review of the facts.

When it is argued that higher proportions of Negro women than men hold white-collar jobs today, it is forgotten that the same holds true of female whites in relation to men—simply because our economy employs more cashiers, "girl fridays," and telephone operators than it does lawyers, physicians, and corporation executives. Women moved into these more numerous white-collar occupations as men took better paying jobs in other sectors of the economy, including blue-collar jobs. It is *not* true, as is often assumed, that female white-collar workers, black or white, earn more than male blue-collar workers. In 1969, annual earnings for Negro men in white-collar, blue-collar, and service (excluding private household) occupations were higher on average than earnings for Negro women in clerical and sales jobs. In the top bracket of the earnings scale, Negro female professional workers rank third, following Negro male professionals and managerial workers. However, these women, who are predominantly elementary and secondary school teachers, nurses, or medical and health technicians, are only 10 per cent of all employed Negro women; they earn on average a mere $17 more per year than Negro male craftsmen and foremen. Twice as many Negro women are still to be found in the lowest paying of all job classifications, private household work.

Thus, the facts simply do not support the notion that the Negro man had a rougher go in the urban labor market than the Negro woman. On the contrary, his economic problems shrivel by comparison with hers. If she had to work, she found a limited range of jobs to choose from, most of them in private households, which paid the lowest wages. In New York City 70 years ago, more than half (53 per cent) of the Negro women in service work earned less than five dollars a week, whereas only 28 per cent of Negro male service workers had earnings that low. Elevator operator, butler, fireman, houseman, even "usefulman," paid better than "general housework, chambermaid, and laundress."

The argument for the Negro female's advantaged labor market position fails precisely where one might expect it to be strongest—in times of economic depression. Consider the facts turned up by the Division of Social Research of the Works Progress Administration (WPA). A thorough study of urban workers on relief in 79 major cities in the early 1930's was published in the two-volume study, *Urban Workers on Relief.* We learn:

1. The single occupational group that had

the heaviest representation among relief applicants was "servants." Women, and particularly Negro women, were disproportionately represented in the unskilled service jobs included in that category. Among Negro women, a large majority were general houseworkers and laundresses.

2. Negro women on relief were twice as apt to be employed at the time of the study as Negro men on relief—but they enjoyed no special economic advantage because of that fact. The WPA researchers point out that the women earned less than men (17 cents an hour against the male's 25 cents an hour). And because she worked fewer than half the median hours her working male counterpart obtained in a week (17 hours for her; 35 for him), her median *weekly* earnings ($2.80) were less than half of what he earned ($6.30).

To argue that Negro women had the edge in the Depression labor market simply because at any given time she was more apt to get some job in unskilled service work is to rest the argument for her superiority on a shallow and incomplete statistic. In any case white men faced the same situation in relation to white females. Negro men may very well have been unemployed for longer stretches, but *when they did get jobs they worked more hours per week and earned substantially more money, such that in the aggregate they may very well have been doing much better by far than Negro women.* What proponents of the "dominant-female" view have never established is crucial: Did the female domestic work more days during the course of a given *year* in and out of depressions? The fact that in a given week she could often locate some job does not prove that she had more work over a longer span. Did she receive anywhere near the annual earnings received by a male laborer? According to Charles S. Johnson, research director for the National Urban League, women domestics in Waterbury, Connecticut were averaging three dollars a day in 1923 in work "that could rarely be secured for more than four days a week." Wages for Negro men averaged $4.38 per day; men in skilled manual jobs earned as much as five dollars and six dollars per day.

3. What the WPA researchers chose to emphasize in their study is even more significant in view of the strenuous attempt scholars have made to stress the differences in the adjustments of blacks and whites to a recession. The WPA study emphasized that *both* Negro and white males were unemployed for longer stretches than their female counterparts because *both* white and Negro men had a more diverse occupational distribution. This meant that, though they enjoyed the higher earnings that jobs in industrial and commercial firms paid in good times, they would suffer longer stretches of unemployment during a recession. It is reasonable to think that the casual service employment which women willingly took was not an acceptable alternative to either the white or black male worker, in any case. Reports issued by the United States Employment Service during the Depression years showed that a large proportion of the job placements in household work were for very short periods, often only for a given day, which supports the WPA's finding that most women obtained casual laboring jobs characterized by high turnover. Household workers in Wisconsin, for example, were so poorly paid that the state set a minimum weekly wage of $6 for a 50 hour week if board alone was furnished. We have no comparable data on the conditions of employment and pay in service jobs available to men, but we can be reasonably sure that the male janitor or porter, for example, would have been guaranteed a job of longer duration at higher pay.

The irony here is that the facts gathered by the WPA research team require something on the order of an about-face in our thinking. If Negro men had made even *further* advances in occupations and earnings, and hence in expectations as well, beyond what they had already achieved, then they would have experienced *longer* stretches of unemployment. They would have been more reluctant to take casual low-paying jobs. *Their problem of finding an acceptable job would have approached in severity that of white males who held the record for unbroken spells of unemployment!*

Clearly, it was because most reform-minded scholars wanted to do the Negro good, not ill, that they were led consistently to emphasize the *differences* between white and black Americans in their performances in the labor market. Only thus could special remedial action urged on the Negro's behalf have a plausible basis. Moreover, the troublesome issue of Negro marital instability had to be explained. If this could be linked to an economic plight not shared by white Americans, then it followed that most scholars would first seek out and then emphasize some critical difference observed in the adjustment of blacks and whites to the labor market.

It is important to keep two facts in mind: First, that an economic explanation was not logically compulsory for understanding family instability. E. Franklin Frazier's early monograph, *The Negro Family in Chicago,* hardly mentions employment handicaps—let alone handicaps peculiar to the Negro—in accounting for the disintegration of families in the slum. If Frazier later changed his mind, it was most probably because others were changing theirs, and his professors at the University of Chicago no longer insisted that the adjustment of Negro migrants—whom Frazier called peasants—fit the same model they had used earlier to explain the adjustment of European peasants who had come to Chicago from Poland and southern Italy. (Then, family disintegration was attributed to the clash between a secular urban and a traditional agrarian ethos.)

Secondly, even granting that the antecedent of an aberrant social pattern might be an aberrant economic pattern, was there one and only one important and critical difference between whites and blacks in their relation to the occupational order? Was it not possible that some other difference had been overlooked that might explain the instability of Negro marriages just as well?

If it is hard to imagine that the working Negro woman could resent her husband, or he her, on the basis of the jobs, wages, and the amount of work she could command in relation to him, then we must turn to another clue in trying to answer the riddle of the urban North's peculiar institution—the matriarchal Negro family. For clearly it was the woman who faced near insurmountable obstacles in getting jobs beyond the level of unskilled domestic work, and this heavy concentration of Negro women in domestic service suggests an intriguing alternative explanation. She had not just a second job, but a job in a second *household,* with a second family. How this competition between obligations to two households could tear at the fabric of her own family's solidarity we can just imagine—not alone in the burden of doing double duty with long hours spent away from her own home, but also in the continual awareness of the differences in living standards, the competition of dual loyalties and possibly of dual affections.

If the status of the employing household mattered to the domestic, how might this have affected her perception of the conditions in her own? Negro women at service in Carlisle, Pennsylvania, a contributor to *Gunton's Magazine* (January, 1896) observed, "will only serve in a Negro family when hard pressed for money, and then for a few days only." If, as the writer suggests, the domestic was accustomed to taking home foodstuffs from her employer's table, such considerations of status would make sense. Might it also, along with all the other invidious comparisons to be made, condition her to think less highly of the breadwinner in her own family? Or, taking the problem from the other end: Did her husband find her efforts at home less than satisfactory because she had to do so much for the other household? It is hard, perhaps impossible, to arrive at clear-cut answers to these questions. We can only hypothesize that if Negro women had had access to a broader range of jobs beyond household work fewer complications would have entered into the picture.

It is instructive that white female houseworkers, including the many European immigrant women who took domestic jobs, seem to have solved the dual-household problem by staying single for as long as they worked, and then quitting domestic service upon marriage. Doubtless the strong sentiments of Catholicism about the requirements of normal family life insured this outcome in the case of the Irish, for example, who had a tradition of delaying marriage until economic conditions permitted. The available evidence on this point is sketchy, but a 1925 study of working women in four cities revealed that domestics in Passaic, New Jersey, who were overwhelmingly native or foreign-born whites, were much more apt to be single at the time of the canvass than were domestics in Jacksonville, Florida, who were overwhelmingly black. Whereas almost half (45 per cent) of Jacksonville domestics were either married, or married but separated, only a quarter (24 per cent) of Passaic's domestics were thus classified. Mary V. Robinson's report to the Women's Bureau in the United States Department of Labor a year earlier established two facts from a survey of applicants for domestic work in Baltimore: Negro women were clearly reluctant to take jobs that required living in. Only 36 per cent of the black women stated a willingness to do so, whereas 80 per cent of white females were prepared to live in. Mary Robinson related this fact to another—namely, the significantly higher proportion of Negro women compared with white females who remained in domestic service after marriage—and she came to a judgment about the difficulties of carrying the work of two households that should not surprise us:

[Matrimony] usually means added responsibilities which tend to demand more time than many women in domestic service are able to find for such important private matters, especially if they are compelled to live in the home of employers or to have the usual hours of labor expected in domestic service. When women live in the homes of their employers, they rarely have opportunity to go to their own homes more than once or twice a week, and can have little private life with their families.

At the turn of the century, a researcher assigned to canvass Sandy Springs, Maryland, reported to the United States Department of Labor that he found a tragic division between the Negro woman's "real family" and her "economic family" (the employing household) that her heavy concentration in domestic work had caused. Noting the heavy turnover of domestic workers and how better wages in the bigger cities north lured girls away, he concluded that "the future of the Negro race would seem to be more in danger from a certain general looseness of the younger generations of women than from lawlessness of the younger generations of men."

Certainly more research is needed to settle this historical issue. Again returning to the 1930 Census we find industrial cities in which a very low proportion of Negro women are holding jobs—Flint, Gary and Youngstown, for example. Perhaps domestic work was harder to find in small industrial cities than in the large northern cities having a wealthier citizenry. Were marriages correspondingly more stable in cities where, regardless of the women's interest in or need of work, jobs for domestics simply did not exist in the number needed? We do not know.

Accepting this alternative view of the Negro family problem does not require that we refuse to consider the Negro male's hardships, or their effect on his role in the family. Certainly if his rents had been lower and his wages higher, fewer of his women would have found it necessary to seek out domestic jobs. And it is quite proper to think that family stress would be closely associated with cyclical business fluctuations that affected the man's employment, as Daniel P. Moynihan showed in his 1965 report, The Negro Family: The Case for National Action. But we still need to know why Negroes, of all groups, were disproportionately affected in their family life by bad times that in their season hit every working-class group, and hit much harder in times past than now. This requires looking for that combination of unique historical experiences peculiar to many Negro Americans. The "peculiar institution" of the south, slavery, was very probably the most important factor in the emergence of the peculiar institution of the urban north, the female-headed family. But if an economic cause is to be sought in addition, we suggest that it may have been the Negro woman's handicaps in the labor market, not the man's.

Part Four
Black Families and the Future

Alternative Family Life Styles

Making sociological predictions about family life is risky. Few, for instance, could have projected what has happened to the American family in the last fifteen years. Certain trends were apparent but the acceleration of those trends caught many by surprise. In the case of the Black family, the research literature is still sparse and biased, and there have been very few attempts to discuss the Black family of the future or alternative family life styles. Certain signs of the future can be seen, however, in existing social conditions for Blacks and in the trends in sexual behavior, fertility patterns, sex role changes, and marital adjustment.

Some adaptations to alternative life styles will no doubt be made because large numbers of Blacks, especially middle-class Blacks, are taking on the values of the majority culture. Family relations in the majority culture are changing and many Blacks will probably follow the trends. However, Blacks as a group will continue to face certain deep-seated and widespread problems. High unemployment among Black men and women will continue to have serious ramifications for family life, especially for lower-class Blacks. All classes, however, will have to adapt to the increasingly critical shortage of men.

Up to this time the shortage of males has been compensated for by a type of serial polygyny, whereby a Black man has more than one wife in a lifetime, although never at the same time. Some men remain married but have relations with other women. This kind of sharing of men may be a necessity for a group with such an imbalanced sex ratio. However, where men and women have been strongly socialized into monogamous values, such sharing gives rise to many conflicts and intensifies the forces leading to marital disruption.

In the future, alternative family life styles should be well thought out and implemented so as to promote individual and group harmony.

This section examines single motherhood and homosexuality as alternative life styles. Single motherhood is a response to the shortage of males; homosexuality is one cause of the shortage. The article by White indicates that increasing numbers of unmarried, middle-class Black women consciously choose to have children out of wedlock. Some will adopt a child, others will bear one with the idea that it is better to be a happy, unmarried mother than a miserable, married one. Benton's article on what it's like to be Black and gay is one of the few accounts of this growing phenomenon among Black men and women. In the final paper in this chapter, Staples attempts to summarize the trends in Black family life and some of the forces behind them.

Public Policy and Black Families

The American belief in the sacredness of the family may account for the fact that this country has rarely had clearly defined plans or policy concerning the family. The closest thing has been the welfare system, which has actually worked to disrupt more families than it kept together. With the continuing decline of the extended family—once a valuable backup to the nuclear family—some sort of family support systems seems necessary, especially for the Black family. The central problems facing Black families more than ever require remedy through well-formulated public policy and through action programs addressed to their needs.

Scott delineates the needs of Black women

in our society. She describes American Black women as a lower-income group with a high rate of unemployment, concentrated in low-level, service-related jobs. Even if jobs were available, unemployed Black women would have problems because quality day care centers are often not accessible to them. Some critics of expanding day care programs argue that taking care of children is a function of the family, not the government. This argument ignores the realities of today's families, where the choice is between having low-cost, government-supervised care of children or making women second-class citizens.

These same critics advocate involuntary birth control and sterilization, especially for low-income Black women, who are stereotyped as irresponsible child breeders. Scott notes that such programs often have higher priority than prenatal health services or sex education programs for Black adolescents. She suggests a number of ways to assist Black women in maintaining healthy families, including elevating their job status and their pay; developing high-quality day care facilities; and promoting research on the mental and physical health problems of Black women, on the needs of the aged Black woman, and on the role of women in the media.

In his article, Staples reviews the past relationship of government to the structure of Black family life. He finds that, in general, the government's efforts have been few in number and have been sporadic, misguided, and ineffective. For the future he sees increasing numbers of female-headed households of below-average income and above-average number of children. He suggests a public policy relevant to Black families, one which includes a guaranteed income, elimination of sex discrimination in employment, community-controlled day care centers, and a child development program.

14

Alternative Family Life Styles

Single Motherhood

Joyce White

This article shows the increasingly changing mood of many American Black women between the ages of 21 and 33. They seem unaffected by any stigma of bearing illegitimate children. Their attitude appears to be a function of several factors; a shortage of eligible Black males, a desire to be mother rather than wife, and feelings about abortion. The author presents case interviews of three Black single mothers.

Ten years ago, all the women whom I knew to be pregnant and unmarried were "girls in trouble." They certainly hadn't planned it that way. And in those days, if a woman wanted to abort, she erroneously thought she could by jumping down two flights of stairs or drinking too much quinine. Today, those methods of coping with unwanted pregnancies are outmoded, and legalized abortions are available in almost every state.

But lately, I've noticed a strange thing. More and more single Black women are having children out of wedlock because they want to. Most don't have a man lined up, either. In the main, they are taking on the challenge of becoming a single mother, despite the availability of abortions.

I first wondered if there really was a trend towards choosing single motherhood while at a cocktail party a few months ago. A group of chic, young Black women, all unmarried, was talking about the subject. All of them said they knew either an unmarried friend or relative who, when faced with pregnancy, had chosen childbirth rather than abortion. As glasses were refilled and conversations became more intense, several said

that if they didn't find the right man to marry they too would opt for unwed motherhood.

Several reasons were behind their voiced decisions. One or two women took a moral stand against abortions, a few said they desired to be a mother more than a wife, and several pointed out that the Black man shortage had reached an epidemic level.

One woman summed up the availability of Black men this way: "The prisons are filled with Black men; the Vietnam War killed a larger percentage of Black men than anybody else; there is the drug problem; and even more insidious, Miss Ann is capturing a fair share *and* Mr. Charlie certainly isn't marrying Sapphire! Every desirable Black man I meet is *already* hooked up with another woman."

When I left the cocktail party, my curiosity about single women as mothers had been fully piqued. I was eager to know if many single Black women were really making this choice, and what influences were responsible. I was even more anxious to find out how on earth did they manage rearing a child alone.

The next day, I got on the phone and called people I hadn't seen in a long time and, after a brief conversation, asked the question: "Do you know a single, solvent Black woman in her late twenties or early thirties who chose childbirth rather than abortion?" In most cases, the answer, yes.

Before the week was over, I had made contact with 12 single mothers or mothers-to-be. Ten of them were willing to talk with me about their experiences—all were between the ages of 21 and

---

33, half were college graduates, three of whom had gone on to graduate school. Of the other five, two had attended college, one for a year, another for three years, and three were high school graduates.

None of the women had gotten pregnant on purpose—although three made ambivalent statements such as "I guess I wanted to get pregnant. I wasn't using any birth control." Three others said that their pregnancy was simply a careless accident; they had either "forgotten to take the Pill that week" or "left my diaphragm at home." Four had become pregnant when they were in their teens, then so naive about sex that they thought pregnancy came from swallowing watermelon seeds or French-kissing. Only two were strongly opposed to abortions.

The three women whose stories follow are individuals, not composites. Their names [have been] changed, [and] in some cases, certain identifying facts have been altered.

Tall, graceful Bernice greeted me at her eleventh floor apartment wearing billowing yellow pants, a tight-fitting, black bodyshirt, a long scarf tied gypsy fashion around her head and holding a burning stick of incense in her hand. Her three-year-old son, Eric, was standing on his tricycle in the center of the room.

While Bernice busied herself with house chores, she talked about her varied career. At the age of 33, she has worked as a biology researcher, a truant officer and school teacher. In her spare time, she dabbles in photography, astrology, poetry and essays and works with SLICK, a cultural organization. Currently a biology lecturer at a New York college, Bernice plans to change her career; she wants to become a full-time booking agent for musicians.

Bernice became deeply involved with a man, had set up an apartment with him and, at the age of 29, ended up pregnant.

"I guess I wanted to get pregnant," she says. "I knew that I was ovulating and I wasn't using any type of birth control. However, when I discovered that I really was pregnant, I panicked, and even went to have an abortion. Abortion wasn't yet legalized in New York. The scene in the abortion waiting room reminded me of a funeral parlor. It seemed that everybody there was dressed in dark blue or black. The reality of what I was about to do finally hit me. I got up and left."

Bernice says that her family, who lives in the South, wasn't jubilant about her pregnancy, but they didn't threaten to disown her. Her problem came from the baby's father as the relationship began to sour. Their relationship lasted less than a year after her son's birth. "He became abusive, jealous, wouldn't take me anywhere or help with chores or with the baby. I don't have any family in New York and had to tend to a new baby and manage a household all alone."

Six months after they split up, Bernice met Harry Whitaker, piano player, arranger and composer and the man with whom she is getting ready to share an apartment.

"I'm not against marriage as an institution or against going through the legal aspects of the ceremony. Marriage makes things simpler. However, I don't know when I will get married, I'm not concerned about it. One day the spirit will hit, Harry and I will say 'this is the day' and off to city hall we'll go. Then we will call up friends and have a party."

Bernice says that she is not worried about what effect her unmarried status will have on her son. "If I have any regrets about breaking off with Eric's father, it's because I know that my son has been affected by not having his father around. At this time I can't say just how he has been affected." Pausing briefly, she said, "I guess you can say there is nothing like the love of your father."

Until he was three, Eric's paternal grandmother took care of him while Bernice worked—now he spends the day at a nearby daycare center. Bernice believes that the daycare center is important for her child's development, but wishes that she could have been a full-time mother until her son was at least two years old. "Since I was the sole support, I had to return to work as quickly as possible. That's one disadvantage of being a single mother."

As I was getting ready to leave, Bernice said with a twinkle in her eye, "My period is four days late, I hope I am pregnant. Harry and I want a girl."

Bernice entered into single motherhood with a good education, a solid career and an optimistic outlook on life. Basha, on the other hand, is a woman who was born and raised in the chaotic throes of a central city.

Basha stood waiting for me at the door of her street-level East Bronx apartment dressed in a long caftan, gelé and a wristful of silver bangles. Glancing nervously at the huddle of young men gathered on the littered street corner, she quickly locked the door and led me to her sparsely furnished room in a crowded seven-room apartment which she shares with her mother, an aunt, two brothers, a sister and her daughter.

Seated on her studio bed, I asked her if she had considered an abortion. "I don't believe in abortions," she answers. "You never know what you are bringing into this world. A child is life. It's something to live for when you are down and out."

Eight months pregnant, 22 years old, with smooth, coffee brown skin, dancing eyes, soft voice and a slim figure despite her bulging stomach, Basha knows how it feels to be "down and out."

In 1968, she graduated from a New York high school with an 85 average and entered a local college as a full-time student. "My mother was very proud of me. She felt that finally one of her five children was going to turn into something."

However, things began to go wrong for Basha. "I became dissatisfied with the course of my life," she recalls with a perplexed look on her face. "I wanted to do something—something that would assert my Blackness.

"I became bored with college. My grades fell and the situation here at home was almost unbearable—seven people live in this apartment. My sister refuses to work and support her child, one of my brothers is suffering from a nervous breakdown and the other one is on drugs. I had to get a job so I could move to my own place."

Until Basha was 18, she attended a Baptist church every Sunday, sang in the choir, taught Sunday school and participated in a variety of church club activities. In 1969, she gave up Christianity, adopted the Hebrew name Basha, and proclaimed herself a Black Israelite.

With three years of college behind her, Basha took a leave from school and started working as an assistant teacher in a daycare center. Then, less than a year after leaving school, still living at home, unmarried, Basha became pregnant by the first man she had sexual intercourse with. "I was a virgin until I was 21," she says with a slight smile.

"Even though I knew about birth control, I wasn't using any," she continues. "I don't believe in the Pill. I'm against all those chemicals in the body." Twisting nervously she says, "I didn't really plan to get pregnant, but I didn't care if it happened."

Confronted with the impending birth, Basha never considered an abortion, but she says that she and the baby's father thought about marriage and bought a license. A few days later, Basha changed her mind, and the license expired.

"Neither one of us has an apartment," she says referring to the baby's father. "He lives in a rooming house and I'm here. Setting up an apartment involves so many things—rent, moving expenses, furniture, plus it costs a lot of money to have a baby. Suppose I had rushed into marriage and things hadn't worked out. I would have been stuck out there with a baby, a new apartment and bills up over my head . . . all alone. At least now I am eligible for Medicaid." (In many cases, if a young woman finds herself jobless, pregnant, unmarried and her man can't be found, Medicaid will pay for all medical and hospital expenses.)

"Anyway," she adds, raising her voice slightly, "as far as I am concerned I *am* married. Marriage is an agreement between two people and you don't need any legal sanctions to make this agreement official. I'm in love with the father of my baby and he's in love with me.

"I know that Tony (the baby's father) will always be there and our child will feel his influence. Children don't have hangups about illegitimacy. Those feelings are instilled by parents and society."

Basha says that one day she may go and stand in front of some judge for that "little piece of paper." Right now she says that she is more concerned about caring for her baby.

"My child will give me a real incentive to leave this neighborhood, to finish college," she says. "I have gotten used to the junkies on the corner, the debris, the dilapidated buildings, the rampant crime. But with a child coming, it's important for me to get out of here. I don't want my child to become used to it."

Three weeks later Basha called and with just a hint of enthusiasm in her voice, announced that she was the mother of a seven-pound boy.

After expressing my best wishes, I asked as tactfully as possible, who was going to keep the baby when she returned to work. "I really don't know how I will manage," she said hesitantly, "but I'm sure that I will work something out."

Janet is a big, brassy Texan. The first time I talked with the 28-year-old freelance writer her delivery date was imminent, and she was preparing for motherhood the way Napoleon waged battles.

As soon as I was inside her Manhattan apartment, Janet pulled out the blender she will use to make baby food, the new washing machine that she bought to wash diapers and the 14 books on child care that she had read.

"I probably won't have another child as a single mother," she says laughingly. "It's too expensive. It takes money to enrich a child's life." She got up and offered me a plate of cookies and iced tea, and then went on. "I plan to stay home and take care of my baby. I'm against leaving children all day with baby-sitters or in daycare centers."

Janet was quick to explain her plans after the baby's birth. She reeled off a list of freelance assignments that she has lined up for the coming year, including articles for such disparate publications as the *New York Daily News* and *Ms.* magazine. Janet has also received a cash advance on a book she is writing. "Everything about this pregnancy, paying off the hospital bills, rent, food, clothing, etcetera, has been planned to the last detail," she says proudly.

Despite her enthusiasm for motherhood, Janet insists that her pregnancy was an accident, but admits that subconsciously she probably desired it. A doctor had told her that she had a hormone deficiency and couldn't have children. Janet proved him wrong.

Faced with pregnancy, Janet didn't have to cope with thoughts of marriage or abortion. The father of the baby was "already involved in a marriage situation," and she never considered abortion. Janet likes children so much that she once looked into the possibility of adopting a child as a single woman. "I'm not against abortions for those who want them," she cautions. "Nobody has the right to tell a woman what she can do with her body. I *am* against forced marriage.

"Let's face it," she adds, echoing the same sentiments I had heard at the cocktail party, "there just aren't enough Black men to go around. Many of my friends who are around say that if they aren't married by the age of 30, they will consider having a child. Furthermore, the whole concept of

marriage is changing. In the next ten years, you will see more and more one-parent families and these will be women who aren't on welfare."

Janet said that during a visit to her family in Texas she had expected neighbors to point their fingers and waggle their tongues, but, surprisingly, everybody was excited about her pregnancy. "I guess they realized that I am a full-grown woman and can handle the responsibilities arising from my actions. If I were 17 and pregnant, it would be a different situation."

Growing somber she says, "Pregnancy is such a beautiful time in a woman's life. It does get lonely when you don't have someone around to share the experience with, to feel the baby's movement and to help make decisions."

A few minutes later, her high spirit restored, Janet followed me to the door talking about the virtues of natural childbirth, breast feeding and the car that she plans to buy after the baby arrives. "A car is very necessary when you have a baby you must be able to move around and show your child things." . . .

A week later, Janet brought in a lusty, eight-pound boy named Jon Amilcar, in honor of Amilcar Cabral, the Mozambique freedom fighter.

When I saw Janet again, she was in a bubbly mood. Her mother and sister came in from Texas to be with her during childbirth and she was without a trace of postpartum blues.

Holding her eight-day-old son like any cautious mother, she says, "I still believe in abortions for those who want them. But every time I look at my son, I realize that he was once a tiny cell which multiplied a million times and turned into a human being. The whole experience is too fantastic for me to destroy. In the future, I'll be careful so I won't get pregnant."

Whether or not these women reflect a "new" crop of Black women is a subject that can be debated for hours. But one thing is for sure: these single mothers were less weighed down by public opinion than women I knew just ten years ago. And even more surprising, all of them felt that they were perfectly capable of rearing a child alone. However, most admitted that their task would be easier if another person was around. One woman, the mother of a nine-month-old girl, captured the sentiments of the group when she said: "I would rather be a happy unmarried mother than a miserable married one."

Case History:
"I'm a Black Homosexual"

Levi Benton

In this article the author discusses, along with the problems of society's acceptance of gay people, the pressures and rejections experienced by Black homosexuals. He compares life-styles and sexual preferences of Black and white gays. Mr. Benton (a pseudonym) is a Black homosexual living in New York City.

A comparison between homosexual attitudes before the Civil Rights Movement of 1954, and since Gay Liberation, shows that many prejudices remain. Black homosexuals who preferred members of their own race before 1954 still do. The same is true with those Whites who preferred Whites. If there seems to be more homosexual integration, that is due to greater freedom of movement for those who always wanted integration, rather than any widespread conversion. (The reference to Afro-American homosexuals as "Black" is arbitrary. The Afro-American homosexual is still a "Negro" for the most part. He thinks "White," and he acts "White." He wants "White" things, total integration, and above all he wants his black pigmentation to be as invisible as possible.)

Those Whites who used to believe that Blacks carry strong genital odors, still think so. Blacks who were sure that body insects are more likely to be transmitted in a White and White or White and Black, rather than a Black and Black relationship, retain that opinion. There is some truth in both convictions. Blacks do not practice oral sex as widely as do Whites, so less emphasis is put on perfuming the genital areas. It is still believed that the hair texture of Whites attracts body insects more than kinky textured Black hair. Neither matter is true for all members of either race, and with better hygiene practices, both can be avoided.

The question of whether venereal disease is more prevalent among Blacks or Whites is still debated among both races. Statistics suggest that Blacks are reported with VD more frequently than Whites. But most Blacks can seldom afford private doctor fees. Municipal and voluntary hospitals are required to report VD cases; private doctors are not, and seldom do. What is alarming is that statistics show a more steady rise of venereal diseases among all homosexuals than among heterosexuals.

Promiscuity among Black homosexuals is a new trend. Before the Civil Rights and Gay Liberation Movements, those Black homosexuals who were not transvestites, or overtly effeminate, lived rather invisible lives. There was a scarcity of Black men. Gay barrooms and cruising trails were "White only" before 1954. Black homosexuals were thus very "marriage" conscious, and such relationships lasted much longer than similar arrangements among Whites. Many Blacks bought their homes and entertained there, rather than in lounges and barrooms. If a Black did not have a permanent lover, he could find one at a drag party in a gay home.

The younger ones are taking advantage of the new freedom, but there are many instances to prove that they are more frustrated and lonely than their elders. The majority of Whites who are homosexually interested in Blacks are misfits.

The young misfit is the White who is not comfortable among other Whites. He might desire a Black mate because he senses an identity between his own feelings of insecurity and the myth of Black inferiority.

He is likely to be unskilled and usually unemployed. He may be a struggling White college student, or may be mentally or physically defective. Even though his Black partner is sound in body and mind, the White misfit clings to the myth of his "superiority."

The truth about integration in the United

From *Sexology* (March 1972): 15–18. Reprinted by permission of the SXO Corp.

States is that Whites who are accepted by their families and society seldom take any interest in Blacks. This is as true with heterosexuals as it is with homosexuals. In the gay life, Whites who have Black friends usually have only Black friends.

There are old White misfits in the gay life, too. Their problem is that the older these White homosexuals get, the more they generally desire young boys. This is not as often true with old Black homosexuals. So the old White homosexual, who shunned and laughed at all Blacks when he was young and desirable, now seeks a young Black lover.

The young Black who accepts the old White usually thinks he is making "Whitey" pay up. This makes it a sugar-daddy relationship. The old White homosexual pays for his lover's education, sheltering, food, and clothing. He becomes a "slave" to the young Black, with all of the incompatibility and mental cruelty which comes with slavery. Five years is about the longest these "marriages" last.

One of the attractions of White men to Black Americans is the stereotyped image of superior Black sexuality, from the days of slave-studding and breeding. It is assumed that since Cassius Clay is more physically beautiful than the average man, he is also more sexually potent. Since Black singing stars have suggestive lyrics in their songs, which they sing with gestures, it is assumed that the Black entertainer must be representative of a whole race. What is really insulting to the humanity of Blacks is that few Whites are attracted to Blacks because a Black may have more power in his brain than in his penis or muscles.

If Blacks get little respect from Whites, even in the gay world, they can find it among themselves at times. Family acceptance of a homosexual is still a problem. If one is passive and introverted, it is simpler to conceal homosexuality and be accepted as "straight." A Black man who dates girls and marries one, is looked upon with less scorn when other Blacks hear that "the boy is living with some old girlish faggot now." It is always the other person who is homosexual.

The Black family—and the Black woman, especially—still requires that a male exhibit some superman qualities. He ought to be physically strong and superior in some sport. If he is, the fact that he may have homosexual traits is secondary.

Mothers and sisters of both races tend to recognize and accept homosexuality in a son or brother more readily. The Black mother will encourage a gay son to excel in a "gay career": hairstyling, teaching, piano, ballet, drama, secretarial work, etc.

A White mother seldom thinks in those terms. She may try to aid her son's emotional adjustment, and even go to gay bars with him. She may do some matchmaking in his interest. If she learns gay terminology, she might refer to her White son as "my daughter." This means that such a man can discuss his problems more freely with his mother.

The same reluctance and fear shown by the Black mother is found in the Black wife. She will tolerate her husband's bisexuality so long as he never admits it to her. Compared to Black heterosexual husbands, the homosexual or bisexual husband is often more considerate, cooperative, and dedicated to family and home. He is likely to be more loving and more successful economically. Once her bisexual husband shows a trait of weakness, however, the Black wife often becomes domineering, leading to a breakup.

Perhaps the greatest rise in the homosexual population reflects tastes acquired during prison terms, and the situation of separated or divorced "straights." These men are often "role players" because they have trouble accepting their homosexuality. Their motive for coming into "the life" is often to escape responsibilities to family and society, and to enjoy homosexual licenses and freedoms. These are the brutes in gay life.

The ex-convict and the divorced also constitute much of the stream of homosexual prostitution. Alleged Black homosexuals are seldom found making their living from prostitution. The "butch," "straight" types solicit up and down the 42nd Streets of America, preying upon lonely homosexuals.

What sort of laws would help the homosexual? It is senseless to make laws prohibiting, or merely permitting something that has existed for centuries. Rather, we should enact statutes which protect the homosexual against crimes such as those committed on him by "straight male studs." There should be laws which protect property rights when a homosexual couple break up, and which guarantee freedom of movement and association for separating homosexuals. There is more harm done by one gay person against another than by police, or the law, or society.

Rehabilitation and social counseling are desperately needed for all homosexuals, to help them adjust to a life of common sense and moderation. The new concept is that a man need not think or act like a woman in order to be a homosexual. The current unisex fashions have contributed to that feeling, and a "Queen" is regarded not only as illegal, but obnoxious even to other homosexuals. As one recently put it, "She is a tired bitch who runs in drag these days."

Counseling is needed for homosexuals in everything from interpersonal relationships for happier unions to the problems of their sexual practices. Not only venereal diseases, but hepatitis, hemorrhoids, hernia, and cancer are on the rise. A great deal of education could come through literary channels which presently exploit homosexuals through pornography and sensationalism.

The Mattachine Society, like the NAACP, has more respect outside its sphere than within. Yet, its aim is to present homosexual life to the world as something which mature, responsible, and decent individuals can practice with moderation. As homosexuals fight for "liberation," they might be reminded that such an organization can help them more than irresponsible activist gestures.

Change and Adaptation in the Black Family

Robert Staples

This article gives special attention to social-psychological trends and the adaptability of the Black family to rapid social changes. The author provides a potpourri of changing social attitudes and habits of the different ideological factions in the Black community. The emphasis is on preserving the Black family in positive ways so as to provide a strong backbone for the Black race.

One of the most fluid institutions in American life is the family. Probably in no other sphere of our society have such rapid and profound changes taken place. While the changes are most significant for white Americans, Blacks too are influenced to some degree by the same forces. Among the most visible trends are the increase in sexual permissiveness, challenges to the traditional concept of woman's role, more divorces, and reductions in the fertility rate. Although Blacks are part of these dynamics, their different history and needs preclude any convergence of their family life style with that of white families.

There is considerable disagreement over whether a revolution in sexual behavior has occurred. Some argue that only the public acknowledgment of past sexual behavior has happened, giving the appearance of change. Yet, it is impossible to deny there is greater sexual permissiveness and a revolution in attitudes. The most significant change has been the sexual liberation of middle-class white women. There are many indications that the double standard of sexual conduct is disappearing or being modified.

This change in male attitudes about female sexuality has had little effect on Black female sexuality, however, since Black women have rarely been subjected to the same sexual restrictions as white women. Previously, the sexual liberation of Black women had been the source of the white American stereotype of Afro-Americans as morally loose. In reality, Black women escaped the fate of many white women who were condemned to premarital chastity and marital frigidity. The healthy attitudes Blacks have toward sex have aided them in avoiding some of the "deviant" sexual actions more common to whites. One finds a much lower incidence of mate swapping, homosexuality, transvestism, pornography, and incest in the Black population. However, Blacks have shared in the general sexual freedom of whites, especially the Black middle class. There is a

Adapted from *Introduction to Black Sociology* (New York: McGraw-Hill, 1976, pp. 136–141. © 1976 by McGraw-Hill Book Company. Reprinted by permission.

greater acceptance of sexual cohabitation, of different forms of sexual expression, of out-of-wedlock births, and so on, among today's Black middle class.

A big part of the sexual revolution has been the challenge to the traditional concept of the woman's role in society. White women are demanding equality in employment and in their legal rights; they are seeking to share responsibility for raising children, and to be freed of the liabilities only women face in the United States. Many Black women see the feminist movement as being anti-male, anti-children, anti-sex, and anti-family; therefore, few Black women are involved in the movement because many of its demands do not seem relevant to their needs. For instance, motherhood and marriage are two institutions that have been denied them in the past. Because they had to work, many were deprived of the time to enjoy their children. Many cannot afford the luxury of marriage, or the conditions of their lives do not provide it.

Many of the methods and goals of the women's liberation movement, however, are important to Black women. As a result of women declaring their independence from the domination of men, there will be a greater acceptance of women heading families by themselves. Perhaps society will then make provisions for eliminating some of the problems associated with female-headed households, for example, child care facilities. Although the demand for equal employment opportunities and income equality for women and men in the same jobs is very important to all women, Black women are more victimized by employment and income discrimination against women. The assumption that women are not supporting their families themselves is one reason they are so low-paid. Because Black women are more likely than white women to be heads of households, they are hurt more by this discriminatory salary structure.

The shortage of Black males available for marriage may force Black women to rethink the idea of the monogamous marriage that lasts forever. There simply are not enough Black males. Perhaps some convergence of white and Black marital patterns is possible. White women, too, face a shortage of 5 million males due to the higher infant mortality rate for white males. Also, the continued failure of marriage to meet the emotional needs of Black women could bring about a willingness to consider more radical life styles.

There is some indication of a homogenization of Black family life styles. This mass family pattern will not be based on the white, middle-class nuclear family model. Rather, the increasing nativist sentiments among Black youth may result in a family system based on a combination of African and Afro-American cultural systems, which will transcend the class and regional variations that now exist. While some white Americans are questioning whether the family as an institution can survive, Blacks may decide that it must become stronger and more relevant to their lives. As the Black youth of America—the group most imbued with the spirit of Black nationalism—becomes the majority of the Black population, this process of Africanizing the Black family may be accelerated. This will depend on whether or not the forces of racial integration and movement into the middle class lead Blacks toward assimilation and acculturation or toward the crystallizing of an Afro-American identity.

Internal Adaptations

The changes in the interior of the Black family, while ideologically in the direction of pan-Africanism, are statistically in the direction of assimilation and acculturation. We can see examples of this phenomenon in the diffusion of Blacks into predominantly white suburbs, in the increase in interracial dating and marriage, in the higher incidence of suicide and mental illness, and in a decline in the extended family pattern, all of which reflect the variation in the Black community. What is surprising, given the pace of racial integration in American society, is that more Blacks have not become assimilated into the majority's mode of behavior. The integration of school systems, desegregation of suburbia, and greater access to knowledge of majority cultural norms through the mass media have provided unprecedented opportunities for Black acculturation.

Yet some Blacks demand separate facilities and organizations on white university campuses, and some Blacks who moved to the suburbs continue their social lives in the inner cities. While the extended family may not live in the same household, it still provides emotional solidarity and other kinds of support. Moreover, the concept of the extended family has broadened to include all members of the Black community. These internal adaptations made by the Black community prevent racial integration from diluting their cultural unity.

In contrast to the demands of the women's liberation movement for emancipation from the passive role ascribed to women, some Black women are discussing adopting the subordinate position of African women. Their contention is that the roles of men and women are different, not unequal. In some of the Black nationalist organizations, women are placed in auxiliary groups, while men take the leadership. Much of this is a reaction to the time when Black women had the leadership of the family thrust upon them and Black men were not allowed to fulfill the ascribed male role. Hence, in some circles it is now believed that Black women should step back and let Black men emerge as the leaders of the family and the race.

Another important adaptation under consideration by some Blacks is adopting polygyny as the Black marriage system. Because there are not enough Black males, the idea is that the sharing of husbands could stabilize Black marriages and provide certain legal benefits to women now deprived of them. At least two Black nationalist organizations are on record as advocates of polygyny for the Black population. The actual number of Black polygynous marriages is unknown, but probably quite low. In African society, the practice of polygyny is closely related to the economic system and people are socialized to accept it, but such marriages are illegal in the United States, and the second wife has no legal benefits.

Problems and Prospects

The problems Black people face have been essentially the same for a century. These problems are not related to family stability, but to the socioeconomic conditions that tear families asunder. In general, the problems have been and still are poverty and racism. While the past decade has produced a decline in racial segregation and white stereotypes of Black inferiority, Blacks still receive discriminatory treatment in every sphere of American life. Moreover, while whites agree that there is discrimination against Blacks, any na-

tional effort toward further remedy for these racist practices has a low priority among white Americans.

Low socioeconomic status continues to plague many Black families. Whereas some Blacks have achieved a higher standard of living as a result of the civil rights movement, many continue to live below the poverty level. A disproportionate number of these Blacks are female heads of families. They have more responsibilities and less income than any other group in American society, yet child care facilities are few and inadequate. Few effective programs are being proposed to meet the needs of this group—one third of all Black families.

Racism is still a problem with interracial marriages. The increased rate of interracial marriages will continue because more Blacks and whites will meet as peers. One reason some Black men will marry white women is because society's standards of beauty are still white. More Black women will marry white men for greater economic security and because they have become disenchanted with Black men. Whatever the reason, these marriages will face many obstacles. In an era of unabated white racism and Black nationalism, many interracial couples will become outcasts in Black communities as well as white. The problems of marital conflict will be compounded by these external pressures.

It is difficult to project the future of Black families because several parallel trends are occurring at once. Many Blacks are entering the middle class as a result of higher education and increased opportunities. At the same time the future is dim for those Blacks in the lower class. Automation and computer technology are rendering obsolete the labor of unskilled Black men and threatening to render them permanently unemployed. The status of Black women is in a state of flux. Some welcome liberation from male control, while others urge a regeneration of Black male leadership. Easier access to contraceptives and abortion may mean a considerable decline in the Black fertility rate. Simultaneously, many Blacks express concern with the implications of genocide in Black family limitation. Whatever the future of Black families, it is time to put to rest all the theories about Black family instability and recognize the crucial role of this institution in the Black struggle for survival.

15

Public Policy and Black Families

Black Female Liberation and Family Action Programs: Some Considerations

Patricia Bell Scott

This paper explores some critical issues of Black female liberation and examines the implications of these issues for family action or advocacy programs. Demographic trends relating to the Black female population are discussed, as well as the impact of these trends on the social, political, and economic plight of Black women. The article concludes with a discussion of strategies that might be used by a family advocate for improving the quality of life for Black women, and thereby furthering the process of human liberation for all Blacks.

The present-day welfare system has been described as "a super-sexist marriage" by a poor, middle-aged, Black mother receiving aid for her dependent children.[1] Her feelings and the plight of many Black welfare mothers are the result of racist and sexist traditions which permeate our societal institutions. Such traditions have distorted American scholarship and encouraged the development of public policies and social programs which have been particularly detrimental to the well-being of Black women.

The purpose of this paper is to explore the problems of Black women in America and to identify those strategies that might be utilized in family action programs to eradicate rather than to compound these problems. It is intended that such a discussion will inspire a more positive and relevant activism among family advocates. For in the case of many low-income Black women, the development of positive and relevant family action programs is a matter of survival and human liberation.

Black Women and the American Social System

Any inquiry into the problems of Black women inevitably focuses upon their exploitation in the economic system. Recent census data indicate that Black women occupy the lowest rung of the economic ladder, with median earnings of $3,042, whereas the median earnings of White women, Black men, and White men are $3,190, $5,405, and $8,332, respectively.[2] Though Black women have always surpassed their White counterpart in labor force participation, they continue to experience high rates of unemployment and are overrepresented in the low-level, service-related jobs. . . .

As consumers of social, medical and health care services, Black women are often shortchanged. In many instances, the programs developed for the dispersal of social services are totally irrelevant to the needs of low-income Black women. Ofttimes social service programs are based upon stereotypes about Black people, ill-defined objectives, and insensitive personnel. Despite the high rates of infant mortality reported in the Census, the establishment of family planning

[1] J. Tillmon, "Welfare is a Women's Issue," in C. Perrucci and D. Targ, eds., *Marriage and the Family: A Critical Analysis and Proposals for Change* (New York: David McKay, 1974), p. 104.

[2] U.S. Bureau of the Census, Current Population Reports, Special Studies, Series P-23, No. 48, *The Social and Economic Status of the Black Population in the United States,* (Washington, D.C.: Government Printing Office, 1973), p. 18.

Abridged and reprinted by permission. Footnotes have been renumbered.

clinics which provide free (and in some instances unwanted) sterilizations has taken priority over the development of adequate prenatal care or comprehensive community health services, and sex education programs for Black adolescents.

Despite the obvious need of numerous working Black mothers for quality day care centers, industry and government have failed to provide on a consistent basis adequate child care facilities. The lack of such facilities has made employment impossible for some women, whereas others have found that the cost of transportation, clothing, food, and day care services tremendously reduces the financial rewards of work.

Black women suffer from mental and physical health problems. These problems emanate from the precarious position that Black women occupy in the American social order. A recent conference in Washington, D.C., sponsored by the Black Women's Community Development Foundation, attempted to deal with and identify some of the "stresses and strains" peculiar to Black women. Participants discussed the increasing suicide rates, the high incidence of hypertension and cardiovascular diseases among Black women. Other ailments of specific concern to Black women are anemia (especially sickle cell anemia), various types of arthritic conditions, and psychological depression. . . .

Any discussion of the economic and social position of Black women in American society would be incomplete without some mention of the malicious stereotypes of Black women which saturate the mass media and American scholarship. The "Sapphire" image of Black womanhood is a caricature of long-standing tradition. As a result of this image of a dominating, emasculating Black woman, many family-life and social scientists have naively accused Black womanhood of castrating Black men, destroying stable family life, and stifling the social and intellectual development of Black children. Such accusations have allowed many public policy-makers to "blame the victim," thereby ignoring the institutional racism and sexism in our economic, educational, and occupational systems.

Another stereotype of long-standing tradition is that of the "super-sexual" Black woman. It is quite likely that the current attempts in many states to force Black women on welfare to submit to sterilization are related to the popular notion of the "promiscuous, Black unwed mother," who continually bears children in order to make money off of the government.

Given the enormity of the problems of Black women in American society, it seems imperative that Black feminism be encouraged by family advocates. This movement, like other movements, is not entirely monolithic; however, many of the problem areas discussed earlier in this paper have been the focus of most of those organizations concerned with Black women. The National Welfare Rights Organization, the National Committee on Household Employment, Domestics United of North Carolina, the National Caucus on the Black Aged, The National Council of Negro Women, The National Black Feminist Organization, and The Black Women's Community Development Foundation of Washington, D.C., are but a few of the organizations concerned with the well-being of the Black American woman. As advocates of human betterment, family practitioners must support their endeavors.

Strategies and Recommendations

There are several strategies that might be utilized by helping professionals to eliminate the "dual burden" of racism and sexism which victimizes Black women. Family advocates should seriously question the objectives and the applicability of program proposals designated for the Black community. Attention should be focused upon the accurate identification of the community's needs by the inclusion of local residents in the developmental process. Such a strategy might result in the establishment of more responsive family action programs.

Ladner, in a study of young Black female adolescents, has reported that the sexual socialization process and the attitudes of Black women toward contraception are decidedly different from those of wider America.[3] Most of these women had negative views of contraception and abortion. With the public exposure of the forced sterilization of poor Black women, it is likely that the attitudes in the Black community toward all kinds of family planning may become suspicious and negative (perhaps, rightly so). Family advocates must protest these forced sterilizations and support the

[3]J. Ladner, *Tomorrow's Tomorrow* (New York: Doubleday, 1971), pp. 262–269.

development of effective sex education programs for adolescents, safe and inexpensive abortions for those women who want them, and adequate prenatal health care for those women who choose to have their babies.

Demographic reports reveal that Black women with a college education have a fertility rate lower than their White counterparts.[4] In light of this finding it might be more applicable for those family advocates concerned with over-population and maximization of all human potential to place more emphasis upon equal opportunity to higher education for Black women.[5]

The grave economic needs of Black women necessitate that family advocates form liaisons with public employment agencies and employers. Such a liaison could encourage the development of more on-the-job and occupational training programs by industry. The family advocate should also put pressure upon those industries which employ Black women in heavy numbers to provide equal pay and minimum wages. Such pressure could take the form of public exposure (for example, letters to the local media), organized protest, and litigation.

With the present excess of females in the Black population, it seems likely that the number of female-headed households will increase. The number of Black women who choose to be single for a lifetime will also increase. It is imperative that family advocates design programs that will not jeopardize these families and individuals for being different. Perhaps the first move in that direction would be to recognize the female-headed family and the single individual as legitimate social units which are not inherently pathological. Such lifestyles can be healthy and functional in spite of the social and economic pressures. Family action programs should be designed that do not stigmatize the unwed mother, and legislation which calls for a decent, guaranteed income should be supported. Family assistance programs that penalize Black women for working to supplement meager incomes or being married to unemployed Black males must be revamped. Such programs have discouraged economic independence and encouraged family dissolution.

Because of the heavy labor-force participation of Black women, family action programs must be involved with the provision of convenient day care facilities for children of working mothers. Family advocates must work for the development of quality day care facilities for the economic and psychosocial needs of Black families.

The promotion of research activities that relate to the mental and physical health problems of Black women and Black people should also be a concern for family action programs. In order to develop effective programs, the family advocate must have knowledge of the specific psychological and health needs of the given population. All vestiges of racism and sexism must be eliminated from the helping professions of social work, psychology, medicine, and law.

With the current interest in aging, family advocates must initiate programs and research that will deal with the needs of the middle-aged and aged Black woman. Such persons will constitute a significant portion of the Black elderly population. Any attempts to deal with the needs of aging Black women will necessitate that more research and attention be given to the earlier phases and conditions of the life span, as many of the problems of the aged Black woman are reflections of earlier economic and health complications.

As advocates for family well-being, some attention must be given to the social responsibility of the American mass media. The commercial proliferation of negative stereotypes of Black womanhood and Black people cannot be allowed to go uncensored. Such stereotypes can inhibit the development of healthy self-concepts in Black children and perpetuate the inaccurate image of Black people held by many members of the American public. Recent participants of a Knoxville, Tennessee, community workshop on the Black family contended that Black parents should carefully censor the television programs and movies Black children view. Perhaps all parents should become more knowledgeable of the images of other people projected before their children in the mass media. Participants in the Knoxville community workshop also suggested economic boycott as another strategy that could be utilized against those movies and television programs that are blatantly racist and/or sexist. Family advocates should encourage and emulate such activism.

[4]R. Farley, *Growth of the Black Population* (Chicago: Markam, 1970), pp. 120–125.

[5]P. Daugherty, Personal recommendation made at Knoxville, Tennessee, Community Workshop, August, 1974.

These recommendations and strategies are but a few of many that might be utilized by family advocates in family action programs to improve the social and economic plight of Black women. Such strategies will advance the goals of the Black female liberation movement, thereby enhancing the process of human liberation for the total Black population. In the eyes of many Black women, this kind of positive activism is long overdue.

Public Policy and the Changing Status of Black Families

Robert Staples

The changing role of the family in this society has been widely studied during the past decade. In this article, the author proposes some specific changes in public policy to help provide the support still needed by many Black families, changes that will enable them to be more effective in their diverse roles.

According to Bell and Vogel (1968), the family contributes its loyalty to the government in exchange for leadership which will provide direct and indirect benefits for the nuclear family. While there is little doubt that Black families have been loyal to the political state in America, it appears that they have derived few reciprocal benefits in return. Although the political system has the power to affect many of the conditions influencing Black family life, it has failed to intervene in the service of the Black population and, in fact, has been more of a negative force in shaping the conditions under which Black families must live. As Billingsley (1968, 177) has stated, "no subsystem has been more oppressive of the Negro people or holds greater promise for their development."

Historically, we find that state, local, and federal governmental bodies have pursued policies that have contributed to the victimization of Black families. Under slavery, marriages between slaves were not legal, since the slave could make no contract. The government did nothing to insure stable marriages among the slave population or to prevent the arbitrary separation of slave couples by their owners. Moreover, the National government was committed to the institution of slavery, a practice which was most inimical to Black family life (Frazier, 1939).

Although this fact may not seem relevant today, it illustrates the federal government's default in protecting the integrity of the slave family. This failure to intervene and its impact is most clearly demonstrated when compared to the laws passed in many South American countries that possessed slaves. While the slave states in North America had slave codes that required slaves to submit to their masters and other white men at all times, the South American governments passed laws that provided for the physical protection and integrity of the slaves, as it did for free citizens (Elkins, 1968). Because the United States government was not as benign, slavery was a more oppressive institution which has left us with a legacy of racial inequality in all spheres of American life—a past that had significant repercussions in the area of Black family life.

In more recent years, some state governments have passed laws which impose middle-class values on lower-income families, many of which are Black. Various state legislatures have passed laws designed to reduce or eliminate welfare benefits to women who have given birth to a child out-of-wedlock. A few states have even attempted to pass laws sterilizing women on welfare who have had more than one "illegitimate" child. All these attempts have failed, as the laws were subsequently invalidated by the courts.

While the welfare system may be viewed as a positive governmental action in assisting families

From *The Family Coordinator* 22 (July 1973): 345–351. © 1973 by National Council on Family Relations. Reprinted by permission.

who are economically deprived, it has often served to tear low-income families asunder. The Aid to Families with Dependent Children (AFDC) program was designed to economically maintain children whose father was absent from the home. Hence, it was available, until recently, only to those familes where the husband/father was not present in the home. A family in need of assistance due to the male breadwinner's unemployment could not receive help unless he "deserted" the family. Many lower-class Black males have been forced to abandon their wives and children in order to satisfy this restrictive governmental welfare policy.

When the federal government finally decided to develop a program to strengthen Black family life, the attempt was made in a very curious way. It began with a report by Daniel Moynihan (1965) who was then an Assistant Secretary of Labor. According to Rainwater and Yancey (1967), Moynihan wanted to have the Black problem redefined by focusing on the instability of the Black family. As an index of Black family deterioration, he used the census reports which revealed that Blacks had more female-headed households, illegitimate children, and divorces than white families. While these characteristics were applicable to only a minority of Black families, Moynihan generalized their effect and influence to the entire Black population.

Since the validity of the Moynihan Report has been dealt with extensively elsewhere (Staples, 1971), our concern here is with the role of the government in formulating a policy for strengthening Black family life. First, we might question the political strategy involved in issuing such a report on the Black family at that particular time or at any time. The Moynihan Study was published at a time when Blacks had defined their problem as deriving from institutionalized white racism. The effect of the Moynihan Report was to redefine the problem as emanating from weaknesses in the Black family, which was the main factor in the alleged deterioration of Black society. In other words, Blacks were largely responsible for their condition, not the legacy of slavery or subsequent racist practices in American life.

Moreover, the national action that Moynihan spoke of was not delineated in the report. At a later time, he did recommend social services and noted that a policy of benign neglect had not been too detrimental. Moreover, he is generally credited with being the creator of one government policy designed to affect the family life of low-income Americans. This policy proposed the creation of a Family Assistance Program [FAP], which was designed to correct the inadequacies of the AFDC system by substituting workfare for welfare. At this time the proposal has not yet been acted on by Congress.

The Family Assistance Program ostensibly was designed to aid families who are not eligible for welfare benefits under the present welfare system. However, the additional benefits seem to be secondary to the strong work requirements contained in the present bill. In fact, the purpose of the plan is to force several million Black welfare mothers to work—mostly at wretchedly paid, menial jobs. This purpose is unmasked by the fact that economic benefits under the proposed plan would actually be lower than those presently given in most state-controlled AFDC programs (Axinn and Levin, 1972).

In a recent study of welfare families, Goodwin (1972) noted that the results of the FAP may be just the opposite of those intended. The past history of work programs have conclusively demonstrated that few of the welfare mothers will find work at all, and those who do are in jobs no better than domestic service. These low-paying jobs will not provide a sufficient income for women to support their families without continued governmental aid. Moreover, being confined to ill-paid jobs that do not enable them to support their families may reinforce the same psychological orientation which presently characterizes low-income families and discourages them from further work activity.

This emphasis on mandatory work requirements is based on the false stereotypes of the poor as lacking the incentive to work because of the economic security provided them by public assistance programs. Yet, Goodwin (1972) found that the poor have just as strong a work ethic as the middle class. In fact, poor Black youth who have grown up in welfare families have a more positive attitude toward the desirability and necessity of work than the children of the white middle class. Furthermore, Black women on welfare see getting a job as far more important than middle-class white women for whom work has little relevance to their upward mobility. However, securing employment for these Black women really depends on the availability of meaningful, decent-paying jobs, not on a training program.

It can reasonably be stated that the federal government's efforts to promote Black family solidarity have been misguided and ineffective. The purpose of this article is to review the changing status of Black families and its implications for a meaningful public policy to strengthen Black family life. In describing the contemporary condition of Black families, we will not attempt to deal with the larger sociological factors responsible for current Black family patterns. Our intent is to point out the changes that are taking place and the public policy that would be relevant to future trends among Black families.

Education, Employment, and Income

Among the principal variables that undergird family life are education, employment, and income. Looking at the 1970 census, we find some absolute progress in certain areas for Black families, little change in their status *vis-a-vis* white families, and the general problems of poverty and unemployment unchanged overall for many Black families. In education, for example, the proportion of Blacks graduating from high school increased slightly. Nevertheless, Blacks were still more likely than whites to be high school dropouts. The median number of school years completed by Black Americans over 24 years of age was 10.0 in contrast to 12.1 for white Americans (U.S. Bureau of the Census, 1971).

There are two important aspects of the education situation to consider in assessing its relevance to Blacks. First, Black women tend to be slightly more educated than Black men at all levels. In the past decade, the educational level of white men increased to reach the average of white women, while Black men continued to lag behind Black women (U.S. Bureau of the Census, 1971). Hence, an increase in the educational level of the Black population will not automatically mean a rise in income or employment opportunities. The fact that much of that increase in education belongs to Black women reduces the mobility level for Blacks because Black women, even educated ones, tend to be concentrated in lower paying jobs than Black men. Another significant factor is

the sexual discrimination that women in our society face in the labor force (Pressman, 1970).

The second important aspect of education is that it does not have the same utility for Blacks as it does for whites. While the yearly incomes of Black college graduates and whites who have completed only elementary school are no longer the same, the equal educational achievements of Blacks and whites still are not reflected in income levels. The 1970 census reveals that Blacks are still paid less for comparable work than whites. While white male professional, managerial, and kindred workers earned $11,108, Blacks in the same occupational category only earned $7,659. Among craftsmen, foremen, and kindred workers the white median was $8,305, the Black median was $5,921. Similar, but smaller, Black–white discrepancies appear in other occupational categories (U.S. Bureau of the Census, 1971). These figures lend substance to the Jencks et al. (1972) argument that education alone will not equalize the income distribution of Blacks and whites. In fact, the relative income gap between Blacks and whites increases with education. While both Blacks and whites incur difficulties due to a low level of education, college-educated whites face fewer barriers to their career aspirations. In computing the estimated lifetime income of Blacks as a percentage of white estimated lifetime income at three educational levels, Siegel (1965) found that the Black elementary school graduate would earn 64 percent of his white counterpart's lifetime income, but the Black college graduate's lifetime earnings would be only 50 percent of his white poor's lifetime income. Hence, highly educated Blacks suffer the brunt of income discrimination more intensely than those with less education.

During the past decade, the median family income for Blacks increased at a faster rate than the median for the population as a whole. Yet, Black family income is still only 60 percent of white family income. The median income for white families in 1970 was $9,961, for Black families only $6,067. Even these figures are misleading because they do not show that Black family incomes must be used to support more family members and that their family income is more often derived from the employment of both the husband and wife. Also, according to the Labor Department, the majority of Black families do not earn the $7,000 a year needed to maintain themselves at a non-poor, intermediate standard of living (U.S. Bureau of the Census, 1971).

Furthermore, about a third of the nation's Black population is still living in official poverty. About a fourth of them are receiving public assistance. The comparable figures for whites were ten and four percent. Almost half of these Black families living in poverty are headed by females. About 41 percent of all Black children are members of these families, who exist on an income of less than $3,700 a year. Only ten percent of white children live in households that are officially defined as poor (U.S. Bureau of the Census, 1971).

The unemployment rate for Blacks in 1971 was at its highest level since 1961. Overall, 9.9 percent of Blacks were officially unemployed compared to 5.4 percent for whites. In the years 1969–1971, Black unemployment increased from 5.8 to 8.7 [percent]. Furthermore, this increase in unemployment during that three-year period was highest among married Black men who were the primary breadwinners in their household. Just as significant is the unemployment rate of Black women who were heads of families and in the labor force. About ten percent of that group was unemployed as compared to six percent of white women. The highest unemployment rates in the country are among Black female teenagers in low-income areas of central cities. Their unemployment rate is about 36.1 percent and has risen as high as 50 percent (U.S. Bureau of the Census, 1971).

What the recent census figures indicate is that the decade of the sixties saw little significant change in the socioeconomic status of Black families. An increase in educational achievements has produced little in economic benefits for most Blacks. Based on the rate of progress in integrating Blacks in the labor force in the past decade, it will take 9.3 years to equalize the participation of Blacks in low-paying office and clerical jobs and a period of 90 years before Black professionals approximate the proportion of Blacks in the population (Purcell and Cavanagh, 1972).

Changing Patterns of Black Family Life

Recent years have brought about significant changes in the marital and family patterns of many Americans. We have witnessed an era of greater sexual permissiveness, alternate family life styles, increased divorce rates, and reductions in the fertility rate. Some of these changes have also occurred among Black families and have implications for any public policy developed to strengthen Black family life.

The sexual revolution has arrived, and Blacks are very much a part of it (Staples, 1972). By the age of 19, over half of the Black females in a recent study had engaged in intercourse. While the proportion of comparable white females was only 23.4 percent, they were engaging in premarital coitus more often and with a larger number of sexual partners. However, a larger number of sexually active Black females were not using reliable contraceptives, and 41 percent had been, or were, pregnant (Zelnik and Kantner, 1972).

One result of this increased premarital sexual activity among Blacks is the large number of Black children born out-of-wedlock. Almost 184 of every 1,000 Black births were illegitimate in the year 1968. However, this rate was lower for Blacks than in the most recent earlier periods. The racial differences in illegitimacy rates also narrowed in the last 20 years (U.S. Bureau of the Census, 1971). One reason for the decline is the easier accessibility to safe, low-cost abortions. Nationwide, Black women received 24 percent of all legal abortions performed in hospitals (Population Council, 1971). In all probability, the Black birth rate will continue to decrease as contraception and abortion readily become available.

When Blacks choose to get married, the same economic and cultural forces that are undermining marital stability in the general population are operative. In the last decade, the annual divorce rate has risen 75 percent. For white women under the age of 30, the chances are nearly one in three that their marriage will end in divorce. Among Black women, their chances are one in two. In 1971, 20 percent of ever-married Black women were separated or divorced compared to six percent of similar white women. The divorce rate of middle-class Blacks is lower, since the more money that a family makes and the higher their educational achievements, the greater are their chances for a "stable" marriage (U.S. Bureau of the Census, 1971).

A combination of the aforementioned factors has increased the proportion of Black households headed by females. The percentage of female-headed families among Blacks increased eight percent in the last decade, from 22 percent to 30 percent. A third of these female household heads worked and had a median income of only $4,396 in 1971. The proportion of Black children living with both parents declined in the last decade, and currently only 64 percent of children in Black families are residing with both parents. It is apparently the increasing pressures of discrimination, urban living, and poverty that cause Black fathers to leave their homes or never marry. At the upper-income level of $15,000 and over, the percentage of Black families headed by a man is similar to that for white families (U.S. Bureau of the Census, 1971).

The fertility rate of Black women is hardly a factor in the increase of female-headed households among Blacks. Between 1961 and 1968, the total birth rate for Black women decreased sharply. The fertility rate of Black women (3.13 child per Black woman) is still higher than the 2.37 birth rate for white women. However, the average number of total births expected by young Black wives (2.6) and young white wives (2.4) are very similar. As more Black women acquire middle-class status or access to birth control and abortion, we can expect racial differentials in fertility to narrow (U.S. Bureau of the Census, 1971). The birth rate of college-educated Black women is actually lower than their white counterparts (Kiser and Frank, 1967).

This statistical picture of marital and family patterns among Blacks indicates a continued trend toward attenuated nuclear families caused by the general changes in the society and the effects of the disadvantaged economic position of large numbers of Black people. An enlightened public policy will address itself to the needs of those families, rather than attempting to mold Black families into idealized middle-class models, which no longer mean much, even for the white middle class. What is needed is a government policy that is devoid of middle-class puritanism, the protestant ethic, and male-chauvinist concepts about family leadership. In the concluding section, we will spell out the elements of such a public policy.

A Public Policy for Black Families

The following elements of a public policy for Black families is a combination of the author's ideas and other recommendations by various Black groups concerned with certain problems of the Black family.

In most proposals to strengthen Black family life, it is common to assert that providing meaningful, gainful employment to Black males is necessary in order to ensure that they will remain with, and support, their families. While this is of concern here, it will not be accorded the highest priority. Although unemployment and low income are key factors in Black family disorganization, there are other cultural and social forces which threaten the continued existence of the Black nuclear family. Among them are weaknesses in the institution of marriage itself, which make it less than a viable solidarity medium for either Blacks or whites. The demographic nature of the Black community will also insure the existence of large numbers of female-headed households among them. Since there are approximately one million more Black females than males, there is less opportunity for many Black women to establish a monogamic nuclear family. Although part of this sex-role differential is due to underenumeration of Black males in the census, there is a shortage of more than a million Black males available to Black women for marriage because of the higher male rates of mortality, incarceration, homosexuality, and intermarriage.

Our focus will be on efforts needed to assist families which may be headed by women. These should include decisive and speedy government action to remove all arbitrary sex-role barriers in obtaining employment and providing opportunities for job mobility for women. Those women in low-income categories should be given subsidized training for jobs which pay decent salaries and are not restricted only to men. Since the economy is not really geared to provide jobs to prepared and willing workers, we would recommend a guaranteed income of $6,000 to a family with at least one parent and three children.

While the above figure has been criticized as being too high and not politically feasible, it seems a reasonable amount in light of the Labor Department's admission that an annual income of $7,000 is required to maintain a family of four at the non-poor but low standard of living in urban areas. This will also free women of their dependency on men to maintain a decent standard of living. Women will be able to enter marriage out of desire, rather than economic need. Although this may not slow down the rising tide of dissolved marriages, it does give women a greater life choice.

To facilitate the entrance of women into the labor force, we also recommend community-controlled, 24-hour child care centers. The Bureau of Labor Statistics shows that a larger proportion of Black women are employed fulltime than white women. This is particularly true of the 16–24-year age group, who are most likely to have very young children with no child care facilities they can afford in which to leave them. These child care services should be provided on a sliding fee scale, based on income, by the Government. They will serve a dual function by freeing working women from the responsibilities of child care and providing employment for women and men who work in the child care centers.

Closely related to the concept of child care centers is the need for the government's commitment to a national comprehensive program of child development. This would provide for the establishment of a national system of child development centers and programs which would provide comprehensive health services, education, recreation, and cultural enrichment for preschool children (Billingsley, 1972).

To further protect Black children, we need to reconsider the traditional methods of child placement. Since caring for other's children on a temporary basis is a time-honored practice in the Black community, there is no reason why the family who accepts a child on a permanent basis should not be subsidized by the government to do so. The idea of subsidized adoption should become a part of public policy and would deal with the paradoxical situation of mothers who do not want to rear their children and families who want them, but cannot afford them. We should also get some community input into foster care arrangements.

For Black women who do not wish to bear children, there should be available safe, free contraceptives or abortion. However, these services should be organized into a community-controlled comprehensive health program and center. This will demonstrate that white society is concerned not with preventing Black children from entering the world, but wants to safeguard the health of the mothers and provide decent health care to those Black children that are born.

Also, any governmental policy to help Black families should recognize the desire of Blacks to control their own community and destiny. Thus, the initial formulation of such a public policy should include a major input from the Black community. Programs imposed by white people on Black families are no longer acceptable or desirable if we wish to establish a policy which will begin to promote the conditions necessary for a strong Black family structure.

In concluding, we might note that public policy has not favored any family which is poor or uneducated, but the Black family has been singled out and discriminated against in employment, housing, education, health, and other services which require special remediation. Although public policy was not designed to disadvantage any particular group, its ineffectiveness has been felt most significantly in the area of lower-income Black family life. This special need of Black families, however, should not distract from the necessity of a major governmental effort on behalf of all families. Work training means nothing unless there is a commitment to provide jobs for all willing to work. And, the provision of jobs will mean little to Black families unless there is a concomitant elimination of racial discrimination in employment and promotional opportunities.

References

Axinn, June, and Herman Levin. "Optimizing Social Policy for Families." *The Family Coordinator,* 1972, 21, 163–170.

Bell, Norman, and Ezra Vogel. *A Modern Introduction to the Family.* New York: Free Press, 1968.

Berry, Mary. *Black Resistance—White Law: A History of Constitutional Racism in America.* New York: Appleton-Century-Crofts, 1971.

Billingsley, Andrew. *Black Families in White America.* Englewood Cliffs, New Jersey: Prentice-Hall, 1968.

Billingsley, Andrew. *Children of the Storm.* New York: Harcourt Brace Jovanovich, 1972.

Elkins, Stanley. *Slavery: A Problem in American Institutional and Intellectual Life.* Chicago: University of Chicago Press, 1968.

Frazier, E. Franklin. *The Negro Family in the United States*. Chicago: University of Chicago Press, 1939.

Goodwin, Leonard. *Do the Poor Want to Work? A Social-Psychological Study of Work Orientations*. Washington, D.C.: Brookings, 1972.

Jencks, Christopher, et al. *Inequality: A Re-Assessment of the Effect of Family and Schooling in America*. New York: Basic Books, 1972.

Kiser, Clyde, and Myrna Frank. "Factors Associated with the Low Fertility of Non-white Women of College Attainment." *Milbank Memorial Fund Quarterly*, October 1967, 425–429.

Moynihan, Daniel P. *The Negro Family: The Case for National Action*. Washington, D.C.: U.S. Department of Labor, 1965.

Population Council Report on Abortions by Age and Race. Washington, D.C.: U.S. Government Printing Office, 1971.

Pressman, Sonia. "Job Discrimination and the Black Woman." *The Crisis*, March 1970, 103–108.

Purcell, Theodore, and Gerald Cavanagh. *Blacks in the Industrial World*. New York: The Free Press, 1972.

Rainwater, Lee, and William Yancey. *The Moynihan Report and the Politics of Controversy*. Cambridge, Massachusetts: The M.I.T. Press, 1967.

Siegel, Paul M. "On the Cost of Being Negro." *Sociological Inquiry*, 1965, 35, 52–55.

Staples, Robert. "Towards a Sociology of the Black Family: A Theoretical and Methodological Assessment." *Journal of Marriage and the Family*, 1971, 33, 19–38.

Staples, Robert. "The Sexuality of Black Women." *Sexual Behavior*, 1972, 2, 4–14.

United States Bureau of the Census, Department of Commerce. *The Social and Economic Status of the Black Population in the United States*, Series P. 23, No. 42. 1971.

Zelnik, Melvin, and John Kantner. "Sexuality, Contraception, and Pregnancy among Young Unwed Females in the United States." A paper prepared for the Commission on Population Growth and the American Future, May 1972.

Selected Bibliography

Abzug, Robert H.
1971 "The Black Family During Reconstruction." In *Key Issues in the Afro-American Experience,* Nathan Huggins et al., eds., pp. 26–39. New York: Harcourt Brace Jovanovich.

Aldridge, Delores P.
1974 "Problems and Approaches to Black Adoptions." *The Family Coordinator* 23:407–410.

Anderson, David
1971 *Children of Special Value. Interracial Adoption in America.* New York: St. Martin's Press.

Andrews, Roberts
1968 "Permanent Placement of Negro Children through Quasi-Adoption." *Child Welfare* 47:583–588.

Aschenbrenner, J.
1973 "Extended Families among Black Americans." *Journal of Comparative Family Studies* 4:257–268.

Axelson, Leland J.
1970 "The Working Wife: Differences in Perception among Negro and White Males." *Journal of Marriage and the Family* 32:457–464.

Baughman, Earl, and W. Grant Dahlstrom
1968 *Negro and White Children: A Psychological Study in the Rural South.* New York: Academic Press.

Bauman, Karl, and Richard Udry
1972 "Powerlessness and Regularity of Contraception in an Urban Negro Male Sample: A Research Note." *Journal of Marriage and the Family* 34:112–114.

Bauman, R., and Richard Udry
1973 "The Difference in Unwanted Births between Blacks and Whites." *Demography* 10:315–328.

Baumrind, D.
1972 "An Exploratory Study of Socialization Effects on Black Children. Some Black-White Comparisons." *Child Development* 43:261–267.

Bayer, Alan E.
1972 "College Impact on Marriage." *Journal of Marriage and the Family* 34:600–610.

Bell, Robert
1965 "Lower Class Negro Mothers and Their Children." *Integrated Education* 2:23–27.

1970 "Comparative Attitudes about Marital Sex among Negro Women in the United States, Great Britain, and Trinidad." *Journal of Comparative Family Studies* 1 (Autumn):71–81.

Benjamin, R.
1971 *Factors Related to Conceptions of the Black Male Familial Role by Black Male Youth.* Mississippi State University Sociological-Anthropological Press Series.

Berger, Alan S., et al.
1973 *Black Families and the Moynihan Report: A Research Evaluation.* Chicago: Institute for Juvenile Research, August.

Bernard, Jessie
1966 *Marriage and Family Among Negroes.* Englewood Cliffs, N.J.: Prentice-Hall.

Biller, Henry
1968 "A Note on Father Absence and Masculine Development in Lower-Class Negro and White Boys." *Child Development* 39:1004–1006.

Billingsley, Andrew
1968   *Black Families in White America.* Englewood Cliffs, N.J.: Prentice-Hall.

E185.86/B5

1969   "Family Functioning in the Low-Income Black Community." *Social Casework* 59:563–572.

1970   "Black Families and White Social Science." *Journal of Social Issues* 26:127–142.

1974   *Black Families and the Struggle for Survival.* New York: Friendship Press.

Billingsley, Andrew, and Amy Tate Billingsley
1965   "Negro Family Life in America." *Social Service Review* 39:310–319.

1966   "Illegitimacy and Patterns of Negro Family Life." In *The Unwed Mothers,* Robert W. Roberts, ed., pp. 131–157. New York: Harper & Row.

Billingsley, Andrew, and Jeanne Giovannoni
1972   *Children of the Storm.* New York: Harcourt Brace Jovanovich.

Billingsley, Andrew, and Marilyn Greene
1974   "Family Life among the Free Black Population in the 18th Century." *Journal of Social and Behavioral Sciences* 20:1–18.

Bims, Hamilton
1973   "Black Man/Black Woman—Closer Together or Further Apart." *Essence,* October–November.

1974   "The Black Family: A Proud Reappraisal." *Ebony* 29:118–127.

Black Women's Community Development Foundation
1970   *Child Development from a Black Perspective.* Washington, D.C.: Black Child Development Education Center.

Blassingame, John   (E443/B55 / 1972)
1972   *The Slave Community.* New York: Oxford.

Brodber, Erna, and Nathaniel Wagner
1970   "The Black Family, Poverty, and Family Planning: Anthropological Impressions." *The Family Coordinator* 19:168–172.

Brooks, Robert
1971   *Sex—Black and White.* New York: Dell.

Busoe, T. V., and P. Busse
1972   "Negro Parental Behavior and Social Class Variables." *Journal of Genetic Psychology* 120:287–294.

Cade, Toni
1970   *The Black Woman: An Anthology.* New York: Signet.

Carter, Barbara
1973   "Reform School Families." *Society* 11:36–43.

Carter, Lewis F.
1968   "Racial-Caste Hypogamy: A Sociological Myth." *Phylon* 29:349–352.

Chisholm, Shirley
1970   "Racism and Anti-feminism." *The Black Scholar* 2:40–45.

1971   "Race, Revolution and Women." *The Black Scholar* 3:17–21.

Clarizio, Harvey
1968   "Maternal Attitude Change Associated with Involvement in Project Head Start." *Journal of Negro Education* 37:106–113.

Clark, Kenneth
1965   *Dark Ghetto.* New York: Harper & Row.

Clark, Milton R.
1974   "The Dance Party as a Socialization Mechanism for Black Urban Preadolescents and Adolescents." *Sociology and Social Research* 58:045–154.

Clarke, H. Courtenay
1974   "Sexual Behavior in an Integrated Multiracial Community." *Journal of Sex Research* 10:1–9.

Clarke, J. W.
1973   "Family Structure and Political Socialization among Urban Black Children." *American Journal of Political Science* 17:302–315.

Collier, L., et al.
1973   "The Effect of the Father Absent Home on Lower Class Black Adolescents." *Educational Quest* 17:11–14.

Comer, J. P.
1970   *The Black Family: An Adaptive Perspective.* New Haven: Child Study Center, Yale University.

Cottle, Thomas J.
1974   *Black Children, White Dreams.* New York: Houghton Mifflin.

Cromwell, Ronald E., et al.
1975   "Ethnic Minority Family Research in an

Urban Setting: A Process of Exchange." *The American Sociologist* 10:141–149.

Dansby, Pearl
1975 "Perceptions of Role and Status of Black Females." *Journal of Social and Behavioral Sciences* 2:31–38.

Davids, A.
1973 "Self-Concept and Mother-Concept in Black and White Preschool Children." *Child Psychiatry and Human Development* 4:30–43.

Davidson, Douglas
1969 "Black Culture and Liberal Sociology." *Berkeley Journal of Sociology* 15:164–183.

Davis, Allison, Burleigh B. Gardner, and Mary Gardner
1941 *Deep South.* Chicago: University of Chicago Press.

Davis, Allison, and Robert Havighurst
1946 "Social Class and Color Differences in Child Rearing." *American Sociological Review* 11:698–710.

Davis, Angela
1971 "Reflections on the Black Woman's Role in the Community of Slaves." *The Black Scholar* 3:2–16.

Day, Beth
1972 *Sexual Life Between Blacks and Whites.* New York: World.

DeRachewitz, Boris
1964 *Black Eros.* New York: Lyle-Stuart.

X Dodson, Jualynne
1976 *To Define Black Womanhood.* Atlanta: Institute of the Black World.

DuBois, W. E. B.
1908 *The Negro American Family.* Atlanta: Atlanta University Press. 325.26/A881P/ no. 13

Edwards, Harry
1968 "Black Muslim and Negro Christian Family Relationships." *Journal of Marriage and the Family* 30:604–611.

English, Richard
1974 "Beyond Pathology: Research and Theoretical Perspectives on Black Families." In *Social Research and the Black Community,* Lawrence Gary, ed., pp. 39–52. Washington, D.C.: Institute for Urban Affairs and Research.

Epstein, C.
1973 "Black and Female: The Double Whammy." *Psychology Today* 7:61, 89.

Erikson, Eric
1964 "Memorandum on Identity and Negro Youth." *Journal of Social Sciences* 20:29–42.

Farley, Reynolds
1966 "Recent Changes in Negro Fertility." *Demography* 3:188–203.

1970 *Growth of the Black Population.* Chicago: Markham.

Farley, Reynolds, and Albert Hermalin
1971 "Family Stability: A Comparison of Trends between Blacks and Whites." *American Sociological Review* 36:1–17.

Feagin, Joe R.
1968 "The Kinship Ties of Negro Urbanites." *Social Science Quarterly* 49.

Fendrich, James, and Leland Axelson
1971 "Marital Status and Political Alienation among Black Veterans." *American Journal of Sociology* 77:245–261.

Fischer, Ann, et al.
1968 "The Occurrence of the Extended Family at the Origin of the Family of Procreation: A Developmental Approach to Negro Family Structure." *Journal of Marriage and the Family* 30:290–300.

Fogel, William, and Stanley Engerman
1974 *Time on the Cross.* Boston: Little, Brown & Co.

Foster, Frances S.
1973 "Changing Concepts of the Black Woman." *Journal of Black Studies* 3:433–454.

Frazier, Franklin E.
1930 "The Negro Slave Family." *The Journal of Negro History* 15:198–206.

1932 *The Free Negro Family.* Nashville, Tennessee: Fisk University Press. (E185.86/F73/1968

1932 *The Negro Family in Chicago.* Chicago: University of Chicago Press. (E185.86/F74/1966

1941 *Negro Youth at the Crossways.* Washington, D.C.: American Council on Education.

1948   "Ethnic Family Patterns: The Negro Family in the United States." *American Journal of Sociology* 54:433–438.

1950   "Problems and Norms of Negro Children and Youth Resulting from Family Disorganization." *Journal of Negro Education* 19:261–277.

1957   *Black Bourgeoisie.* New York: Collier Books.

1961   "Sex Life of the African and American Negro." In *The Encyclopedia of Sexual Behavior,* Albert Ellis and Albert Arbarnel, eds., pp. 769–775. New York: Hawthorn Books.

Fricke, Harriet
1965   "Interracial Adoption: The Little Revolution." *Social Work* 10:92–97.

Furstenburg, Frank
1970   "Premarital Pregnancy among Black Teenagers." *Transaction* 7:52–55.

1972   "Attitudes toward Abortion among Young Blacks." *Studies in Family Planning* 3:66–69.

Furstenburg, Frank, et al.
1969   "Birth Control Knowledge and Attitudes among Unmarried Pregnant Adolescents." *Journal of Marriage and the Family* 31:34–42.

Gebhard, Paul, et al.
1958   *Pregnancy, Birth and Abortion.* New York: Harper & Row.

Geismar, Ludwig, and Ursula Gerhart
1968   "Social Class, Ethnicity and Family Functioning: Exploring Some Issues Raised by the Moynihan Report." *Journal of Marriage and the Family* 30:480–487.

Glick, Paul, and Karen Mills
1974   "Black Families: Marriage Patterns and Living Arrangements." A paper presented at the W.E.B. DuBois Conference on American Blacks, Atlanta, Ga.

Goldscheider, Calvin, and Peter Uhlenberg
1969   "Minority Group Status and Fertility." *American Journal of Sociology* 74:361–372.

Grier, William, and Price Cobbs
1968   *Black Rage.* New York: Basic Books.

Grow, Lucille, and Deborah Shapiro
1974   *Black Children—White Parents: A Study of Transracial Adoption.* New York: Child Welfare League of America.

Gullattee, Alyce, ed.
1972   *The Black Family: Fact or Fantasy.* Washington, D.C.: National Medical Association.

Gustarvus, Susan, and Kent Mommsen
1973   "Black–White Differentials in Family Size Preferences among Youth." *Pacific Sociological Review* 16:107–119.

Gutman, Herbert G.
1975   *Slavery and the Numbers Game: A Critique of Time on the Cross.* Urbana: University of Illinois Press.

E185.86/G77 1976   *The Black Family in Slavery and in Freedom.* New York: Pantheon Books.

Hall, Gwendolyn M.
1970   "The Myth of Benevolent Spanish Slave Law." *Negro Digest* 19:31–38.

Halpern, Florence
1972   *Survival Black/White.* Elmsford, New York: Pergamon Press.

Halsell, Grace
1972   *Black–White Sex.* New York: William Morrow.

Hammond, Boone, and Joyce Ladner
1969   "Socialization into Sexual Behavior in a Negro Slum Ghetto." In *The Individual, Sex and Society,* Carlfred Broderick and Jessie Bernard, eds., pp. 41–52. Baltimore: Johns Hopkins University Press.

Hannerz, Ulf
1969   *Soulside.* New York: Columbia University Press.

Hare, Nathan
1976   "For a Better Black Family." *Ebony* 32:62.

1976   "What Black Intellectuals Misunderstand about the Black Family." *Black World* (March):4–14.

Hare, Nathan, and Julia Hare
1970   "Black Women, 1970." *Transaction* 8:65–68.

Harrison, Algea
1974   "Dilemma of Growing Up Black and Female." *The Journal of Social and Behavioral Sciences* 20:28–40.

Heiss, Jerald
1972 "On the Transmission of Marital Instability in Black Families." *American Sociological Review* 37:82–92.
1975 *The Case of the Black Family: A Sociological Inquiry.* New York: Columbia University Press.

Henriques, Fernando
1975 *Children of Conflict: A Study of Interracial Sex and Marriage.* New York: E. P. Dutton.

Hernton, Calvin
1971 "Social Struggle and Sexual Conflict: Black Sexuality and the Contemporary Ideology of Black Power." In *Sexuality: A Search for Perspective,* B. Grummon and A. Barclay, eds., pp. 126–139. New York: Van Nostrand.
1972 *Coming Together.* New York: Random House.

Hershberg, Theodore
1971 "Free Blacks in Antebellum Philadelphia. A Study of Ex-Slaves, Freeborn and Socio-Economic Decline." *Journal of Social History* 5:183–209.

Herskovits, Melville J.
1958 *The Myth of the Negro Past.* Boston: Beacon Press.

Herzog, Elizabeth, et al.
1971 *Families for Black Children.* Washington, D.C.: Department of Health, Education and Welfare, Office of Child Development.

Hess, Robert, and Virginia Shipman
1965 "Early Experience and the Socialization of Cognitive Modes in Children." *Child Development* 36:869–886.

Hill, Robert
1972 *The Strengths of Black Families.* New York: Emerson-Hall. (E185.86 / H66 / 1972

Hobson, Sheila
1971 "The Black Family: Together in Every Sense." *Tuesday* (April):12–14, 28–32.

Hudgins, John
1972 "Is Birth Control Genocide?" *The Black Scholar* 4:34–37.

Jackson, Jacquelyne
1969 "Negro Aged Parents and Adult Children: Their Affective Relationships." *Varia* 2:1–14.

1971 "Sex and Social Class Variations in Black Aged Parent–Adult Child Relationships." *Aging and Human Development* 2:96–107.
1972 "Comparative Life Styles and Family and Friend Relationships among Older Black Women." *The Family Coordinator* 21:477–486.
1972 "Marital Life among Older Black Couples." *The Family Coordinator* 21:21–28.
1973 "Black Women in a Racist Society." In *Racism and Mental Health,* Charles Willie et al., eds., pp. 185–268. Pittsburgh: University of Pittsburgh Press.
1975 *Aging and Black Women.* Washington, D.C.: College and University Press.

Jackson, Lorraine B.
1975 "The Attitudes of Black Females Toward Upper and Lower Class Black Males." *The Journal of Black Psychology* 1:53–64.

Jacobs, Douglas, et al.
1974 "A Prospective Study of the Psychological Effects of Therapeutic Abortion." *Comprehensive Psychiatry* 15:423–434.

Johnson, Charles
1934 *Shadow of the Plantation.* Chicago: University of Chicago Press.
1941 *Growing Up in the Black Belt.* Washington, D.C.: The American Council on Education.

Johnson, Leanor B.
1974 "Afro-American Premarital Sex Attitudes and Behavior: A Comparison with Midwestern and Scandinavian Whites." Ph.D. dissertation, Purdue University.

Johnson, Willa D., and Thomas L. Green, eds.
1975 *Perspectives on Afro-American Women.* Washington, D.C.: ECCA Publications.

Jones, J.
1971 "The Conflicting Role of the Black Woman in White Society." *American Journal of Orthopsychiatry* 41:250.

Jordan, Winthrop
1968 *White Over Black: American Attitudes toward the Negro, 1550–1812.* Durham: University of North Carolina Press.

Kamii, Constance, and Norma Radin
1967 "Class Differences in the Socialization Practices of Negro Mothers." *Journal of Marriage and the Family* 29:302–310.

Kammeyer, K. C. W., et al.
1974   "Family Planning Services and the Distribution of Black Americans." *Social Problems* 21:674–689.

Kantner, John F., and Melvin Zelnik
1972   "Sexual Experience of Young Unmarried Women in the United States." *Family Planning Perspectives* 4:9–17.
1973   "Contraception and Pregnancy: Experience of Young Unmarried Women in the United States." *Family Planning Perspectives* 5:21–35.

Keller, P. A., and E. J. Murray
1973   "Imitative Aggression with Adult Male and Female Models in Father-Absent and Father-Present Negro Boys." *Journal of Genetic Psychology* 122:217–221.

King, Karl
1967   "A Comparison of the Negro and White Family Power Structure in Low-Income Families." *Child and Family* 6:65–74.
1969   "Adolescent Perception of Power Structure in the Negro Family." *Journal of Marriage and the Family* 31:751–755.

King, Mae
1973   "The Politics of Sexual Stereotypes." *The Black Scholar* 4:12–23.

Kiser, Clyde, and Myrna Frank
1967   "Factors Associated with the Low Fertility of Non-White Women of College Attainment." *Milbank Memorial Fund Quarterly* 2:425–429.

Kiser, Clyde, ed.
1970   *Demographic Aspects of the Black Community.* New York: Milbank Memorial Fund Quarterly.

Kronus, Sidney J.
1971   *The Black Middle Class.* Columbus, Ohio: Charles V. Merrill.

Kulesky, William, and Augelita Obordo
1972   "A Racial Comparison of Teenage Girls' Projections for Marriage and Procreation." *Journal of Marriage and the Family* 34:75–84.

Kunkel, Peter, and Sara Kennard
1971   *Sprout Spring: A Black Community.* Chicago: Rand McNally.

Kunz, Phillip R., and Merlin B. Brinkerhoff
1969   "Differential Childlessness by Color: The Destruction of a Cultural Belief." *Journal of Marriage and the Family* 31:713–719.

Ladner, Joyce
1971   *Tomorrow's Tomorrow: The Black Woman.* Garden City, New York: Doubleday.
1972   "The Legacy of Black Womanhood." *Tuesday* (1972):4–5, 18–20.
1974   "Black Women in Poverty." *The Journal of Social and Behavioral Sciences* 20:41–51.

Lammermeier, Paul J.
1973   "The Urban Black Family of the Nineteenth Century: A Study of Black Family Structure in the Ohio Valley, 1850–1880." *Journal of Marriage and the Family* 35:440–456.

Larue, Linda
1970   "The Black Movement and Women's Liberation." *The Black Scholar* 1:36–42.

Lawrence, Margaret M.
1974   *Young Inner City Families.* New York: Behavioral Publications.

Lee, Irene, and Marjorie Stith
1969   "Opinions about Sex Education Held by Low-Income Negro Mothers." *Journal of Home Economics* 61:359–362.

Lerner, Gerta
1972   *Black Women in White America: A Documentary History.* New York: Pantheon Books.

Lieberman, Leonard
1973   "The Emerging Model of the Black Family." *International Journal of Sociology of the Family* 3:10–22.

Liebow, Elliot
1966   *Tally's Corner.* Boston: Little, Brown.
1970   "Attitudes Toward Marriage and Family among Black Males in Tally's Corner." *Milbank Memorial Fund Quarterly* 4:151–180.

Little, W. B., C. T. Kenny, and M. H. Middleton
1973   "Differences in Intelligence, Age, Educational Levels of Parents and Home Stability." *Journal of Genetic Psychology* 123:241–250.

Lopata, Helena
1973 "Social Relations of Black and White Wid-
       owed Women in a Northern Metropolis."
       American Journal of Sociology 76:1003–
       1010.

Mack, Delores
1971 "Where the Black Matriarchy Theorists
       Went Wrong." *Psychology Today* 4:24.

Mackie, J. B., et al.
1974 "The Father's Influence on the Intellectual
       Level of Black Ghetto Children." *American
       Journal of Public Health* 64:615–616.

Malveaux, Julianne
1973 "Polar Entities Apart: What Black College
       Coeds Think About the Brothers." *Es-
       sence* 4:48–49.

Matthews, Basil
1971 *The Crisis of the West Indian Family.* West-
       port, Conn.: Greenwood.

Mayo, Julia
1973 "The New Black Feminism: A Minority Re-
       port." In *Contemporary Sexual Behavior:
       Critical Issues in the 1970's,* Joseph Zubin
       and John Money, eds., pp. 175–186. Bal-
       timore: Johns Hopkins University Press.

McCormick, E. Patricia
1975 *Attitudes toward Abortion: Experiences of
       Selected Black and White Women.* Lex-
       ington, Mass.: Lexington Books.

McLaughlin, Clara
1975 *Black Parents Handbook, A Guide on Preg-
       nancy, Birth and Child Care.* New York:
       Harcourt Brace Jovanovich.

Meyers, Lena Wright
1975 "Black Women: Selectivity among Roles
       and References Groups in Maintenance of
       Self-Esteem." *Journal of Social and Be-
       havioral Sciences* 21:39–47.

Miao, Greta
1974 "Marital Instability and Unemployment
       among Whites and Non-Whites: The
       Moynihan Report Revisited—Again." *Jour-
       nal of Marriage and the Family* 36:77–86.

Michielutte, R., et al.
1971 "Outcome of Illegitimate Conceptions in a
       Black Population." *Obstetrics and
       Gynecology* 38:583–588.

Milner, Christina, and Richard Milner
1972 *Black Players.* Boston: Little, Brown & Co.

Mommsen, Kent
1973 "Differentials in Fertility among Black Doc-
       torates." *Social Biology* 20:20–29.

Monahan, Thomas
1966 "Interracial Marriage and Divorce in the
       State of Hawaii." *Eugenics Quarterly*
       13:40–47.

1970 "Are Interracial Marriages Really Less Sta-
       ble?" *Social Forces* 48:461–473.

1970 "Interracial Marriage Data for Philadelphia
       and Pennsylvania." *Demography* 7:287–
       299.

1971 "Interracial Marriage and Divorce in Kan-
       sas and the Question of Instability of Mixed
       Marriages." *Journal of Comparative Fam-
       ily Studies* 2:107–120.

1971 "Interracial Marriage in the United States:
       Some Data on Upstate New York." *Interna-
       tional Journal of Sociology of the Family*
       1:94–105.

1973 "Marriage Across Racial Lines in Indiana."
       Journal of Marriage and the Family
       35:632–640.

Moss, M. K.
1973 "Belief Similarity and Interracial Attrac-
       tion." *Journal of Personality* 41:192–205.

Murray, Albert
1970 *The Omni-Americans.* New York: Out-
       erbridge and Diensterey.

Murray, Pauli
1970 "The Liberation of Black Women." In
       Voices of the New Feminism, Mary Lou
       Thompson, ed., pp. 87–103. Boston:
       Beacon Press.

National Conference of Black Social Workers
1971 *The Black Family.* Philadelphia: MMS Pub-
       lic Relations.

Newman, Dorothy U.
1971 "The Middle Income Black Family: Are
       They Middle Class?" *Tuesday* (October):8–
       10.

Nobles, Wade
1974 "African Root and American Fruit: The
       Black Family." *Journal of Social and Be-
       havioral Sciences* 20:52–64.

Nolle, David
1972   "Changes in Black Sons and Daughters: A Panel Analysis of Black Adolescents' Orientation toward their Parents." *Journal of Marriage and the Family* 34:443–447.

Oblinger, Carl
1972   "Vestiges of Poverty: Black Families and Fragments of Black Families in Southeastern Pennsylvania, 1830–1860." Family History Newsletter, Department of History. Baltimore: Johns Hopkins University.

Parker, Maude
1970   "Growing Up Black." In *Sex in the Childhood years,* Isadore Rubin and Lester Kirkendall, eds., pp. 161–168. New York: Association Press.
1974   "Black Identity: Sex Education for Blacks in the Central City." *School Health Review* (November–December):10–16.

Parrish, Milton
1974   "Black Woman's Guide to the Black Man." *Essence* 4:56–57.

Paulme, Denise, ed.
1963   *Women of Tropical Africa.* Berkeley: University of California Press.

Perkins, Eugene
1975   *Home Is a Dirty Street: The Social Oppression of Black Children.* Chicago: Third World Press.

Peters, Marie
1974   "The Black Family: Perpetuating the Myths: An Analysis of Family Sociology Textbooks Treatment of Black Families." *The Family Coordinator* 23:349–359.

Petroni, Frank
1971   "Teenage Interracial Dating." *Transaction* 9:52–59.

Pettigrew, Thomas, et al.
1966   "Color Gradations and Attitudes among Middle-Income Negroes." *American Sociological Review* 31:365–374.

Pomeroy, R., and A. Torres
1972   "Family Planning Practices of Low-Income Women in Two Communities." *American Journal of Public Health* 62:1123–1129.

Porterfield, Ernest
1973   "Mixed Marriage." *Psychology Today* 6:71–78.

Poussaint, Alvin
1971   "Blacks and the Sexual Revolution." *Ebony* 26:112–122.
1972   "Sex and the Black Male." *Ebony* 27:114–122.

Poussaint, Alvin, and James Comer
1974   *Black Child Care.* New York: Simon and Schuster.

Poussaint, Ann Ashmore
1974   "Can Black Marriages Survive Modern Pressures?" *Ebony* 29:97–102.

Powdermaker, Hortense
1939   *After Freedom: A Cultural Study in the Deep South.* New York: Viking Press.

Presser, Harriet
1971   "The Timing of First Birth, Female Roles and Black Fertility." *Milbank Memorial Fund Quarterly* 49:329–361.

Proctor, Samuel D.
1972   "Stability of the Black Family and the Black Community." In *Families of the Future,* pp. 104–115. Ames: Iowa State University Press.

Radcliffe-Brown, A. R., and Darryl Forde
1950   *African Systems of Kinship and Marriage.* New York: Oxford University Press.

Rainwater, Lee
1964   *Family Design.* Chicago: Aldine.
1966   "The Crucible of Identity: The Lower-Class Negro Family." *Daedalus* 95:258–264.
1966   "Some Aspects of Lower-Class Sexual Behavior." *Journal of Social Issues* 22:96–108.
1970   *Behind Ghetto Walls: Negro Families in a Federal Slum.* Chicago: Aldine.

Rainwater, Lee, and William Yancey
1967   *The Moynihan Report and the Politics of Controversy.* Cambridge, Mass.: M.I.T. Press. (E185.86/U54/R3/1967)

Raver, John
1970   "Boy, Girl, Black, White." *Time* (April 6): 30–36.

Reed, Fred, and J. Richard Udry
1973   "Female Work, Fertility and Contraceptive Use in a Biracial Sample." *Journal of Marriage and the Family* 35:597–603.

Reed, Julia
1970   "Marriage and Fertility in Black Female Teachers." *The Black Scholar* 1:22–28.

Reid, Inez
1972   *Together Black Women.* New York: Emerson-Hall.

Reiner, B. S.
1968   "The Real World of the Teenage Negro Mother." *Child Welfare* 47:391–396.

Reiss, I. L.
1964   "Premarital Sexual Permissiveness among Negroes and Whites." *American Sociological Review* 29:688–698.

1968   *The Social Context of Premarital Sexual Permissiveness.* New York: Holt, Rinehart, and Winston.

Renne, Karen
1970   "Correlates of Dissatisfaction in Marriage." *Journal of Marriage and the Family* 32:54–67.

Rickman, Geraldine A.
1974   "Natural Alliance: The New Role for Black Women." *Civil Rights Digest* 6:57–65.

Rodman, Hyman
1971   *Lower Class Families.* New York: Oxford University Press.

Rodman, Hyman, et al.
1971   "Lower-Class Attitudes toward Deviant Family Patterns: A Cross-Cultural Study." *Journal of Marriage and the Family* 31:315–321.

Rooks, Evelyn, and Karl King
1973   "A Study of the Marriage Role Expectations of Black Adolescents." *Adolescence* 8:317–323.

Rosenberg, Bernard, and Joseph Bensman
1968   "Sexual Patterns in Three Ethnic Subcultures of an American Underclass." *Annals of the American Academy of Political and Social Science* (March):61–75.

Ross, J. A.
1973   "Influence of Expert and Peer upon Negro Mothers of Low Socio-economic Status." *Journal of Social Psychology* 89:79–84.

Ross-Harrison, Phyllis, and Barbara Wyden
1973   *The Black Child: A Parents' Guide.* New York: Wyden.

Ryan, William
1971   *Blaming the Victim.* New York: Pantheon Books.

Sager, C., et al.
1970   *The Black Ghetto Family in Therapy.* New York: Grove Press.

Scanzoni, John
1971   *The Black Family in Modern Society.* Boston: Allyn and Bacon. (E 185.86 / S28 / 1977

Schockley, Ann
1974   "The New Black Feminists." *Northwest Journal of African and Black American Studies* 2:1–5.

Schulman, Gary
1974   "Race, Sex and Violence. A Laboratory Test of the Sexual Threat of the Black Male Hypothesis." *American Journal of Sociology* 79:1260–1277.

Schulz, David
1969   *Coming Up Black.* Englewood Cliffs, N.J.: Prentice-Hall.

1969   "Variations in the Father Role in Complete Families of the Negro Lower Class." *Social Science Quarterly* 49:651–659.

Scott, Patricia Bell
1976   "Teaching about Black Families through Black Literature." *Journal of Home Economics* 68:22–24.

Seckels, Robert J.
1972   *Race, Marriage and the Law.* Albuquerque: University of New Mexico Press.

Shimkin, Demitri, et al., eds.
1976   *The Extended Family in Black Societies.* The Hague: Mouton Publishers.

Silverstein, Barry, and Ronald Krate
1975   *Children of the Dark Ghetto.* New York: Praeger.

Slim, Iceberg
1969   *Pimp, The Story of My Life.* Los Angeles: Holloway House.

Sly, David F.
1970   "Minority Group Status and Fertility." *American Journal of Sociology* 76:448–450.

Smith, Mary
1968   "Birth Control and the Negro Woman." *Ebony* 23:29–37.

Smith, Raymond

1970   "The Nuclear Family in Afro-American Kinship." *Journal of Comparative Family
Studies* 1:55–70.

Sommerville, Rose

1970   "Contemporary Family Materials: Black
Family Patterns." *The Family Coordinator*
19:279–286.

Spanier, Graham, and Carol Fishel

1973   "The Housing Project and Familial Functions: Consequences for Low-Income, Urban Families." *The Family Coordinator*
22:235–240.

Stack, Carol B.

1972   "Black Kindreds: Parenthood and Personal Kindreds among Urban Blacks."
Journal of Comparative Family Studies
3:194–206.

1974   *All Our Kin: Strategies for Survival in a
Black Community.* New York: Harper &
Row. (E 185 · 86 / S 697 / 1974)

Stampp, Kenneth

1956   *The Peculiar Institution.* New York: Vintage.

Staples, Robert

1966   "Sex Life of Middle Class Negroes." *Sexology* 33:86–89.

1966   "What's Wrong with the Negro Family?"
Progressive World 20:32–37.

1967   *The Lower Income Negro Family in St.
Paul.* St. Paul: Urban League.

1967   "Sex Behavior of Lower Income Negroes."
Sexology 34:52–55.

1968   "Negro–White Sex: Fact and Fiction." *Sexology* 35:46–51.

1969   "Reconstruction of the Black Lower-Class
Family: The Role of the Social Worker."
Bayviewer 5:14–18.

1969   "Research on the Negro Family: A Source
for Family Practitioners." *The Family Coordinator* 18:202–210.

1970   "Educating the Black Male at Various
Class Levels for Marital Roles." *The Family
Coordinator* 19:164–167.

⌐   "A Study of the Influence of Liberal-Con-
        ᵛative Attitudes on the Premarital Sex-
        ᵃndards of Different Racial, Sex-
        ᵃnd Social Class Groupings." Ph.D.
        ᵗation, University of Minnesota.

1971   "Ideological Conflict in Family Analysis."
The Black Scholar 3:42–45.

1971   "Some Comments on Black Women and
Women's Liberation." *The Black Scholar*
1:53–54.

1971   "The Myth of the Black Matriarchy." *The
Black Scholar* 2:2–9.

1971   "Towards a Sociology of the Black Family:
A Decade of Theory and Research." *Journal of Marriage and the Family* 33:19–38.

1972   "The Influence of Race on Reactions to a
Hypothetical Premarital Pregnancy." *Journal of Social and Behavioral Science*
18:32–35.

1972   "The Matricentric Family: A Cross-Cultural
Examination." *Journal of Marriage and the
Family* 34:156–165.

1972   "Research on Black Sexuality: Its Implications for Family Life, Education, and Public
Policy." *The Family Coordinator* 21:183–
188.

1973   *The Black Woman in America.* Chicago:
Nelson-Hall.

1973   "Sex and the Black Middle Class." *Ebony*
28:106–114.

1974   "The Black Family in Evolutionary Perspective." *The Black Scholar* 5:2–10.

1974   "Black Sexuality." In *Sexuality and Human
Values,* Mary Calderone, ed., pp. 62–71.
New York: Association Press.

1975   "The Status of Black Women: Sex, Marriage and the Family." In *Perspectives on
Afro-American Women,* W. Johnson and
Thomas L. Green, eds., pp. 45–48. Washington, D.C.: ECCA Publications.

1976   "The Black Family." In *American Minority
Family Life Styles,* Charles Mindel and
Robert Habenstein, eds., pp. 222–247.
New York: Elsevier Press.

1976   "Changes in the American and Afro-American Family. Their Implications for Social
and Economic Policy." In *Proceedings of
the National Conference of Catholic
Bishops Hearing on "The Family,"* pp. 4–9.
Washington, D.C.

1976   "Mental Health and Black Family Life." In
Mental Health: A Black Perspective, Lawrence Gary, ed. Washington, D.C.: Institute
for Urban Affairs and Research.

1976   "Race and Family Violence: The Internal Colonialism Perspective." In *Crime and the Black Community,* L. Gary, ed., pp. 85–96. Washington, D.C.: Institute for Urban Affairs and Research.

Steinman, Anne, and David I. Fox
1970   "Attitudes toward Women's Family Role among Black and White Undergraduates." *The Family Coordinator* 19:363–367.

Stimpson, Catherine
1971   "Thy Neighbor's Wife, Thy Neighbor's Servants: Women's Liberation and Black Civil Rights." In *Women in Sexist Society,* Vivian Gorsick and Barbara Moran, eds., pp. 622–657. New York: Basic Books.

Stuart, Irving, and Lawrence E. Abt
1973   *Interracial Marriage: Expectations and Realities.* New York: Grossman Publishers.

Stuker, Patricia, and Richie S. Gilliard
1970   "Personal Sexual Attitudes and Behavior in Blacks and Whites." *Psychological Reports* 27:753–754.

Swan, L. Alex
1974   "Moynihan: A Methodological Note." *Journal of Afro-American Issues* 2:11–20.

Swelt, J. A.
1974   "Differentials in Marital Instability of the Black Population." *Phylon, Review of Race and Culture* 35:323–331.

Ten Houten, Warren
1970   "The Black Family: Myth and Reality." *Psychiatry* (May):145–173.

Thomas, Alexander, and Samuel Sillen
1972   *Racism and Psychiatry.* New York: Brunner.

Thomas, Charles W.
1970   "On Being a Black Man." In *Black America,* John Szwed, ed., pp. 219–229. New York: Basic Books.

Thomas, George B.
1974   *Young Black Adults: Liberation and Family Attitudes.* New York: Friendship Press.

Thompson, Daniel, and W. Thompson
1960   *The Eighth Generation: Culture and Personalities of New Orleans Negroes.* New York: Harper & Row.

Tuck, Samuel, Jr.
1971   "Working with Black Fathers." *American Journal of Orthopsychiatry* 41:465.

Turner, Barbara, and Castellano Turner
1974   "The Political Implications of Social Stereotyping of Women and Men among Black and White College Students." *Sociology and Social Research* 58:155–162.

Turner, Clarence Rollo
1972   "Some Theoretical and Conceptual Considerations for Black Family Studies." *Black Lines* 2:13–28.

Udry, J. Richard
1970   "Frequency of Intercourse on Day of the Week." *Journal of Sex Research* 6:229–234.

Udry, J. Richard, et al.
1970   "Social Class, Social Mobility and Prematurity: A Test of the Childhood Environment Hypothesis for Negro Women." *Journal of Health and Social Behavior* 2:190–195.

1971   "Skin Color, Status, and Mate Selection." *American Journal of Sociology* 76:722–733.

Uhlenberg, Peter
1966   "Negro Fertility Patterns in the United States." *Berkeley Journal of Sociology* 11:54–66.

1974   "Cohort Variations in Family Life Cycle Experiences of U.S. Females." *Journal of Marriage and the Family* 36:284–292.

U.S. Bureau of the Census
1972   Current Population Reports Series, No. 42, p. 23. *The Social and Economic Status of the Black Population in the United States, 1974.* Washington, D.C.: U.S. Government Printing Office.

U.S. Department of Labor
1971   *The Negro in the West: The Negro Family.* Washington, D.C.: Department of Labor.

U.S. Population Council
1972   *Report on Abortions by Age and Race.* Washington, D.C.: U.S. Population Council.

Veevers, J.E.
1971   "Differential Childlessness by Color: A Future Examination." *Social Biology* 18:285–291.

Velasco-Rice, Jesus, and Lizbeth Mynko
1973 "Suicide and Marital Status: A Changing Relationship." *Journal of Marriage and the Family* 35:239–244.

Vontress, Clement
1971 "The Black Male Personality." *The Black Scholar* 2:10–17.

Washington, Joseph
1970 *Marriage in Black and White.* Boston: Beacon Press.

Wasserman, Herbert
1972 "A Comparative Study of School Performance among Boys from Broken and Intact Families." *Journal of Negro Education* 16:137–140.

Watkins, Mel, and Jay David
1970 *To Be A Black Woman: Portraits in Facts and Fiction.* New York: William Morrow.

Weisbord, Robert G.
1975 *Genocide? Birth Control and the Black American.* Westport, Conn.: Greenwood Press.

Westoff, Charles F.
1970 "Contraceptive Practice among Urban Blacks in the United States, 1965." *Milbank Memorial Fund Quarterly* 48.

Westoff, Charles F., and Leslie Westoff
1971 *From Now to Zero.* Boston: Little, Brown & Co.

Weston, Peter, and Martha Mednick
1970 "Race, Social Class and the Motive to Avoid Success in Women." *Journal of Cross-Cultural Psychology* 1:284–291.

White, Priscilla, and Patricia Scott
1975 "The Role of Black Women in Black Families: Teaching about Black Families on a Predominantly White Campus." In *Perspectives on Afro-American Women,* W. Johnson and T. Green, eds., pp. 187–195. Washington, D.C.: ECCA Publications.

Wilkinson, Doris Y., ed.
1976 *Black Male/White Female.* Cambridge, Mass.: Schenkman.

Williams, Leon
1972 "Sex, Racism and Social Work." In *Human Sexuality and Social Work,* Harvey Gochros and Leroy Schultz, eds., pp. 75–82. New York: Association Press.

Willie, Charles V.
1970 *The Family Life of Black People.* Columbus, Ohio: Charles V. Merrill.

1976 *A New Look at Black Families.* New York: General Hall.

Willie, Charles V., and Joan Levy
1972 "Black Is Lonely." *Psychology Today* 6:50–52.

Woods, Sister Frances Jerome
1972 *Marginality and Identity: A Colored Creole Family Through Ten Generations.* Baton Rouge: Louisiana State University Press.

Yancey, William
1972 "Going Down Home: Family Structure and the Urban Trap." *Social Science Quarterly* 52:893–906.

Young, Louis C.
1974 "Are Black Men Taking Care of Business?" *Essence* 4:40–41.

Young, Virginia
1970 "Family and Childhood in a Southern Negro Community." *American Anthropologist* 72:269–288.

CF 380/C9/W66/1972

Wheeler, W. H. The Black Family in perspective (E 185. 86/W44/1973)
Blassingame, John & M. F. Berry. Long memory: the Black Experience in America (E 185. 5/B47/1982)
Martin, Elmer. The black extended family (E 185. 86/M37/1978)
Wallace, Michele. Black macho and the myth of the Superwoman. (E 185. 86/W34/1979